￣ヿ'S COLLE(

U.S. DIPLOMACY
SINCE 1900

Fourth Edition

ROBERT D. SCHULZINGER

New York   Oxford
OXFORD UNIVERSITY PRESS
1998

*For my niece and nephews
Sara, Ari, Jonathan, and Joshua*

Oxford University Press

Oxford   New York
Athens   Auckland   Bangkok   Bogota   Bombay   Buenos Aires
Calcutta   Cape Town   Dar es Salaam   Delhi   Florence   Hong Kong
Istanbul   Karachi   Kuala Lumpur   Madras   Madrid   Melbourne
Mexico City   Nairobi   Paris   Singapore   Taipei   Tokyo   Toronto   Warsaw

and associated companies in
Berlin   Ibadan

Copyright © 1984, 1990, 1994, 1998 by Oxford University Press, Inc.

Published by Oxford University Press, Inc.
198 Madison Avenue, New York, New York 10016

Oxford is a registered trademark of Oxford University Press

Library of Congress Cataloging-in-Publication Data
Schulzinger, Robert D., 1945–
U.S. diplomacy since 1900 / Robert D. Schulzinger. –– 4th ed.
p.   cm.
Rev. ed. of: American diplomacy in the twentieth century. 3rd ed.
1993.
Includes bibliographical references and index.
ISBN 0-19-510630-X. –– ISBN 0-19-510631-8 (pbk.)
1. United States––Foreign relations—20th century.
I. Schulzinger, Robert D., 1945–   American diplomacy in the
twentieth century.   II. Title.
E744.S399   1998
327.73'009'04––dc21   97-29533
                                                      CIP

ISBN 0-19-510631-8 (paper)
0-19-510630-X (cloth)

1   3   5   7   9   8   6   4   2
Printed in the United States of America
on acid-free paper

Preface

The approach of a new century is a good time to see the past hundred years in proper perspective. The fourth edition of this book tries to understand the changes and continuity of American foreign relations from the time of the Spanish-American war until the post–Cold War era. To that end I have greatly revised the first chapter, "The Setting of American Foreign Policy" to show connections across the twentieth century. I have also made substantial revisions in chapter fourteen, which tells story from 1977 to 1988 and contains revised assessments of the Reagan administration's record in light of new scholarship. I have provided an entirely new concluding chapter—fifteen, "Toward the Twenty-First Century"—which discusses American foreign relations after the Cold War. It provides balanced coverage of both the Bush and Clinton administrations' efforts to come to grips with the remarkable changes in international affairs after the Cold War. It addresses the search for a new world order, the disorders of worldwide ethnic strife, the American effort to promote democracy and free markets, the U.S. attempt to foster stability in former communist regions of the world, and the quest to create a new paradigm for American diplomacy in the next century.

In the preface to the third edition of 1994 I noted that the writing of diplomacy history had been revitalized in the past decade. The new work, informed by the contributions of related social sciences, continues to appear. I have updated the Selected Bibliography to include the best books published in the last four years.

As in earlier revisions, I have incorporated suggestions from many of the students and their professors who have used this book. I also thank three friends in the diplomatic history profession who have used this book in their classrooms and have commented on new material included in this edition: Diane B. Kunz, Michael Schaller, and Thomas W. Zeiler.

Boulder, Colorado   R.D.S.
January 1997

Preface to the Third Edition

The writing of the second edition of *American Diplomacy in the Twentieth Century* was finished at the end of 1988. In the last paragraph of that edition I predicted that "the new Bush administration faced challenges as daunting as any in the century." Neither I, nor anyone else, however, anticipated the monumental changes in world politics and American foreign policy that were to occur with breathtaking speed after 1988. The Cold War ended, the Soviet Union died, and communism collapsed. Containment, the principal focus of American foreign policy since 1945, had succeeded, probably beyond the wildest imagination of its architects and practitioners. In the aftermath of this success the United States remained the world's only superpower, but American foreign policy lacked the sharp definition of the Cold War years.

Accordingly, the third edition of this book tries to put the end of the Cold War and the future of American foreign policy in the context of the twentieth century. To that end, the first chapter, "The Setting of American Foreign Policy," has been considerably revised to show connections across the twentieth century. In addition, I have completely rewritten the final chapters of the book. I believe that the process of detente, begun after 1969, represented a significant turning point in the Cold War and that the brief revival of tensions between the United States and the Soviet Union after 1978 represented only a temporary interruption. Therefore, I have combined the material on the foreign policies of the Carter and Reagan administrations' handling of foreign affairs into a single chapter, fourteen. I also have written an entirely new chapter, fifteen, for this edition. It begins with the election of George Bush to the presidency in 1988 and concludes with his defeat by Bill Clinton in 1992. It discusses the end of the Cold War, the hopes

for a new world order, the apparent achievement of international cooperation in reversing Iraq's aggression against Kuwait, and the grim reality of
American diplomacy in a disorderly world. Like the second edition, this third
edition ends with a discussion of the complicated international environment
that the new administration faces.

At the same time that international relations have undergone vast
changes, the writing of American diplomatic history has been revitalized. I
have therefore made extensive changes in the Selected Bibliography. It now
includes material on new theoretical approaches to the history of American
foreign relations, as well as the best works published since 1988. Most of the
new books deal with events since the Second World War, but there has also
been significant recent scholarship on many aspects of U.S. foreign relations
before 1945, for example, relations within the Western Hemisphere, Wilsonianism, and the Second World War. These, too, are in the bibliographical
essay.

The suggestions of many students who have used this textbook have been
incorporated into this edition. I also thank three friends in the diplomatic
history profession for their extremely insightful critical comments on the
new material in this edition: Diane B. Kunz, Michael Schaller, and Thomas
W. Zeiler.

Boulder, Colorado   R.D.S.
January 1993

Preface to the First Edition

Whenever I answer the all-purpose icebreaker "And what do *you* do," with "I'm a professor of American diplomatic history," a sure, swift sneer comes back: "I didn't know the United States had a foreign policy." *American Diplomacy in the Twentieth Century* is my effort to show that it does. It traces the record of the foreign relations of the United States from their modern beginnings in the 1890s to the present.

This book tells what has happened, who has made decisions, how they have done it, what their critics and supporters have said, how Americans remember what their leaders have done, and what difference those recollections made for current actions. It begins with an explanation titled "The Setting of American Foreign Policy," a chapter devoted to the international environment in which diplomats have operated, the types of people who have been in charge, their relations with nongovernmental supporters and detractors, and the ideas which have moved officials, commentators, and critics. Thirteen narrative chapters follow. Each can be read in its own right, but the coherence of foreign policy becomes most clear if readers keep in mind the framework laid out at the beginning.

Readers will notice the extra attention paid historiography—analysis of the controversies among writers over the causes, significance, and consequences of events. These capsule evaluations of the writings of professors, diplomats, politicians, reporters, and columnists demonstrate the ongoing conversation between present and past. They appear throughout the narrative rather than being packaged discreetly at the back of the book because memory, whether accurate or flawed, always affects current actions. To understand American foreign relations at any time in the century requires unraveling the way contemporaries recalled earlier diplomatic episodes. More than anything, historiography suggests that what happens today affects our interpretation of a living past which, in turn, alters our perception of the morning's headlines.

Many people and institutions helped make this book possible. Four close friends, all scholars of recent American history, read the manuscript and made it better with their suggestions. Leonard Dinnerstein, Bruce Kuklick, Leo Ribuffo, and Michael Schaller all provided unstinting encouragement with their comprehensive comments on early drafts. Useful details, interpretations, and approaches also came from the following fellow researchers, friends, and students: Robert Blum, Robert Dallek, Alton Frye, Lloyd Gardner, Daniel Guttman, Walter Hixson, Richard Immerman, James Jankowski, Melvyn Leffler, John McCamant, James Nugent, William Olson, Bradford Perkins, Robert Pois, Barry Rubin, Lee Scamehorn, Ronald Steel, Peter Van Ness, and William Wei. During the summer of 1981, I directed a National Endowment for the Humanities Summer Seminar on "The War in Vietnam and Its Legacy." I was privileged to try out my ideas on recent foreign policy on the participants, many of whom helped me sharpen my concepts. I am most grateful to five seminar participants for their perceptive comments: Frank Burdick, Dorothy Donnelly, John Hellmann, Milton Katz, and Marianna Sullivan.

Nancy Lane, my editor at Oxford, deserves special praise. She has been enthusiastic about this project from the beginning, always has had the right word to say, and kept the book moving along. No author could want more. Abby Levine, Oxford's copy editor, also made this book better.

Generous financial support came from the University of Colorado's Council on Research and Creative Work, the Council on Foreign Relations, and the National Endowment for the Humanities. My thanks to all.

The manuscript was typed, retyped, and typed again by Tina Ament, Holly Hammond, Sandy Marsh, Carol Watson, and Dolores Young.

Marie Manes, good friend and gifted writer, has been a never-ending source of inspiration. As always, my parents have been a great strength with their reassurance, extra bedroom, and indispensable editorial help. My sisters Ellen Adler and Jane Fox and their husbands Bill and Michael can always be counted on for good food, good talk, and good perspective. I've dedicated this book to their children, a happy quartet whom I like very much. I expect them to read it and promote it.

Boulder, Colorado   R.D.S.
April 1983

Contents

CHAPTER ONE

The Setting of American Foreign Policy

AN AGE OF INTERDEPENDENCE AND IMPERIALISM

American foreign policy in the twentieth century has sought to assure United States supremacy in the Western Hemisphere while at the same time asserting American power and influence widely around the globe. Until the end of the Second World War, U.S. foreign policy makers acted to make certain that the United States became a great power, the equal of the major European nations. During the Cold War era, the United States surpassed the Europeans and contended with the Soviet Union, the other so-called superpower, for mastery of world politics. In the post–Cold War years, the United States stood at the apex of an international hierarchy. America's preeminence throughout the twentieth century has caused some critical observers at home and abroad to question whether it uses its military and political influence wisely.

Since 1900, most officials in charge of setting American foreign policy have consistently sought to involve the United States deeply in political developments far beyond the water's edge. Yet constant tension and competition has broken out among the architects of American foreign policy for preeminence in setting America's course in world affairs. Outside the executive branch, members of Congress, the press, and well-spoken and powerful figures outside the government have all sought to influence the direction of the United States in foreign affairs.

The power of many nations has waxed and waned, but much of the international environment has remained constant throughout the twentieth century. Nations have competed and cooperated during a period of rapid technological change and improved communications. These developments have seemed to shrink the size of the world. As international commerce has increased, the world's economies have grown ever more interdependent. In recent decades, Americans have openly accepted the challenges of a shrinking world. In 1976, the two hundredth anniversary of the Declaration of Independence, one fifth of the members of congress expressed their willingness to sign a Declaration of Interdependence with the rest of the world. In 1996, half a decade after the end of the Cold War, Deputy Secretary of State Strobe Talbott noted that "in an increasingly interdependent world Americans have a growing stake in how other countries govern, or misgovern themselves. The larger and more close-knit the community of nations that choose democratic forms of government, the safer and more prosperous Americans will be."

Identical arguments about the knitting together of the world's regions and resources and similar suspicions of "rabid nationalism" filled the air earlier in the century. In 1910, Norman Angell, a British peace reformer, surveyed the world economy in the generation after 1880 and decided that foreign conquest no longer made sense. "The cause of this profound change," he assured skittish citizens, "is due mainly to the complex financial interdependence of the capitals of the world."

The last decades of the nineteenth century have aptly been called an "age of imperialism," an epoch which has continued, with some modifications, until the present. The major powers of Western Europe, joined by Russia, Japan, and the United States, alternately combined with and opposed one another for preeminence throughout the world. Earlier in the nineteenth century, the United States had maintained a pose of bored indifference to Old World quarrels outside the Western Hemisphere. This aloof neutrality derived from preoccupation with the creation of a Yankee empire on the North American continent. English-speaking settlers, mostly Protestant and white but many taking black slaves with them, moved west to subjugate, displace, and kill native American Indians and Spanish-language Mexicans. Officials in Washington responded to calls for continental "manifest destiny" with wars against Great Britain (1812–1815), Mexico (1846–1848), native American Indians (1783–1890), and Spain (1898), and threats against and purchases from France (1791–1799, 1803, 1867), Spain (1783–1898), Britain (1818–1848), Russia (1821–1867), and Mexico (1825–1853). These expansionist thrusts provided vast territory and an enormous internal market. The triumph of American arms and the submission of nonwhite, non-Protestant peoples left a legacy of cultural supremacy for the twentieth century.

Having completed the conquest of North America, the United States by the 1890s participated fully in the struggle of the great powers around the world. To observers in Europe, and even to some Americans who wanted to see their country become a great power, the conduct of American diplomacy imitated Europe's outward thrust. In the 1890s, the United States grandly expanded the scope of the Monroe Doctrine in the midst of a dispute between Venezuela and Great Britain (1893), added the Hawaiian Islands to its possessions (1897), and fought "a splendid little war" with Spain (1898). That brief passage of arms left the United States in possession of the islands of Puerto Rico, Cuba, and the Philippines. The expansion into the Pacific provided "vast and varied opportunities for further increases of American exports" into China, the diplomat W. W. Rockhill asserted. Cushman Davis, chairman of the Senate Committee on Foreign Relations, thought that the newly acquired Pacific islands meant that "we can commercially [do] what we please" in Asia.

While some Americans, like the assistant secretary of the navy, Theodore Roosevelt, or his friend, Massachusetts senator Henry Cabot Lodge, or his teacher, Adm. Alfred Thayer Mahan, comfortably acknowledged that they were "imperialists," others did not like this label. For some, like the industrialist Andrew Carnegie, the seizure of territory by the United States marked a departure from the traditions of republican rule. Carnegie's brand of antiimperialism led him to combine with men like the other senator from Massachusetts, George Frisbee Hoar, to block the annexation of the Philippines. Americans who supported administering the islands found a champion in President William McKinley, who assured a group of visiting Methodist ministers that a night on his knees left him with God's clear instruction "that there was nothing left for us to do but to take them all, and to educate the Filipinos, and uplift and civilize and Christianize them." Such moralizers were not as proud of the imperialist identification as Roosevelt and his circle.

Americans who resisted the tag of imperialism recalled how previous diplomats had sought to distinguish their conduct from that of the Europeans. After all, that premise underlay the Monroe Doctrine proclaimed in 1823. President James Monroe then declared in his message to Congress that the United States would remain aloof from European quarrels because its democratic social system differed from the autocracies of Europe. Smugness like that often made Americans seem overbearing to nineteenth-century Europeans. Some of them, like Britain's prime minister at the time of the American Civil War, Lord Palmerston, poked fun at a nation of slaveholders claiming to be democrats. Nevertheless, many Americans liked to believe that their country conducted a "democratic" foreign policy. And advocates of a more active American role in world affairs were loath to acknowledge similarities between their actions and those of other great powers.

Even Theodore Roosevelt, who happily called himself an imperialist, stressed the altruistic aims of his forward foreign policy. While Europeans spoke of bringing the benefits of "civilization" to benighted races of the world, they seldom lost sight of the competitive nature of the race for pre-eminence. Americans, on the other hand, often implied they differed from the Europeans in having the best interests of the world at heart. Americans proclaimed that the United States had entered the race to prevent the bad Europeans from conquering the world. Instead, the United States, richer and more republican than everyone else, could do more to mediate disputes among other countries than any other imperial state. This conviction gave a missionary flavor to American diplomacy, irritated Europeans, and bewildered people in the rest of the world.

HOW AMERICANS MAKE FOREIGN POLICY

Government Officials

Who has been in charge of American foreign policy? How have they created it? At the top, of course, stands the president. At times, notably under the two Roosevelts, Woodrow Wilson, Herbert Hoover, John F. Kennedy, and Richard M. Nixon, the president himself has been someone who has thought deeply about foreign affairs, or at least as deeply as Americans ever think about such matters. Other occupants of the White House have also conducted foreign policy, and some have presided over crises, over successes and failures of magnificent proportions. Nonetheless, the remainder of twentieth-century presidents have not put an individual stamp upon the conduct of America's foreign relations.

While these six presidents have had distinctive notions of what to do in foreign affairs, most of the elections in which they ran for the highest office turned on domestic issues. Exceptions prove the rule. When foreign affairs received attention during presidential contests, voters had trouble distinguishing the views of Democrats and Republicans. Two presidential campaigns, 1916 and 1940, occurred while the United States stood neutral in world wars. Both times the rivals expressed interest in the outcome while assuring the voters that the United States would not fight. Foreign affairs questions have arisen in other presidential elections, especially those after the Second World War, but rarely, if ever, has foreign policy been the decisive issue.

In office, the chief executive divides his attention between foreign and domestic concerns. Many presidents, including those who claimed no special diplomatic expertise, enjoyed the drama of meeting other rulers. Foreign travel gave them a sense of accomplishment, the image of activity, and relief from carping critics. Woodrow Wilson conducted a campaignlike swing through Europe after the First World War. Herbert Hoover went to Latin America to show that the United States no longer sought domination in the hemisphere. Franklin D. Roosevelt served longer than any president and traveled more than his predecessors. Before the Second World War, he cruised the Caribbean and South America. During the war the navy and air force took him to conferences in the North Atlantic, North Africa, Iran, and the Soviet Crimea. With the arrival of airplanes, presidents became even more peripatetic. Truman followed FDR in traveling to summit conferences. Dwight D. Eisenhower, a popular figure to Americans with his wide grin and upraised arms, aroused audiences around the globe. John F. Kennedy started the practice of sending his wife to mend fences. Lyndon B. Johnson, Richard M. Nixon, Gerald Ford, Jimmy Carter, and George Bush all seemed to cheer up and recover their vigor when they quit the capital and the country.

Since a president cannot spend all of his time dealing with foreign affairs, he assembles a staff of subordinates who do that. The principal aide entrusted with foreign affairs has been the secretary of state. In the twentieth century, several of them—John Hay (1898–1905), Robert Lansing (1915–1919), Charles Evans Hughes (1921–1925), Dean Acheson (1949–1953), John Foster Dulles (1953–1959), Henry Kissinger (1973–1977), and James Baker (1989–1992)—have left records of achievement. The others have been less memorable, recalled primarily because they occupied the premier position in the president's cabinet.

All secretaries of state want to be the government's foremost initiator of foreign policies, but they have shared their authority with other functionaries. In the process, secretaries have sometimes become jealous of competitors—the heads of the Treasury, Commerce, Agriculture, and War and Navy (later Defense) departments. Since no one can draw a clear line separating foreign and domestic policies of the government, remaining cabinet secretaries reason that they have the right to pursue their own goals overseas. Hence the Commerce or Treasury secretaries have handled questions of international economics. Military leaders, who realize that diplomacy rests on the forces under their command, believe that their voices should reach the president's ear.

Sometimes the president mediates disputes among his cabinet departments through his personal staff. In the post–World War II era, originators of numerous schemes for reform of the apparatus of foreign policy noticed that the president himself had a set of personal and private advisers who whispered foreign policy instructions in his ear. The process began early in the twentieth century. Theodore Roosevelt had what he called a *kitchen cabinet*, made up of personal friends who went outside the traditional channels of the executive departments to advise him on what to do abroad. In the two world wars, special presidential envoys and advisers—men like Edward M. House, who advised Woodrow Wilson, and Harry Hopkins, who worked with Franklin D. Roosevelt—achieved positions of dominance in the conduct of foreign policy. Their easy access to the president caused tremors of envy in the corridors of the Department of State, whose professional staff found themselves shunted aside by presidents who wanted to control foreign policy.

As the United States came to adopt an ever more active role in world politics, where every move made had effects on every other state in the world, the president's special adviser took on even more tasks. The National Security Act, passed in 1947 to make some sense out of the confused lines of authority in foreign affairs, established a National Security Council headed by an official who was to be the president's chief of staff in foreign affairs. The national security adviser made few waves until the 1960s, but in the administration of John F. Kennedy he became a dominant figure. From McGeorge Bundy (1961–1965), to Walt Whitman Rostow (1965–1969), to Henry Kissinger (1969–1975), to Zbigniew Brzezinski (1977–1981), the modern national security adviser was a college professor with geopolitical inclinations who wanted the United States to pursue an activist role. From his original duties as housekeeper of foreign affairs, the national security adviser became the official who maintained direction in American foreign policy.

If the executive branch of the government speaks with several voices on foreign affairs, the problem becomes still more complicated when Congress gets involved. All modern presidents have wanted to use Congress to ratify their foreign policies, but none has wanted to share power with the lawmakers. Legislators have been permitted to lead cheers for a president's conduct, and sometimes the Senate and House have acted as mediators between the chief executive and the public at large. But members of Congress do not always passively accept their role as the meek upholders of the president's undertakings. Sometimes congressmen have their own projects in foreign affairs. Issues which involve foreign and domestic affairs together, such as immigration and trade, always have attracted congressional scrutiny. Usually the interests of the representatives have diverged from those of the executive because congressmen bend to constituents' wishes while presidents often look to the effects of immigration restriction or trade barriers on events overseas. Occasionally, when Congress has tried to conduct trade or immigration policy, the president and his advisers have sighed and said, in effect, "Well, what can you expect from a parochial group who care only about 'low policy'? We in the foreign affairs department look to a greater question of 'high policy.'" Distinctions between "high" and "low" policy were imports from Europe, where the aristocratic diplomats of the eighteenth and nineteenth centuries claimed that they paid attention to the "high" questions of war and peace. "Low" issues of trade and the movement of individuals were subjects fit only for the money-conscious middle class.

Unfortunately for the self-esteem of American diplomats, Congress refused to keep to "low" questions. During and after the First World War, in the period before the Second World War, in the early Cold War, and during the war in Vietnam, lawmakers became interested in the "higher" questions of whether and how the United States should get involved in foreign conflicts. Sometimes legislators accused the president and his secretaries of state of aping the Europeans by getting the country involved in foreign wars. At other times, senators and representatives did not think that the president had been militant enough. Now and then Congress went on investigatory binges, calling officials to testify why they "lost" China, why they thought it a good idea to slip Fidel Castro a poisoned cigar, or why they overthrew the government of Chile. In each episode of congressional attempt to control foreign policy, the president and his advisers responded with a combination of disdain and fear, vowing all the while to quiet Congress.

Outsiders

Much as officials might like it to be the case, foreign policy is by no means the exclusive realm of the government. Some critics of American diplomacy even suggest that the government really is not the prime mover in diplomacy. Instead, a group of dissenters, often called *revisionists*, pointed to the domination of the foreign policy of the United States by businesses which long for markets. These charges, first raised by antiimperialists in the 1890s, gained currency through revisionist writers like Charles Beard and Harry Elmer Barnes in the twenties and thirties and were revived in the post–World War II years by an enthusiastic group of diplomatic historians influenced by William Appleman Williams. In an important work, *The Tragedy of American Diplomacy*, first published in 1959, Williams argues that twentieth-century American diplomacy has sadly been characterized by continuing attempts to find markets for goods which could not be sold at home. Business leaders and farmers, who also wanted to export their products, persuaded Washington to adopt an "Open Door" policy which called upon all of the nations of the world to offer a "fair field and no favor" to the goods produced by all industrialized nations. According to this view, the Open Door policy that resulted was made up of equal measures of avarice, hypocrisy, and a stubborn refusal to acknowledge what actually went on in the rest of the world.

While revisionists occasionally overlooked any foreign policy impulses *other* than the urge to expand exports, they did open eyes to the role played by nongovernmental spokesmen in setting diplomatic goals. Government has never been a simple puppet of great interests, dancing to a tune set by the Rockefeller family, as some critics claim, but neither has it ignored the needs of powerful interests. Sometimes officials hope outsiders will be still and accept policies set by their "betters." But on other occasions, people in Washington have eagerly followed the lines set down by planners who did not hold public office. In fact, no one can untangle officeholders and private citizens. A "foreign policy establishment" arose, made up of men (and much later women) who alternated tours of government service with stints in private institutions—law firms, banking houses, universities, research foundations and institutions, or industrial corporations. Several secretaries of state— Elihu Root (1905–1909), Philander C. Knox (1909–1913), Robert Lansing (1915–1920), Charles Evans Hughes (1921–1925), Henry L. Stimson (1929–1933), Dean Acheson (1949–1953), John Foster Dulles (1953–1959), William P. Rogers (1969–1973), and Cyrus Vance (1977–1980)—came from elite New York law offices. Edward Stettinius (1944–1945) had been president of United States Steel; Dean Rusk (1961–1968) came from the Rockefeller Foundation; Alexander Haig (1981–1982) had headed United Technologies, a major supplier of modern weaponry; and George P. Shultz (1982–1989) was president of the Bechtel Corporation, a multinational construction firm, before returning to Washington. Important officials of the Commerce, Defense, and Treasury departments, which had major roles in setting foreign policy, came from heavy industry (Secretary of Commerce Herbert Hoover [mining] and Secretaries of Defense Charles Wilson and Robert McNamara [automobiles] and Caspar Weinberger [international construction]). Investment banking supplied Secretary of Defense James Forrestal. Secretary of the Treasury Andrew Mellon (1921–1929) made his fortune in aluminum and banking.

Much of the theorizing about foreign affairs originates in the minds of journalists, academics (in universities and private research organizations like the Council on Foreign Relations, the Brookings Institution, or the American Enterprise Institute), international lawyers, political activists, or religious leaders who did not take jobs in the government. The daily business of conducting foreign affairs demands so much attention that officeholders rely on the ideas of outsiders with the leisure to create plans for the future. Some of these figures, men like the columnist Walter Lippmann, editor of *Foreign Affairs* Hamilton Fish Armstrong, or Columbia professor James T. Shotwell, exercised influence while taking only minor government positions for short times. Others—*Time* publisher Henry Luce or Reinhold Niebuhr, the neoorthodox theologian—never joined the government but made their views known. Still other professors—Henry Kissinger, Zbigniew Brzezinski, or James Schlesinger—established solid academic reputations before turning full time to public affairs.

FUNDAMENTAL INTERESTS

Regardless of their positions in private life, opinion molders have served the function of setting limits of acceptable or responsible debate on foreign policy. Their theories have given foreign policy a sense of consistency, undisturbed by changes in presidential administrations and sometimes impervious to alterations in the world as a whole. Not that there has been unanimity in views among the establishment over the course of the century. Some thinkers, such as Andrew Carnegie, advocated "internationalism"—a belief in international cooperation to solve world difficulties—while others, like Henry Cabot Lodge, favored "nationalism"—an approach which paid less attention to the desires of other nations. Adm. Alfred Thayer Mahan and civilian strategists Nicholas John Spyckman and Bernard Brodie emphasized the role of force in international relations while Brooks Adams stressed economic power and Elihu Root praised the gently soothing effects of international organization. Woodrow Wilson paid attention to moral appeals to others. Some "realists" of the fifties like Hans Morgenthau urged diplomats to concentrate attention on influencing the conduct of other governments. "Idealists" like Franklin Roosevelt's undersecretary of state, Sumner Welles, thought it was shortsighted to neglect the attitudes and activites of foreign citizens in favor of what their governments did. Many more differences in the advice of the foreign policy experts occurred over the century, and they will be discussed later, but no one should overlook the near unanimity of opinion among foreign policy advisers on certain fundamentals. First, they believed that foreign affairs matter to mature minds. Next, they felt that America was superior to other nations. Third, they feared that other countries presented dangers. And finally, they shared an optimistic faith that American military strength, wealth, and political values could be artfully applied to improve the lot of the world's peoples.

A belief in the importance of foreign policy has not always been as obvious as it seems today. During the eighteenth century, Americans took comfort in Tom Paine's 1776 call in *Common Sense* for North American colonies to separate themselves from a Europe constantly embroiled in stupid quarrels and wars. One of the mainstays of American diplomacy in the nineteenth century, the Monroe Doctrine, rested on a belief that the United States should have as little as possible to do with the great power game of nations.

By the twentieth century, few Americans believed their country could ignore the rest of the world. Even "isolationists" such as the America First Committee in 1940 or conservative Republican senator Robert A. Taft of Ohio in 1950 thought the rest of the world affected the United States; they simply had less enthusiasm than did their counterparts among internationalists for the way the United States affected the rest of the world.

A widespread faith in the superiority of the United States moved diplomats. Historians have stressed the missionary and moralistic flourishes of American diplomacy. A former diplomat turned scholar, George Kennan, traced this urge to make the rest of the world over into the American image to the deep strains of Puritanism running through American culture. While Puritan self-righteousness undoubtedly has characterized American history, it is a mistake to think that such ideas as Manifest Destiny or "defending the free world" derived from seventeenth-century theologians like Cotton Mather or Jonathan Edwards. Instead, it makes more sense to consider American messianism a form of the nationalistic exuberance which afflicted all of the great powers at the end of the nineteenth century.

Whatever the sources of the sense of mission—an urge to mask insecurities, a carry-over from a Puritan past, the natural inclination of powerful nations to force others to conform to their will—Americans imposed their views on others. Despite recognition of the need for cooperation, consultation, and partnership, American diplomacy has been bedeviled by an urge to lead. When Americans speak of international consensus or compromise, as they did in negotiations establishing a League of Nations in 1919, the United Nations in 1945, or the General Agreement on Tariffs and Trade in 1948, they hope to bring other nations round to their way of viewing problems.

Of course, it is the essence of diplomacy to yield on the form of one's demands while retaining the substance of one's claims, and shrewd negotiators try to make other nations see things their way. American diplomats followed this pattern, and their missionary style added spice to their approach. Customarily, Americans believed that their country stood above others' quarrels. This aloofness is both moral and economic, but whatever its origin, its consequences are clear. American diplomats like to see their country as the balance wheel of the international system, mediating disputes among other nations.

Sometimes the sense of moral superiority has made Americans want to withdraw in disgust from the world's woes. The neutrality laws of the thirties, the America First Committee preceding entry into the Second World War, and suspicion of members of the United Nations in the seventies and eighties arose, in part, from a fear that other countries carried corruption. More often than not, though, American disappointments with international events led to a redoubling of reform efforts. The creation of the League, the UN, or alliance commitments to international monetary reform after 1945 and the beginning of economic assistance for poor countries represented ways of painting the international environment in American hues.

At the turn of the century, Americans such as Theodore Roosevelt or his secretaries of state, John Hay and Elihu Root, who advocated making their country a preeminent world power, did so from two contrary sources. They reckoned that America's strength made it equal to European great powers. But they also knew that the United States differed from Europe. In the words of some theorists, the country was "unique." Woodrow Wilson and his secretaries of state, William Jennings Bryan and Robert Lansing, held this view. Since the United States had been blessed with two oceans separating it from Europe, it had not developed the traditional animosities of the Old World. Lacking a warrior class, the United States also escaped Europe's militarism. Finally, the blessings of prosperity appeared more widespread in the United States than in Europe. No great class cleavages rent American society, so there were fewer impulses to engage in foreign adventures.

We know that this view of American society overlooked many details. While separated from Europe, Americans had their share of local animosities, directed toward neighbors to the south. The lack of a hereditary warrior class did not make the United States any less bloodthirsty in its call for the humbling of the enemies. Few reputable historians speak nowadays about the absence of class divisions in the United States, and even at the end of the nineteenth century, when a business leader looked to an aggressive overseas policy, he did so precisely because he hoped it would diminish class tensions at home.

Whether correct or not, the grip of this idealized portrait of the United States and its foreign policy had its effects on diplomacy. Americans went abroad serenely sure of the harmony of their society. They offered economic aid, political guidance, and diplomatic mediation to anyone who requested them and many who did not. Nationalist China, Korea, the Philippines, Japan, Greece, Italy, Morocco, Jordan, Israel, and Liberia—different countries around the world have, at various times, requested, received, and gratefully acknowledged American financial assistance and diplomatic protection. But the United States arrived without invitation or soon wore out its welcome in the Dominican Republic, Iran, Lebanon, Zaire, and Angola, to name a few.

Time and time again Americans found that other nations resented their preachings. The British, an ally during the Second World War, came to dread American lectures on the shape of the postwar world. Charles de Gaulle, president of France from 1958 to 1969, looked forward to a "Europe from the Atlantic to the Urals" which excluded the United States. During the Cold War, neutralists like India or Egypt which opted out of the struggle between the United States and the Soviet Union resisted Washington's blandishments to join an anti-Communist alignment.

Americans found themselves especially ill-equipped to respond effectively to revolutionary nationalism. These upheavals often followed the lead of men and women who wanted nothing more than to be left alone. Americans, who distinguished between themselves and other foreigners, could understand why Cubans, Chinese, or Russians might want *other* nationals to go away. But Americans could never comprehend why overseas revolutionaries wanted *Americans* to steer clear. Having only recently convinced themselves that the rest of the world needed the attention of the United States lest it fall into barbarism, Americans were shocked to learn that parts of the world did not want to listen to them. Whenever nationalist revolutions occurred in the twentieth century, Americans responded that the people in charge had temporarily lost their good judgment. Eventually, Americans hoped revolutionaries would come to see things as the United States did. In the meantime, Washington did what it could to make life difficult for those who took power—in Mexico in 1913, in Russia in 1917, in China in 1949, in Guatemala in 1954, in Cuba in 1959, in Iran in 1979, or in Nicaragua after 1980.

In its relations with other great powers which did not undergo revolutionary upheavals, American diplomacy followed a traditional mode. Anyone familiar with the behavior of the European states in their struggles for mastery of the continent would have no difficulty in following America's relations with the great powers in the twentieth century. The United States used its wealth and military might to gain influence. It entered two world wars, revived the economies of Europe with the Marshall Plan, created the North Atlantic Treaty Organization, and looked with approval on the formation of the European Economic Community as a sort of embryonic United States of Europe.

American diplomacy in the twentieth century resembled Britain's in the nineteenth. Just as Britain sought to ensure that no single power was strong enough to dominate Europe, so did the United States in the twentieth century try to make sure that no other nation was strong enough to unite other countries against the United States. The Atlantic Ocean provided a sense of security that enabled Americans to tell Europeans how to conduct their affairs, acting all the while like a sort of honest broker. American attitudes toward Europe were filtered through the prism of the "special relationship" with Great Britain. Throughout the twentieth century, the United States and Great Britain, despite a good deal of bickering, have been aligned together on most international questions. By the Second World War, however, it no longer was a relationship of equals. Instead, the United States became the leader of the English-speaking peoples.

As the United States became more involved in European politics after the Second World War, attention encompassed the whole world. The Cold War—the competition between the Soviet Union and the United States and between the alternative economic systems of capitalism and communism—framed foreign relations. Americans imbued the Soviets with awesome powers and detected evil intentions toward world domination. World politics became a "great game" for preeminence, just as it had been at the turn of the century. The stakes, however, rose steeply after the development of atomic weapons. When, around 1960, both the United States and the Soviet Union acquired the capacity to destroy life in each other's countries, the rivalry took on a grisly aspect.

American diplomats tended to see the remainder of the world as sub-
sidiary theaters of the Cold War. Communism became the enemy, and Americans thought that Marxist governments and movements everywhere took orders from the Kremlin in Moscow. In the 1970s, a subtler view emerged, and
some experts, diplomats, and politicians awoke to the fissures of communism. China, for many years a place where Americans hoped to find friends,
wounded American pride when it turned to Marxism in 1949. In the seventies, however, the United States "normalized" relations with Beijing to "play
the China card" against the Soviets. Recent American diplomats have had a
more difficult time distinguishing between other revolutionary movements
and the Soviet Union, astonishing allies and students of the rest of the world
with the assertion that all the turbulence in the world emanated from the
Soviet Union.

The end of the Cold War and the death of the Soviet Union in the years
1989 to 1991 revealed that Moscow had not been the only source of disorder in the world after 1945. The promise of democratic institutions, free
markets, and Western prosperity did not materialize quickly after the Cold
War. Furthermore, communism left a bitter legacy in Eastern Europe, Russia, and Eurasia, sometimes sinking into interethnic tension, national rivalry,
and despair. The noncommunist regions of the world also continued to experience revolution, war, and famine after the end of the Cold War. Without the organizing principle of anticommunism, Americans approached with
difficulty the problems of creating a coherent and consistent post–Cold War
foreign policy. Most Americans believed it necessary for the United States to
remain deeply involved in foreign affairs, though a significant minority
wanted to turn inward. Yet beyond believing in the continuing importance
of U.S. involvement in the world, Americans did not know precisely what
they wanted to do to minimize world disorder after the Cold War.

Outside government, the rise to world power after 1945 drew a mixed
reaction. For the first twenty years of the Cold War, broad consensus existed
that the United States had to counter the Soviet Union everywhere in the
world. To be sure, not everyone enlisted in the Cold War, and some doubters
held their peace only because they feared the wrath of authorities. Nonetheless, the consensus collapsed during the tragic war in Vietnam, and Americans engaged in a debate on the proper role of world politics. Like earlier
eruptions of public concern, these controversies failed to reach a united conclusion. The United States left Vietnam eventually, but each successive administration drew a different lesson from the engagement. Jimmy Carter,
president from 1977 to 1981, acknowledged that the episode had been a mistake, an adventure, and an arrogant application of American power. Republican Ronald Reagan, who followed in 1981, preferred to think of the
war in Vietnam as a "noble cause" in which the United States had refused

to commit itself fully for victory. The Reagan administration promised an assertive America, able to take the initiative in the Cold War from the Soviets. The end of the Cold War and the death of Soviet-style communism came with a suddenness that surprised but also deeply satisfied most Americans. They welcomed the triumph of Western-style ideals of democracy, human rights, and the abundance promised by free markets. Yet they also were uneasy about their nation's role in a disorderly post–Cold War world. The United States struggled to find a sharp focus for its foreign affairs as it approached the twenty-first century. Most people believed that their prosperity and safety depended upon continuous American engagement in world affairs, although they did not agree on the precise depth or nature of that participation. A few people actually looked back in appreciation at the clarity created by the Cold War competition between the United States and the Soviet Union. A majority of Americans did not share this nostalgia, as they never wished to endure an encore of the decades-long terror of the prospect of nuclear destruction. While they were encouraged that much of the anxiety of the Cold War had passed, Americans were not free from apprehension about their nation's future role in the world. Many other nations continued to look to the United States for leadership and admired its political institutions and robust culture and economy. Some other countries resented or feared American power and preeminence. Friends, competitors, rivals, and foes all acknowledged, however—as Americans had done throughout the century—that the United States exercised great influence over the shape of international relations.

CHAPTER TWO

The United States as a World Power, 1898–1908

.

Modern American diplomacy dates from the war with Spain in 1898. The brief, four-month passage of arms between a major new imperial power and a decrepit empire left the United States in possession of Cuba and Puerto Rico in the Caribbean and the Philippines and Guam in the Pacific. More important than the specific territorial acquisitions, the war permitted the United States to compete equally with the Europeans in the race for pre-eminence in world politics.

The war with Spain did not occur accidentally. Both the immediate aim of the war—the eviction of the Spanish from Cuba—and its long-term implications—catapulting the United States into the first rank of world powers—had roots of more than half a century. Southern slaveholders in the United States had coveted Cuba before the Civil War. Cuba remained an island of desire even after slavery was eliminated. Ulysses S. Grant's secretary of state, Hamilton Fish, cast longing glances in that direction. Grant even tried to buy outright the country of Santo Domingo in 1869. Yet the reasons for insular expansion changed in the late nineteenth century.

Before the Civil War, the justification for seizing the islands of the Caribbean was the need for more slave territory. In the years after the Civil War, Americans looked outward in order to trade more effectively abroad. Much argument has gone on over whether Americans wanted to trade with the islands they eventually acquired from Spain. After all, some critics of the idea of a foreign policy based upon trade expansion have argued, there really was very little the Cubans or Puerto Ricans could buy from the United

States. Even the overseas investment by Americans went other places than Cuba.

But the islands of the Caribbean were important for the navy, the protection of a proposed canal across the Isthmus of Panama, and to show that the United States was a power to be reckoned with. The modern American navy, the forerunner of the military establishment of the twentieth century, came to life in the 1880s. From then until the end of the century, the United States built capital ships while naval officers developed the theories of modern warfare. Admirals Alfred Thayer Mahan and Stephen C. Luce became the two most notable advocates of a strong navy. Mahan developed the idea that whichever nation controlled the seas controlled the course of world politics. He saw strong links between the navy and overseas trade. Each required the other: a flourishing trade made a large navy necessary, while the larger the fleet, the more trade was possible.

Advocates of a grand navy found allies among traders who wanted ships to carry goods abroad. Joseph C. Hendrix, president of the American Bankers' Association, expressed the view of many businessmen when he observed that "we have the Anglo-Saxon thirst for wide markets growing upon us." Demands to rid the United States of surplus production grew in the aftermath of the Panic of 1893. A strike at the Pullman Sleeping Car Company near Chicago, a march by veterans demanding payment of a Civil War bonus, and mass demonstrations by unemployed workers sent shivers down the spines of the business community. *The New York Tribune* anguished over "social restlessness . . . arraying class against class and filling the land with a nondescript socialism as dangerous and revolutionary as it is imbecile and grotesque." As Brooks Adams, a disillusioned scion of a distinguished family, mourned, there was a "law of civilization and decay": societies either expanded or they died. Josiah Strong, a popular commentator on current events, pointed the way out: "Overproduction compels a quest for ultimate supremacy in the markets of the world. . . . The United States is to become the mighty workshop of the world and our people the hands of mankind."

An expansionist desire to look outward coincided with urges to convert others to what came to be known as "the American way of life." The most numerous groups of Americans who wanted to spread the word about the United States overseas were, of course, missionaries. By 1900, some seven thousand Americans were teaching the gospel and, incidentally, the benefits of American republicanism, in over thirty countries around the world.

Missionaries helped get the message across in the Far East, especially China. Americans had been trading with the Chinese since the *Empress of China* had sailed into Guangzhou (Canton) in 1784. Since the Treaty of Wangxia of 1844, the United States had been one of the non-Chinese powers permitted to open trade with ports on the mainland. Over the remainder of the nineteenth century, American missionaries accompanied American traders in China. Together they sent home word of developments abroad, and they encouraged the American government to take a greater interest in the competition for advantage in China.

Closer to home, in the Western Hemisphere, Americans had less to worry about from the competition of the European powers. By the end of the nineteenth century, the Europeans had all quit the New World at the prodding of the United States, and because the Latins themselves had evicted them. While the United States was engaged in the Civil War, the French under Napoleon III had a brief fling at establishing a New World empire in Mexico. In 1867, however, the Mexicans expelled the French and executed an ineffectual Hapsburg prince, Maximilian, whom the French had made emperor.

In the late nineties, it was Spain's turn to lose its final foothold in the New World. The Spanish empire was the first one to be established in the Western Hemisphere. It was outlived by the British, French, Dutch, and even Danish empires, but the demise of New Spain was far more spectacular than the fall of other European colonial societies. The end came quickly in a 123-day land and sea fight which ended with American ownership of the Philippine Islands, taken because President McKinley thought he heard God's voice. The revolution in Cuba, which had gone on intermittently since 1868, was the proximate cause of the American decision to fight. For people alive in 1898 as well as for historians, the question of why President William McKinley asked Congress to declare war against Spain on April 11, 1898, provoked argument. On the one side were those who saw the burst of imperialism of the war as somehow accidental. According to this view, put forward by Margaret Leech in her biography *In the Days of McKinley* (1959), the president was an unwitting participant in the movement to expand the power of the United States abroad. He opted for war only to preserve the unity of his party in the face of a clamor for a strong policy on the part of the sensational yellow press led by Joseph Pulitzer of the *New York World* and William Randolph Hearst of the *New York American*. McKinley also was supposed to have listened to the voices raised by American businessmen who dreaded the prospect of the Cuban revolution endangering their belongings in the islands. This accidental view of the war with Spain sees McKinley as essentially a weak-willed politician responding to demands inside the country to do something, anything, in order to stanch the hemorrhage in Cuba.

A more sinister view of the origins of the war with Spain, expressed by such historians as Julius W. Pratt and Walter Millis in the twenties and thirties and by leftists like Philip Foner in the sixties, holds that the war with Spain marked the culmination of the traditional American policy of expansion. To these writers, it mattered little that McKinley was a weak and vacil-

lating leader without a clearly thought-out foreign policy. Even if he only responded to the pressure brought to bear by elements within the Republican
party and the business community, that was enough to set the United States
on a course devoted to imperial expansion.

A third interpretation is that the imperialism of the late 1890s was both
accidental and conscious. In a phrase made famous by a respected historian
of American diplomacy, Samuel Flagg Bemis, who taught at Yale University
for over thirty years, the three years after the Spanish-American War were a
"great aberration" in American history. He implied that the United States
took leave of its traditional values in foreign policy when it embarked on its
imperial adventure with Spain. Bemis suggested that the excursion into rivalry with the Europeans was short-lived, however, and by 1902, when the
Senate passed the Teller Amendment (Henry M. Teller, D., Colo.), which
promised the eventual independence of the nation of Cuba, the country had
abandoned the attempt to compete with the Europeans as a colonial master
over the poorer, nonwhite regions of the world. The notion of a great aberration has few adherents nowadays, but Bemis's insistence that the United
States had a gentler, more humanitarian foreign policy than Europeans has
dominated the thinking of American diplomats over the years.

In Europe and in America, then, at the end of the nineteenth century,
there was a growing awareness that the pace of international relations had
quickened recently. Another, more ominous sense also gripped diplomats.
Thoughtful observers of international politics like Elihu Root, a lawyer who
became secretary of state in 1905, believed that if things were left to take
their course, war might erupt. This fear even penetrated the mind of the
czar of Russia, Nicholas II. He called a meeting of the diplomats of Europe
and America at the Hague on his birthday, May 18, 1899, to discuss ways to
make the world a more peaceable kingdom.

The Hague Conference of 1899 attracted delegates from twenty-six countries, all of the "civilized" world at the time. Along with its successor conference in the Dutch city eight years later, the meeting at the Hague set the
pattern for schemes of reform of international politics in the twentieth century. At the Hague, delegates sipped tea and wrote plans to make modern
warfare less horrible. They wrote rules for the use of such weapons as balloons, explained how prisoners should be treated, and provided some limited protection for civilians during times of war. The conference did nothing at all to prevent the outbreak of war, its ostensible purpose. This pattern
remained for the rest of the twentieth century—international meetings which
began with high hopes for a revolutionary change in the way in which diplomacy was done ended in acrimony with few of their original goals achieved.

This, then, was the world of international relations at the turn of the century. At least seven rapidly industrializing nations (the United States, Great
Britain, France, Germany, Italy, Russia, and Japan) whose governments were

in the hands of newly enriched elites confronted one another. They depended to one degree or another upon the support of their newly franchised populations. These governments competed far from home in nonindustrial lands inhabited by nonwhite peoples.

EXPANDING THE PACIFIC EMPIRE: THE OPEN DOOR POLICY

After the United States crushed Spain, Americans and foreigners saw American power rivaling Europe's. New Yorkers recalled the glories of Rome and Napoleon by erecting a triumphal arch in Central Park through which passed Adm. George Dewey, the hero of Manila Bay. Across the country, editorials praised the "new empire." Englishmen discovered some new virtues in an America they once had scorned. Colonial Secretary Joseph Chamberlain pro38sed an alliance between the United States and Great Britain in terms that would have brought calls for his examination by a psychiatrist ten years before. "Even war itself would be cheaply purchased," he said, "if in a great and noble cause the Stars and Stripes and the Union Jack were to wave together over an Anglo-Saxon Alliance." In Latin America, newspapers voiced concern over the "colossus of the North," while across the Pacific, too, Chinese and Japanese diplomats acknowledged that the United States had become a "world power."

What did it mean to be a world power in 1900? For European nations such as Britain, France, Russia, or Germany, the answer was easy. World powers had empires around the globe, and they demanded to be consulted wherever boundaries changed. Their merchants and bankers could be found in the remotest regions, and citizens of less fortunate lands paid them timid respect.

Having taken the Philippines, Guam, Puerto Rico, and Cuba from Spain, the United States too possessed a fledgling empire. Its merchants were just as active as those of Europe. While debate raged in Congress and the country at large over whether the United States should keep its new acquisitions, Massachusetts Republican Henry Cabot Lodge put the case for empire and world power to his colleagues in the Senate. He likened a nation to an athlete who "does not win a race by habitually sitting in an armchair." To anti-imperialists like Andrew Carnegie or Democratic presidential candidate William Jennings Bryan, who wondered why enter the race in the first place, Lodge replied that it built character: "This necessity for watching over the welfare of another people will improve our civil service, raise the tone of public life, and make broader and better our politics."

Across the Pacific in China was one place where the athletic American empire joined the race. "We believe our interests in the Pacific Ocean are as great as those of any power," Secretary of State John Hay observed. In

1844, Americans gained the right to trade in the Treaty of Wangxia, which Caleb Cushing of Massachusetts negotiated with the Chinese government. China opened to the Americans the same ports it had allowed the British to enter two years before at the end of the Opium War. Americans and Britishers also won the right of "extraterritoriality," or exemption from Chinese law. The Chinese had not wanted to trade with Britain, but having lost the war they had no choice. Nor did the Chinese consider the Americans to be any more "civilized" than the "barbarous" British, who had forced opium upon China. Cushing's demand to receive equal treatment with the British was scorned as "jackal diplomacy" by the Chinese, who taunted the Americans for arriving after the fight to demand the spoils of war. For the remainder of the nineteenth century, Americans managed to ignore the jibe. Out of the natural tendency of people to think well of themselves, American merchants, missionaries, and diplomats in China thought that they had come there to protect the Chinese from the designs of greedy Europeans. Charles Denby, the American minister in China, predicted to Ohio Republican senator John Sherman in 1897 that "the statesmen of China will understand that in our case foreign control does not mean territorial absorption nor governmental interference, while both these results are possible, or even probable, in dealing with European powers."

Chaos ruled China in the 1890s. The Chinese shocked everyone, including themselves, by losing a war with Japan in 1895. Europeans and Americans who watched the speedy collapse of the Chinese armed forces felt "nothing but disgust . . . for the weakness and incompetence by the Chinese." One English expert on China, Lord Charles Beresford, crisscrossed America in early 1899 promoting his book, *The Break-Up of China,* which predicted that the Asian nation would soon fall to the European empires the way Africa had done in the last two decades. If China were to be "sliced like a watermelon," he informed his audiences, Americans must be prepared to take their share. They should be especially wary of the designs of the Russians.

Surprisingly, Americans did not rush to carve China. Ambassador Edwin Conger and railroad promoters James Hill and Edward H. Harriman remembered the bitter debate in 1898 before taking the Philippines. Although they longed for the riches of the East, they recalled how President William McKinley had been forced to promise that the United States eventually would offer independence to the Philippines. If the American public had to be fooled in this way into accepting the "responsibilities of empire," then the future of imperial America seemed dim. There was one way, however, that the United States matched the other world powers. Economically, the United States held its own with anyone, and the ports on the west coast placed it closer to China than was Europe. If taking colonies held political risks in the United States, an "informal empire" based on the principles of free trade gave Americans a leg up on their rivals.

In September 1899, the American government moved to establish a "fair field and no favor" for foreign merchants and investors in China. Without consulting the Chinese government, Secretary of State John Hay sent notes to all other imperial powers asking them to maintain an "Open Door" for traders of all nations inside their Chinese spheres of influence. Hay had been persuaded by an American diplomat in China, W. W. Rockhill, that since American goods could be sold more cheaply in China than those of any other power, the Open Door policy would work to the advantage of the United States. Receiving no answer from Europe and Japan, Hay took silence for assent and proclaimed China open to trade.

The next year, 1900, Hay again wrote notes to the major European powers when China erupted in the Boxer Rebellion. This popular rising against foreign domination of China initially won the support of China's empress dowager, Cixi, who hoped the Boxers (the Society of the Righteous Fists) could rid her country of the humiliating presence of the Europeans, Japanese, and Americans. When the rebels laid siege in June to the German embassy, capturing the foreign diplomats, the empress dowager distanced herself from the Boxers. For fifty-five days the diplomats were prisoners of angry nationalists while a joint expedition of Japanese, Russian, British, and American marines marched from the coast to rescue them. As the diplomats and their families languished under house arrest, the secretary of state sent his second Open Door notes to the powers on July 2, asking them not to dismantle China in their anger over the envoys' capture. The respondents coolly acknowledged his notes and made vague promises to respect China's territorial integrity if the others followed suit. That was enough for the American secretary of state, who publicly proclaimed China's safety. Privately, he approved a contingency plan to seize a Chinese port for the United States in case the other powers broke their word.

Hay has been called "naive," "moralistic," and "easily gulled" by historians. His cavalier assurance that the other powers had accepted the Open Door policy when in fact they had made polite murmurings was seen by former diplomat George Kennan in *American Diplomacy* (1951) as a flagrant example of American misunderstanding of how diplomacy is done. Thomas McCormick, writing from a radical revisionist perspective in *The China Market* (1967), however, argues that Hay's critics underestimated him. The secretary had a weak diplomatic hand since he knew that the United States would not use force in China. Still he wanted an informal empire. Making the most of a bad situation, he maneuvered the other imperial states into taking account of what Americans had to say.

For Europeans his diplomacy seemed hypocritical and self-serving. The British liked the Open Door, but for different reasons than did the Americans. For British merchants, the new policy meant that they, the world's premier traders, would sweep the field. For Russians, Germans, and Japanese,

United States troops firing on Philippine nationalists.
(National Archives)

there was no such saving feature to America's attempt at moral suasion. The Open Door notes suggested to them that the United States had in charge of its foreign affairs a man who did not fully appreciate the vast changes which were occurring in China. The powers might agree to humor him, but they would pursue their own ends in China without taking orders from the United States.

The Europeans knew that the United States was engaged in the bloody suppression of a nationalist movement in its newly conquered Asian territory of the Philippines. This was one explanation of their failure to take seriously American demands that they forgo territorial ambitions in China. From 1899 until his capture in 1901, Emilio Aguinaldo led two hundred thousand independence fighters against the American occupiers of the islands. Aguinaldo's forces had fought the Spanish before the American arrival, and he was puzzled that the new colonial masters did not seem to want immediately to offer national freedom.

The United States sent 126,000 troops, who engaged in a fierce guerrilla war against the nationalists. Four thousand American soldiers and about five times that many Filipinos lost their lives in battle. *The Springfield Republican,* an antiimperialist newspaper, published reports of American officers ordering the murder of unarmed women, children, and infirm men. Filipino *insurrectos* complained of being subjected to a slow, painful water torture. One American officer who served in the war told a reporter, "We must bury all qualms . . . and have no scruples about exterminating this other race standing in the way of progress and enlightenment, if it is necessary." Two commissions, headed respectively by Jacob Gould Schurman, president of Cornell University, and William Howard Taft, an Ohio Republican politician, investigated conditions in the Philippines in 1900 and 1901. They heard an American anthropologist assert that "the great mass of the people here are ignorant. They have a very vague idea of either independence or liberty as such." Taft privately complained to his boss, President Theodore Roosevelt, that stories of atrocities ruined the morale of the American soldiers.

THE RISE OF THEODORE ROOSEVELT

Theodore Roosevelt, who took office in September 1901 when an assassin shot President McKinley, had a clearer idea than many presidents about what he wanted to accomplish in foreign affairs, He advocated "progressivism," a mixture of nationalism, moralism, racism, social Darwinism (the competition of the fittest peoples), uplift, and social planning. Suspicious of businessmen, he sometimes advanced their interests because he thought that might project American power. He divided the world according to race and culture. "Civilized" states could expect courteous treatment from the United States while "backwards" ones had to watch their step.

As a Progressive, Roosevelt believed in the power of the government to regulate at home and abroad. As a nationalist, he thought the United States superior to its rivals. In the nineties, he had joined Henry Cabot Lodge and Adm. Alfred Thayer Mahan, the architect of the modern American navy, in demanding a large American fleet, a war with Spain, and a canal across the Isthmus of Panama. As Howard Beale writes, "Though he valued the blessings of peace, he craved the excitement of war." The prospect of leading troops against Spain made him leave his comfortable job as assistant secretary of the navy to join the army in 1898. He had more fun charging up San Juan Hill at the head of his Rough Riders than he had at any time in his life since he left his ranch in North Dakota in his twenties. Blood was part of the thrill. "Did I tell you," he wrote Lodge, "that I killed a Spaniard with my own hands?"

How to assess such a man? Some recent historians, writing in a complex era, long for Roosevelt's panacea. In *Velvet on Iron* (1979), Frederick Marks calls him "a peacemaker in a bellicose age." A more typical view was expressed earlier by Howard Beale in the most thorough examination of Roosevelt's diplomacy, *Theodore Roosevelt and the Rise of America to World Power* (1956). Beale acknowledges Roosevelt's grasp, energy, and intelligence but admits that "the trouble lay not in his abilities but in his values." He was a bombastic nationalist who influenced America's course "that by mid-century was to bring her face to face with grave dangers."

For all of his strutting, however, Roosevelt had a strategy. He wanted the United States to act as a great power, fully the equal of the imperial states of Europe. Consequently, he created the Panama Canal, policed the Western Hemisphere, built up the navy, mediated the war between Russia and Japan in 1905, called for the Second Peace Conference at the Hague in 1907, and took a seat at the 1906 Algeciras Conference which decided the fate of Morocco. While maintaining that the United States was fully the equal of the other great powers of the world, TR sought to maintain good personal relationships with all of the European diplomats in Washington. He referred to the British ambassador, Cecil Spring-Rice, as "Springy," and the ambassador from Germany, Speck von Sternberg, as "Specky." The French ambassador, Jules Jusserand, had a forbidding presence that rebuffed nicknames, but Roosevelt included him on his rambles through Rock Creek Park.

Roosevelt, a racist and social Darwinist, thought it obvious that the fiercest competition in the modern world took place between different races. He spoke of an English-speaking "race," comparing it favorably to "backward" Chinese, Latins whose "day is over," or blacks kept down by their own "vice and criminality" and their "shiftlessness and laziness." Shortly before he became president, he thrilled a crowd in Minnesota with, "It is our duty people living people living in barbarism to see that they are freed from their chains, and we can free them only by destroying barbarism itself. . . . Exactly as it is the duty of a civilized power scrupulously to respect the rights of weaker civilized powers . . . so it is its duty to put down savagery and barbarism."

The Trans-Isthmian Canal

Roosevelt showed how he would put down savagery and barbarism in the Western Hemisphere. Consider his maneuverings to have the United States build and fortify a canal across the Isthmus of Panama. In 1850, the United States and Great Britain had agreed that neither power would build such a canal on its own. Ever since that Clayton-Bulwer Treaty, American diplomats and politicians had kicked themselves for having yielded such an important right to the British government. Not that it mattered very much before the technology of digging a lock-type canal of some thirty miles in length had been developed. But in the post–Civil War era, it became possible for the first time to create a canal with locks across the Isthmus.

The first group to try to do so was the French company which had completed the sea-level Suez Canal in 1869. Ferdinand de Lesseps, the creator of the Suez Canal, lost his money and his sanity in the effort to dig across the northern Colombian province of Panama. The bankruptcy of the Panama Canal Company became a major scandal in France in 1889, and it also provided the United States with an opportunity to annul the Clayton-Bulwer agreement and cut its own canal.

After the war with Spain, the United States was firmly committed to a canal, but the question was whether the ditch would be dug across Panama, where it would be shorter but would require locks, or across Nicaragua, where it would be longer but use a sea-level path. For the reorganized French company, which had been digging for fifteen years in Panama, the only way to recover at least part of its investment was for the Americans to select a route through Panama. If the Americans chose Panama, then they would buy the equipment left by the French.

While a special commission under Adm. J. C. Walker studied the preferred route, Secretary Hay negotiated with the British to allow the United States a free hand in digging a ditch between the Atlantic and Pacific oceans. Hay worked out two treaties with the British ambassador in Washington, Julian Pauncefote. In the first Hay-Pauncefote agreement, initialed in February 1900, the British agreed to an American canal but insisted that the waterway be neutral and unfortified. When Roosevelt became president, he refused to submit this treaty to the Senate and sent Hay back to Pauncefote with instructions to get a treaty which allowed the Americans to construct a canal and protect it with its own navies. Faced with the obvious determination on the part of Roosevelt to have a canal with or without British agreement, Pauncefote capitulated in 1901. The second Hay-Pauncefote agreement gave Americans everything they had asked for, although the British did insist that the tolls levied against them be the same as the ones levied on American ships.

Now that the United States had a free hand, the French company went to work making certain that the canal would be built across the territory where its equipment lay rusting. A French mining engineer, Philippe Bunau-Varilla, who had not seen Panama for the previous fifteen years, became the company's chief representative in the United States. Bunau-Varilla hired a Wall Street lawyer, William Nelson Cromwell, to lobby for the Panama route. As the Senate debated, the House passed the Hepburn bill, which recommended the route across Nicaragua. Bunau-Varilla and Cromwell placed on the desk of each senator a Nicaraguan postage stamp showing the volcano Momotombo in full eruption in the middle of the lake through which the canal would pass. On June 28, 1902, Congress approved the Panama route and the purchase of the French company for $40 million.

The question changed to how would the United States come to terms with the government of Colombia, which was sovereign in Panama. In January 1903, John Hay signed an agreement with Thomas Herrán, the Colombian minister to the United States. In return for a payment of $10 million and an annual rent of $250,000, the United States would have the right to lease for ninety-nine years a canal zone six miles wide across the Isthmus of Panama.

The Senate of Colombia rejected this treaty unanimously, hoping for more money from the United States. When Theodore Roosevelt learned that Colombia had turned down the treaty, he was outraged. He lashed the Colombians as "inefficient bandits" and "a corrupt pithecoid community." Cromwell, who visited the president, emerged to report, "President Roosevelt is determined to have the Panama Canal route." If necessary, he would help Panama secede from Colombia.

Some businessmen in the province of Panama also were alarmed at their Colombian Senate's decision to reject the treaty. These men had holdings in the French canal company, and they saw that a rejection of the treaty would ruin them. What if the Roosevelt administration decided after all on the Nicaraguan route? In order to prevent the loss of their investment, a junta in Panama City conspired with Philippe Bunau-Varilla to detach the province of Panama from Colombia. Once an independent Panama came into being, it could sign its own treaty, letting the United States build the canal. Legitimate nationalists who had long chafed under Colombian rule also joined the revolution. The successful secession of 1903 capped a sixty-year drive for independence which had seen at least four previous uprisings. A Panamanian diplomat remarked years later that his country became independent through "the interests and sentiments of the people of Panama, not the arbitrariness of Roosevelt." But TR played a major, dishonorable role.

While the junta in Panama City organized a revolt, Cromwell and Bunau-Varilla pressured the U.S. government to recognize revolutionary Panama. Bunau-Varilla went to the White House on October 10, 1903, to ask Roosevelt's help. Roosevelt later told a cheering crowd of students at Berkeley, "I took the isthmus," and in a way he did. When the revolutionaries proclaimed their independence on November 1, 1903, Roosevelt made certain that the American ship *Nashville* stood off the coast to prevent a Colombian landing. Two days later, a fleet of six American ships menaced the coast.

Events moved fast in Washington after the junta declared independence. Bunau-Varilla, although a French citizen and never having resided in Panama, named himself the foreign minister of the new government. The nationalists in Panama City wired him the news in New York that their rebellion had succeeded and told him that a delegation was on its way to Washington to negotiate a treaty with the United States. Bunau-Varilla had no intention, however, of waiting until the Panamanians, some of whom might be nationalists, arrived. They might try to get a treaty more favorable to their nation than the one which Colombia had rejected. The Frenchman feared that Roosevelt would spurn the Panamanians if they upped the ante, leaving his company stranded. Bunau-Varilla scurried to Washington on the night of November 8 and met with Hay the next morning. He carried with him a draft of a treaty which he got Hay to sign before the Panamanians arrived. When they showed up at Washington's Union Station on November 18, they were shocked. One of them was so angry at Bunau-Varilla that he punched him in the nose; another fainted when he learned what the United States had gained from Panama.

Later, Panamanians denounced the Hay–Bunau-Varilla agreement as "the treaty no Panamanian signed." Under its terms, the United States received a permanent lease upon a canal-zone territory ten miles wide. The United States would pay the same $10 million and $250,000 per year promised Colombia. Bunau-Varilla, wishing to sweeten the deal, included language allowing the United States to act "as if it were sovereign" in the zone. This grant of quasi-sovereignty bedeviled relations between the United States and Panama for seventy-five years until a treaty restored control of the canal to Panama in 1978. In the United States at the time, a few opposing Democrats denounced Roosevelt and the treaty. William Randolph Hearst's Democratic *Chicago American* called it "a rough-riding assault upon another republic over the shattered wreckage of international law and diplomatic usage." But such voices were few. Most Americans, *Public Opinion* asserted, wanted "an Isthmian canal above all things." The Senate ratified the treaty on February 23, 1904. TR knew the popularity of this accomplishment. He wrote a campaign manager in the 1904 election, "Can you tell our speakers to dwell more on the Panama Canal? We have not a stronger card."

The Army Corps of Engineers spent the next ten years in the mud, contracting yellow fever and supervising construction. While the army boasted of its campaign to eradicate the disease, it also hired some thirty thousand black laborers from the West Indies to perform the truly backbreaking work of digging the canal at ten cents an hour, ten hours a day, six days a week. "Segregation by color . . . became established policy." Thousands died from fatigue, overwork, and bad food. Those who survived suffered the contempt of their army foremen who complained that West Indians were "wasteful . . . stupid . . . possessed with unutterable hatred of exertion other than conversation." In 1906, Roosevelt became the first American president to leave the country while in office, sailing to Panama in November to look at the canal. He climbed into a giant ninety-five-ton Bucyrus steam shovel to have his picture taken watching "the dirt fly."

Theodore Roosevelt personally digging the Panama Canal, 1906.
(Library of Congress)

Expanding the Monroe Doctrine

Once the United States had purchased the rights to the Isthmus, the protection of the area took on importance. James Monroe had announced that the United States would block any new European colonies in the Western Hemisphere in 1823. No American statesman had made much of the doctrine during the first fifty years of its existence, but in the 1890s it had become a major principle of American foreign policy. During a border dispute between the government of Venezuela and British Guiana over the headwaters of the Orinoco River, the American secretary of state, Richard Olney, interjected himself as mediator in the controversy without having been asked for his opinion by either side. In one of the most famous comments ever made on United States dominance of the Western Hemisphere, Olney bluntly informed the British government that "the United States is practically sovereign in this hemisphere and its fiat is law upon the subjects to which it confines its interposition."

Ten years later, Roosevelt showed how many hemisphere subjects the United States considered relevant. After the war with Spain, Roosevelt did not fear direct rule from Europe, but economic ties between Europe and Latin America gave him pause. On the one hand, European lending and investment in the Western Hemisphere made business more difficult for American firms. Therefore, the United States government might support governments in the Caribbean and South America which wanted to evict European bankers and replace their funds with dollars from New York. On the other hand, lenders in Europe and the United States had to stick together in a common front against borrowers. Should the Latin American nations default on their European loan, the investments of Americans might be next.

In 1902, the government of Venezuela stopped payment on some $12.5 million in loans from European, mostly German, bankers. The dictator of Venezuela, Cipriano Castro, who had long denounced Europeans and the United States in equally harsh terms, became embroiled with the German kaiser, William II. At first, the United States paid no attention, as Roosevelt personally liked the kaiser and detested Castro. He told his friend, German ambassador "Specky" von Sternberg, "If any South American state misbehaves toward any European country, let the European country spank it." The chastisement began in December when the Germans and British sent a fleet to Venezuela, shelled the coast, and imposed a blockade. Roosevelt was pleased, but the *Literary Digest* reported that many American newspapers "think that the allies have gone too far." Roosevelt also worried that a Venezuelan capitulation in the face of European armed force would give an excessive boost to the German prestige in the Western Hemisphere. Accordingly, he urged arbitration upon Venezuela and the Europeans. The two sides took their case to the International Tribunal at the Hague which ruled in February 1904, upholding the claims of Germany and Britain against hapless Venezuela. In 1916, in the midst of his campaign to have the United States declare war against Germany, Roosevelt added a twist to the story of the Venezuelan dispute when he claimed that the Germans had actually intended to seize a port on the coast. "I took action accordingly," he said. "I assembled our battle fleet . . . for maneuvers, with instructions that the fleet . . . should be ready to sail at an hour's notice."

Two years after the Venezuelan affair, in December 1904, the president formally appointed the United States "the policeman of the west." The occasion was another financial row in the Caribbean. The Dominican Republic had placed its finances in the hands of an American financial concern optimistically calling itself the "Santo Domingo Improvement Company." In

1901, the government of the Dominican Republic threw out the American financiers, who appealed to the State Department for help in recovering $4.5 million. Belgian bankers also pressed suits, and the American minister in Santo Domingo, "an eager friend of intervention," reported that the government was considering inviting the Germans to establish a naval base on the island. Roosevelt himself warned in the spring of 1904 that he might have "to do what a policeman has to do."

The president waited until his resounding electoral victory in November. When Congress convened in December, he used the situation in Santo Domingo to announce his corollary to the Monroe Doctrine. He decried the "chronic wrongdoing, or . . . impotence which results in a general loosening of ties of civilized society." He told Congress that "in the western hemisphere the adherence of the United States to the Monroe Doctrine may force the United States, however reluctantly, in flagrant cases of such wrongdoing or impotence, to the exercise of an international police power." In these words, Roosevelt had transformed the Monroe Doctrine from a warning to the Europeans not to intervene in the Western Hemisphere into an American commitment to intervene whenever the United States saw "chronic wrongdoing" among its neighbors.

Three weeks after he spoke, the State Department opened discussions with the government of the Dominican Republic designed to establish American control over Dominican customs and tax receipts. A compliant Dominican government agreed and readily signed a treaty in February 1905, but Democrats in the Senate prevented its ratification. Roosevelt then acted informally, appointing an American as controller of the Dominican customs and stationing the navy off the coast just to make sure. On February 25, 1907, the two nations signed and ratified the treaty. While testifying for the agreement, the new secretary of state, Elihu Root, explained how the Panama Canal required the United States to "police the surrounding premises."

Historians and strategists have argued for three-quarters of a century over whether the canal and the Roosevelt Corollary resulted from economic pressures or from defenses against real or imagined threats from other great powers. Writing in the midst of worries over German expansion in the Second World War, Nicholas John Spyckman argued in *America's Strategy in World Politics* (1941) that Roosevelt's diplomacy in the Western Hemisphere rested on a clear-headed acknowledgment that modern European navies could attack the United States unless it turned the Caribbean into an American lake and protected the canal. Robert E. Osgood confirms that view in *Ideals and SelfInterest in American Foreign Relations* (1952). While faulting Roosevelt for nationalistic bravado, Osgood says that the decisions on the canal and the corollary came from the president's realistic assessment of the dangers of war. Other historians, while not denying Roosevelt's jingoism, point to the role of businessmen in advocating the canal and urging a policeman's role on the United States. Walter LaFeber in *The New Empire* (1963) and *The Panama Canal* (1979) suggests that the "Yankee colossus," as the Latin Americans came to call the United States, acquired its domination because private American citizens saw the hemisphere as a rich new market. In *Tragedy of American Diplomacy* (1962) William Appleman Williams supports this view.

Roosevelt on Asia and Russia

But Roosevelt himself never clearly distinguished between economic and strategic motives in his foreign policy. He thought that many businessmen had far too narrow a view of the national interest: they were "lazy [and] preferred ease to the strenuous life." At the same time, he believed that American businessmen were superior to those of other nations. Sometimes he sought to stiffen the spines of American businessmen and have them aggressively seek markets they might otherwise ignore. In China, he thought that American business could be the stalking horse for the government. He encouraged a reluctant J. P. Morgan in 1905 to back a railroad in China even though it was a bad investment. The president fulminated against businessmen who took only a short view. Even if the American-China Development Corporation lost money, U.S. businessmen could maintain an American presence in a country where the United States could not use force.

Roosevelt was especially concerned that the United States was losing influence in China to Russia, which had moved into Manchuria after 1900. In the war between Russia and Japan of 1904 and 1905, the rest of the world watched as those two nations fought to determine the major imperial power in China. When the war broke, the United States sided with the Japanese. Russia had enjoyed good relations with the United States in the eighteenth and nineteenth centuries, when it had supported the American definition of neutral rights. The United States had also supported the call of Czar Nicholas II for the peace conference at the Hague in 1899. But in the Roosevelt administration, relations deteriorated badly. A pogrom against Jews in the south Russian city of Kishinev in 1903 sent shock waves across the Atlantic Ocean. Jewish immigration from Russia had risen throughout the decade of the 1890s, and it shot up dramatically after the attack, which killed forty-nine people. From 1890 to 1910, some 1.5 million Jews left Russia for the United States. President Roosevelt denounced the pogrom and with it the entire government of Russia as a "barbarous despotism."

When Japan attacked the Russian fleet at Port Arthur without warning on February 8, 1904, the American public reacted gleefully. Elihu Root asked the president, "Was not the way the Jap began the fight bully?" He admired their "perfect preparation and willingness to take action," and newspapers chimed in with high praise for Japanese cleverness. Just as the reputation of Russia had sunk in the United States at the end of the nineteenth century, that of the Japanese had risen over the years. Some Americans felt flattered by the Japanese imitation of the habits of the West. Hundreds of Japanese had attended universities in the United States, going home full of enthusiasm for American science, business methods, and political structure. But not all Japanese were so loved by Americans. While hundreds of students came to American universities to learn techniques which they could apply back home, thirty thousand more Japanese came to America as laborers, where they encountered nativist demands for their exclusion, segregation, and repatriation. When the Japanese vanquished the Russians, American feelings toward them were thus mixed. On the one hand, Americans admired the Japanese capacity to learn from the West and improve themselves. On the other hand, deep strains of racism turned the Japanese into a threatening people who might overtake the West.

The war with Japan helped create a revolution in Russia which threatened to topple the czar's despotism in early 1905. It also had immediate and longterm effects upon American thinking about Russia. The initial American reaction to the "democratic" uprising in St. Petersburg in 1905 was enthusiasm for the reformers, who seemed to want to imitate the democratic form of government favored in the United States. Roosevelt himself thought the revolution was an encouraging sign, and it made him more favorably disposed toward the Russian side in the war. Americans quickly discovered, however, that the revolution was not the "liberal" movement they hoped would become the standard for the world. The ambassador in St. Petersburg reported the alarming presence of socialists, Communists, and communitarians in the leadership of the revolutionary forces. The czar might have been "stupid, cruel, despotic," but the radicals who longed to replace him were worse. The government's shakiness made Roosevelt want to mediate an end to the war with Japan, while his alarm at the radicals foreshadowed later American uneasiness with a new generation of Russian revolutionaries twelve years later.

Roosevelt's attitudes toward the war typified the views of others. Along with his countrymen, the president detested Russian despotism and felt flattered by the Japanese imitation of American habits, but at the same time he feared the Japanese. Neither complete Japanese nor Russian victories pleased him. He injected himself as a mediator in the war in order to make sure that the United States had a say in the future of China. Roosevelt worried that no matter what the outcome, it would leave China at the mercy of either Japan or Russia. In either case, the United States and the Western European powers would find themselves frozen out of deciding what the future of China would look like. He tried, therefore, to stop the two powers from completing their conquest of China. Roosevelt hoped that his mediation would cause the combatants to draw back from dismembering China, but even if he did not succeed, he wanted to demonstrate to the Chinese that the United States had their best interest at heart. He would be an honest broker to the belligerents; to the Chinese, he would be a protector.

In June 1905, Roosevelt asked representatives of Russia and Japan to meet with him at Portsmouth, New Hampshire, to end the conflict. Exhausted by war, both powers accepted, and the peace conference assembled on August 9 in the midst of the hottest summer in New England history. The Japanese wanted the Russians to pay a huge indemnity, yield a free hand in North China and Manchuria, and hand over their lease on the Liaodong (Liaotung) Peninsula, the base at Port Arthur, and Sakhalin Island. Roosevelt felt the Japanese had a right to expect an indemnity from the Russians, but he did not want the Japanese to take over the Russian port. Under the terms of the Open Door policy, Roosevelt also was worried about the Japanese desire for a free hand in the north of China. Russia refused to provide an indemnity, or all territory demanded.

The conversations at Portsmouth therefore did not go smoothly. The United States was contemptuous of the Russians and a little afraid of the Japanese. Russia had lost the war and was convulsed by revolution at home. For their part, the financially spent Japanese could no longer press their advantage. Both sides sullenly accepted a compromise Roosevelt presented on August 28. Japan dropped demands for an indemnity and agreed to accept only half of Sakhalin in return for virtual control of North China and Manchuria. In 1906, Roosevelt won the Nobel Peace Prize for his work. The next year, however, Russia and Japan quietly buried the hatchet and agreed jointly to dismember North China and Manchuria. The United States found itself out in the cold.

Japanese nationalists thought that Roosevelt had deprived them of their just gains, and an ugly riot broke out in Tokyo. Protestors demanded that the government reject American mediation and take every inch demanded of the czar. The crowd denounced Roosevelt and hanged an effigy of the American president in front of the United States embassy. The Japanese government had helped organize the rally against the United States, but once the people had blown off steam, officials dropped opposition to the treaty.

Racial disagreements between the United States and Japan continued after the Russo-Japanese War. In October 1906, the school board of San Francisco sent Japanese children to segregated schools in that city. There happened to be fewer than two hundred Japanese students in the district, but the board decided anyway that these children were a disrupting influence upon the lives of the rest of the scholars. Japan angrily protested to the Department of State in Washington about the segregation order. Elihu Root, the conservative New York lawyer who had succeeded John Hay as secretary of state upon Hay's death in 1905, thought the school board had gone too far. He had no special concern for the feelings of Japanese in America, but Root believed that the United States could not afford to offend the government of Japan. Roosevelt as well was furious with the San Franciscans, denouncing the segregation order as a "wicked absurdity." He summoned the California congressional delegation to the White House on January 3, 1907, to reveal his plan to have San Francisco drop segregation while he stopped further immigration from Japan. He let the Japanese ambassador know that he personally disapproved of the segregation order, believed that the Californians were bigots, and wanted the Japanese to continue to have good relations with the United States.

Eventually, in the winter of 1906–1907, Roosevelt worked out a gentlemen's agreement with the San Francisco school board and the government of Japan. The Californians would return the Japanese school children to their regular classrooms, and the Japanese government would finally ban emigration to the United States. The Japanese would not have to suffer the indignity of being singled out, as had the Chinese, as members of a race which could not enter the United States. Under the gentlemen's agreement, no Japanese came directly to the United States for the next two decades.

A Great Power Everywhere

Theodore Roosevelt also involved the United States in European conflicts which traditionally had not interested the American government. One of these involved Morocco. By the early twentieth century, this sand dune in North Africa, officially part of the Ottoman empire, had fallen under the control of France. The German emperor, William II, thought that France should yield a share of the direction of Moroccan affairs to Germany. In March 1905, the kaiser showed up in Tangier and offered a toast to the bey of Morocco which pledged support to him in resisting the French. France complained that the Germans were fishing in troubled waters, and William II replied by asking President Roosevelt to intervene on his side. Roosevelt, eager to see the United States assume a prominent role in world affairs, readily agreed to invite the great powers to a conference at Algeciras on the Spanish coast.

No one could say that the United States had a direct interest in what happened in Morocco, but Theodore Roosevelt insisted that the American government receive an invitation to the conference which assembled at the Spanish port city in January 1906. He reasonsed that if the United States truly was a world power with interests everywhere around the globe, then America should be included in the conferences which drew up the boundaries. Brushing aside the objection that the Monroe Doctrine had formerly prevented the United States from involvement in European politics, Roosevelt asserted he participated "to keep matters on an even keel in Europe."

On another occasion in the Roosevelt administration, the United States led the way in calling a general conference of the major nations. In the summer of 1906, Americans joined forty-three other countries at the Hague to complete the work of the First Hague Peace Conference of 1899. The Second Hague Conference continued the work of the first in setting the rules of war. New weapons developed over the previous decade made the work of the conference all the harder. What would the diplomats, admirals, and generals have to say about the new battleships, poison gas, and war from balloons in the air? All the participants worried that these new techniques of destruction might ruin them in a coming war. They also hoped, however, that the new weaponry would be exactly what they needed to overcome their opponents. The American delegation, led by John W. Foster, a former secretary of state and a grandfather of a future one, John Foster Dulles, led the way in establishing some new rules. Poison gas was outlawed, but the powers could not agree on other new frightening weapons—the submarine, the aerial balloon, the airplane, or the battleship. The admirals and generals refused to ban these modern instruments of destruction. They thought that the advantages they could gain from using these weapons would outweigh any dangers which might ensue.

The Hague Conference made a start in creating a predictable world through the codification of international law. Reformers expected the court to grow into what Andrew Carnegie called a League of Peace or a League of Nations. Some reformers anticipated the birth of an international congress to enforce the judgments of the Hague court. Richard Bartholdt, one of the organizers of the American Society of International Law in 1906, confidently predicted that in due time an international congress would grow and become "more perfect in form and accomplish for nations what a Federal union like ours accomplished for the constituent states."

Secretary of State Elihu Root, who lent his name to the creation of the American Society of International Law, had more modest hopes. At the beginning of the twentieth century, international law was nothing more than the treaties previously drawn up between states. Nations might agree to regulate their affairs with one another according to treaties, and the courts of two nations might rule that the treaties had the force of law. Root proposed to make the treaties conducted by individual states available to every nation. He suggested that a central organization record all treaties nations had drafted with one another. Registration of treaties would fulfill several functions: it would set standards for other nations to uphold in their treaties, permit the Hague court to make judgments, and eliminate the practice of "secret treaties," agreements with clauses known only to the nations signing them. Reformers believed that this kind of treaty created discord and resentment among states since nations could only fear that secret clauses contained threats. The reformers of international law acknowledged that strong states would still rule the world once treaties were codified. Still, the growing body of international law could make the world more predictable for the weak as well as the strong. Lesser nations would have to respect the mighty, but they had less to fear from their caprice.

As secretary of state, Root began a campaign of arbitration treaties for the United States. Under terms of these agreements signed with twenty-four states throughout the world, each party agreed to bring outstanding disputes between them to the world court at the Hague. In this way, Root sought to offer some respect to the world court.

Root's career as a jurist was a curious one. Early in the Roosevelt administration, he had served as one of the president's hand-picked panelists on an arbitration board deciding the boundary between Alaska and Canada. Seated alongside Root for the Americans were Henry Cabot Lodge and a former senator from the state of Washington, two intense nationalists. The dispute arose over control of the Lynn Canal and the port city of Sitka. Once gold had been discovered in the Klondike River basin of Alaska in 1899, it became important to Alaskans and Canadians alike that they have access to the sea.

The Canadians insisted to both the British government in London and the American State Department in Washington that the ports on the coast belonged to Canada. Otherwise, there would be no way that Canadian gold could be shipped out without going through Alaska. The British government did not favor the Canadian claims as the Foreign Office in London thought good relations with the United States mattered more than did satisfying the demands of their lower dominion. The British agreed to bring the case before a mock arbitration panel in order to quiet the Canadians. Roosevelt could appoint men to the panel who were bound to support the Alaskan claims. The British side of the delegation consisted of two Canadians and an English judge, Richard C. E. Alverstone. Since the Americans would hold for their side and the Canadians for the claims of the Yukon, Alverstone had the final say. He held for the United States, outraging the Canadians. London supported the Americans in the controversy since it did not wish the growing entente between the two countries to be jeopardized to satisfy Ottawa's parochial interests. Canadians grumbled that the defection of the British meant that Canada had no choice but to seek control of its own affairs. Eventually, in 1921, Canada gained such independence.

The British capitulation to the United States in 1903, however, indicated that they had decided that the Western Hemisphere belonged to the Americans. Britain's period of "splendid isolation" had left it threatened by other powers. It needed friends, and America seemed a good candidate. Insofar as the British had ambitions in world politics, they would be satisfied in Europe first, then in the Middle East, and then in Africa and Asia. The United States and the British would become good friends but only at the cost of a division of the world into spheres.

In 1907, Roosevelt decided literally to show the flag. He had the American navy, which he happily called the "Great White Fleet," travel to Europe, Africa, and Asia to impress world leaders with American might. When the fleet was halfway around the world, the American Congress, in a cost-cutting mood, threatened to stop payment for such imperial pomp. Undaunted, Roosevelt informed Congress that the fleet could stay abroad, demonstrating that the United States was indeed a premier nation, if the money did not arrive to bring it back to the United States. Of course Congress relented, and the Great White Fleet sailed home triumphantly.

When Roosevelt turned over his office to William Howard Taft, his hand-picked successor, on March 4, 1909, he had laid the foundations for subsequent progressive diplomacy. He bequeathed an enthusiastic American nationalism that distrusted the flag-waving of other countries. Valuing stability and the capacity to influence the future above all else, the makers of foreign policy saw other peoples' nationalism, revolutionary fervor, and great power rivalry as threats to a predictable world order.

CHAPTER THREE

The Diplomacy of the Dollar, 1909–1920

In the 1920s, the term *dollar diplomacy* became a curse mouthed by liberals, radicals, and muckrakers who damned the foreign policies of William Howard Taft and Woodrow Wilson. One reform-minded author, Scott Nearing, wrote a book called *Dollar Diplomacy* to prove how Taft and Wilson had boosted the fortunes of selfish Wall Street plutocrats at the expense of the people of China, Central America, Mexico, and the Caribbean. Critics even discovered forgotten virtues in the nationalism of Theodore Roosevelt. If the flamboyant Rough Rider had been bombastic, at least he was fun to watch. Taft, with his countinghouse mentality, appeared dull, and Wilson, with his sermons to foreigners who did not want to listen, seemed a hypocrite.

Self-satisfied and good-natured, William Howard Taft never seemed bothered by the criticism. He thought his quieter, less martial, more realistic conduct of foreign relations surpassed that of his predecessor. His secretary of state, Philander C. Knox, a former corporation lawyer, proudly spoke of dollar diplomacy, thinking it represented an advance in the way the United States conducted its foreign affairs. Instead of dwelling on conflicts among nations and preparing for war, Knox urged support for international traders and investors who knit the world together. Of course, any government tries to shield its citizens working abroad, yet dollar diplomacy went far beyond protesting harassment by foreigners of Americans. Instead, Knox elevated international businessmen to the position where they, rather than diplomats, represented the best interests of the United States overseas. In contrast to Theodore Roosevelt, who tolerated businessmen but thought them too weak and cowardly to do much good for the American cause overseas, Knox believed that business leaders actually were morally superior to flag-waving military men. Their very caution made them better advocates for the United States. They hated war, loved predictability, and supposedly built bridges across frontiers.

In a sense, dollar diplomacy recalled the earliest traditions of American foreign policy. In the eighteenth century, one of the reasons the United States had separated from Great Britain and Europe was an American suspicion that the Europeans spent too much time on war and peace and too little effort on commerce. In his pamphlet *Common Sense,* Tom Paine had warned that Britain and Europe were corrupt because they had kept business and the expansion of trade in a subordinate role. In the "model treaty" drafted by the Second Continental Congress in 1776 to serve as basis of all subsequent United States relations with foreign nations, the principal form of interaction with other nations was supposed to be commercial. The model treaty elevated the status of the "most-favored-nation clause," under which the United States and its trading partners agreed to extend the same privileges to one another that they extended to all other states. In the eighteenth and nineteenth centuries, mostfavored-nation status became the major aim of American diplomats in the treaties signed then with the great powers of Europe. Americans did not always succeed in gaining these clauses, but they never stopped trying.

In the early twentieth century, that status became only one of a variety of strategies which the United States would pursue in helping its overseas traders and investors. Under Taft, the government also tried to make certain that United States traders would be welcomed alongside those of every other nation and American bankers got their share of the booming market for foreign loans. As European and American railroad promoters and mining companies cast longing glances toward the remaining underdeveloped regions of the world, Knox believed that the rest of the world had finally caught up with the American way of diplomacy. As in Paine's day, Knox's promotion of business abroad became a way of placing international relations on a more peaceable foundation than that of dynastic rivalry.

Taft operated at a time when the expansion of European and American capital abroad helped ignite nationalistic resentments against the imperial powers. Revolutions erupted in Asia and Central America, the two regions most attractive to American investors. The pace picked up under Woodrow Wilson, who clung to a belief that the United States was somehow more moral than the imperial powers of Europe. "In Wilson's completely liberal ideology, imperialism and militarism were seen as essentially European phenomena associated with a past America had escaped," writes historian N. Gordon Levin in *Woodrow Wilson and World Politics* (1968). This notion of "American exceptionalism" served United States interests, for it enabled Wilson to claim "a mission to lead mankind." His first secretary of state, three-time Democratic presidential candidate William Jennings Bryan, did not fit the mold of a worldly eastern lawyer as chief diplomat. Wilson's appointment of the Nebraska-born "Great Commoner" raised eyebrows among the sophisticated. To journalist Walter Lippmann, the new secretary seemed "irresistibly funny," a man who "moved in a world that has ceased to exist." The *New York Sun* urged the president to "seize upon the windpipe of Bryanism at the very start and . . . throttle that persistent fatal thing." Six weeks after taking over the State Department, Bryan served White Rock water and grape juice, but no wine or liquor, at a farewell reception for Britain's ambassador. "Grape juice diplomacy" became a derisive phrase among Bryan's detractors. One of his friends remarked that he provoked "wholehearted, comprehensive, constitutional, fundamental, temperamental, special, religious, anatomical, gastronomic, and sartorical disagreement."

For all of his midwestern naiveté, Bryan as much as Wilson believed that the United States occupied a special place in God's favor. When it came to explaining their duties to foreigners, he obediently followed his chief's instructions. After he resigned in 1915, his place was taken by a more traditional diplomat, Robert Lansing, a well-connected but nonpolitical lawyer. Lansing did not enjoy Bryan's base within the Democratic party, and by the time he became secretary, Wilson had acquired enough confidence in his own diplomatic skills that he wanted a clerk as his principal foreign policy adviser. Lansing performed this secondary role with some misgivings as Wilson grappled with the changes nationalism and revolution brought to world politics.

AMERICA, CHINA, AND THE PROBLEM OF REVOLUTION, 1909–1915

One place the Taft administration sought to practice dollar diplomacy was China, where Knox moved quickly to distinguish his policy from Roosevelt's. The Rough Rider had quietly dropped the Open Door policy in the wake of the Russo-Japanese War, acknowledging that Japan's and Russia's proximity to China gave them the power to do what they wanted in Manchuria. While the American consul general in Mukden, Willard Straight, complained that the Russo-Japanese rapprochement of 1908 effectively froze the United States out of North China, Roosevelt thought there was little the United States could do about it. The principal American interest in the Far East was the protection of the Philippines, which could be done by mollifying Japan.

Taft and Knox paid more attention than had TR to Straight, who returned to Washington to become chief of the Division of Far Eastern Affairs, and Huntington Wilson, the first assistant secretary of state. Both men detested Japan and promoted China. They encouraged Knox to urge American investment in China to counter the influence of Japan and Russia. The Chinese government in Beijing (Peking) also hoped that investment from the United States and perhaps Great Britain would check Japanese expansion.

The American effort to enter the investment market of North China began in the summer of 1909. Taft cabled Prince Chun, the Chinese regent, asking him to grant American investors an equal share of a loan being floated in Europe to construct a railroad in southern China. In 1910, the Europeans reluctantly acceded to Chinese and American importunities and allowed Americans to invest. About the same time, Willard Straight left the State Department to represent the American bankers who wanted to build railroads in Manchuria. He went to Europe and China to obtain agreement for his sponsors to join a consortium building a trans-Manchurian railroad from Chinchow to Aigun. In October, Chinese representatives in Manchuria authorized Straight's group to finance the road.

While Straight worked the private sector, Knox proceeded along a diplomatic front to establish an open door for investment and make the United States the savior of China. The State Department proposed the "neutralization" or "internationalization" of all railroads in Manchuria and North China. Japan was the obvious target of this scheme which would force the island empire to yield its exclusive control of the South Manchurian railroad. Knox hoped that Russia and Great Britain would welcome the chance to block Japan. Unfortunately for his plan, their fears of Japanese military power exceeded their greed. Britain had been allied with Japan since 1902, when London felt the need for friends in remote places. British support for the neutralization plan would jeopardize the alliance. Knox had no better luck with Russia, which drew closer to Japan in the face of the neutralization plan. The Russians feared Japanese retaliation while expecting that their agreement with Japan over the exploitation of North China offered more protection than agreeing to American proposals.

Having been rebuffed by the British and Russians, the Taft administration kept at it. The next area in which it sought to have American businessmen participate was in direct loans to the government of China to meet its operating expenses and stabilize its currency. The finances of China, like those of so many dying empires, were in disarray at the turn of the century. As the government lost control of outlying districts and as its expenses mounted, it found itself deeply in debt. As had been the case for the Ottoman empire, Egypt, or Morocco in the late nineteenth century, the Chinese discovered that the only readily available source of funds was the bankers of the outside powers.

Chinese government officials knew what had happened in North Africa in the previous decades when the local governments had borrowed in Europe. In some cases, the debts had led to seizures of the customs houses. In others, European powers had established protectorates over the debtor. Chinese diplomats feared the same fate, so they actively encouraged the Americans to join the consortium making loans for their currency. The more participants in the consortium, the Chinese reasoned, the easier to play one against another. Tang Shao, a leader of the Manchurian railroad, also detected a more impartial attitude on the part of the United States. He complained that "the great powers of Europe, aside from Germany, openly give to Japan the advantage over us and conclude with her agreements to our detriment, but the United States continues to have in the Far East a national policy independent of all foreign alliances."

The American government wanted New York bankers to join in loans to China, with Knox insisting that participation would preserve the Open Door. He encouraged Straight to alert bankers to their patriotic obligations to join the loan consortium organized in support of China's government. The secretary of state passed the word that "when we support the open door in China that is not so-called dollar diplomacy, but the recognition of a high moral duty."

Duty, perhaps, but bankers saw no reason to bear the major burden of morality. They scorned the meager promise of 5-percent interest, doubted the Chinese would pay even that modest amount, and wondered if Washington used them as a "wedge" to gain preeminence in China. Nonetheless, Knox carried the day in persuading them that if the United States did not participate in the loans, then the empire would fall apart. In 1911, the American firms of J. P. Morgan and Kuhn Loeb and Company made over $2 million available for the Chinese government.

The government tried, but the transfusion of money could not revive the Manchu empire. In April 1911, China underwent one of the revolutions which convulsed it in the twentieth century. Under the leadership of Sun Yat-sen, an American-educated doctor, Chinese revolutionaries overthrew the monarchy and created a republic. For Americans, the initial success of the revolutionaries represented a vast improvement over the empire. Knox thought revolution in China a far better thing for American interests than the Boxer Rebellion of 1900. The earlier uprising had been a nationalistic, antiforeign movement. While the earlier Boxers opposed the government of China, their animosity toward the authorities derived from the government's having turned the country over to the foreigners. The republicans of 1911 opposed the corruption of the court itself, arguing that China should use the West as a model. Sun's government would resemble the American system in outward form. American officials were flattered by the Chinese mimicry.

The pompous pride Americans felt when the Chinese emulated them clouded the American judgment about their revolution. Unwilling or unable to recognize that Chinese republicans took only those elements from the American experience which they believed to be most relevant to their own, the Americans thought instead that the Chinese wanted to become like the United States. When it later became clear that the republicans remained proud of their own heritage and resented the West as much as had the Boxers, lovers of China felt betrayed. How dare the Chinese try to find their own way of organizing their society?

The response to the Chinese revolution followed the pattern set by the Russian revolution of 1905. For the remainder of the century, Americans maintained ambivalent feelings toward nationalist upheavals. During these eruptions, the reaction became a short-lived initial burst of enthusiasm as Yankees heard echoes of their own eighteenth-century revolution. Americans longed to see themselves as a model, and they considered Europe a source of reaction and autocracy. But this complacency soon collapsed under the weight of revolutionary nationalism. When revolutionaries turned against the United States as bad or even worse than European nations, Americans reacted with wounded pride. At this point, they usually believed that the revolution had been captured by "fanatics" who lacked the sense of balance or perspective needed to run a modern state. They rejected the possibility of organizing a modern society on any lines other than those laid down in the United States and began to think that the revolutionaries did not know what they were doing. As revolutions turned radical, the United States opposed them.

In the aftermath of the Chinese revolution of 1911, Secretary of State Knox redoubled his efforts to have Wall Street bankers loan money to the new republic, hoping to influence it in favor of "moderation" and the United States. For his part, Sun Yat-sen would have the Western consortium continue to loan money so long as the terms of the loan could be revised in China's favor. The European powers, on the other hand, demurred, suspecting the independence of the new republican government. They resisted according diplomatic recognition to the republic for a year after the revolution, while negotiations to refinance the loan bogged down.

By the time a new agreement was reached in early 1913, the Taft administration was a lame duck, having been defeated in November 1912 in a threeway race with former president Roosevelt, running as a Progressive, and the winner, the Democrats' Woodrow Wilson. During the election campaign, foreign affairs had not been an issue. Instead the more progressive candidates, Roosevelt and Wilson, had complained about the probusiness attitude of the leader they both called "lazy." Wilson, the former governor of New Jersey and president of Princeton University before that, had campaigned for the "New Freedom," a vague promise of government intervention to protect middle-class Americans from the grip of large, heartless business interests. As a college professor, Wilson had written extensively on the structure of American government but had thought little about the problems of foreign affairs. His views were the standard opinions of Democratic politicians of the day: a commitment to low tariffs and free trade, a resentment of Theodore Roosevelt's nationalistic flourishes, and a reluctance to hold formal colonies.

A week after he took office on March 4, 1913, Wilson reversed Taft's support of the American bankers' participation in the China loan consortium. After March 13, he told the press, J. P. Morgan's bank, and the American minister in Beijing, American financiers would be on their own in China. For Wilson's admirers, this abrupt reversal cancelled dollar diplomacy and made him, in the words of Arthur Link, "the first effective anti-imperialist statesman of the twentieth century." Link, the comprehensive biographer of Wilson, argues that he broke up the consortium because he "utterly detested the exploitative imperialist system" and the consortium "threatened the political independence of China." Few others have expressed quite so rosy a view of Wilson's China policy. William A. Williams's *Tragedy of American Diplomacy* (1962) describes the new loan policy in China as a different sort of turning point. Williams notes that bankers themselves had grown weary of the constant hectoring from Taft and Knox to commit funds to worthless projects. Moreover, Wilson actually freed the American bankers from having to associate with their European counterparts. Committed to a belief that the United States was exceptional in world politics, Wilson hoped that the Chinese might distinguish between the Americans and the more exploitative Europeans.

For all of Wilson's scorn for Theodore Roosevelt's boyish temper, the new president's Asian policy actually followed Roosevelt's attempt to reach an accommodation with Japan. Joint ventures with Japan cast a spell over American financiers for the next year. When, however, Europe erupted into war in August 1914, the Japanese saw their opportunity to exploit China without the help of any other power, including the United States. Wilson himself became preoccupied with events in Mexico and Europe in 1914 and 1915, as we shall see shortly, and the United States found itself without influence in China. In 1915, Japan presented the "Twenty-One Demands," which required that China become a virtual protectorate of Japan. Despite Lansing's protests, Japan got its way from 1915 to 1919.

INTERVENTION AND DOLLAR DIPLOMACY IN CENTRAL AMERICA AND THE CARIBBEAN

The United States government had an easier time getting its way through dollar diplomacy closer to home where it had less competition from imperial rivals. Taft and Knox sent the American marines to occupy Nicaragua and the Dominican Republic, took over the custom receipts of Guatemala and Honduras, and meddled in Mexico. The Wilson administration occupied the Dominican Republic and Haiti and nearly fought a war with America's southern neighbor, Mexico. In each case the United States intervened to prevent what was called "anarchy." Often intervention made things worse, as the government assisted private traders and investors who hoped to steal a march on competition from Europe. Taft and Wilson went beyond the Roosevelt Corollary to the Monroe Doctrine by intervening in Central America before there was a hint of the "chronic wrongdoing" which Roosevelt had insisted called for the United States to wield its policeman's stick.

The case of Nicaragua provided one of the longest running episodes of American interventions in the hemisphere. In 1909, American businessmen helped a local junta overthrow the dictatorship of José Zaleya, who had led the country since 1893. A nationalist, Zaleya had been a thorn in the side of the United States, waging wars with his neighbors Honduras, El Salvador, and Guatemala. Worse, from the American point of view, he financed his country's national debt through European banks in May 1909. Under the terms of this agreement, Europeans had control over the customs revenues, and their governments could intervene directly should the Central American country default on its debt.

American landholders and miners in Nicaragua accordingly sought ways to rid the country of Zaleya, and in 1909 they financed a revolution against him. The rebels, led by Juan Estrada, conducted a guerrilla campaign, and during one of the military engagements, Zaleya's troops captured and executed two United States citizens fighting with the insurgents. In Washington, Knox responded by denouncing Zaleya to Nicaragua's chargé d'affaires as a "blot on the history of Nicaragua." The secretary then broke diplomatic relations and announced the United States would welcome a victory of the insurrection. Faced with American support of his opponents, Zaleya resigned and fled to Mexico.

By August 1910, the guerrillas had triumphed and installed as president Adolfo Díaz, who once had worked as a bookkeeper for an American mining firm in the country. American businessmen there welcomed Díaz's assumption of power, but they let him know that if he was to maintain the nation's finances, he must look to the United States for help. Knox thought that an American loan would end the residual British interests in that country. In June 1911, Knox signed an accord with the Nicaraguan minister to Washington, Salvador Castrillo, that would turn the latter's country into a protectorate of the United States.

Under the terms of the Knox-Castrillo Convention, the United States refunded the Nicaraguan debt with an American loan. As collateral, the Cen-

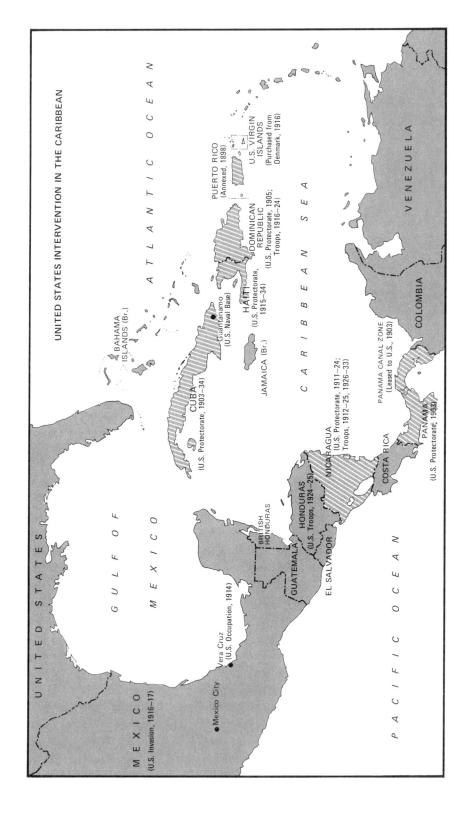

UNITED STATES INTERVENTION IN THE CARIBBEAN

UNITED STATES

GULF OF
MEXICO

MEXICO
(U.S. Invasion, 1916–17)

●Mexico City

Vera Cruz
(U.S. Occupation, 1914)

BAHAMA
ISLANDS (Br.)

CUBA
(U.S. Protectorate, 1903–34)

Guantánamo
(U.S. Naval Base)

JAMAICA (Br.)

HAITI
(U.S. Protectorate,
1915–34)

DOMINICAN
REPUBLIC
(U.S. Protectorate, 1905;
Troops, 1916–24)

PUERTO RICO
(Annexed, 1898)

U.S. VIRGIN
ISLANDS
(Purchased from
Denmark, 1916)

ATLANTIC OCEAN

CARIBBEAN SEA

GUATEMALA

BRITISH
HONDURAS

HONDURAS
(U.S. Troops, 1924–25)

EL SALVADOR

NICARAGUA
(U.S. Protectorate, 1911–24;
Troops, 1912–25, 1926–33)

COSTA RICA

PANAMA CANAL ZONE
(Leased to U.S., 1903)

PANAMA
(U.S. Protectorate, 1903)

COLOMBIA

VENEZUELA

PACIFIC OCEAN

tral American nation pledged its customs receipts, and the commissioner of customs became an official approved by the American government. Knox had no respect for the self-restraint of any of these "banana-republic" politicians and claimed that placing the customs house under control of the United States would remove an incentive to oust the new government by eliminating the prize of the tariff revenues.

Less than a month after signing the convention, the Managua government defaulted on the debts contracted with the Europeans in 1909. The Department of State unofficially encouraged American bankers to step into the breach. They did so by providing a short-term credit of a million dollars and a promise to negotiate a settlement with the European creditors. Americans also took over control of the Nicaraguan customs house. In December 1911, Knox appointed an American army officer on leave of absence from his command to take charge of the collection of customs duties in Nicaragua.

While all of these activities occurred in Central America, the Senate considered the Knox-Castrillo agreement, which would make them formal. Democrats objected, accusing Knox of wishing to extend the power of the United States too broadly. Furthermore, the Senate was jealous of its authority to make treaties and believed that the convention would limit its control of foreign affairs. In May 1912, senators turned back the Knox-Castrillo pact. American bankers, however, continued their supervision of the customs houses of Nicaragua. With the connivance of Taft and Knox, the Amer-

United States marines on the move in Nicaragua.
(National Archives)

icans maintained a sort of informal protectorate over the finances. The Senate, which had worried that it had yielded too much power to the executive branch, discovered that the administration did not care whether it approved its actions or not.

In Nicaragua itself, American domination aroused resentment from nationalists led by former president Zaleya. In July 1912, they attacked the government in Managua, and Díaz wired Washington for assistance to put down the revolt. American bankers also desperately wanted assistance because they feared that their own holdings in the country might be appropriated. Taft sent a flotilla of eight American warships bearing a force of twenty-five hundred marines, and sailors landed to crush the revolt. After Díaz was saved, one hundred marines remained to guard the American legation, and an American warship remained stationed off the coast as a warning to the revolutionaries. Díaz's control had been restored, but he could never be safe so long as his treasury was insecure. Furthermore, American lenders wanted greater assurance than their supervision of the country's customs houses that they would receive repayment. In early 1913, they encouraged Díaz to negotiate a new treaty with the United States to underwrite their loans. In February, the two countries signed a treaty under which the United States received naval bases and the right to build and operate a canal across the country. In return for these favors, the United States would pay, not loan, Nicaragua $3 million. Wilson became president in March, and he submitted the treaty to the Senate with an additional guarantee of Washington's right to intervene. This new Bryan-Chamorro Treaty was not ratified until 1916, when the Senate dropped the intervention clause. Wilson sent American warships to patrol Nicaraguan waters during the 1916 presidential election.

While the affair was the most spectacular extension of American power in the Caribbean during the Taft administration, the United States also took over tax collection of the other nations of Central America. All of the Central American countries except El Salvador had defaulted on their debts to Europeans. Knox reasoned that these creditors might seize control of the customs houses unless some arrangements were made to refund debts. At the same time Knox was negotiating American control over Nicaragua's tariff revenues, he also offered to reorganize Honduras's finances. The American minister in Honduras took a hand in negotiating an agreement between the government and its creditors. Most lenders were European bankers who knew that their governments never would support an intervention in Central America if it meant coming into conflict with the United States. So in return for a payment of a few cents on the dollar, the creditors agreed to refund the debt. Even this token payment exceeded the means of the Hondurans, but the American minister promised that the United States would provide the money to pay the European debts. In return, the customs houses would come under United States control. In January 1911, Knox signed a treaty establishing American control over the customs houses, but the United States Senate as well as the Honduran Congress rejected it. In the case of the Senate, Democrats objected to the idea of the United States dollar diplomacy, while in Honduras, the Congress thought that the government had turned the country over to the Yankees.

Knox tried again in Costa Rica and Guatemala to extend United States control over customs receipts. In both cases, however, the countries refused his offer. In 1911, the prospect of an American attempt to take over the customs houses forced Costa Rica to conclude an agreement with European creditors to repay part of the debt. Guatemala's president also felt pressure from the State Department to negotiate an agreement with his foreign creditors. The State Department wanted American bankers to refund the debt of Guatemala. Despite their best efforts, the Americans never could get Guatemala to agree to a refunding program, and the scheme died.

The United States also took over the island Hispaniola, shared by the Dominican Republic and Haiti. In 1912, Taft sent marines to the Dominican Republic, the country where Roosevelt had invoked his corollary and seized the customs. A revolution broke out, forcing the closure of seven customs houses operated by the Americans under the terms of the 1907 treaty. In September, Taft sent a contingent of 750 marines to force the resignation of a corrupt Dominican president and supervise a new election. The troops came home to the United States in December, but the Wilson administration kept a close watch on politics in the Dominican Republic. In September 1913, a threat of another revolution brought an American squadron to the coast. Things calmed down until May 1916, when the next insurrection occurred. The American navy landed sailors, while the commanding admiral threatened to bombard the capital, Santo Domingo, unless the insurgents surrendered. At the same time, the State Department worked out a treaty giving the United States effective control over Santo Domingo's tax collections and spending. Even this was not enough for a worried President Wilson, who feared German intervention in the country. At the end of 1916, when it appeared likely that the United States would soon enter the European war against Germany, Wilson proclaimed the military occupation of the Dominican Republic. The American navy remained to govern there until 1922.

Haiti had also attracted the American navy. Political murder and revolutionary upheaval had tormented that nation ever since the slave rebellion of Touissant L'Ouverture had thrown out the French in the beginning of the nineteenth century. A depressed economy had not encouraged Americans to invest, and such commerce as existed there was in the hands of a few French and German expatriates. Chronic instability often spilled over to the

Dominican Republic, where Americans were deeply involved. Once war broke out in Europe, the Wilson administration feared that European control could lead to a German fleet in Haiti threatening the approaches to the Panama Canal. Wilson therefore opened negotiations for an American receivership of Haitian customs. The response in Haiti was another bloody revolution, which toppled the government of Guillaume Sam in July 1915. Wilson, who had once described nonwhite countries as living in the "childhood of political development" and dismissed democracy for them as a "curse," dispatched two thousand marines to impose martial law on Haiti. At the same time, Secretary of State Lansing drafted a treaty with a compliant Haitian government granting the United States control of the country's finances. The American navy stayed there until 1934.

If Knox's attempts to get Americans included in the financial arrangements of other nations represented one side of American diplomacy, an even stranger episode occurred when Massachusetts Republican Henry Cabot Lodge, the chairman of the Senate Foreign Relations Committee, injected himself into the debate. The so-called Lodge Corollary to the Monroe Doctrine went beyond Roosevelt's gloss, excluding private foreign companies as well as foreign governments from the Western Hemisphere. Under Lodge's prescription, the New World was to become a commercial as well as a strategic sphere of influence for the United States.

The issue arose over a Japanese attempt to purchase an American tract of land and a fishing concession off the coast of Mexico's Baja California in 1912. In one sense, Lodge raised an issue which had been settled the previous year. In 1911, a group of Japanese in San Francisco had opened negotiations with Mexico to purchase the rights off Baja. The State Department had blocked the sale, fearing that it would result in the establishment of a Japanese colony in the Western Hemisphere. The matter seemed a dead issue until 1912, when Lodge revived it by pointing out that outsiders could appear at any time. Lodge's speech denouncing the threat of "some great eastern power" taking possession of Baja got picked up by one of William Randolph Hearst's papers. Soon the *Los Angeles Examiner* announced that the Japanese government was ready to set up a naval base in Magdalena Bay on the Baja Peninsula. The very next day, the Japanese government denied such plans. Knox, at the State Department, said he did not think the Japanese were moving to Mexico either, and he privately asked Lodge to be quiet. The Massachusetts senator refused to be silenced, and he called the Senate Foreign Relations Committee together to warn Japan. The committee reported a resolution to the entire Senate opposing the transfer of strategic sites in the Western Hemisphere to private companies outside the New World. The senate passed his thinly veiled attack on Japan on August 2, 1912, by the vote of fifty-one to four. The proclamation of the Lodge Corollary did more than serve notice on Japan, which in fact ignored it. It also demonstrated some of Lodge's prickliness, which became a major factor after the election of 1918, when the Republicans once again controlled the Senate and Lodge once more became the chairman of the Foreign Relations Committee.

CONFRONTING REVOLUTIONARY NATIONALISM IN MEXICO

The Mexican Revolution of 1910–1917 caused an earthquake in United States foreign policy. Taft and Wilson both meddled in Mexican affairs to outflank Europeans and maintain a favorable climate for United States investors. Neither reckoned the depths of nationalism among the Mexicans, nor did American presidents seem to realize the damage they could do to the United States by attempting to dominate Mexico's politics and economy. The story deserves detailed explanation, for it later recurred in different form in other lands.

As a weak neighbor, inhabited by a largely nonwhite and Catholic population, Mexico had drawn the scorn and attracted the greed of expansionists north of the border in the nineteenth century. In a war waged against Mexico from 1846 to 1848, the United States had stripped its southern neighbor of nearly one-third of its total land area. Later, after the Civil War, the United States helped Mexican revolutionaries, led by Benito Juárez, depose and execute the Austrian duke Maximilian, whom the French had installed as emperor of the country. Juárez had little luck with his own rule, losing the support of the United States, and abdicating his presidency to Porfirio Díaz in 1877.

Díaz was one of those "modernizers" of recent history who have sought to drag their countries into the world's economy by selling or giving away their nations' resources to overseas investors. Díaz looked to North Americans to dig the mines, build the railroads, and create plantations in Mexico. Over the next twenty years, the Guggenheim family sank millions into Mexican mines, E. H. Harriman purchased most of the railroads of Mexico, and scores of American landlords took over control of the countryside, owning over half of the available land. All the while, Díaz borrowed money to construct government buildings and stabilize the nation's currency in the credit markets of the United States and Europe. English investors also actively participated in the exploitation of the natural resources of Mexico, and by 1910, a British company had begun exploring for oil.

While Díaz had encumbered nearly two-thirds of Mexico's wealth with debts and concessions to foreigners, he had also engaged in a ruthless campaign of suppression of the nation's Indian population. In addition, his government was exceedingly corrupt, with ministers demanding kickbacks from the foreign investors before allowing them to bid on government projects or permitting them to look for minerals in the country. Still, outside businessmen accepted these restraints upon their actions with good humor and grace because they rightly believed that they would eventually recoup all of the money they had invested in the country.

For the American government, Díaz was exactly the kind of leader they hoped to see in a neighbor. While he might suppress his own people and demand payoffs from the foreigners who invested in his country, he kept his word. The concessions eventually were granted, and best of all, he paid his debts to foreign bankers. This reputation for probity meant that Mexico was not likely to become an arena for intervention by the Europeans.

By the twentieth century, however, Díaz was losing his grip. Some members of the Mexican middle class thought that they had been overlooked in the boom. Only the president's friends and relatives profited by the expansion of overseas investment in the country, and urban merchants and professionals lacking close connections with him felt cheated. In 1910, a revolution broke out among the mostly mestizo (mixed Indian and white) population of south central Mexico. In the following year, the middle class joined the opposition and in 1911 the president had to flee the country for Paris.

The revolutionaries called themselves Constitutionalists, since they promised a republican form of government based upon a written constitution. They installed a bemused and scholarly lawyer, Francisco Madero, as president and set about dismantling the state established by Díaz. Very quickly, Madero ran into difficulties, whipsawed between radicals who wished to see an immediate end to all vestiges of Díaz's rule and members of the old regime. Army officers sneered at the Constitutionalists as woolly minded reformers, while common soldiers worried about losing their jobs.

The foreign community in Mexico also feared that the new rulers would be less sympathetic to their exploitation of resources than Díaz had been. These fears proved well founded, for if Madero himself lacked spine, his party contained stronger personalities who thought that Díaz had plundered the country with concessions to foreigners. For these more nationalistic members of the Constitutionalist party, the aim of the revolution was to return Mexico's wealth to Mexico. They would renege on the concessions for the mineral and oil companies. Those claims which were not actually being explored and mined by the foreigners would revert to the government of Mexico. Where the concessionaires were actually at work extracting minerals and petroleum from the soil, the tax would go up. Some radicals also wanted to redistribute the land of the large plantation holders. North Americans and the Catholic church, the greatest holders of land in Mexico, faced expropriation of their property.

Naturally, expatriates in Mexico worried their privileged position would vanish if Madero stayed in power. Led by Lord Cowdray, local representative of a British oil firm, British minister Sir Francis Strong, and Henry Lane Wilson, the United States minister to Mexico, they plotted with disgruntled officers to oust the government of Francisco Madero. The man they selected to lead the assault on the Constitutionalist government was Victoriano Huerta, one of Díaz's trusted generals who had grown disgusted with the government's hostility to the armed forces. In late 1912, the plotters met, and in early 1913 they moved. In February, troops loyal to Huerta surrounded the presidential palace in Mexico City and arrested and murdered Madero. Huerta became president of Mexico and quickly applied for diplomatic recognition of his country by the European powers and by the United States. Great Britain recognized the government, but the United States demurred. The coup occurred only three weeks before Woodrow Wilson took office as president, and the Taft administration left the recognition question to its successor.

When Woodrow Wilson took office, he refused diplomatic recognition of Huerta's government, reversing the traditional practice of accrediting the diplomats of any regime which seemed strong enough to establish effective control over a country. There was no question that Huerta had effective control over Mexico, but Wilson detested his coup d'état. Wilson also wondered why the American business interests had married themselves to the British. The president believed that the rise of a Constitutionalist party in Mexico represented the best hope that country ever had of establishing a tradition of democratic rule on United States lines. He became incensed when he learned of the part that Henry Lane Wilson, the American minister, had played in the sordid murder of Madero. Woodrow Wilson recalled Wilson as his minister in August 1913 and replaced him with John Lind, a former Democratic governor of Minnesota who had close ties to Secretary of State Bryan.

Sending Lind to Mexico City by itself did not mean that the United States recognized Huerta's authority. Instead, Lind carried a proposal to settle the civil war in Mexico on terms drawn up by officials of the Southern Pacific Railroad and the Phelps Dodge Mining Company. These businesses had originally supported Huerta, but now that the United States refused to extend recognition, investors believed that something had to be done to secure official American backing. The proposal they drafted would have the American embassy in Mexico City arrange a nationwide election to decide between the Huerta government and the Constitutionalist opposition. Neither side in the Mexican civil war had sought mediation and neither wanted it, but Woodrow Wilson believed that a militant policy would force both to accept his proposal.

John Lind also had authority to offer a loan to the Mexican government if it would accept supervision of its election. Lind arrived in Mexico City on August 11 and went to the foreign minister, Federico Gamboa, with the proposal for American-supervised elections and a loan, or bribe, to Huerta to effect the plan. Gamboa replied with a blistering nationalistic note, denouncing interference while in effect yielding to pressure. The foreign secretary repudiated the right of an American president to interfere in Mexican elections because it would "compromise for an indefinite future, our destinies as a sovereign entity and all the future elections for president would be submitted to the veto of any President of the United States of America. And such an enormity, Mr. Confidential Agent, no government will ever attempt to perpetuate . . . unless some monstrous and almost impossible cataclysm should occur in the conscience of the Mexican people." Gamboa also turned down the offer of a loan, sniffing, "When the dignity of the nation is at stake, I believe that there are not loans enough to induce those charged by law to maintain it to permit it to be lessened."

Indignant though Gamboa might have been, he did concede an important point, because he noted that President Huerta would not succeed himself when an election occurred. Lind told Wilson that the ban on Huerta's seeking a second term represented a substantial victory for the United States. The ambassador's dispatch did not reach Washington until the evening of August 27, and on that afternoon Wilson had taken the nearly unprecedented step of personally addressing Congress on the state of United States–Mexican relations. He unveiled the proposal which Lind had taken to Huerta, and he denounced the Mexican president for having rejected all of it. The United States now should change course with the Mexicans and follow a policy of "watchful waiting" until the Mexican government paid respectful attention to what the Americans had to say. He pledged that the United States would "follow the best practice of nations in the matter of neutrality" and not export arms to either side of the civil war. (Wilson was to regret he ever mentioned the "best practice of nations" because his interpretation was demonstrably wrong. Two years later, during World War I, Americans exported arms to Britain and France, and supporters of Germany flung Wilson's words back at him.)

Lind's message relaxed Wilson, and over the next five weeks the crisis between the United States and Mexico eased. Then, in October, Huerta reversed his earlier, more conciliatory course and sent his gendarmes into the Mexican Chamber of Deputies, arresting 110 Maderista members, and proclaiming a full-scale military dictatorship. Wilson considered Huerta's move a slap in the face and accused the Mexican of breaking faith with him personally. Beyond that, Wilson sat down at his own typewriter and dashed off a note to the State Department telling Bryan to take a hard line with the Europeans, who the president believed had encouraged Huerta to seize the Parliament.

The State Department never sent Wilson's note to the European powers, but he delivered it himself to the world in a famous speech at Mobile, Alabama, on October 27. He said that one day soon Latin American would be freed from the thralldom of "foreign interests." These remarks were a veiled reference to Wilson's opposition to the British concessionaires and a warning that the United States was about to take action to oust them from Mexico. He also attempted to assure the Mexicans that his opposition to the British did not mean that the United States coveted the territory.

The British found Wilson's attitude hypocritical. Foreign Secretary Sir Edward Grey wanted assurances from the United States that if the government of Huerta were overthrown, the United States would undertake to protect British property. Wilson calmed Grey's representative by explaining that any government which the United States approved of would surely protect the rights of property holders. He then affirmed that his policy in the Western Hemisphere would be to "teach the South American republics to elect good men."

Poor Wilson. The Mexicans proved to be very slow learners in electing good men, and they resented American instruction. The American president was baffled that the Constitutionalist "first chief," Venustiano Carranza, rebuffed an offer for joint cooperation against the Huerta government. When Wilson sent William Bayard Hale to meet wth Carranza at the dusty border town of Nogales, Sonora, in November 1913, Hale carried a scheme for American support for the Constitutionalists in return for Carranza's promise to participate in elections under American guidance. Carranza thought Mexican elections were no business of the United States, and he told Hale that all he wanted from the Americans was recognition of his status as a belligerent and the right to buy arms. As talks between the Constitutionalists and Hale deteriorated into name-calling, Carranza demanded recognition as the only legitimate government. For his part, the American left in a sour mood, met a squad of reporters, and denounced Carranza's government as "the gentlemen across the border who are with such admirable skill preventing their friends from helping them."

Wilson was so angry with Carranza's treatment of Hale that he refused to provide arms for the Constitutionalists. By the beginning of 1914, however, the president realized that he either must let Carranza purchase weapons in the United States or else carry out his threat to depose Huerta. After negotiations lasting a month, the United States finally lifted the arms embargo against Mexico in February. Carranza could now receive weapons, and the Wilson administration had become identified with the revolution. In both Washington and Mexico City, foes of the Huerta government confidently expected that the dictator would soon pass into oblivion. It did not happen that way, partly because support for Carranza provided Huerta with a means of rallying nationalists to his cause. The Church, landed interests, and businesses, which formerly had been lukewarm toward Huerta, now changed their tune and actively offered their support. By March, John Lind was sending frantic messages to Washington that it was up to Wilson to fulfill his promise to end European domination of Huerta's government.

In April, Wilson found an excuse to send troops. The incident which sparked the American intervention has been called "an affair of honor," but it more resembled a bad opera. On April 10, the paymaster and crew of U.S.S. *Dolphin,* visiting the port of Tampico, were arrested by a colonel when they landed their small boat without permission from the federal troops. When the officer in charge of the Huertista forces learned of the Americans' arrest, he immediately ordered their release and personally apologized to Adm. Henry T. Mayo, the commander of the American squadron stationed off Vera Cruz. The matter would have been settled had not Admiral Mayo demanded a twenty-one gun salute from the Mexicans to salve the honor of the United States. In Washington, Wilson backed Mayo, and a preposterous exchange ensued between Lind in Vera Cruz and Huerta in Mexico City. The Mexican president noted the absurdity of the American demand for a salute from a government it did not recognize. He would agree to his forces saluting the Americans, if the Yankees would respond to each volley with a shot of their own. An insulted Wilson decided finally to rid Mexico of Huerta by force of arms.

Wilson went before a joint session of Congress on the afternoon of April 20 and recounted the Tampico incident. Two days later, he ordered the American navy to land at Vera Cruz and occupy the city. Mexican forces made up of naval cadets and civilians resisted. By April 23, the Americans had gained control of the port of Vera Cruz; Mexicans had suffered 126 killed and 195 wounded while Americans had lost 19 dead and 71 wounded.

Reaction came swiftly at home and abroad, with most people who took a stand on the issue believing that Wilson had behaved badly. The *Economist* of London sneered, "If war is to be made on points of punctilio raised by admirals and generals and if the Government of the United States is to set the example of this return to mediaeval conditions, it will be a bad day for civilization." Wilson received protests of his action from the American peace movement. The Federal Council of Churches, the Socialist party, and the AntiImperialist League all denounced the move into Mexico. Andrew Carnegie wrote Wilson an angry letter as did the liberal editor of the *Nation,*

Oswald Garrison Villard, and the president of Harvard, Charles W. Eliot. Even conservative Republicans who casually took a nationalistic position on international affairs, men such as former president William Howard Taft and former secretary of state Elihu Root, opposed the occupation of Mexican territory, with Taft complaining that Wilson had sent the navy to Vera Cruz as the most cynical sort of electioneering.

Not surprisingly, Latin Americans expressed outrage. Street demonstrations broke out in Uruguay, Chile, Costa Rica, and Guatemala. In Mexico itself, Wilson's intervention accomplished the almost impossible feat of unifying the Constitutionalists and the Huertistas. Carranza, the Constitutionalist leader, condemned the American invasion and announced that his troops would fight and expel the invaders.

In this atmosphere anything was possible. Secretary of War Lindley M. Garrison urged Wilson to send the army from the coast to Mexico City immediately. Then the ambassadors of Argentina, Brazil, and Chile offered mediation between the United States and Mexico. Despite the irony of the United States negotiating with a government it did not recognize, Wilson believed that accepting the proposition from the so-called ABC powers would hasten the downfall of the Huerta government. Talks convened at Niagara Falls, Canada, from May to July. While the conversations continued, the civil war in Mexico proceeded with the Constitutionalist forces driving closer to Mexico City. Huerta frantically informed the conference that unless something were done to stop Carranza in his tracks, the Constitutionalists would triumph.

Carranza took the capital on July 20, five days after Huerta resigned the presidency and fled. With a Constitutionalist provisional government, it might have seemed as if the aims of Wilson's diplomacy had been accomplished. Yet so personally insulted was Wilson, and so angry that the first chief would not accept American guidance, that immediately upon Carranza's installation as president the United States looked around for a more malleable replacement. Such a man was found in a Constitutionalist general, Francisco "Pancho" Villa, who had been feuding with the first chief.

In Washington, Wilson and Secretary of State Bryan welcomed Villa's breach with the Constitutionalist leadership, because they believed that here was a man who could assume the presidency of Mexico and be friendly to the United States. They even deceived themselves into thinking that Villa would actually be better for Mexico than would Carranza because he would order more land distributed to the downtrodden Mexican peasantry.

Villa gave the outward appearance of accepting a new constitutional convention, but on September 23, three weeks before the assembly was scheduled to open, he declared war. The convention attempted to install Villa as president. All Constitutionalist generals were forced to choose sides, and most decided to throw their lot in with Carranza. Villa was left to form an alliance with Emiliano Zapata, a peasant leader who had been waging his own war south of Mexico City for several years.

The United States enlisted on backing the Villa-Zapata forces on the grounds that they would be easier for North Americans to control. That prediction proved absolutely wrong. Moreover, the open support given to Carranza's enemies inflamed the first chief's hostility to the United States.

In the first nine months of 1915, Carranza's regrouped armed forces successfully pushed Villa's army out of Mexico and northward toward the United States border. Wilson's government fell into confusion. Early in February, Wilson did what he should have done the previous fall and proclaimed that now the United States was strictly neutral in the civil war and the Mexicans should settle their own differences. This pledge found little support in Mexico, for now Villa was unhappy that the Americans had abandoned him while Carranza thought that he deserved support. On June 2, Wilson said that unless the Carranzista and Villista factions concluded a cease-fire, the Americans would intervene. Again, Carranza dismissed Wilson's efforts as unjustified interference while Villa said that he was willing to accept American mediation.

Thus, in June 1915, it seemed as if Wilson had finally adopted the advice of the interventionists. Over the summer, however, American foreign policy took another turn. The United States now became embroiled in conflict with Germany over neutral rights in the North Atlantic. If, as seemed possible during the summer of 1915, the United States and Germany were to fight one another, the Americans could not fight Mexico at the same time. In August, Wilson finally decided that the United States must recognize the Carranza government. After two months of further negotiation with the South American republics, most of whom were reactionary regimes which opposed Carranza, the United States as well as these Latin republics extended recognition. On October 19, the United States finally extended formal recognition to Carranza, thereby ensuring the enmity of the Villa forces as well as American Catholics alarmed by Constitutionalist anticlericalism. Wilson found the Catholic opposition especially annoying, and he thought about issuing a public denunciation of the Catholic church until dissuaded by his personal adviser, Col. Edward M. House.

Villa now felt betrayed. Driven northward by the federal troops, on March 9, 1916, he crossed the border into the United States and attacked the town of Columbus, New Mexico. His forces killed nineteen Americans, and the pressure on Wilson to invade Mexico finally achieved fruition. On March 15, an American punitive expedition led by Gen. John J. "Black Jack" Pershing drove into Mexico to begin a ridiculous three-month scramble to find and capture Villa. Carranza had been willing enough to let the Americans into

General John J. "Black Jack" Pershing in futile pursuit of Pancho Villa.
(National Archives)

Mexico when he thought they would send a small force which would quickly rid him of his main rival. Instead of a quick expedition, however, the Americans sent more than eleven thousand officers and men. They marched three hundred miles into Mexico and still could not find their tormentor. By the middle of April, Mexico's president had had enough of North Americans on his soil, especially after a pitched battle occurred on April 12 at the town of Parral. There Pershing's forces killed forty Mexicans. Carranza demanded that the Americans leave. Then Villa struck again in the United States, crossing into Texas and attacking some soldiers at Glen Spring, fifteen miles north of the Rio Grande.

The governor of Texas called for the occupation of all of northern Mexico. Wilson federalized the National Guard, dispatched one hundred thousand of them to patrol the border, and sent American warships to Mexican ports on the east and west coast. On June 21, a battle erupted between Pershing's forces and those of Mexican general Felix G. Gomez near Carrizál, Mexico. The Americans attacked a force of two hundred and fifty federal troops, fully expecting the Mexicans to turn and run. Instead they resisted, killing twelve Americans and capturing twenty-three. In Washington, news of this encounter was treated as an ambush of the Americans, although Pershing's troops had in fact been the aggressors. On July 4, Carranza offered to open negotiations and Washington agreed to appoint a Joint High Commission.

The United States would withdraw its troops only if American economic interests, petroleum, and mining were protected and if the taxes on United States citizens in Mexico were lowered. Unable to reach an agreement on these points, the Joint High Commission disbanded on January 15, 1917. The commission had not ended the dispute, but it had kept Mexican affairs quiet during the presidential election campaign of 1916. Now that the commission had failed in its larger work, Wilson had to either finally withdraw the expeditionary force or proceed with a full occupation of Mexico. In early 1917, however, the United States faced the prospect of war with Germany, which made another one against Mexico less likely. In January, Wilson decided that Carranza would have his way and the American forces would withdraw on the 27th. The first chief had won his victory over a stubborn American president. The Mexicans had not been deterred from writing their own Constitution while the invasion went forward. This progressive document phased out foreign control of Mexico's mineral wealth, curtailed absentee ownership of land, and reduced Church control over education. The Mexicans had elected a constitutional assembly in October, and it had drafted a new fundamental law in December and January. Mexico chose a new Congress and confirmed Carranza as president on March 11. Two days later, the United States extended formal recognition.

Relations between the United States and Mexico continued to be bad for a generation after Wilson's misguided tampering in that country's revolution. American interference in Mexico typified an attitude toward nationalist revolution around the globe. While the United States sometimes opposed reactionary governments and demanded that European nations stay out of the internal affairs of revolutionary states, Washington insisted that revolutionaries follow a model of "development" based on that of the United States.

CHAPTER FOUR

The Politics of Neutrality, 1914–1917

THE SHOCK OF WAR

The First World War was the worst thing that ever happened to Europe. By the time it ended in November 1918, eight to ten million people had been killed and millions of other soldiers had been maimed by machine guns and paralyzed by deadly poisoned gas. Veterans never wanted to repeat the horror of months in muddy trenches battling more against lice, rats, and gangrene than the enemy. Combat changed the shape of European society. Millions of homeless civilians wandered forlornly around the countryside looking for sanctuary. *Refugee,* a new word describing their plight, slipped into the language and was heard often after the Great War. Revolution swept away the old German, Austrian, and Russian empires. Governments which survived intact feared that they might collapse next. Both winners and losers emerged weaker, poorer, and more fearful of their neighbors.

Perhaps the most shocking thing about the conflagration was that few people on either side of the Atlantic expected it to break out and almost no one thought it would last as long and cost as much as it did. Americans at first denied the significance of combat in Europe. President Wilson considered his countrymen special. His sense of American "exceptionalism" made him first want to stay clear of the conflict and later compelled him to enter the fray. Both in the early days of neutrality and during the subsequent movement toward belligerency, the president repeated that the "uniqueness" of the United States lent his nation's diplomacy a moral quality Europeans lacked. In the first two years of the war, Wilson believed the Europeans engaged in a traditional fight which held no interests for Americans. Later, when he called for a declaration of war against Germany, he insisted that the United States fought to change completely the shape of world politics.

Wilson, American diplomats in Europe, and the general public seemed as bewildered as Europeans when war came in August 1914. While American reformers of international law had pointed out the dangers of the system of alliances developed in Europe at the turn of the century, they balanced their warnings with other, more optimistic, assessments of the shape of things to come. Internationalists noticed that the world had grown more interdependent, more knit together, over the previous half-century. They were pleased that a letter could be mailed anywhere in the inhabited world and reach a destination anywhere else on the globe, a happy state of affairs never repeated after 1914. They noticed the growth of bodies like the International Postal Organization and the World Health Organization, which suggested that nations had learned that their fates depended upon one another. The growth of trade among major powers also persuaded optimists that countries would not risk their economic well-being by fighting.

This rosy picture of the future blackened in the summer of 1914. On June 28, the heir to the throne of the Austro-Hungarian empire, Archduke Franz Ferdinand, was gunned down in the Bosnian town of Sarajevo by Slavic nationalists lurking in the crowd. The archduke had traveled to this dreary spot to show that the Hapsburg empire intended to retain control over the Slavs who had been annexed to the empire in 1908. The government of Serbia, one of the states created from the wreckage of the Ottoman Turkish empire, supported the killers, thereby suffering the wrath of Austrians who sent an ultimatum demanding an apology. The summer crisis of 1914 seemed no different from many other divisions which had afflicted Europeans since the turn of the century. None of these encounters in North Africa or the Balkans had led to a major war.

While war shocked Europeans, they should have expected it. For the previous generation, they had erected a system of alliances, contended with one another in Africa, Asia and the Middle East, and indulged in an orgy of nationalistic hatreds. The alliance of Germany and Austria in the 1870s was soon followed by a pact between Russia and France. Both powers detested and feared the new German empire. In 1902, Britain, alarmed by the challenge of Germany's naval construction, ended years of isolation with an informal naval agreeement with France and a formal alliance with Japan. "Panslavism," a mystical potpourri of assertions of superiority of "natural" Russian and Slavic culture and religion over the "decadent materialism" and "nationalism" of Western Europeans, addled the minds of Russian publicists. Many of them encouraged the czar to champion demands for independence from the AustroHungarian empire coming from Slavic peoples living in the Balkans.

In the July 1914 crisis, European nations seemed bent upon ending their insecurities and fears for the future. The alliances developed since the 1870s went into force. Once Austria presented the Serbians with an ultimatum on July 24, Germany backed its partner with a so-called blank check. Berlin told Vienna that whatever it would do against the Serbs would receive full support. Germany even promised Austria aid in a war against Russia. From the issuance of this letter until August 1, events followed an inexorable pattern. First the Russians, then the Germans, and then the French mobilized their troops. On August 1, Austria and Russia declared war on one another, with their two allies, Germany and France respectively, quickly following. After German armed forces swept through Belgium on the first of August, the British government declared war on Germany. The ostensible reason for Britain's action was Germany's violation of Belgium's neutrality, established in 1831. More important, however, was Britain's commitment to France. Since 1904, the British and the French had engaged in an informal entente. Though no formal alliance bound the countries, British and French generals had coordinated their policies over the previous years. When hostilities erupted, British politicians concluded it would be dishonest and unfriendly to the French not to join their fight. On August 4, Parliament voted for war.

NEUTRALITY

The first official American reaction to combat was the president's declaration of neutrality. When Wilson issued the customary order keeping the United States out of battle, he exceeded the traditional declaration and asked the American public to stay neutral "in thought as well as in deed." For years after Wilson made this request for the strictest sort of neutrality, he was the object of sneers from nationalists for imposing impossible conditions upon the public. The idea that Americans would not damn the side they thought at fault and should not lead cheers for possible victors struck a critic like Theodore Roosevelt as silly. Roosevelt, who never forgave Wilson for his victory in 1912, declared that Wilson's neutrality proclamation was "cowardly and unworthy."

This assault on Wilson did not take his interpretation of the causes of the conflict seriously. From August to December, Wilson developed his notions of why war had occurred. He concluded that all the powers were more or less equally responsible for it and that this fight was a recent example of conflicts which had marred European politics for centuries. In the fall, Wilson remarked that bloodshed resulted from "the competing alliances" leading Europeans into a quarrel. No right or wrong side could be found to the arguments between blocs, so Americans should maintain cordial relations with all belligerent powers. While the United States would do nothing to insult either side, combatants themselves would also have to respect the rights of the United States. Wilson demanded that Europeans permit Americans to trade with all the powers who fought.

The president expressed a widespread popular belief that politically the United States and Europe were distinct, but in fact commerce had drawn them together since the American Civil War. American grain helped raise living standards; the nation's cotton and wool kept English textile mills humming; and American copper, coal, and iron, in both raw and finished form, helped the industrialization of Western Europe. Once war broke out prices shot up for American farm products. European investment banking houses, especially in Britain, owned major portions of burgeoning American industrial firms. This growing interdependence, in which the United States provided raw materials and semifinished goods to a Europe which returned hundreds of millions in capital, created an American stake in the outcome of the European war.

By taking a stand on the right of Americans to trade, Wilson thought he followed a traditional approach to neutrality. He did, but old principles made little sense under modern conditions. In the eighteenth century, American diplomats had insisted on four requirements when other nations sent their armies against each other. First, neutral ships had the right to carry "non-contraband" goods to any belligerent power. Second, "contraband" had a narrow definition as those items which actually could be used for making war. Third, blockades had to be real to be recognized by the neutrals. A strong naval power which blockaded its enemy's ports would actually have to station ships outside them. The power could not simply say that ports were under blockade and then raid the high seas for all ships bound there. In practice, the American insistence upon the principle that blockades be "real" to be "effective" had Great Britain, a strong naval power, as its target. British practice had been to use its superior navy to station ships in mid-ocean and then stop all vessels bound for its enemies. Finally, civilians had the right to travel freely to the belligerent nations on the passenger ships of the combatants without fear of interference.

This large, old-fashioned conception of the rights of neutrals involved Wilson in trouble with the Germans and British. It also led to a rift with his own secretary of state, William Jennings Bryan, who never accepted his superior's insistence on the protection of American citizens wanting to travel to the war zone. Bryan, the "prince of Christian peace," probably had a keener appreciation of the nature of warfare and a more realistic grasp of world politics than did Woodrow Wilson. The secretary of state knew that modern conditions and weapons had changed the way nations fought. The distinction between civilian and soldier vanished in the twentieth century, and the European conflagration allowed no sanctuary to neutrals. This might be sad, but it was the way combat occurred. If Americans wanted safety, Bryan urged them to steer clear of the fight.

Bryan concluded that Germany's use of submarines meant that the United States would have to adopt a new policy toward searches and seizures on the seas. Under the traditional assumptions of international law, a power declaring a blockade had to warn a vessel of an impending search, and a boarding party had to go onto the neutral vessel. Once an underwater warship was developed, the possibility of boarding neutral ships evaporated. In order for a submarine to do its deadly work, it had to stay submerged, for if it surfaced, it could not defend itself.

In early 1915, the German navy banned all ships from a war zone around the British Isles. If any neutral vessels sailed into the forbidden area, German U-boats would sink them without warning. Wilson considered this practice a violation of the rights of neutrals, and he vowed to make Germany change its policy. For Bryan, Germany's declaration may have been an insult, but it represented a natural and realistic consequence of the changes in military hardware. Bryan insisted that if Washington truly wished to avoid the possibility of a war over the rights of neutrals, then American ships should accept the blockade. If Americans wanted to travel to Europe, they should do so at their own risk.

The secretary resigned over his disagreement with Wilson's advocacy of old-fashioned strict neutrality. His departure from government came after Germany sank the British liner *Lusitania* on May 7, 1915. This passenger ship carried a cargo of weapons bound for Britain, which is one reason it exploded and sank like a boulder in the Irish Sea twenty miles from the British coast. Nonetheless, the loss of 128 American lives infuriated the public.

"It was as if one of two pugilists had suddenly lashed out at a ringside spectator," writes Patrick Devlin, a member of the British House of Lords, who provided an exhaustive account of Woodrow Wilson's neutrality in *Too Proud to Fight* (1975). Three days later, Wilson calmed the nerves of Americans shouting for vengeance when he assured an assembly of four thousand recently naturalized citizens at Philadelphia that "there is such a thing as a man being too proud to fight. There is such a thing as a nation being so right that it does not need to convince others by force that it is right." Then on May 13, Wilson banged out a brutal protest to Germany on his own typewriter without consulting Bryan. He demanded a German "disavowal" of submarine warfare, reparations for the *Lusitania* sinking, and a promise not to do it again. He sent an even stiffer note in early June, again without paying attention to Bryan's worries that he was moving the United States toward war. Annoyed as much by the president's snub as he was convinced that Wilson would provoke bloodshed, Bryan resigned on June 9, 1915. The president replaced him with Robert Lansing, a dull, conventional lawyer who was a counselor, or second in command at the State Department. Lacking Bryan's authority with the Democratic party and unsure of his own grasp of the nuances of diplomacy, Lansing acted as Wilson's spokesman over the next three years.

Wilson's protest over the sinking of the *Lusitania* opened a series of diplomatic remonstrances with Germany over submarine warfare. On August 19, 1915, a German submarine sank without warning the *Arabic*, a large British liner, killing forty-four passengers including two American citizens. Wilson intimated that he would break off diplomatic relations with Germany unless it stopped torpedoing passenger ships. This complaint brought forth the *Arabic* pledge; the German government promised that "liners will not be sunk by our submarines without warning." Some "mistakes" occurred over the next few months, and on March 24, 1916, a German submarine torpedoed the *Sussex*, a British channel steamer on its regular run from Folkestone to Dieppe. Eighty lives were lost, including those of four Americans. Wilson issued an ultimatum; unless Germany stopped "its present practice of submarine warfare," the United States would break relations with Germany. On May 5, Germany provided the Sussex pledge, offering to suspend unrestricted submarine warfare if the United States could compel the British to lift their blockade. Berlin reserved the right to resume unrestricted U-boat attacks if the United States failed to change British policy.

Domestic Opposition

Bryan's opposition to Wilson's narrow neutrality represented only one sort of dissent from administration policy. Critics on both the left and the right raised alarms. Theodore Roosevelt led the chorus of nationalists. Writing in the *Kansas City Star,* the only outlet he had in the early years of the war for his views, TR began excoriating the Germans for their conduct. He called their invasion of Belgium a barbarous campaign of looting, rape, and destruction of precious artifacts. The German burning of the library in the Belgian university town of Louvain outraged Roosevelt, who demanded the United States enter the war to preserve a "righteous peace."

Roosevelt, who exulted in fighting, argued the American position as a great nation demanded that the United States take part to earn a place in the peace which would follow. His attitude blended progressive reform of world politics with a nationalist's weary acceptance of business as usual. On the one hand, he thought that the United States almost single-handedly could change the way nations behaved toward one another—hence his emphasis upon a righteous peace. On the other hand, he chided Wilson for turning up his nose at the corruption of the European state system. Instead, Roo-

Preparedness at Plattsburgh, summer 1915.
(National Archives)

sevelt thought that the United States could not make the Europeans any more peaceful than they were, so it might as well join the fight to keep an eye on them.

Roosevelt's insistence that the United States have a say in the outcome of the war found an echo in the cries of army general Leonard Wood, the Navy League, and the Army League for American armament or "preparedness." In early 1915, hundreds of wealthy men pledged thousands of dollars to bring a group of undergraduates from the most prestigious universities on the east coast to the Plattsburgh army camp on the shores of New York's Lake Champlain to receive training as officers. The United States army provided the instructors for this privately financed campaign to nudge Wilson and Congress into enlarging the armed forces.

The president responded with a preparedness movement of his own, designed to quiet the complaints from the nationalists on the right while keeping dissident Democrats in line. In December 1915, he asked Congress for $500 million for the navy to add ten battleships and one hundred submarines over the next ten years. In June 1916, after Wilson had crisscrossed the country speaking in favor of preparedness, Congress passed the National Defense

Act, doubling the size of the army to 200,000 men and 110,000 officers. In August, it followed with a navy bill and a shipping act enlarging the merchant marine.

Wilson struggled to balance the demands of nationalists calling for more arms with warnings from Progressives, pacifists, and socialists that preparedness invariably would bring a war favored by big business and deadly to reform and civil liberties in the United States. Socialist party leader Eugene Debs, who polled over nine hundred thousand votes for president in 1912, former secretary of state Bryan, editor Oswald Garrison Villard of the liberal weekly the *Nation,* and Wisconsin's Progressive senator Robert LaFollette, led a movement against the military buildup. Other Progressives were not so sure. The editorial board of the *New Republic,* the Progressive weekly started by Willard Straight in 1912 and including Herbert Croly, Nathaniel Weyl, and Walter Lippmann, who had backed Roosevelt's bid for the presidency in 1912, swung round to Wilson's side during the preparedness battles of 1916. Reasoning that the president had steered a moderate course between competing pressure groups and fearing to abandon a reform-minded president to nationalists, Croly, Weyl, and Lippmann decided to help Wilson wage a "Progressive war."

American ethnic groups also tugged the president in different directions. On one side were supporters of the British position, descendants of settlers from the British Isles. Americans prefer not to think of Anglo-Saxons as an ethnic group since they have largely controlled the government of the United States and have regarded themselves as the "true Americans." Still, an ethnic group is what they are. Many aspiring American plutocratic families had married their daughters to impoverished scions of the British aristocracy in the late nineteenth century, strengthening the bonds of the "English-speaking peoples." New York banks, many of which were controlled by Anglo-Saxons, arranged loans of $2.25 billion to the Allies in the first two and one half years of the war, giving the house of Morgan and the National City Bank and others a stake in the success of the Allied cause. Wilson's pleas to remain neutral in thought as well as deed made little sense to men whose families and fortunes depended on Britain's success.

Arrayed against the supporters of the British and French were other ethnic groups, Irish, Germans, and Jews, each of which had its own reasons for wishing the Allies ill. The Irish, who had come to the United States in the middle of the nineteenth century to escape famine and persecution at the hands of the British empire, naturally had no reason to support the British. Throughout the years before the United States entered the war, the Irish warned against tying American policy to the British. Ethnic Germans in the United States opposed a foreign policy which seemed to lean toward the British, and many Jewish Americans also dissented from the bias shown by the Wilson administration toward the Allied side. American Jews held no special brief for Germany, although many of the leaders of the American Jewish community were indeed of German descent and had family ties there. The major concern of the Jewish Americans, however, was with the czarist government of Russia. Until the revolution of March 1917, they had dismissed claims of British supporters that the war would be fought for democracy and in opposition to authoritarianism. The Russian government of the czar seemed to be excessively authoritarian as well as anti-Semitic. American Jews thus saw no reason to support any policy which might align the United States with the Russians.

In this environment of conflicting interpretations of the war, Wilson could follow his neutral path. The public babel also made it easier for him to take exclusive control of foreign policy. Since the general public did not speak with a single voice on the war, Wilson thought that he could direct foreign affairs himself. This job became all the easier after the resignation of Secretary of State Bryan. For all of his faults and his differences with the president, Bryan was a public figure with a commanding presence.

American Mediation Efforts

Wilson could not act alone, however, no matter how much he wanted to; he needed a trusted confidant. He found the appropriate aide in the person of Edward M. House, a political fixer from Texas who had longed to direct great events from his childhood. As a boy, he had dreamed of someday telling the politicians what to do. As a young man, he had decided not to enter politics because his health was not up to it, but he was strong enough to direct affairs from behind the scenes. He even had produced a poor novel, *Philip Dru, Administrator,* setting down his hopes for the future. Dru, a character who resembled the melancholic House, found himself called upon to tell the great men of the world how to behave once a world war broke out. Bumbling politicians turned to Dru, who shuttled between the belligerents and forced them to end the fighting and put the future of world politics in the hands of serene experts, administrators like himself, who made the world more peaceful.

House, who held an honorary colonelcy from Texas, found himself living his novel when be became the private foreign policy adviser to Woodrow Wilson. House's major trip to the European capitals came in January and February 1916, where he arranged one of the strangest episodes in modern diplomacy. He went to London, Paris, and Berlin trying to negotiate an end to a war which by this time had dragged on for twenty months and had cost over four million lives. The quick end which all of the European leaders expected had not occurred, nor had the war been fought as a series of short engagements with troops rushing across the landscape. Instead, front lines had become fixed early, and troops had settled down to months of trench warfare. By the winter of 1915–1916, armies had dug into cold, damp, muddy slits in the earth. Soldiers got cold feet, dysentery, and trench mouth when they stayed put, and when they reluctantly followed their officers' orders to climb over the top and expose themselves to the enemy, things got worse. Armed only with rifles, infantrymen confronted machine-gun fire and artillery barrages. Thirty thousand men could die in one day of combat in northeastern France, and at the end of eight hours of slaughter, the front lines might have moved four hundred yards.

Along with this horrible human suffering, the governments of France and Great Britain had also come to the end of their financial ropes by early 1916. Each had stripped its citizens of their holdings of overseas investments and used the proceeds to buy supplies in the United States. By 1916, the Western Allies had exhausted these resources. Conditions were nearly as bad for the Germans, who slowly starved to death under pressure from the British blockade. They could not trade at all with the Western Hemisphere, and all material for the conduct of the war had to come from production inside Germany. Yet Germans were in France and Belgium, and no Allied troops occupied German soil. In the east as well, the German army stood inside the Russian empire.

As each side seemed incapable of defeating the other, and as both approached the brink of starvation, Wilson believed that they might be ready for mediation from the United States. He hoped that he could persuade the belligerents to restore the situation which existed before the war while at the same time eliminating what he considered the major cause—the system of alliances and the arms race which had grown up early in the twentieth century. Wilson thought that unless the war stopped and the Europeans dropped their alliances, the United States would fight whether Americans wanted to or not.

In this atmosphere, heavy with exhaustion and suspicion, Wilson sent his confidential agent, Colonel House, to Europe in the first months of 1916. House supported the cause of the Allies, especially the British, in the war, believing that Germany threatened the security of the continent. Unlike the president, who considered all the powers to be equally at fault in creating conditions leading to the war, House held the Germans responsible and considered their behavior in Belgium the war's most barbarous act.

When House arrived in London on January 19, 1916, he spoke with British Foreign Secretary Sir Edward Grey, who impressed upon him the desperation of the Allied situation. Grey wondered if the British and the French could hold out against the Germans for another year. The foreign secretary wanted the United States to enter the war on the side of the British and the

French even though he knew that the president could not support some Allied war aims. Grey was well aware that Wilson opposed secret pledges such as the two Western powers had made to Italy to assure it the restoration of territory in the Tyrol and on the Adriatic coast at the expense of the Austrian empire.

Grey believed that if the Americans could not be persuaded to join the fight as actual allies of the British and the French, that would not be the worst thing in the world. The Americans might be coaxed to come in as arbiters, fighting alongside Britain and France but not formally allied with them. If Americans wished to retain a shred of the old virtue and not be seen as fighting for the same goals as Western powers, the Allies could easily wink at such hypocrisy. From the British point of view, the important thing was to make sure that the Americans took up arms against Germany. Fresh American troops backed up by the world's premier economy would be enough to turn the tide. Everything else would be simply window dressing, and the British could wait until the eventual outcome before deciding what to do with Americans at the peace settlement.

The scheme which Grey drew up to encourage the United States would satisfy the American desire to act as a mediator. The United States would publicly ask the belligerents to stop fighting and attend a peace conference presided over by American diplomats. To provide the necessary goodwill among the enemies, the conference would not begin until the battle lines were restored to the positions occupied before the war broke out. In other words, the Germans were supposed to withdraw their troops from northern France, Belgium, and Poland before peace talks began. Obviously, Grey knew that the Germans would not accept this proposal. They had outlined their war aims, which consisted of taking French territory, creating a new pro-German state in the Lowlands, and pushing the Russians further to the east. The size of the German appetite meant that they never would settle for a return to the status quo before the war unless the Allies defeated them. Therein lay the beauty of the plan. The United States would ask each belligerent to accept the peace conference with the warning that if one side agreed and the other did not, the Americans would enter the war on behalf of the nations which signaled acceptance. Since the British were bound to say yes, and since they could deliver the French, only the Germans would be left out. Grey fully expected a German rejection which would produce an American entry in the war alongside London and Paris.

It is still puzzling why Edward House, by no means a naive or foolish man, pushed Grey's proposal. He signed a note with the British foreign secretary on February 22, which became known as the House-Grey Memorandum. The two forwarded it to Wilson in Washington advising him to endorse it. House knew that the memorandum would bring the United States into

the war, and that is precisely why he agreed. He feared that the howl for preparedness emanating from the Republican opposition signaled a loss of support for Wilson. To regain popular approval, Wilson had to be seen to be
active in the Great War. If Grey's proposal were adopted as Wilson's own,
the United States would appear to come into the war for its own principles
rather than simply as an accessory to the Allies.

Wilson toyed with it but eventually modified the plan out of recognition.
He thought that it would be workable only if there could be a realistic
prospect of German agreement. He learned from his ambassador in Berlin,
John W. Gerard, that the Germans certainly would reject such an obvious
British ploy to recruit Americans into their alliance. Wilson had scant respect
for Gerard; early in the war the president had angrily scrawled on a dispatch
from Berlin, "I wish they'd hand this idiot his passport." But the president
shrank from endorsing the House-Grey Memorandum because he reasoned
that Gerard told the truth and the Germans would reject it. Wilson thought
that he could not enlist that part of the public opposed to joining the war
on the side of the Allies with such a transparent scheme. Wilson turned the
House-Grey Memorandum into a vague American offer of mediation which
neither side took seriously.

THE ELECTION OF 1916

Over the next six months, Wilson sought support for reelection in November 1916. The election was one of those rare events in American political
history in which the outcome actually turned on foreign affairs. Voters took
an unusual interest in the course of the war in Europe as they wondered
whether they might be called upon to fight.

On the Republican side, former president Theodore Roosevelt thought
that the war would catapult him back into the White House. After all, he reasoned, he had a fine reputation as a foreign policy leader, and he had kept
his name before the public by his constant charges of "cowardice" on Wilson's part. Roosevelt's hope to win the nomination in 1916 did not reckon
with the depth of the resentment many Republicans felt toward him for running as a Progressive in 1912. They thought that he had ruined the chances
of William Howard Taft and had assured the election of Wilson, the man
Roosevelt detested. Roosevelt's efforts to win the presidential nomination
fell apart in the spring of 1916. Unable to gain the nod himself, he vowed
to make certain that whoever the party did put forward would follow his foreign policy prescriptions. The Republicans nominated U.S. Supreme Court
Justice Charles Evans Hughes, a New Yorker, who had been friendly to the
former president and whom President Taft had appointed to the Court in

1910. Therefore, he was acceptable to the leadership of the party. During the campaign, Hughes sought to embarrass Wilson by portraying him as not responding to the threat posed by the war. The Republican ran on a platform of increasing American preparedness. Roosevelt offered support by touring the country denouncing the "hyphenated Americans," German and Irish, who opposed Great Britain.

Of course, Germans and Irish in the United States did not believe that Wilson was so supportive of their attitudes toward the war. The president's campaign stressed what he had done over the past year to boost the nation's military. At the same time, he argued that the campaign for preparedness had meant that the United States would not have to use its soldiers. Now that the United States was prepared to fight, it would never have to do so. One of his campaign managers, Joseph Tumulty, got so carried away with the idea that preparedness actually had prevented the United States from entering the war that he coined the slogan "He kept us out of war." The president was not happy that his supporters would make such a blatant appeal to the noninterventionist voters because he thought that someday the United States might actually have to fight. But he kept his doubts to himself and never ordered his backers not to utter the phrase, preferring instead to take the high road while his surrogates appealed to the basic fears of the public.

Most perceptive observers of American politics seemed certain that the challenger would win in November. The country was traditionally Republican; there was a single Republican candidate opposing the president in 1916 whereas there had been two in 1912, and voters seemed weary of the movement for Progressive reform which had been the major accomplishment of the Democratic administration. Insofar as voters thought at all about events in Europe, Hughes also seemed to have the more consistent position. He argued more forthrightly for preparedness, and he could take the offensive against Wilson. The challenger could accuse the incumbent of every sin without at the same time saying what he would have done better. Wilson, on the other hand, occupied a confused middle position, favoring preparedness while preserving neutrality. He would have the United States both in the war and aloof from it. Expecting victory, Hughes went to sleep on the night of Tuesday, November 6, thinking that voters had given him the prize. Wilson too felt the sting of rejection as the returns from the East and the Midwest showed him the loser. Not until the middle of Wednesday, when the late tallies arrived from California and Ohio, had Wilson eked out a victory.

The results were so close that any number of factors might have contributed to Wilson's triumph. Certainly his supporters' cry that he had kept the country out of war had done its bit. Ethnic groups opposed to the United States entering the war on the side of the British were delighted that the incumbent promised less intervention than the Republicans had in mind. But as is often the case in American elections, once the president had been returned to office, voters had little say in what he did. Since it really was impossible to determine with clarity what the public thought, Wilson himself created policy on the basis of what his advisers said foreign governments did and what he believed.

MOVING TOWARD WAR

All of the dreadful trends in the Great War intensified in the winter of 1916–1917. Both Germany and the Allies seemed to be more exhausted than ever before, and they both looked for ways finally to defeat the other side. By that winter, the conflict became for the first time a "total war." On both sides of the front, the military authorities took complete control of their societies. Conscription started in Germany and France before 1914, but the British had traditionally relied upon volunteers to fill their armies. For the first two years, there were enough young men who enlisted in the British armed forces, out of a combination of patriotism, a desire to go along with their peers, and a fear of social ridicule if they shirked. By the middle of 1916, however, these inducements, strong as they were, could not encourage enough young Englishmen to sign up. For the first time since the Napoleonic conflicts, the British government had to establish a conscription law. At the same time, the British cabinet, led by the Liberal party's prime minister, Henry Asquith, fell, replaced by a coalition of Liberals and Conservatives with a radical member of the Liberals, David Lloyd George, as its head. Lloyd George turned the British domestic economy over to the Ministry of Supply. All production in the country was directed by the government. All able-bodied men had to register for work in either the military or in weapons plants.

The same process went on in all of the belligerent countries, reaching its peak in Germany. There the military itself took charge of organizing the domestic economy. Unlike Great Britain, where civilians ran the Supply Ministry, the German army and the navy took over the procurement of goods. The general staff led by generals Erich von Ludendorff and Paul von Hindenburg faced appalling shortages of everything necessary to run a modern fighting force. The British blockade had reduced the food supply. Since the army needed to be fed at a level approaching that of peacetime, civilians ate turnips. Similarly, the armed forces preempted the fuel supply. The First World War was the first conflict during which petroleum became important, and Germany lost access to sources of fuel in Russia and the United States. It made do with the coal they had in northwestern Germany and occupied

France. The military also gobbled the nation's entire production of clothing.

By December 1916, the Ludendorff and Hindenburg staff worried about surviving another year of fighting. Even if the government continued to expropriate the bulk of production, Germany would die of the effects of the British blockade in late 1917. The generals hoped, however, to win the war by committing the reserves and overwhelming the British and French in a final offensive in 1917. Submarines would impose a counterblockade against Great Britain, sinking every ship bound for British ports. Since the British had not lifted their blockade, a condition of the Sussex pledge of May 1916, the Germans could resume unrestricted submarine warfare. The kaiser's generals and admirals recognized the obvious risks of provoking the United States by unleashing the U-boats, but they thought the possible gains made it worthwhile. From a strictly military point of view, Ludendorff argued that the United States could not effectively join the war before his troops could vanquish their enemies. Even if the Americans stood alongside the Allies, it would take Washington at least a year to put an effective army on the field.

For Ludendorff and Hindenburg, the choice was clear: either declare unrestricted submarine warfare and antagonize the United States, or face slow starvation. The situation looked far murkier to civilians. Chancellor Theobald von Bethmann-Hollweg, a gloomy man who had been predicting disaster ever since August 1914, saw his fears coming true in late 1916. He pressed negotiations as the only alternative to mutual starvation of the two sides. Should fighting drag on, Germany faced defeat, revolution, and political collapse. The German Catholic Center party and the Social Democrats, both of which had greeted the outbreak of combat with varying degrees of enthusiasm in 1914, now swung round to the nearly heretical view that hostilities should end with a return to the pre-1914 borders.

To do so required the assent of the kaiser, William II, one of the oddest men to lead a nation in the twentieth century. Temperamental, brought up to admire the military virtues and horses, not stupid but badly educated, William suffered from a massive inferiority complex and insisted on getting his own way. He had succeeded to the throne in 1892 and almost immediately picked a fight with Otto von Bismarck, the Iron Chancellor who had created the modern German empire. Bismarck stayed on for two miserable years after William became emperor, but his influence was never the same. After Bismarck gave up in 1894, the kaiser chose a succession of small-minded men as chancellor, none of whom risked offending the monarchy. A sweet air of decay settled over the court in Berlin before the Great War, with the emperor surrounded by sycophants whose principal occupation was assuring William of his brilliance while terrifying him with tales of the plots of the Russians, French, and British.

The kaiser resented bad news from anyone, and a weak hand wringer like Bethmann-Hollweg had little success in explaining that the war must end. Ludendorff and Hindenburg outargued the whimpering chancellor at the kaiser's country retreat of Pless over the Christmas holidays of 1916. Mocking Bethmann-Hollweg's fears as the product of an unhealthy physique, the generals pointed out that the Allies had rebuffed a German peace initiative in early December. It seemed as if the Allies insisted upon a German surrender. In that case, why not try one last roll of the dice: resume unrestricted U-boat warfare and launch an offensive in the west?

The kaiser accepted the generals' logic, and on January 31, 1917, the German Foreign Ministry let the United States know that Germany was no longer bound by the Sussex pledge. Germany proclaimed Great Britain under blockade and said all neutral ships traveled there at the risk of being sunk without warning. Only a British agreement to lift the stranglehold on Germany's food imports would stay the order.

THE FINAL DECISION TO FIGHT

The reaction in Washington to the news that the Germans were again going to sink American vessels en route to Britain seemed surprisingly quiet. For pro-British members of Wilson's government, men such as Lansing and House, the German action was just what they had been waiting for. Now, surely the president would see the danger posed by German power, and he would want the United States to join the fight. A brooding Wilson, however, still did not know for sure that war with Germany was the best solution. He hoped to force Berlin to reverse its unconditional submarine warfare policy by another threat to break relations or by arming merchant ships on their way to Britain.

Nonetheless, the Germans' announcement that they would soon resume their attacks on American shipping forced Wilson to do something. Wilson thought that if the public would not stand for attacks by Germany on American shipping, then it might be better to ask Congress for a declaration of war before the inevitable war whoops forced his hand. Besides, Wilson heard frantic pleas from his two major foreign affairs advisers, Lansing and House, both of whom wanted him to end the stalemate and oppose Germany. Never a tolerant man, Wilson lost what little patience he had for the opponents of a strong anti-German policy as he surveyed the reaction to his plan to arm American merchant ships. When he recommended a law for that armament to the Senate on February 26, he blew up in disgust at the reaction of Progressive antiwar senators. Led by Senator Robert LaFollette of Wisconsin, some ten senators filibustered against the bill, preventing it from coming to a vote. Wilson denounced the Progressives as a "little group of willful men who have rendered the great government of the United States helpless and contemptible," and he decided to arm the American merchant fleet on his own without waiting for congressional approval.

Another episode which led Wilson finally to ask for a declaration from Congress was Germany's grand mistake in promising Mexico a share of the spoils if it would fight the United States. Berlin's reasoning for inviting Mexico into an alliance made military sense. The kaiser expected the Americans to join the war eventually anyway. When the United States did fight, the important thing was to make certain that the United States did not have enough forces to turn the tide in Europe. The longer Americans were kept preoccupied, the more time the Germans would have to overwhelm the British and French armies on the western front. Consequently, Arthur Zimmermann, the German undersecretary of foreign affairs, cabled his ambassador in Mexico City, telling him to offer the Mexicans a chunk of the United States if they would declare war on the United States once the Yankees joined the allies. Germany would see to it that Mexico received all of the territory, except for California, lost to the United States in the 1840s.

The Mexican government probably never would have accepted the offer in the first place, but it never had the chance to reject it. A gleeful naval intelligence officer intercepted the Zimmermann telegram as it made its way to Mexico City. Thrilled with the document, London knew it could use the purloined telegram to persuade Washington to fight at their side. A copy went to American ambassador Walter Hines Page, a supporter of the Allied cause, who immediately forwarded it to Lansing as proof of German duplicity.

Wilson himself realized that the evidence of the German attempts at persuasion of the Mexicans would whip up patriotic frenzy, and he changed his mind on why the war should be fought. No longer did he rest complaints on the preservation of neutral rights. While still important, shipping took second place to spreading democratic values. By March, Wilson believed that Germany's government was more immoral than that of other belligerents. The fact that Germany was an autocratic monarchy offended the president, an Anglophile, who admired English liberals advocating a democratic foreign policy. The Union for Democratic Control for Foreign Policy, led by liberal reformer E. D. Morel, who had exposed the horrors of Belgian rule in the Congo in 1904, argued that popular diplomacy could smash the alliance system and end the arms race. The president seemed to agree. Wilson also finally accepted the suggestion of Lansing and House that Germany represented a threat to the physical and economic security of the United States. If Germany defeated the British and the French, it would be in a position to organize the economies of Europe as it pleased. The United States would not be able to trade with the occupied lands of Europe, except as Berlin permitted. The Germans might also take over the colonies of the Allies, ending American hopes to see the Open Door policy applied around the world.

Some time during the last week of March, Wilson made up his mind that the United States had to fight Germany, and he went to Congress on April 3, 1917. Promising a battle "for democracy, for the right of those who submit to authority to have a voice in their own governments, for the rights and liberties, for a universal dominion of right by such a concert of free peoples as shall bring peace and safety to all nations and make the world itself at last free," the president received a prolonged ovation by both houses, which quickly voted the declaration. Such dissent as was heard came from a few Progressives, led by Senator LaFollette, who feared what might happen at home. He reminded colleagues of the sorry history of conscription in the United States; riots and inequities had besmirched the draft during the Civil War. He recalled traditional American intolerance for pacifists; critics of the Mexican War and Northern dissenters during the Civil War had gone to jail for their unpopular opinions. Worst of all, LaFollette predicted that joining the Allies would kill Progressive reform at home and turn the government over to the richest and most reactionary men in the country. Outside Congress, another Progressive, Randolph Bourne, warned his fellow liberals that "the American intellectuals . . . seem to have forgotten that the real enemy is War rather than Imperial Germany."

The president himself acknowledged these dangers to progressivism. There is a famous story, which may or may not be true, about Wilson's anguish on the eve of his address to Congress. Frank Cobb, the editor of the *New York World,* reported ten years later that he visited the president the night before his speech to Congress and found him "uncanny" in his predictions. "Once I lead these people into war, . . . they'll forget there was ever such a thing as tolerance. To fight you must be brutal and ruthless, and the spirit of ruthless brutality will enter into the very fabric of our national life."

In an article in the *Journal of American History* in 1971, historian Jerold Auerbach, who searched the White House records, casts some doubts on whether Cobb ever visited the president that evening. Whether Wilson made all of those startling predictions, he should have said these things. The war did kill tolerance, Progressive reform, and eventually, three years after its declaration, generated a public revulsion against ever having joined the fight in the first place.

INTERPRETING AMERICA'S ENTRY

Entry into World War I marked a great departure in United States foreign relations. Americans knew that at the time and have argued over it ever since, asking why Wilson made his decision, questioning his reasoning, and proposing alternatives. These arguments represent more than making work for professors filling learned journals with complicated theories; the memory of how the United States fought in 1917 affected the conduct of American diplomacy for generations.

Woodrow Wilson's official biographer, journalist Ray Stannard Baker, presented a standard interpretation in the 1920s when he argued in *Woodrow Wilson* that the president abandoned neutrality for belligerency for exactly the reasons he cited in his message. Unrestricted submarine warfare represented a "barbarous" affront to international law, and the United States fought to preserve its traditional understanding of the rights of neutrals. Stress on eighteenth-century rights seemed outmoded even as Baker wrote, for many American liberals had become disillusioned with the failures of Wilson's diplomacy to achieve any real improvements in world politics in the twenties. During the twenties, liberals licked wounds and punctured pompous pretensions; a decade later, during the Depression, their views received a sympathetic hearing. Stressing economic factors and the malevolent influence of bankers and munitions manufacturers, a school of "revisionists" carried the day after 1919. Such writers as Harry Elmer Barnes (*Genesis of the World War* [1926]), Charles Tansill (*America Goes to War* [1938]), C. Hartley Grattan (*Why We Fought* [1929]), and J. Kenneth Tunnel (*Shall It Be Again?* [1922]) shifted the focus from President Wilson, whom they considered sanctimonious and slow, to the house of Morgan and the Bethlehem Steel Company, which they charged with leading the country into combat to protect their investments in British securities. In the midst of the Depression, two reporters, H. C. Engelbrecht and F. C. Hanighen, published *Merchants of Death,* an account of influence exercised by arms manufacturers and the bankers who financed the war efforts of the European belligerents. They argued that Britain and France purchased cannon, ships, ammunition, or the steel to make them in the United States with money supplied by New York lenders. By late 1916, it appeared that Germany might win the war, in which case loans never would be repaid and future deliveries cancelled. To keep business humming and assure repayment, a cabal of industrialists and bankers persuaded President Wilson's closest advisers that the United States should join forces with the allies against Germany. The idea that a business conspiracy led an unwitting nation into bloodshed attracted congressional interest in 1934 when a special committee, chaired by Progressive Republican senator Gerald Nye of North Dakota, investigated the origins of the 1917 war. Nye's panel assailed businessmen, whose reputation in the midst of the Depression had reached new lows anyway, for misleading the country into war, and prepared the ground for revised neutrality laws designed to prevent a recurrence.

By the time the United States fought the Second World War, conventional wisdom had turned again, as Americans once again saw Germany as a threat. In 1941, the struggles of 1917 seemed less futile, although few students paid much attention to legalistic quarrels over the rights of neutrals. "Geopolitics," the study of the importance of geography and might in world affairs, dominated the serious study of international relations in the era of the Second World War, and it affected the interpretations of the entry into the First. Walter Lippmann, active as a thrice-weekly columnist for the *New York Herald Tribune*, presented a new gloss on American neutrality in a book he wrote in 1943, *American Foreign Policy: Shield of the Republic*. He acknowledged that Wilson thought he had fought for neutral rights, and he chastised the president for excessive legalism. Lippmann claimed that the country fought the right enemy for the wrong reasons, and he would have preferred to have seen the president base his message on the physical threat posed by imperial Germany.

Lippmann's interpretation attracted sympathetic followers among such advocates of "realism" in foreign affairs as George Kennan *(American Diplomacy)*, Hans Morgenthau *(In Defense of the National Interest)*, and Robert Endicott Osgood *(Ideals and Self Interest in America's Foreign Relations)* in the 1950s. None of the realists had anything good to say about Wilson, for while they thought the United States should have fought the First World War, they argued that Wilson did more harm than good by basing his decision on the rights of neutrals. Force and power were things which set the realists' blood racing.

Almost inevitably, the pendulum swung back in favor of an appreciation of the subtleties of Wilson's mind. What was surprising was that both Wilson's admirers and his detractors in the sixties and seventies gave him credit for a shrewd grasp of what went on in the world. According to Arthur Link, the president's fullest biographer, his diplomacy represented a "higher realism" and an appreciation of what the world might be like if American power were applied effectively. For Link in *Wilson the Diplomatist* (1956) or *Woodrow Wilson: Revolution, War and Peace* (1979), the president's view of foreign affairs did not look backward to the classical age of neutrality but forward to a world reformed through American guidance. Patrick Devlin, a British writer who also thought well of Wilson despite misgivings about the brittleness of his character, came to essentially the same conclusions in *Too Proud to Fight* (1975).

Revisionists on the left, led by William Appleman Williams, paid Wilson the respect of taking his ideas seriously while disapproving of the results of his policies. In *The Tragedy of American Diplomacy* (1962), Williams rejected the earlier revisionist claim that the president was led by the nose by the "merchants of death." Instead, Williams insisted that Wilson made the decision on his own to expand American influence in the emerging interdependent world economy. N. Gordon Levin followed a similar path in *Woodrow Wilson and World Politics* (1968), where he suggested that Wilson set the stage for subsequent American thought on politics. Levin felt Wilson was committed to a belief in American "exceptionalism" and certain that the United States had the power to act as the balance wheel of international politics, and he accused Wilson of bringing the United States into war to apply his notions of "liberalcapitalist-internationalism" around the world. Williams and Levin both wrote that Wilson's expansionism left a bitter legacy. From this modern revisionist point of view, Wilsonianism encouraged Americans to embark on a fruitless quest to create stability, put down revolution, and expand American commerce. While saddened by the results, Williams, Levin, and other revisionists respected Wilson as a serious thinker on international affairs who led the country into war with his eyes open to the consequences.

Whatever their differing interpretations of the reasons for American involvement in the Great War, historians agree that the decisions of 1916 and 1917 prepared the way for most of what came afterward in the history of American foreign relations. Once the United States joined the fight, Americans no longer were special, despite what they might think to themselves or say to others. The United States had become a great power like the others.

CHAPTER FIVE

America in the Great War,
1917–1918

On April 2, 1917, the United States joined the enemies of Germany, but President Wilson carefully pointed out that America fought as an "associate," not an "ally," of Britain, France, and Russia. The distinction affected both America's self-image and European attitudes. For the president, the United States fought for nobler aims than the Europeans, and he wanted to make certain that it stood aside from the deals struck by Europeans before the war. "Secret diplomacy" had caused the war, he proclaimed, and his country would have no part of it.

America's posture seemed supercilious to its partners, but the British and French longed so desperately for American help that they swallowed complaints about America's refusal to enter an alliance. Privately Europeans mocked Washington's aloofness. Transatlantic relations suffered more since Gen. Tasker Bliss, the American representative on the Supreme War Council, an organization designed to coordinate strategy among the powers fighting the Germans, lacked authority to discuss political plans for ending the war. Bliss, an accomplished linguist and amateur classical scholar, would have loved to have done so. He considered himself the intellectual superior of his counterparts on the British and French general staffs, and if their governments let them debate political questions, he felt he should be allowed to do the same thing. But Wilson refused, and Bliss could speak only about the role of fresh American troops.

RELATIONS WITH JAPAN AND CHINA

While the United States wanted no meeting of the minds with Europeans, Wilson and Lansing abandoned a firm stand on principles in the Far East to placate Japan in July 1917. Japan had declared war on Germany in the fall of 1914 even though the Japanese-British alliance did not require either power to join its ally's fight unless attacked in Asia. Japan saw the European war, though, as a splendid opportunity to complete its dominance of China. In the fall of 1914, Japan quickly seized the German leasehold on Kiaow-chow. Early in 1915, Japan went further and issued what became known as the TwentyOne Demands. Japan insisted that China recognize Japanese pre-eminence in the lands which Germany had yielded and, more ominously, required agreement to accept only Nipponese bankers as sources of capital. Even worse, China was supposed to clear all of its overseas diplomatic business with the Japanese ambassador.

A frightened and indignant Chinese government did not know how to handle this ultimatum. The Great War reduced effectiveness of the traditional technique of setting major powers at one another's throats. Now Europeans were preoccupied with combat, and Americans had made it clear since 1900 that they would send no troops to Asia. Therefore, China temporized as best it could, refusing to put all of its foreign affairs in the hands of Japan but acknowledging Japanese dominance of Shandong (Shantung). It also agreed to follow Japan's lead and declare war on Germany. Not that there were any Germans to fight in Asia, but Beijing reasoned that it could have a seat at the peace conference if it declared opposition to the Germans. The Japanese happily accepted the Chinese as allies, expecting them to become Japan's willing clients in the peace conference.

That was the situation in the Far East when the United States entered the war in the spring of 1917. All American experts on Asia feared that Japan might have ambitions on the American possessions in the Philippines. Instead of becoming the steppingstone to China, the islands had become a morass swallowing American resources, and now, in the midst of war, Washington had to protect the very islands it had once coveted. When the Japanese foreign minister, Baron Kikujiro Ishii, went on a round-the-world trip in the summer of 1917, the United States wanted assurances that Japan did not intend to supplant the United States in the Philippines. Ishii was willing to make such a declaration provided that he got something in return. Secretary of State Robert Lansing came through with a document which acknowledged Japan's preeminence in much of China. As a sort of after-thought, the secretary insisted that the two nations agree to respect the Open Door in China, a grotesque addition to a cynical document. How could the United States continue to support the notion of an Open Door in China while at the same time agreeing to Japan's conquest of the German lease-holds? The contradiction bedeviled American policy toward Japan and China during the war and in the peace conference which followed. At the time, in the summer of 1917, Lansing told Wilson that the United States had no choice in the midst of the war, for if it refused to recognize the Japanese in

Shantung, they might abandon the struggle against Germany and turn on the United States in the Philippines. Lansing also told Wilson to regard the agreement with Ishii as something concluded under duress. If, as the president hoped, the end of the war saw the total reorganization of world politics, then the United States could force the Japanese to back down from their hold on the coast of China.

REVOLUTION IN RUSSIA

While Americans assembled an army to send to Europe, a revolution grew in Russia. In March, before the declaration of war, the czar lost his crown, helping Wilson present the war as a fight of democrats against autocrats. Some of the Russian revolutionaries who wished to prosecute the war against Germany more vigorously thought that the government of the czar had been seized by a pro-German clique, but fighting harder against Germany was not uppermost in the mind of the bulk of Russians, who longed for an end to a horrible war. The government which replaced the czar remained in the war, undermining its popular support while gaining prestige in America.

The overthrow of the czar by an apparently liberal government headed by a lawyer, Alexander Kerensky, seemed to answer Wilson's hopes for a more democratic Russia. Americans who felt uneasy about fighting alongside an autocratic regime to rid the world of German dictatorship sloughed off their fear of hypocrisy. Kerensky's announcement that his forces would wage war more vigorously soothed the nerves of Western generals. But their leader's eagerness to fight Germans disappointed many war-weary Russian peasants and workers who, over the spring and summer of 1917, threw down their weapons and, in the words of Vladimir Lenin, head of the most radical faction of the Social Democratic party, the Bolsheviks, "voted with their feet" against war. By August, thousands of disgruntled, hungry veterans flooded the major cities of Russia where they listened attentively to the Bolsheviks call for "all power to the Soviets [worker-peasant councils dominated by the radicals that were set up in the spring of 1917]." Kerensky's government, once the hope of Western liberals, became a hollow shell bereft of an army, unable to fight the Germans, and incapable of meeting the peasants' calls for land and citizens' cries for food.

The success of the Bolshevik Revolution in November 1917 shook these easy optimistic assumptions about the future of Russia. Lenin had thought about international relations for a long time before his uprising was successful. He took power vowing to change world politics and end imperial rivalries and war in terms that challenged Woodrow Wilson's. Lenin proclaimed that the war signaled "the death throes" of capitalism and that a

Bolshevik leader Vladimir Lenin addresses a crowd during the Russian revolution.
(Library of Congress)

world revolution would sweep aside "the imperialist order." The Russian leader knew that whatever popular support his revolution had earned among his people depended upon his ability to bring the Russian soldiers home, so he called for an immediate cease-fire. The Allies viewed that move as a terrible blow. A Russian surrender would free hundreds of thousands of German troops to rush to the fighting in France. Even worse horrors were in store for the Western liberal democrats when they contemplated what the Bolsheviks, who hoped that their revolution would sweep over the rest of the world, would do to international relations in general. The rising of the world's working class would destroy all governments and replace them with international unity among laboring men and women. Bolsheviks had opposed the world war from the very beginning, saying it represented a grab for territory among the imperial powers. None of the workers would gain from the war; only industrialists with international interests profited from it.

The United States and Communist Revolution After 1917

From the triumph of Lenin's Bolshevik party on November 7, 1917, to the present, the United States has opposed Communist movements and governments throughout the world. Since 1945, Washington's confrontation with the Soviet Union has stood at the center of United States foreign policy. What has there been about communism and revolution that provokes dismay among American policymakers?

Generations of Western anti-Communists have offered a straightforward answer: Communism represented one variety of "totalitarianism." Like the other face of totalitarianism, fascism or nazism, communism supposedly marries brutal suppressions of human rights at home to limitless appetites for other peoples' lands. Communist revolutionaries everywhere are said to make up an army, more or less directed by the Soviet Union, which looks forward to conquering the world and eliminating political, cultural and religious freedom. In 1983 President Ronald Reagan called Moscow "the focus of evil in the world." Under such circumstances, a great democratic power like the United States would abdicate moral responsibilities if it did not wage political warfare against the Soviet Union and communism.

Some aspects of Soviet history since 1917 support this grim view of the meaning of communism. Successive governments have imprisoned and murdered their subjects. Political, religious, and cultural liberties, as practiced in some parliamentary democracies, are scorned in the Soviet Union as the false promises of "bourgeois democracy." Communist regimes created by the Soviet Union in Eastern Europe after the Second World War have similar contempt for human rights. And Communist governments in lands not controlled by the Soviet Union—China, Indochina, and Cuba—have taken power with the sword, jailing, killing, and exiling millions of citizens whose backgrounds, behavior, or opinions displease the authorities. Moreover, armies from Communist states have indeed crossed their borders to attack, invade, and occupy other lands, sometimes, but not always, without provocation.

Russia attacked Finland in 1939, annexed Latvia, Lithuania, and Estonia the following year, and imposed friendly governments in Eastern Europe after the Second World War. The Red Army crushed revolts in Hungary in 1956 and Czechoslovakia in 1968, and entered Afghanistan in 1979. Moscow sponsored the imposition of martial law in Poland in 1981. China annexed Tibet in 1959 and invaded another Communist state, Vietnam, in 1979. Vietnam, for its part, occupied neighboring Cambodia the same year. Revolutionary Cuba, as well, sent troops to Ethiopia and Angola in Africa to help fellow revolutionaries.

And yet, are the sorry human rights records and nonchalant regard for international frontiers of the Communist states sufficient reasons for Washington to wage a holy war against communism and revolution? Revolutionaries themselves reject Washington's indictments of their violations of human rights as so much hypocritical cant. Stories of indignities perpetrated in the United States on blacks, Indians, Hispanics, and political radicals form a staple of the Soviet press. Western critics of relentless competition with communism also point out that the United States often helps dictators it likes in Latin America, the Middle East, Africa, and Asia exile, silence, arrest, maim, and murder thousands of their own people. Complicating matters further, Washington has occasionally downplayed its objections to communism by formally or tacitly allying with one or another revolutionary government. The United States and the Soviet Union jointly fought against Hitler's Germany. America supported Communist Yugoslavia against the Soviet Union in 1948, and the People's Republic of China became an "honorary member" of the North Atlantic Treaty Organization (NATO) in 1979.

While ideological competition between communism and capitalism and dictatorship and democracy explains some of the decades-long American animosity for communism and revolution, it overlooks the most important part of the story. If Russia had not undergone a revolution and if the world had never heard of Karl Marx, the United States, as the world's major economic and military power since at least 1945, would have resisted challenges to its preponderance. Since 1917, many of these challenges have come from revolutionaries. They complain that the current structure of world politics, created by Europeans and Americans, discriminates against the poor, the weak, and the newly independent. They threaten to rewrite the rules of world commerce to the detriment of the rich, which often frightens American, European, and Japanese businesses, even if the worst rarely materializes. United States policymakers take the threats seriously, though, as they have considered revolutionary communism an obstacle to a stable, predictable world in which American views, people, ships, planes, products, and investments are welcome everywhere.

THE FOURTEEN POINTS

Bolshevik insistence that the nation-state was doomed terrified traditional politicians the world over. On the one hand, David Lloyd George in Britain and Georges Clemenceau in France might dismiss Lenin as a raving crank, whom they doubted could last more than six months in Russia; on the other hand, they feared he just might be serious. If the Russian Revolution spread, the nations in Europe would be threatened. Since Lenin seemed so eager to conclude a peace agreement with the enemy, the leaders of the Western states thought that in reality he was an agent of the German general staff. Yet, the working classes in France and Great Britain might not think that the appeal of the Russian Revolution was just a thinly veiled ploy of German propaganda. Therefore, something had to be done and done quickly by the allies to neutralize the appeal of the revolutionaries. For his part, Wilson saw that the threat to the durability of the European governments posed by bolshevism represented an opportunity for the United States to exert leadership. As a standoffish associated power, the United States could appeal over the heads of the European governments to their populations and announce an American challenge to the way the Bolsheviks wanted to alter relations among nations.

Wilson explained what he wanted in a speech to Congress on January 18 in which he included his famous Fourteen Points. While the talk represented what the president had been thinking about international affairs since the war began, it owed its shape to a group of experts who had been assembled early in the war by Col. Edward M. House. The president's confidential foreign affairs adviser thought that the diplomacy of the war was too important to be left to the Department of State. Diplomats were well enough equipped to handle the daily problems which arose in coalition warfare. They were too busy, however, to address long-term problems which the United States had to face. House thought that the United States would remain a part of the struggle for international dominance long after the world war was over. He concluded that the government had to plan for the future. Since the State Department had neither time to draft proposals nor highly trained thinkers who might do the job, he went outside the government. He found the people he wanted in universities and writing for journals of opinion. He asked his brother-in-law, Sidney Mizes, to head a research organization made up of whatever experts could be found on the question of international affairs. Mizes obligingly set up something called "the Inquiry" and assembled a staff of experts to make the plans for the future foreign policy of the United States. Among the prominent scholars and journalists who joined the group were Isaiah Bowman, the head of the American Geographical Society; Archibald Carey Coolidge, a professor of history at Harvard and one of the few Americans who knew anything about conditions in the Balkans; and Walter Lippmann, a brilliant young editor at *The New Republic.*

Lippmann helped write the Fourteen Points speech. The address offered a variety of general and specific remedies for the problems presented by the war. It called for a "New Diplomacy" consisting of "open covenants openly arrived at." The secret treaties which had bedeviled European diplomacy in the years before the world war were to be cast aside by the United States and any other powers which advocated the liberal peace program. Next, Wilson committed himself to uphold the rights of nations which were subjugated by the great empires of Europe. Of course, Wilson did not mean that all of the peoples under the thrall of the British and French empires were to be immediately flung into independence. The president doubted that most non-white nations could govern themselves; besides, such a stance would not win friends for the liberal peace program among Europeans. What self-determination did imply was that the peoples which made up parts of the *enemies'* empires had the right to organize independent nations. The multinational Austro-Hungarian and Ottoman Turkish empires would fare worst under this scheme. Wilson promised independence to the Czechs and the South Slavs who were included in the Austrian empire. He pledged an end to Turkish control over their possessions in the Balkans. The Germans would also have some subject nations taken from them: an independent Poland with access to the sea would be made up of lands taken from Germany, Austria, and Russia.

Wilson hoped his Fourteen Points would appeal to German "moderates" and "liberals." The peace he proposed left Germany more or less intact after the war, but it did threaten some reduction in territory. Besides creating Poland partially from Germany, Wilson returned to France the provinces of Alsace and Lorraine, lost to Germany in 1871. One of the most deeply held French war aims was the recovery of these two conquered territories, and Wilson expected Paris to continue the fight until they were defeated or had recovered these two Rhineland territories. In the Fourteen Points, however, Wilson did not include another of the Gaullic demands—stripping of all German land west of the Rhine River. He proposed returning Alsace-Lorraine because he believed that its inhabitants really wanted French citizenship. Yet he refused to change border lines simply because the French insisted on more physical security.

One of the schemes the French had for increasing their safety had them disarming Germany and occupying its territory with their own troops. Wilson thought disarmament was fine but balked at occupying Germany. The Fourteen Points proposed general disarmament after the war. True, Germans and Austrians were expected to give up their armed forces first, but Wilson expected the other states of the world to lay down their weapons as well.

The president was not so naive as to think that all of these radical changes in international relations could happen immediately after fighting stopped. He thought that the announcement of a liberal program would arouse considerable public support. His speech was designed, of course, to lessen the appeal from the Bolshevik call to smash the international system, so it had to be somewhat visionary. But Wilson also included what he thought was a practical method of resolving vexing international problems. The most important element of his peace program was a general international organization. This world body, open to membership to all independent states, was expected to regulate whatever peace treaty was adopted. It would supervise the disarmament of all the world's states and be in charge of the movement toward independence of colonies taken from the defeated powers. Moreover, the proposed League of Nations had power over all disputes among states including those which did not arise from the peace treaty.

The League of Nations represented the centerpiece of Wilson's plans for the postwar world. From the time he first proposed it in January 1918 until the Senate finally rejected the Treaty of Versailles containing the League Covenant, Wilson hoped that it could transform international relations. If the problem of the prewar period arose from competing alliances angrily confronting one another, creating suspicion and insecurity, the League could change that. It substituted "collective security" for the frail protection of alliances and the instability of a balance of power. The League also fulfilled the dreams of the reformers of international law. Led in the United States by Elihu Root, international lawyers hoped that the world might create an authority superseding individual nations. A new international organization took the process begun at the Hague conferences to its logical conclusions by regulating relations among nations in the future.

INTERVENTION IN RUSSIA

If the Fourteen Points speech was Wilson's way of stopping the spread of bolshevism, the Allies had more immediate means of strangling that revolution. In June 1918, British, French, Japanese, and American troops intervened in the civil war in Russia in an attempt to topple Lenin. The war had broken out almost immediately after the Soviets had yielded about one-quarter of their territory under the terms of their peace treaty made with the Germans at Brest-Litovsk in March 1918. The treaty attracted criticism even among Communists, and the foreign minister, Leon Trotsky, resigned his position rather than agree to such a humiliating peace. Lenin, on the other hand, thought that it did not matter how much he gave to the Germans, for they could not retain territory for long once the revolution occurred. The remnants of the old regime, as well as the supporters of the recently deposed provisional government of Alexander Kerensky, also thought that the treaty proved that the Bolsheviks were the agents of the Germans.

The old regime's supporters in Russia embarked upon a civil war with the Bolsheviks in the spring of 1918. The counterrevolutionaries were an odd alliance; some wanted to restore the czar, others wanted to bring back Kerensky, while still others hoped to see the Russian empire break up into independent states in the Ukraine and the Baltic. But all of the Whites, as they were called, were united by their hatred for the Reds, or Bolsheviks, and all of the Whites wanted Allied support. The White forces promised they would continue Russia's war against the Germans, which would relieve the pressure upon the Western powers. In June, therefore, the French, British, Japanese, and Americans sent troops to Siberia to help the anti-Bolsheviks in their war.

Since 1919, American policymakers and historians have argued over the motives of the intervention of the United States in the Russian civil war. The issue has become international as well, with the Soviets claiming that the Americans invaded their country in order to reverse their revolution. Some American writers have maintained that the troops entering Russia in June 1918 began a half-century of antirevolutionary crusading. William A. Williams claimed in 1964 that intervention was undertaken "to provide direct and indirect aid to the anti-Bolshevik forces in Russia." Writing later in *America Confronts a Revolutionary World* (1978), he suggests that the troops went to Russia to inaugurate "a half-century of futile confrontation" with communism. Another revisionist, N. Gordon Levin, expresses similar themes differently in *Woodrow Wilson and World Politics* (1968). The decision to intervene in Siberia "was based primarily on the Wilsonian desire to use American influence in support of Russian liberal nationalism against the interrelated threats posed both by German imperialism and Russian Bolshevism." Other historians are less harsh. George F. Kennan, a former Foreign Service officer who spent ten years off and on in the Soviet Union from the mid-thirties to the early fifties learning to hate the Soviets, wrote several accounts of American intervention in the Russian civil war and concludes that the Wilson administration was more misinformed than nasty. Help for the Czech legionnaires, whom Americans thought a far more effective fighting force than was actually the case, prompted the invasion. "The president's decision was taken against an inaccurate pattern of information, partly out of date, partly erroneous." In *The Decision to Intervene* (1956) and *Russia and the West Under Lenin and Stalin* (1965), Kennan considers the intervention an example of the regrettable Wilsonian tendency to exaggerate Yankee influence over events. Historian Betty Miller Unterberger offers another explanation: the United States joined the invading armies to maintain good relations with allies Britain and France while keeping a watchful eye on Japan's Siberian ambitions. Writing in *America's Siberian Expedition* (1956), she affirms: "When the allies insisted on going into Siberia, [Wilson] finally yielded" to have a say in the operation. She describes "the guiding motive of American policy" in Siberia as "the maintenance of the open door free from Japanese imperialistic designs."

When Allied forces reached Siberia, they found that their mission had changed into offering protection to a group of Czech prisoners of war. Approximately seventy thousand Czech members of the Austrian army had been captured by the czarist government of Russia, but the Czechs had never wanted to fight the Russians in the first place. Their own aims had been to see the establishment of a separate Czech state from the ruins of the Hapsburg empire, and they wanted to fight *against* Austria. Once the chaos of the civil war in Russia broke out, the Czechs created a fantastic scheme to fight their way across eastern Russia and Siberia, embark at the Pacific port of Vladivostock for San Francisco, sail the Atlantic Ocean, and then join the Western allies fighting the Germans in France. As a measure of the non-chalance of the Americans stationed in Russia at this time, they saw nothing wrong with this plan. If only the Allies could secure the trans-Siberian railroad, the legionnaires would fight their way to the coast. The Bolsheviks in Moscow, of course, thought everything was wrong with the Czechs' ideas, and they watched angrily as the Allied forces joined with the White armies and the legionnaires. The Czechs, however, never did make it to the western front. They spent so much time fighting the Reds in Siberia that by the time they left the country, the war against Germany was over.

THE WAR AT HOME

In the United States, the war saw an end to Progressive reforms, a crusade against dissenters, and encouragement for the wealthy. As the war proceeded, the United States government engaged in a propaganda campaign at home against Germans. At the president's request, a former Progressive newspaper editor from Cleveland, George Creel, established a Committee on Public Information to win the public over to the Allied cause. The CPI published pamphlets and placed newspaper stories about the threats to democratic institutions posed by the "Hun." German soldiers were depicted as subhuman beasts who had embarked upon a campaign of pillage, burning, rape, and murder in their occupations of Belgium and France.

The CPI also led the crusade to purge German influences from American life. Sauerkraut became "liberty cabbage," the German language ceased being taught in the American public schools, and well-known figures with German names anglicized them. Those who persisted in supporting Berlin were vilified. Hugo Munsterberg, a German professor of psychology and philosophy at Harvard University, was muzzled by the university during the war. The psychologist looked like a cartoonist's model of a German professor, with a goatee, flashing eyes, and paunch. Pompous, delighting to be called by a whole range of fancy-sounding titles, he had no political sense. He made pro-German statements until the president of Harvard, Charles Eliot, told him to be silent or be fired. H. L. Mencken, the Baltimore journalist, also learned to curb his tongue in the face of public disapproval of his pro-German sentiments. Mencken had acquired a reputation before the world war as a skillful lampooner of the foibles of the American middle class, whom he dubbed the *booboisie*. During the war, he concluded that the Wilson administration engaged in a gigantic swindle of the hopes of the public. He charged that Wilson embarked on a crusade to remake world politics in order to deify himself. Mencken called Wilson a "devious and foolish fellow" and a promoter of "buncombe." For a while, the newspaperman put these nasty characterizations of the president into print in the *Baltimore Sun,* but once the United States actually entered the war, his editor told him to choose less inflammatory subjects. He directed his attention to the development of the speech patterns of Americans and what made their language different from the one the English spoke. His *American Language* appeared in 1918 and quickly became a classic.

A darker fate awaited radicals who dissented from the war. Congress passed a Sedition Act in June 1917 making it a crime to "encourage" opposition to conscription. Socialist leader Eugene V. Debs went to jail for shouting, "the master class has always declared the wars; the subject class has always fought the battles." Less famous leftists suffered more. Frank Little, a one-eyed organizer for the Industrial Workers of the World (Wobblies or IWW), used crutches to mount a platform in Butte, Montana, to speak against the draft on July 30, 1917. Two nights later, a mob pulled him from bed and hanged him from a nearby tree. One of Montana's senators placed the blame on Washington, since "had [Little] been arrested and put in jail for his seditious and incendiary talk he would not have been lynched." In early September, Justice Department agents fanned out in raids on Wobbly headquarters across the country. They seized everything from correspondence to desks to furnishings. A treason trial opened in Chicago the following April. Radical journalist John Reed, recently returned from covering the Russian Revolution, mocked the judge as having "the face of Andrew Jackson three years dead." Reed, the author of *Ten Days That Shook the World* (an eyewitness account of the Bolshevik revolution), probably confirmed the worst fears of the prosecutors when he described the defendants as "101 lumberjacks, harvest hands and editors who believed that the wealth of the world belongs to him who creates it. . . . The IWW trial looked like a meeting of the Central Executive Committee of the All Russian Soviet." A jury found them all guilty.

Washington's spending, taxing, and industrial policy comforted businessmen who previously had feared progressivism. The government paid for the war by borrowing heavily from banks and wealthy individuals. Despite the memory of objections raised during the Civil War to a financing program that excluded ordinary citizens, Treasury Secretary William Gibbs McAdoo, the president's son-in-law, offered bonds in denominations of $10,000 and more. People of average income could not purchase these notes, and the interest on them of 4 percent more than offset the income tax of $1\frac{1}{2}$ percent levied in 1917. Congress addressed the need for central control over production and distribution with the creation of the War Industries Board (WIB), headed by Wall Street speculator Bernard M. Baruch. The WIB

Socialist leader Eugene V. Debs denounces a war of the plutocrats.
(National Archives)

set prices and wages, forbade strikes, assured profits, allocated markets, rationed consumer goods, adjusted railroad timetables, and purchased supplies for the war effort. Treasury Secretary McAdoo, "economic czar" Baruch, and Food Administrator Herbert Hoover, a mining engineer with experience in Latin America, Asia, and Africa, eased the qualms of business leaders.

The three million young men drafted into the armed forces in 1917 and 1918 encountered a less enthusiastic welcome. Before their departure for Europe, they underwent an extensive series of psychological and intelligence tests. Lewis Terman, a Stanford University psychologist and academic entrepreneur, saw an opportunity he had dreamed of for years in the millions of young soldiers who would submit to anything the army asked of them. He and the American Psychological Association convinced the army to administer a series of Intelligence Quotient (IQ) tests. Psychological examiners rushed to army camps where they supervised separate series of questions for literate and illiterate conscripts. Far from measuring innate abilities, the questions probed acquaintance with American culture. Examiners inquired of the literates' grasp of baseball, their familiarity with American painting, or their ability to recall the names of American poets. Illiterate draftees, many of whom had never taken a test before or even held a pencil in their hands, were subjected to a bewildering torrent of shouted instructions to "start," "write," "hurry up," and "stop" as they puzzled over how to complete unfinished drawings of animals, houses, tennis players, or elegantly dressed people at dinner parties. Not surprisingly, men from "native" or "old" immigrant stock scored most heavily in the "superior" range, while recent immigrants often bore the stigma of an "inferior" test score. Over half of the Russian, Italian, or Polish draftees showed up as "inferior" while 80 percent of the blacks, most of whom came from rural Southern backgrounds, fell into the "inferior" category. These results stimulated the already strong movement to restrict Eastern and Southern European immigration to the United States.

THE END OF THE WAR IN THE WEST

The war in the west ended because the German strategy of overwhelming the Allies before the Americans could make a difference failed. The Hun offensive of 1917 achieved little. Trench warfare, which had killed hundreds of thousands of men in a single day throughout the early years of the war, continued in 1917, and French troops, some of whom had mutinied during the horrible fighting of 1917, remained demoralized. But they held off the ill-fed Germans throughout the summer of 1917. Only in the spring of 1918 could the Germans release some of their troops from duty in Russia to try

American doughboys in the French mud, 1918.
(National Archives)

to overwhelm the Allies in the west. But the very harshness of the peace which Germany exacted from the Russians worked in favor of the west. The kaiser had to leave over one hundred thousand men behind to occupy the territory they had acquired from the Russian empire. The German spring 1918 offensive did not get underway until early summer, and by that time the American Expeditionary Force had reached France.

The first Americans had already been in the field by the winter of 1917, but it was not until the following summer that the force reached its full strength of one and a half million men. Commanding general John J. "Black Jack" Pershing's arrival cheered the French and British. Pershing did not help his historical reputation any by his futile campaign to rid his troops of the vice of women. Actually, the general himself thought that his men should be regular visitors to the camp followers accompanying the army, but this permissiveness proved too much for blue-nosed Progressive reformers, who forced Pershing to issue a standing order forbidding prostitution in the army camps.

While Pershing led the American Expeditionary Force, overall command of Allied and associated powers forces in France went to French general Ferdinand Foch. Tall, thin, imperious, with one of the largest mustaches ever worn by a military man, Foch looked the part of the commander of a coalition. Pershing could not stand him for just that reason, but Foch did a creditable job of integrating the American forces into the tired British and French contingents. The "doughboys" went to the center of the fighting, separating the French and British troops from one another. They had not gotten on well with each other since war had begun, and it seemed a good idea to treat them like unruly children.

Britons and Frenchmen had little time to bicker in the summer of 1918, when the German army launched its final offensive in the west. By August, the Hun had pushed to within forty miles of Paris, the closest they had been to the French capital since the fall of 1914. Then the American troops began to make a difference, and for the first time in four years armies covered miles, not yards, every day. At Château-Thierry, American and French troops were able to throw back the German attack. Since the German army had steeled itself for this one last assault on the western front, it quickly lost its strength. Fresh and healthy Americans began a counteroffensive in late August which gathered momentum in September. By the end of the month, the German army fell back in disarray, and its leaders sought an end to the conflagration. Panic erupted among the general staff who realized that the army was a spent force. If battle continued much longer, the Allies might sweep into the homeland. Even worse, the army might suffer dismemberment by the victors, and the public might turn against the generals, charging them with losing a war. From the point of view of Hindenburg and Ludendorff, it was more important to preserve the integrity of the army than to win. Wars could be fought again if the army remained intact, but if it was destroyed, then the control the general staff exercised over the affairs of the government would end.

Besides, both the German commanders and the government had paid attention to what Wilson had promised about war aims over the past nine months. While they believed that some of Wilson's moderate peace platform was propaganda designed to soften them, surely the president meant most of what he said, and he would be more generous than the British and the French. If only because the United States had entered later and had not suffered the same kinds of losses as had the two Western Allies, the Americans would not be driven by the same desire for vengeance. Wilson had clearly distinguished the United States from the aims of the Allies, and the Germans also thought it very significant that the president had refused to join a formal alliance with the British and the French.

Germany's hope for lenient treatment ran afoul of a change of heart by the president. As combat had gone on, Wilson had added another cause and no longer considered the complicated system of alliances as the sole root of the debacle. The enemy's own autocracy contributed to it, and Wilson now believed that unless democratic governments were set up throughout Europe and America, conflict would be continuous. Never mind the fact that Wilson's belief in the pacific nature of democracy had been found wanting over the centuries. Wilson could well label the Germans more aggressive because of their form of government, as he noticed that the army fought with diminishing support from the people. In late 1917, the leader of the Catholic Center party in Germany, Mathias Erzberger, had called for immediate peace but had been ignored by the generals. Moreover, the president considered the German emperor a part of a military establishment that had to go if the power of the military ever were to be broken. Wilson became convinced that Kaiser William II so loved to play soldier and dress in splendid uniforms that he accepted as true whatever his commanders had to say.

ARRANGING THE ARMISTICE

Consequently, when the enemy showed signs in October of wanting to end the fighting on terms Wilson had proposed the previous January, the president greeted the overtures coolly. He looked forward to an end of the carnage on the battlefield but was just as eager not to outrun the tenuous support given him by the British and the French. Since Wilson knew that his troops had actually been the major force which had turned the tide in battle, he could influence the British and the French. He wanted to apply pressure sparingly, however, because he knew that if he used too heavy a hand the allies would turn surly. Therefore, in October Wilson tried to steer a middle course between generosity and harshness toward the enemy.

If anything, however, in the armistice negotiations of October, Wilson chose the side of harshness. He wanted to keep the French and British in line, and he believed that a harsh truce would lead to allied acceptance of American leadership. When the Germans formally asked the Americans on October 24, 1918, if they could lay down their arms on the basis of Wilson's Fourteen Points, the president imposed tough conditions. He pointed out that the United States was only one of the three major states opposing the Germans. Before any cease-fire could be concluded, it had to be acceptable to all parties. In order to bring the European allies into line, Wilson pressed their requirement that the Germans could not resume hostilities after the truce took effect. According to the French, protection rested on complete disarmament of the enemy and an Allied occupation of Germany. Wilson would not go so far, but he agreed that for the armistice to hold, the Germans would have to promise not to resume the battle. The enemy would be physically restrained from war through retention of the Allied blockade and by forcing the German soldiers on the western front to give up their guns.

They would turn over their artillery, tanks, and airplanes to the victors and would keep their small arms for use against the rise of left-wing revolution.

Having set military conditions for acceptance of an end to the fighting, Wilson also demanded changes in Germany's "monarchical autocracy." He combined his own prejudices against authoritarianism with a desire to make the British and French happy. The president sent word to the enemy through Colonel House that the United States would not open any kind of negotiations with the German kaiser. Only if he abdicated and turned the government over to a republic would the United States consider a cease-fire.

The news that Americans insisted upon ending the kaiser's regime received a mixed reaction in Berlin. Understandably, William II himself was horrified at giving up the throne. He wanted to defy the American proposal and continue the war; he feared that the eventual verdict of history would be that he was a cowardly incompetent who fled when times got rough. (In fact, this was one of the few insights the kaiser ever had into himself.) The only factor which might lead William II to abdicate was his sense that if the war indeed was lost, he might be tried as a criminal by victorious Allies. Over the previous year, an enormous "hang the kaiser" spirit had arisen in Britain and France. William II shrank from facing this kind of vengeance. The emperor received another shock from his own armed forces. Gen. Ludendorff thought that the kaiser should clear out. He and most other army leaders concluded that the military situation looked grim for the German army at the end of October. If battle continued for as much as another month, the Allies would overwhelm the Germans, thrust into the homeland itself, and set up an occupation every bit as brutal as the one the Germans had imposed upon the Russians. Even worse, the Allies would completely disarm the German army and render it helpless. Finally, to continue battle ran the risk of mutiny inside the armed forces. Ludendorff and other conservative generals worried about the rise of bolshevism in the German army. They remembered that the Russian army had turned to the Communists as a result of the defeats that it had suffered. The same thing might happen to the German forces. For all of these reasons, the general staff urged the kaiser to abandon his throne on November 2, 1918.

Initially, William II abdicated in favor of a regent, Prince Max of Baden, who would preserve the monarchy. But this solution proved unacceptable to Americans, republicans within Germany, and militarists. For Washington, the idea of regency suggested an intact German autocracy, and that had been a cause of the war. For German republicans, the regency of Prince Max looked equally unappealing. It meant that in the future some relative of the discredited emperor might wear the crown. The democratic parties would continue to have to watch from the sidelines as court and army conducted affairs. The republicans believed that if Germany's defeat could not force their countrymen into acknowledging the need for parliamentary democracy, nothing ever could. The army, strangely enough, took the side of republican politicians in this factional battle. In early November, the generals needed someone to blame, and republican parties in Parliament made excellent scapegoats.

On November 11, 1918, the Germans and the Western Allies signed a cease-fire at 11:00 in the morning. After the guns fell silent on the western front, statisticians counted ten million dead and five million wounded among the belligerents. France had suffered the most, losing one-third of its young male population. The British and Germans had done nearly as badly. It took another half-century before European nations recovered from this vast devastation.

The war left a legacy of national resentment, suspicion, and lust for vengeance. These hatreds coincided with other, newer emotions. Soldiers in the trenches quickly shed some of their romantic ideas about the glories of warfare as they produced a generation of disillusioned poets. Ezra Pound spoke the words of many angry veterans in 1920 when he mourned:

> There died a myriad,
> And of the very best, among them,
> For an old bitch gone in the teeth
> For a botched civilization.

Young men who had served in the mud and slime, who had seen their friends die horrible deaths from the machine gun, suffer the crippling effects of gas attacks, or have gangrenous limbs amputated, lost their faith in the sense of their officers and came to hate politicians. At the end of the war, some French and British troops, and a great many more German soldiers, thought that the Bolshevik attempt to sweep aside the corrupt structure of international relations was the only sensible method of restructuring world politics. Far more of these disillusioned troops turned from leaders and placed their hopes instead on the reforms of the American president, Woodrow Wilson. Thus Wilson emerged as the most popular figure in Europe on Armistice Day, 1918. Despite their growing disillusionment and desire for vengeance, many Europeans thought that Wilson could redeem them.

THE ELECTION OF 1918

But back home in the United States, Wilson did not enjoy the same appeal. He could have recognized the slide in his own popularity, but he chose to ignore it. A few days before the armistice was signed, the congressional elections took place; the Democratic party suffered a huge defeat and lost control of the Senate. The Republicans had already captured the House in the election of 1916. Consequently, Wilson did not possess a congressional majority to support his overseas moves.

Popular enthusiasm for Wilson's call for the United States to redeem world politics waned by the fall of 1918. Soldiers longed to return home, where their relatives heard horrifying tales of swindles in war plants and profiteering among defense contractors. In the election campaign of 1918, opposition Republicans renewed earlier charges by Theodore Roosevelt that Wilson's war policy ignored basic interests in favor of vague schemes for international reform. In addition, the 1918 election occurred six years after the Democrats gained the presidency, a time when the incumbent party customarily suffers sizable defeats. Despite Wilson's pleas for Democratic candidates, voters took out their frustrations, war weariness, and impatience with the president's high-sounding rhetoric by electing Republican majorities in both House and Senate.

The president himself did not see the election of 1918 as a personal repudiation, despite having campaigned for a Congress committed to his foreign policy. In a breathtaking reversal, he distanced himself from defeated Democrats, calling it their loss, not his. Throughout his career, Wilson thought he was somehow superior to other politicians. If his fellow Democrats had lost at the polls, it represented only a public repudiation of their own personal failings, and it had nothing whatever to do with Wilson's grand design for world politics. Moreover, the president did not feel compelled to pay attention to the public, even if it had voted to reject his reforms. While Wilson thought he had the nation's best interests at heart, he thought the people were easily misled and lacked the patience to conduct an appropriate foreign policy. Just as he had said that he would teach the Latin American nations to elect good men, he believed that North Americans needed instructions from their leaders.

If anything, the Democrats' electoral rout of 1918 augmented Wilson's self-confidence. He no longer needed to share power with congressional Democrats, and he would never yield to Republicans. A complicated mixture of moralist and partisan, he believed that many in his own party were small-minded time servers but that *all* Republicans put their party interests above the common good. Now that the Republicans controlled both houses of Congress, he felt no compunction about ignoring what they had to say about foreign affairs.

His disdain for his political rivals was heightened by his personal hatred of Henry Cabot Lodge, chairman of the Senate Foreign Relations Committee. Lodge of Massachusetts was as proud of his own academic accomplishments as the president was of his. He scorned Wilson's moralizing, his dis-

Senator Henry Cabot Lodge (R., Mass.), spokesman for conservative internationalism
and Chairman of the Senate Foreign Relations Committee, 1919–1924.
(Library of Congress)

dain for ordinary politicians, and his vanity—all qualities Lodge proudly
flaunted. The senator believed that Wilson *thought* he was better than others, while Lodge *knew* that actually he surpassed his own colleagues. Worst
of all, Wilson had seized the presidency from Lodge's old friend and men-
tor, Theodore Roosevelt. Envy is the most corrosive emotion. In their battles over postwar American foreign policy, the president suffered as much
from the Massachusetts man's baiting as the senator resented Wilson's
usurpation. Lodge, quicker of tongue than his rival, mocked Wilson's pro-
nouncements during Senate debates.

Wilson should have paid more respectful attention to the election returns, as it would have saved him from shocking public defeat over the peace
he eventually negotiated in 1919. The vote represented attitudes toward the
war as well as toward repudiated officeholders. After only eighteen months

of fighting, Americans had grown tired. They resented the widespread profiteering that had taken place. Government contracts for uniforms, rifles, motorized vehicles, and ships had allowed some manufacturers to make fortunes. Those who actually went to France wallowed in patriotism, but this
feeling did not necessarily translate into votes for Wilson's program. Front-
line soldiers believed their job was to fight, win as quickly as possible, and
then return home. Calls for world reform left them cold.

In voting for a Republican Congress, the public repudiated the Progressive attempts at reform which Wilson had advocated since 1912. Of course,
Congress passed no new domestic legislation in the year and a half of the
war. Many Democrats, however, were still identified with legislative reforms,
while the newly elected Congress had other ideas. The movement for restriction on the number and sort of immigrants who could enter the United
States got a boost from the election. Already in 1915, Congress had passed
a law cutting the flow of immigrants into the United States. It set a literacy
test for all new entrants. Congress expressed the common racist belief that
the shorter and darker someone was, the worse American citizen he made.
Wilson had vetoed the 1915 bill, but new lawmakers vowed to push for restrictions on immigrants. The majority also favored prohibition of alcohol,
stricter enforcement of the Sedition Act, and an end to economic regulations. Wilson would have had a hard time working with this Republican majority under the best of circumstances.

The American election reflected a movement toward political extremism
which was experienced by all the victorious powers. Similar polls took place
in Great Britain, France, and Italy in late 1918. In each case, incumbent parties lost ground to militants of the right and left. As peace began, then, it
seemed as if Wilson, with his liberal faith in the rational ability of human beings to resolve their differences, would be swept aside. Unwilling or even unable to admit that these elections represented a mockery of his New Diplomacy, Wilson promised to go to the Paris Peace Conference to finish the job
of making "the world safe for democracy."

CHAPTER SIX

Politics and Diplomacy of Peacemaking, 1919–1920

PREPARING FOR THE CONFERENCE

Woodrow Wilson arrived in Brest, France, aboard the *George Washington* on Friday, December 13, 1918. The president did not appear to be a superstitious man, but maybe he should have drawn a different lesson from the date of his arrival than the one he did. It was a measure of his quirky independence of mind that he thought that Friday the thirteenth was a *lucky* day for him. His name had thirteen letters, so why should not thirteen be his number? Others might say that he was whistling past the graveyard.

Years later, after his mission to remake world politics had failed and his presidency lay in ruins, journalists and historians wondered why Wilson decided to go to the peace conference in the first place. If only he had stayed home and remained above the political battles, he would not have been so wounded by the defeat of the Treaty of Versailles in the United States Senate. According to historian Thomas A. Bailey, who wrote the standard account of the failed peace process (*Woodrow Wilson and the Lost Peace* [1944]), Wilson might even have done better by trying to fight for a treaty others had drafted since he would have been in a better position to compromise. His political opponents among the Republicans would not have seen the agreement as the handiwork of a man they despised.

Such criticism meant nothing to Wilson. He had decided upon the signing of the armistice that he had personally to take charge of the negotiations. The harshness of the terms of the agreement that ended the fighting made the president uneasy. Wilson went to Paris to keep watch over the French and British who lusted for more vengeance. He also thought that all

Europe looked to him to create a peace based on the New Diplomacy. From Wilson's vantage point, the alternative was either bolshevism or a reversion to the Old Diplomacy of the men who had gotten Europe into its war. No other American leader, President Wilson believed, had the prestige among ordinary Europeans to force their diplomats to yield to the New Diplomacy of the United States, nor did Wilson trust any other American diplomats to come up with a peace agreement.

Wilson chose the delegation that accompanied him to Paris carefully. The secretary of state, Robert Lansing; his personal confidant, Edward M. House; the general who had represented the United States in the Supreme War Council, Tasker Bliss; and one experienced diplomat, Henry White, former ambassador to Italy and the only registered Republican among the group, constituted the president's chosen few. None of them had any independent political authority. Wilson brusquely turned aside suggestions that he include any Republican of stature since the most frequent candidates proposed, former secretary of state Elihu Root and chairman of the Foreign Relations Committee Henry Cabot Lodge, had flaws. The president objected to Root as too conservative and too attached to the old ways of conducting diplomacy to be of any use, and he rejected Lodge out of hand as a venomous rival. To have the senator take part would invite a stalking horse for Theodore Roosevelt, and although the former president was only a shadow of himself (he died the next year), Wilson wanted no one close to TR making the peace.

While Wilson's four envoys lacked power, they had some experience in foreign affairs. As the conference developed, two of them, House and Lans-

United States delegation to the Paris Peace Conference, 1919. (l. to r.) Edward M. House, Robert Lansing, Woodrow Wilson, Henry White, Tasker Bliss.
(Library of Congress)

ing, forgot that they owed their jobs to Wilson and differed from their chief. House thought his trips to Europe qualified him to take the initiative, and Lansing resented Wilson's continuous jibes at the secretary's legalistic dullness. Of all the delegates, Bliss probably had the greatest experience with the powers, having sat on the Supreme War Council in London for the previous eighteen months. French general Ferdinand Foch, perhaps compensating for his hatred of Pershing, thought well of Bliss, and even the British generals, most of whom were witless reactionaries, acknowledged Bliss's grasp of world politics. The same could not be said of Henry White, one of the first generation of professional diplomats in the United States. As a junior secretary in London, White went out shooting in the grouse lands with English politicians who called him "good old Harry," principally because he could always be relied upon to laugh at cruel jokes about his glacial thought processes and his American naiveté. (Similar barbs flew from the Europeans toward the head of the American delegation to negotiate the peace, Wilson himself, when the conference got down to serious business in January 1919.)

Before that could happen, Woodrow Wilson went on a triumphal tour of France, Britain, and Italy. Everywhere the reception was the same: Wilson stood in an open car listening to the cheers of hundreds of thousands of wellwishers who regarded him as the savior of Europe. European politicians were astounded by the sight. Here were French and Italian crowds made up of citizens who could not comprehend a word of what Wilson, who spoke no language other than English, had to say. And yet the multitudes responded to his message that the slaughter of 1914–1918 had to be the last war that the world would ever see. He insisted that the only way to make certain that Europeans did not rush to murder one another again was to adopt the Fourteen Points as the basis for the new peace. Wilson, speaking through interpreters, urged his admiring crowds to pressure their own national leaders to adopt the liberal program, implying that he had come to Europe to save the Old World from its worst nationalistic tendencies. No wonder the leaders of Britain and France watched the spectacle of Wilson's tour with amused disdain, tinged with envy. Georges Clemenceau, the French prime minister, who was seventyeight years old at the time, had seen everything he wanted to see and knew more people than he wanted to meet, put it this way: "God has given man Ten Commandments. He broke every one. President Wilson has his Fourteen Points. We shall see."

While the president basked in the warm glow of the crowds' adulation and the French and the British prime ministers were asking themselves how long it would be before their fickle countrymen turned against the naive American, the staffs of the great powers were hard at work in Paris. The official delegation of the Americans to the peace conference was only five men, but there was a large support staff. Only the French, who hosted the conference, had more experts on the scene than the Americans. The British too were well represented, but since it was a simple one day's journey home to London, they could keep a subordinate staff in the capital.

The American experts who had joined Colonel House's Inquiry came en masse to Paris to take over one of the finest hotels, the Crillon, and lay the groundwork for the liberal peace program. Throughout December and January, they typed memoranda on territorial settlements, disarmament, the future of Germany and Austria, the fate of the defeated powers' colonies, and the structure of the new international organization. The American specialists, led by Walter Lippmann, Archibald Carey Coolidge, Isaiah Bowman, and Thomas Lamont, a Morgan partner working for the Treasury, met for breakfast every day with their counterparts in the British contingent. The experts discovered that the Atlantic was no barrier to a common understanding of international relations, and they all hoped that Wilson would succeed. Even Englishmen brought up in the methods of the Old Diplomacy, such as Harold Nicolson or Robert Cecil, went to work each morning with a bounce in their steps because the president inspired the belief that a new permanent peace would follow their work.

The high spirits did not last long; once the president returned to Paris for the opening of the conference, he set about ignoring the reams of paper churned out by the experts. That slight would have been bad enough, but worse was to come for liberals looking to the future. Wilson succumbed to demands from the British, French, and Italians that the meetings exclude the defeated Germans. Clemenceau even refused his former enemies the right to have observers patrolling the halls of the conference. The French premier had learned, as had every French schoolchild of the nineteenth century, that the Congress of Vienna, which had ended the wars of Napoleon in 1815, had been a success for France despite its having lost the war. At Vienna, the French representative, the Count de Talleyrand, one of the most masterfully adaptive politicians of all time, preserved much of his country's territory by playing upon the vanity and fears of revolution of the Austrian foreign minister, Count Klemens von Metternich. Clemenceau wanted no German diplomat skulking about the Paris meetings whispering about the danger of bolshevism.

Wilson was willing to keep the Germans from the deliberations although he had come to Europe intending to create a peace of equals. He also believed that the more hands which took part in the drafting of the peace treaty, the more compromises he would have to make. He predicted that Germans in the corridors would outrage the French, British, and Italians, who would dig in their heels, refuse to bargain, and posture for their countrymen. Without Germans present to remind their victims of all the pain caused by the war, Wilson thought that he could soothe the passions of the

Allies, explain that they had to look to the future, and prevent hurt feelings among the defeated. The best way to assure the peace of Europe would be to agree that a new international organization, committed to "open diplomacy," would stand willing to adjust all disputes after the treaty was signed. Once the powers reached agreement and presented their work to the Germans for their signature and the defeated empire made a good faith effort to uphold the treaty, then Germany would be invited to join the new international organization as a full member.

THE FEAR OF REVOLUTION

Time was short in 1919. Wilson had taken an unprecedented step by leaving the country, but he was not so dense as to imagine that he could abandon Washington without seeing his domestic position challenged. The underwater cable existed but that still was not the same as being there. Living out of a suitcase three thousand miles from the White House made Wilson want to draft the treaty as quickly as possible. The European leaders did not have to worry about absenting themselves from their offices, yet a more ominous specter disturbed their sleep—bolshevism.

The revolution in Russia had not fallen under its own weight in 1918 nor had the White armies overcome the Reds. Revolution might spread to the rest of Europe, starting with the defeated countries. German sailors waving red flags had mutinied aboard their ships at Kiel when the war ended in November 1918. A more ominous event occurred in January 1919, when the left wing of the German Social Democratic party tried to seize control of the government in Berlin. Led by Karl Liebknecht, a German, and Rosa Luxemburg of the Polish Social Democratic party, the left had consistently opposed the war in Germany. After the armistice, the two radicals had joined to form the new Spartacist group of Germany, taking with them the Independent Socialists, who had also opposed the war. The Spartacists had no use for the more conservative socialists who had formed the German republic in November 1918, with Liebknecht's newspaper *Di Rote Fahn* (The Red Flag) denouncing the government as the "traitors of the revolution" and "bloodhounds." On Christmas Eve 1918, radical sailors had captured the headquarters of the regular Socialist newspaper and held the Socialist commander of Berlin prisoner. With the new year, the radical members of the government quit, thereby signaling a general Spartacist rising. On January 8, the newly formed Communist party of Germany joined the Spartacist group in calling for armed insurrection against the government. Armed bands of Spartacists took to the streets and called upon the soldiers to join them in toppling the majority Socialist government of Philipp Schneidemann and Friedrich Ebert. That government turned to the generals for help in crushing the uprising. The head of the Berlin police, Socialist minister Gustav Noske, gathered an army of several thousand conservative officers and soldiers. They marched on Berlin the night of January 10 and began a campaign of terror against the left. The troops rounded up all the members of the Spartacist movement they could find, capturing Liebknecht and Luxemburg on the 15th. The former was shot "while trying to escape" while the Polish revolutionary was beaten senseless and thrown into a canal to drown.

The rising of the left had been crushed in Germany, but that did not give much comfort to other Europeans who feared communism, Germany, or anything unpredictable. The correspondent of Britain's liberal *Manchester Guardian* described the situation in Berlin on January 15 in a way which sent chills down the spines of conservatives. "The coalition between Government, Socialists, the middle classes, Pan Germans, and the militarists is for the moment perfect, and Germany is now under control of the same elements which applauded and carried out the war. They have crushed, or are in a fair way of crushing, the political sections which combatted the German war party for years. It is a fact which will scarcely fail to affect Germany's international position. There is no reason at all to believe that the government's military victory will make for internal peace, order and stability."

In Paris the news of the Spartacist rising sent the diplomats into a frenzied search for a speedy peace treaty. Wilson, Lloyd George, and Clemenceau all knew that other revolutions could break out at any minute among other defeated powers. For Wilson, the rising meant that Germany had to recover economically as quickly as possible. He wanted the French to permit lifting the blockade of Germany's ports. But French treasury minister Louis-Lucien Klotz refused to consider it until the Germans turned over their gold to the West.

WRITING THE TREATY

Fearing revolution, the diplomats at Paris reasoned that the quickest path to a treaty was to have it drawn up by the major powers and then presented to the entire assembly. As in Wilson's acquiescence to the exclusion of Germany from the entire conference, this decision made sense. Obviously, no one expected the plenary sessions, at which over thirty nations were represented, actually to set down details. The solution let the great powers do the job.

A Council of Ten consisting of the leaders of the United States, Great Britain, France, Italy, and Japan and their foreign ministers was set up. Even this group proved too large to draft language, so it was reduced to a Coun-

The Big Four at Paris. (l. to r.) Vittorio Orlando, David Lloyd George, Georges
Clemenceau, Woodrow Wilson. *(Library of Congress)*

cil of Four including the heads of government of the obvious big powers:
David Lloyd George of Great Britain, Georges Clemenceau of France, Vittorio Orlando of Italy, and Woodrow Wilson of the United States. These men
did the real work.

Once the idea of the Council of Four was firmly established in February,
it dealt a serious blow to the hopes of the liberals who believed in the president's program. In a single stroke, the leaders of the major powers had denied the equality of all states. Now it was clear that the world was not only
divided into victors and vanquished, which in itself was a departure from the
program of a "peace without victors," but also that four states were the important ones. Other nations arrayed against Germany mattered less or not
at all. The fact that the Big Four meetings involved only the leaders themselves, accompanied by interpreters, assured that the staffs of the delegations, which had done so much of the background studies, would be ignored.

This neglect of subordinates would not have been so bad had Wilson had
a better grasp of the situation. Experts on the Inquiry and the British delegation might resent being kept in the dark, and Edward House and Robert
Lansing might object that the president paid no attention to their advice,

but all of these complaints could easily have been sloughed off as the jealousies of proud men left with nothing to do. The problem with the operations of the Council of Four was that Wilson was out of his depths, and did not know it, in the personal negotiations with Lloyd George, Orlando, and Clemenceau.

One member of the British delegation, Harold Nicolson, confided that when Wilson was confronted with "the swift arrows of Clemenceau's Latin intellect" or with "the king-fisher darts of Mr. Lloyd George's intuition," he seemed "a trifle slow witted." Another Englishman, John Maynard Keynes, a brilliant young member of the Treasury, grew disgusted with Wilson's compromises and blamed them on his mind. "The president's slowness amongst the Europeans was noteworthy. He could not all in a minute take in what the rest were saying, size up the situation with a glance, frame a reply, and meet the case with a slight change of ground; and he was liable therefore to defeat by the mere swiftness, apprehension, and agility of Lloyd George. There can seldom have been a statesman of the first rank more incompetent than the president in the agilities of the council chamber."

But it was not primarily the coarseness of Wilson's mind which put him at such a substantial disadvantage in his conversations. Rather, the Europeans came with concrete proposals to advance individual causes, while he had to create general solutions to everyone's problems. He saw his job as mediating the disputes of other powers. To be successful, he had to win all arguments. For the Europeans to win, they had simply to gain their individual ends. Finally, Wilson had to compromise with the Europeans to gain their support for the centerpiece of his new system, the League of Nations. Unless all of the nations of the world were willing to join the new international organization, Wilson feared that the entire structure would crash to the ground.

The president explained that the League of Nations would substitute a universal alliance, committed to something called "collective security," for the competitive, partial alliances he believed had been mostly responsible for the coming of the war. Under collective security, each member of the general international organization agreed that a threat to another member represented a threat to its own interests, and each pledged aid, just as parties to a military pact promised to assist one another. Collective security, however, eliminated partial groupings of nations, and, so the theory went, statesmen would have less reason to fear their neighbors. Nationalist critics of collective security like Sen. Hiram Johnson (R., Calif.) charged that it subordinated the national interest to the interests of other states, while Progressives, radicals, and defeated Germans complained that it represented a smokescreen which hid the fact that the victors of the Great War kept their feet on the necks of the losers.

CENTRAL EUROPEAN TERRITORIAL
CHANGES AFTER WORLD WAR I

— · — · — Postwar Boundaries

German Losses

Russian Losses

Bulgarian Losses

The Former Austria-Hungary

NORWAY

SWEDEN

FINLAND

Leningrad

ESTONIA

NORTH

SEA

DENMARK

BALTIC

LATVIA

SCHLESWIG

SEA

Memel

LITHUANIA

U. S. S. R.

(RUSSIA)

Danzig

EAST
PRUSSIA

NETHERLANDS

Berlin

WEST
PRUSSIA

BELGIUM

Rhine R.

GERMANY

Posen

Warsaw

POLAND

RUHR

LUX.

SAAR

Prague

GALICIA

UKRAINE

Paris

LORRAINE

CZECHOSLOVAKIA

RUTHENIA

BESSARABIA

Dniester R.

FRANCE

ALSACE

Danube R.

Vienna

Pruth R.

SWITZ.

AUSTRIA

Budapest

RUMANIA

Geneva

TIROL

HUNGARY

TRANSYLVANIA

Trieste

Fiume

BOSNIA

ITALY

Belgrade

Bucharest

BLACK

YUGOSLAVIA

SERBIA

SEA

CORSICA

ADRIATIC SEA

MONTENEGRO

BULGARIA

Rome

Constantinople

SARDINIA

ALBANIA

TURKEY

GREECE

Athens

SICILY

CRETE

MEDITERRANEAN

SEA

The war had undermined the moral authority of European colonial rule in Africa, the Middle East, and Asia. Opposition leaders of the British, French, and Italian labor or socialist parties, touched by Wilson's idealism or Lenin's radicalism, urged eventual independence of their own colonies as well as the overseas dependencies of the vanquished central powers. Anticolonial sentiment had fermented in Europe for a generation. In 1902, British journalist John A. Hobson, a liberal, published his study, *Imperialism,* claiming that overseas expansion served only the interests of a small group of finance capitalists to the detriment of the rest of the nation. Lenin's influential pamphlet *Imperialism: The Highest Stage of Capitalism* (1916) enlarged on Hobson with the assertion that imperial rivalries led to the Great War, the death throes of the capitalist order. Wilson's call for self-determination in his Fourteen Points, while consciously avoiding mention of independence for nonwhite peoples, also offered hope to anticolonialists.

But no government official among the European or Japanese victors spoke openly of yielding colonies in 1919. In fact, these nations hoped to add conquered German and Turkish territory to their own empires. At the Paris Peace Conference, they threw a sop to liberals by acquiescing in Wilson's proposal for a "mandate" system in which victors seized German or Turkish territories not for themselves but in the name of the world community or League of Nations. Commercial motives lurked beneath Wilson's lofty rhetoric. He expected that American merchants would trade freely in the mandates, while they had been barred from outright dependencies.

The conference created three types of mandates, A, B, and C. "A" mandate status applied to Ottoman territory in the Middle East, for example, Palestine, Syria, or Iraq, places which "had reached a stage of development where their existence as independent nations can be provisionally recognized." Britain assumed an "A" mandate over Palestine and Iraq while France took charge in Syria-Lebanon. Both promised eventual independence. "B" mandates applied to "peoples, especially those of central Africa . . . at such a stage that the mandatory must be responsible for the administration of the territory." No one expected such "B" mandates as Tanganyika in East Africa, given to Britain, or the Cameroons in West Africa, placed under French administration, to rule themselves before the remainder of Britain and France's colonies. Eternal bondage awaited "C" mandates. These were forlorn places "such as southwest Africa and certain of the Pacific islands, which, owing to the spareness of their population or their small size or their remoteness from the centers of civilization," would forever remain under foreign control. The government of South Africa took over Germany's ownership of phosphate-rich Southwest Africa, Japan ruled Germany's Pacific islands north of the equator, and Australia and New Zealand divided the "C" mandate south of that line.

Wilson's greatest difficulties at Paris came from the French, Italians, and Japanese. The British, led by Lloyd George, at least appeared to have a liberal government which shared many of the principles that Wilson advanced. The French were another story. Clemenceau's ideas on world politics and the Germans, like those of most Frenchmen of his generation, had been formed by the French defeat in the war with Prussia in 1871. The war of 1914 only confirmed his fear that the Germans would stop at nothing to strip France of its territory. At the conference, Clemenceau was dominated by one passion—to make Germany pay for the war and prevent it from attacking France again. He wanted the conference to assure French security with a military guarantee of its borders, and he insisted that Germany be totally disarmed. His attitude toward reparation was expressed simply as "Les boches peyera tout" ("The Germans will pay for everything"). Of course, he, as did Wilson, wanted to see the lost provinces of Alsace and Lorraine restored. Clemenceau also intended to strip the west bank of the Rhine from Germany and place it under French control.

As nominal host, Clemenceau had advantages over Wilson. The French premier could wait patiently until the public love affair with the American president cooled. After all, Clemenceau did not have to look over his shoulder about what happened back home; he was home. Clemenceau set the pace, knowing that eventually Wilson would beg to have the work completed. The Frenchman chaired meetings by sleeping when issues which did not concern him appeared, conserving his strength until questions interesting to France arose, at which time the "tiger" sprang into action. Thus did he wear down the much younger American president.

For Orlando of Italy, the peace conference represented a means of receiving the spoils promised when Italy had allied with Britain and France in 1915. In the secret Treaty of London, the two allies had promised Rome a huge chunk of Austria should it join them. Before 1914, Italy had been a nominal ally of the Central Powers—Germany and Austria—but the Italians had remained neutral in 1914, saying that their agreement was only a defense agreement. Now, in 1919, Orlando wanted the passes in the Alps as well as the coast of the Adriatic Sea even though neither region was populated with ethnic Italians and the residents of the Alps preferred to remain part of Austria while those on the Adriatic wished to join Yugoslavia. Wilson had no qualms about offering Austrians to the Italians, for the German speakers were, after all, enemy nations, but southern Slavs presented another problem. If Wilson yielded on the question of Trieste and the Dalmatian coast, he might void his promise of self-determination to the subject peoples of the Austrian empire. At one point in April, Orlando threatened to leave the conference and return to Italy. Fine, said Wilson, once the prime minister returned home he would discover that the Italian public had more faith in the judgment of the president of the United States than they did in that of their own premier. Wilson asked the Italian public to repudiate their prime minister and turn instead to the moderate peace program, but to his surprise the Italians, having forgotten their earlier enthusiasm, jeered at his pleas for generosity. They wanted Trieste or they would not become part of the new world system. Wilson prevailed eventually, since Italy was weak and did not receive the support of the French and the British. Yugoslavia emerged as an independent state with Fiume as its Adriatic port. But the settlement embittered the Italians, and three years later they turned to Fascist leader Benito Mussolini who promised to erase the stain on Italy's honor.

The Japanese also called for their share of the spoils of war. Wilson had never been happy with the Lansing-Ishii agreement of 1917 confirming Japan's preeminence in former German leaseholds. There was nothing which the United States could do about it in the midst of hostilities, but once the guns stopped, Wilson tried to turn the peninsula of Shandong over to China. This commendable urge to advance self-determination foundered on racial politics. In April, Japan offered an article to the peace treaty recognizing the formal equality of all races in the world. The move, as clever as it was cynical, reflected Japan's hope to expose the limits of Wilson's commitment to selfdetermination. He obviously had not intended the doctrine to be extended to nonwhite regions of the world, and the Japanese knew that the article would embarrass the Americans. Complaints came immediately from the head of the Australian component of the British delegation, who considered the pledge of racial equality a thinly veiled attempt to invalidate Australia's own laws excluding Japanese immigrants. The British government supported the Australian position, as Lloyd George feared Australia's defection from the consolidated imperial delegation. South Africa, another member of the delegation, also might quit Paris if the conference embraced racial equality. Lloyd George did not want to *oppose* rights for nonwhites, for that would seem crude, but such a stipulation might give unwanted encouragement to nonwhite regions of the empire. The British were in a quandary. The Japanese who asked for the declaration of a formal equality were allied to the British under the terms of a 1902 treaty. To turn their back on racial equality could strain that treaty, stranding the British without a naval partner in the Far East.

To resolve the problem, Lloyd George suggested a deal worthy of the Congress of Vienna. The conference could not endorse racial equality, but it could offer Japan something of far greater practical value—confirmation of their hold over Shandong. Wilson felt relieved to go along with this proposal, liberating him from an uncomfortable spot. He trembled as Japan threatened to leave the conference and stay in Shandong while refusing to join the new world organization. The president had enough presence of mind to realize an appeal to the Japanese people over the head of their government would produce a frostier reception than a similar plea had earned in Italy. In early May, diplomats agreed that Japan could stay in China, running the government and railroads of the province, until a referendum took place in 1922. News of this agreement reached China on May 4, igniting an angry demonstration by thousands of student radicals who surged through the streets of the northern capital, Beijing (Peking), denoucing the agreement as a cowardly surrender to the Japanese. Among those taking part was a young librarian at Beijing University, Mao Zedong, who later called the May Fourth movement "the birthday party" of Chinese communism.

The compromise with Italy and with Japan occurred in April and May, after Wilson returned to the conference from a brief three-week journey home to Washington. The trip had been anticipated since Wilson had been out of the country for two and a half months when he went home in February. While he was gone, he left matters in the hands of Lansing and House, a pair who could not get along without the president acting as referee. The proud, dull, dour Lansing resented House's lightning intelligence, his ability to keep several issues in mind at once, his good spirits, and his way of wooing the Europeans.

Back in Washington, Wilson did very little to make the Republican leadership in Congress think any better of him, and he suffered a rebuke when Lodge led thirty-nine Republican senators in a round robin attack on America's participation in the League of Nations. More bad news came when the local papers criticized the secrecy of the conference as a repudiation of his liberal New Diplomacy. His headaches got worse, as they always did when he encountered opposition; he may even have suffered one of a series of ministrokes that began in his days as president of Princeton.

In Paris, however, things went more smoothly with the president out of the way and House pressing to wrap up the treaty before he got back. Breaking with the Europeans, House came to believe that the Bolsheviks had to be included or the work would be useless. He encouraged William C. Bullitt, a pampered young Philadelphia playboy attached to the American delegation, to travel to Moscow to sound out the Soviet leaders. Bullitt met with Lenin and Trotsky and discovered that they wanted an invitation to the peace conference. The American believed that the Whites could never win the civil war and predicted that if the Western powers left Russia the Soviets would stop exporting their revolution. The young diplomat was appalled at the devastation he saw in Russia, with hundreds of thousands dead in the war, crops in flame, and mass starvation in the cities. He expected Russia would require at least a decade to recover from the damages, so it did not pose as much of a threat to the stability of the rest of Europe as conservative politicians feared. What threat remained could be suitably contained, however, only if the Soviets could be included in the order created at Paris.

House agreed with Bullitt's assessment of the Soviet Union, but he could not move without first satisfying Clemenceau's requirements for French security. In Wilson's absence, House dangled the carrot of German reparations before the French premier's hungry eyes. Originally, Wilson had balked at the notion of Germany being compelled to pay the entire cost of the war, claiming that it would be vindictive, would imply that Germany had caused the war in the first place, and would cause the Germans to thirst for revenge. Besides, he thought that a requirement of huge reparations would exceed Germany's capacity to repay. Either Germany would default or the United States, the only nation with a functioning economy, would pick up the tab.

House saw the point of the president's fears, but he also thought that the French had to have their pound of flesh, and any scheme other than reparations might be worse. The proposal to establish a protectorate over the west bank of the Rhine, another of Clemenceau's brainchildren, would rankle the Germans as deeply as the German seizure of Alsace-Lorraine in 1871 had wounded the French. Nor would the United States ever agree to a formal military alliance with France. Consequently, France's good will had to be purchased in cash. French pride would also be soothed if the peace conference agreed that Germany bore total responsibility for the war. Hence, in Wilson's absence, House agreed that Germany would be held responsible for the cost of the war; what that price was would be decided later.

Having decided to bill Germany for the devastation, diplomats cast about for a way to justify this departure from the liberal program. They decided that the treaty should label Germany the aggressor in 1914. Article 231 of the peace treaty asserted that Germany alone had started the war; therefore, it was responsible for paying damages to the victors. When the news of this "war guilt" clause reached Germany, all parties from the right to the left denounced it. Some representatives of the new republic indicated they would not sign a treaty which contained such insulting language, and the Socialist foreign minister published the diplomatic correspondence of the imperial government dating back to the establishment of the empire in 1870 to prove Germany's good intentions. The Soviet government already had begun publishing the correspondence of the czars, embarrassing the old regime's French allies. German republicans hoped that the same stigma would attach to the governments and that the anti-German judgment of the peace treaty would be overturned. To most Germans, the war guilt clause meant that the treaty was solely a victor's political propaganda document signed to libel them.

When Wilson returned to Paris, he learned of House's compromise with the French. The president did not repudiate the agreement, but he did not like it either. Jealous of House's success, he never again gave his adviser his confidence. At the same time, the French press, which heretofore had condemned the president as a dreamer, now began flattering him. He appeared to be a "statesman" who "understood" the French desire for security, and a man blessed with great "foresight." Wilson, as susceptible to compliments as anybody, purred. He found that he was getting along better with the French now too.

But the cloud of revolution still hung over the conference after Wilson returned from Washington. New revolutionary governments took power in the southern German state of Bavaria and in the former Hungarian province of the Austrian empire. The Bavarian Communists held power for only days before being crushed by right-wing veterans commanded from Berlin. The revolution in Hungary was more serious. There the Communists, led by Bela Kún, held power for over one hundred days from February to May 1919. In the midst of this Hungarian Soviet interval, the peace delegates dispatched Gen. Jan Smuts, the minister of defense in the South African government, to find out what the new Bolshevik government wanted. While in Budapest, Smuts learned that Kún had come to power in part because of the Hungarian desire for territory awarded in Rumania. The representative of the conference spent his time in the Hungarian capital lamenting the cold, the broken windows, the unkempt lawns, the dirty children, and the thievery. Smuts despised the new foreign secretary of Hungary, calling him "a little oily Jew—fur-coat rather moth-eaten—stringy green-tie—dirty collar." Another member of the delegation, Charles Seymour, one of the academic experts on the staff of the Inquiry, said that something had to be done to stop the spread of revolution or "it looks as if Vienna would be the next to go Bolshevik and after that Prague." The prompt action which the victors were prepared to take was to provide a buffer of League of Nations troops between Hungary and Rumania. The Communists in Hungary dithered and thought it was not enough. Finally, the right-wing forces overwhelmed Kún's government in mid-May, sending the leader to Moscow.

Hungary was a small irritant compared to the Soviet Union. When William Bullitt returned from Moscow in April, he rushed to see Lloyd George to inform him of the interest the Bolsheviks had in an invitation to the peace conference. Bullitt announced that the revolutionaries were desperate to see an end to the civil war. Lenin and Trotsky wanted a meeting with representatives of the Western powers and the Whites and a withdrawal of the foreign troops. Bullitt himself was thrilled at the flexibility he saw in the Soviets, and he hoped to ignite a spark in Wilson too. But the president left the young diplomat cooling his heels for days, eventually flatly refusing an audience because of "flu." An enraged Bullitt suspected that the president had only a diplomatic illness, and he resigned in disgust from the Foreign Service, saying he was going to "go to the beach and watch the world go to hell." Lecturers are fond of reporting "He went, and it did," but maybe not because the American government had lost his services.

Wilson did indeed have the flu when he refused to speak with the envoy. Exhaustion combined with the opposition from other diplomats brought about the worst attacks of headaches the president had had in years. To have seen Bullitt would have meant more rows with Lloyd George and Clemenceau, and the president did not feel up to it. Besides, by April the president did not want to have to listen to anyone with a different view on the subject than his own.

For the next two months, Wilson and the leaders of Britain, France, and Italy worked out the final details. The American president often withdrew to type out drafts of the articles on his own battered typewriter. Finally, in early May, a document was ready to submit to the defeated Germans. A German delegation of 160 headed by Count Ulrich von Brockdorff-Rantzau saw the result for the first time on May 1. They were horrified at the size of the indemnity exacted from them and the territory they lost in Eastern Europe. The "Polish corridor" establishing a link to the sea for the new state grated on their nerves. The treaty also stripped Germany of all colonies in Africa and the Pacific.

Brockdorff-Rantzau complained bitterly that the peace agreement was a harsh "diktat" toward the Germans as the Treaty of Brest-Litovsk had been toward the defeated Bolsheviks. The Germans were not alone in complaining about the harshness of the terms of peace. Several of the young, hopeful members of the delegations joined William Bullitt in protest resignations. Adolf Berle on the American staff accused the president of violating his ideals; Joseph Fuller complained that America had "bartered away her principles in a series of compromises with the interests of imperialism and revenge"; John Storck declared that the accords would make Germany "eager for revenge"; and George Bernard Noble predicted that the result "would be provocative of future wars." Lansing rejected all of these resignations, fearing the public storm they would provoke. On the British side, Harold Nicolson kept his misgivings to his diary, but John Maynard Keynes left with a public blast; his book *The Economic Consequences of the Peace* came out the next year. He wrote in bitterness, after seeing his plans for a liberal economic settlement dashed on the rocks of French desires for vengeance and Wilson's inability to stop Clemenceau and Lloyd George. Widely read in the twenty years after the Paris Conference, the book helped create a general public disillusionment among English-speaking readers with the results of the peace conference, and it lay the foundations for a belief that Germany had been badly mistreated by the delegates at Paris.

Staff members' doubts did not penetrate to Woodrow Wilson or the other heads of government. The president believed that the draft's flaws could be cured when the League of Nations took shape and Lloyd George and Clemenceau had gotten what they wanted. On Saturday, June 28, five years after Gavrilo Princep shot the Austrian archduke and his wife in Sarajevo, the peace treaty was signed in a ceremony at the Hall of Mirrors in the Palace of Versailles. It was a festive occasion, but a miasma of fantasy hung over the proceedings. Harold Nicolson, who had been making glum remarks about the proceedings for months, found it ironic that a document designed to establish the new order would be presented to the world in a palace of Louis XIV and called the scene a "horrible humiliation" of the Germans. Others in the Allied delegations were less squeamish as they crowded around the German representatives to ask for their autographs.

THE TREATY COMES HOME

When Woodrow Wilson brought the agreement home in July, he expected the Senate would ratify it quickly and give him credit for having negotiated it. Most newspapers also predicted ratification, and the public wanted the Senate to approve it. A majority of senators polled in July agreed that they would vote yes even if they had to make changes. Nevertheless, the leader of the opposition, Henry Cabot Lodge, grumbled, "I read [Wilson's] speeches and they are all in the clouds and all full of sentiments that lead nowhere." Lodge did not foresee a flat rejection of the document, but he had served notice when the president returned to Washington in February and March that the Senate would insist on its own version. In March, Lodge had led a group of thirtynine senators, seven more than the one-third necessary to block an agreement, in a round robin declaration about the peace treaty. The thirty-nine held that before they would approve the work of the peace conference, it would have to pass their scrutiny as not violating the basic national interests of the United States. Specifically, they wanted to see guarantees of American superiority in the Western Hemisphere expressed in acknowledgment of the Monroe Doctrine. They also opposed Article X of the League of Nations covenant, which required member states to use troops if called upon by the League. Senators, jealous of the prerogatives of Congress, saw the article as a way around their control of the war power.

In the summer of 1919, Lodge expected a delay to help Wilson's opponents. The public's enthusiasm would cool, and the president and the Democrats might wear themselves out in their campaign for the document. Consequently, Lodge decided to give the accord the most exhaustive appraisal that any agreement ever had. He personally read all two hundred pages into the *Congressional Record* in a two-week marathon which emptied the hearing room of spectators, senators, and even stenographers.

The attrition of the boredom was followed by the complaints of the disillusioned. Lodge held hearings, something which the Senate Foreign Relations Committee had never done before for a peace agreement. For six weeks in August and September, the committee listened to experts highlight the flaws. William Bullitt returned from his early retirement on the French Riviera to report how the president had wrecked any chances for accommodation with the new Bolshevik government. Other witnesses predicted a new war as a result of German resentment. Some said that the League of Nations would force the United States to engage in continuous warfare. One witness who testified was the Idaho Progressive Republican William Borah, who led a group of "Irreconcilables," so named because they would not accept the treaty under any terms. Borah told the committee that Wilson had committed the United States to a twentieth-century version of the Holy Alliance which Czar Alexander I had created to stamp out revolution in Europe after the Napoleonic wars. Borah worried that the United States would become the guarantor of the old empires of Britain and France. Germany and the Soviet Union, excluded from the new order, would conspire to wreck the settlement.

Faced with delays and mutterings about his lapses from idealism, Wilson decided to counterattack with a public speaking tour. In September 1919 he covered eight thousand miles in twenty-two days, delivering thirty-six speeches and standing up in cars for a dozen parades. At every stop he appealed to the public for support and mocked the opponents who predicted that the League would have American troops in combat in faraway places. American soldiers would go to war only in places where the United States had interests. As he told his audience in Salt Lake City, "If you want to put out a fire in Utah you do not send to Oklahoma for the fire engine. If you want to put out a fire in the Balkans . . . you do not send to the United States for troops." He brought his audience to tears when he told them that if the League of Nations were rejected, a war would erupt in which "there would not be a merely seven and a half million men slain. The very existence of civilization would be in the balance." Finally, in Pueblo, Colorado, on September 26 he gave his last speech, recalling the mothers who had grabbed his hand, shed tears, and cried, "God bless you, Mr. President." "Why," he asked, "should they weep upon my hand and call down the blessings of God upon me? Because they believe that their boys died for something that vastly transcends any of the immediate and palpable objectives of the war. They believe and rightly believe that their sons saved the liberty of the world." At the end of his speech, the president collapsed with a serious stroke, and four days later his life was in danger.

For the next six weeks Wilson could do no work, and he never recovered fully from this latest in a series of blood clots in his brain. Throughout October and early November, his wife, Edith Bolling Wilson, became in effect acting president. She shielded her husband from the importunities of his colleagues, and grew jealous of his advisers. When Robert Lansing thought that as secretary of state he should hold a cabinet meeting in the president's absence, Mrs. Wilson was outraged. She reported Lansing's disloyalty to her husband, who summarily fired him and put Bainbridge Colby in charge of the State Department. Wilson also broke finally with Colonel House during this period.

With Wilson on the sidelines, the Republican opposition mounted. Lodge announced that he would vote yes only if reservations guaranteeing the Monroe Doctrine and the right of Congress to declare war and repudiating the Shandong agreement giving the peninsula to the Japanese went into law. The first roll call in November was on the agreement with the Lodge reservation. The Democrats joined with the Irreconcilables to vote it down fifty-five to thirty-nine. Then the senators took up the original treaty without reservations. There Lodge joined with the Irreconcilables, and the vote was thirty-eight for, fifty-three against. Wilson had recovered enough to know of the vote and, surprisingly, was not discouraged by the defeat, thinking that public pressure would force a reversal at the next session of Congress. The treaty came up again on March 19, 1920. This time Senate Democratic leaders begged the president to allow the loyal Democrats to vote for a version containing the Lodge reservations, but Wilson was adamant. To accept something amended by his brilliant enemy would mean that the final product would be Lodge's, not his. Besides, the president clung to the forlorn hope that he would win another nomination by his party for the presidency. Once nominated, he would turn the campaign into a "solemn referendum" on the Paris peace and the League. Under orders from the president to vote against the Lodge reservations, Democrats joined with the Irreconcilables to defeat it. In the March roll call, forty-nine voted for the treaty and thirty-five against it. Its supporters were seven votes short of a two-thirds majority.

THE ELECTION OF 1920

Wilson did not get his wish for the Democrats' nomination for a third term. Party leaders recognized that the tide had turned against him in the election of 1918. Wilson still had not fully recovered from the effects of his stroke in the spring of 1920, so it would be impossible for him to campaign. Furthermore, his commands to the Democrats in the Senate made his fellow party members want to drop him. His son-in-law, William Gibbs McAdoo, the secretary of the treasury, tried for the nomination in his stead. The party turned him back, too. They nominated the governor of Ohio, James M. Cox, a popular vote getter in an important state. As a governor, Cox did not have wide experience in foreign affairs, which was just as well from the point of view of the party's leaders. During the campaign Cox would be unlikely to open old wounds about the peace treaty. As a vice-presidential nominee, the Democrats selected the former assistant secretary of the navy, Franklin D. Roosevelt. This Democratic Roosevelt had some international experience, and it was he who would carry the banner for the League of Nations in the "solemn referendum" of the 1920 election.

The Republicans believed that 1920 was their year. The country was normally Republican, and their party had scored large gains in the 1918 elections. They selected another Ohioan, Sen. Warren G. Harding, whose principal qualifications were that he had no enemies and that he looked like a president. His campaign manager followed the advice of Senator Bose Penrose of Pennsylvania who urged, "Keep Warren at home. Don't let him make any speeches. If he goes out on a tour, somebody's sure to ask him questions, and Warren's just the sort of damn fool to try to answer them." Harding made most of his speeches from the porch of his house in Marion. No one could tell where he stood on the League of Nations or the peace treaty. His only contribution during the campaign was a word which passed into the American political lexicon when he said that "America's present need is not heroics but healing, not nostrums but normalcy." In the last week of the campaign, thirty-one prominent Republicans stated that they were sure Harding favored the League. The president of Columbia University, Nicholas Murray Butler, and Henry L. Stimson, Elihu Root, and former nominee Charles Evan Hughes all expressed certainty that the United States would participate in some form of League.

Harding himself was not sure. He swamped Cox with a majority of over 60 percent of the votes, seven million more than the Democrat received. Upon learning of his landslide, Harding came to his front porch and told his supporters that the League of Nations was now "deceased." In office, Harding did nothing to revive it, and the United States did not ratify the rest of the Versailles Treaty. Instead, on July 2, 1921, Congress ended the war with Germany. A month later, the United States and Germany signed the Treaty of Berlin, which gave Washington all rights it would have had under the Versailles agreement. American diplomats made similar agreements with Austria and with Hungary the same month.

HISTORIANS' ASSESSMENTS OF WILSON

Wilson left office a broken man, with only a few loyal supporters to keep alive his vision of a new world order reformed through American efforts. History was kinder than contemporaries who thought that Wilson was a "bombastic pedagogue," as H. L. Mencken put it. By the time of the Second World

War, the League of Nations seemed to have missed a chance to fill the peace-making role Wilson had expected of it, and Americans looked back with a guilty conscience to their repudiation of the work of the Paris Conference. Paul Birdsall, a journalist, took another look at the treatymaking in *Versailles: Twenty Years After* (1940), which appeared on the eve of the Second World War. The peace no longer appeared as harsh as it had before the rise of Hitler, and Birdsall thought that the Allies, under Wilson's direction, had actually held back from excessive demands. Birdsall implies that Europe would have been safer in the thirties had the United States participated in the League of Nations. Thomas Bailey makes the point more strongly in two books on the peace process written in the midst of the Second World War. Both *Woodrow Wilson and the Lost Peace* (1944) and *Woodrow Wilson and the Great Betrayal* (1945) try to apply the lessons of 1919 and 1920 to the plans for the end of the Second World War. While Bailey damns Wilson's stubborn refusal to reach an accommodation with his Republican opponents, which led to "the supreme infanticide" of the president—destruction of his own brainchild—the historian lauds the aims of Wilson's internationalism. After the Second World War, when American foreign policy became unashamedly "internationalist," Wilson's plans for the postwar order carried the day. Arthur Link, his fullest biographer, notes in *Wilson the Dipolomatist* (1956) and *War, Revolution and Peace* (1979) that the world would have been a better place had the treaty been approved as drafted. Dissent concentrated on Wilson's methods, not his intentions. William A. Williams's *Tragedy of American Diplomacy* (1962) argues that Henry Cabot Lodge and William Borah offered alternative visions which might have cost less in the long run. William C. Widenor's *Henry Cabot Lodge and the Search for American Foreign Policy* (1980) maintains that Lodge had a vision of an active American diplomacy which acknowledged limits Wilson often ignored.

Subsequent arguments over American foreign policy often seemed to elaborate Wilson's themes. When Richard M. Nixon moved into the White House in 1969, he asked to have Wilson's old desk moved into the president's office as a symbol of continuity in foreign policy. Nixon often remarked that he only tried to implement the high moral principles of Woodrow Wilson. The irony was inescapable: a president who would later be driven from office as a criminal put his feet on the desk of a man sent home because he was too much a moralist. In fact, Nixon's debt to Wilson struck the appropriate note. For half a century after the Senate rejected the Treaty of Versailles, Wilson's attitudes toward Europe, Latin America, and Asia, his hopes for international organizations, and his fears of revolution set the tone of American foreign policy.

CHAPTER SEVEN

The Triumph of Conservative Internationalism, 1921–1929

SEIZING POSTWAR ECONOMIC OPPORTUNITIES

Warren Harding knew nothing and cared little about foreign affairs. Maybe American power after the world war. As secretary of state, he chose Charles Evans Hughes, the Republican standard bearer in 1916 and a leading internationalist. For commerce secretary, he picked one of the rising stars of the country, Herbert Hoover, a former mining engineer with a reputation for humanitarianism acquired by feeding Belgium and Russia during the Great War. The president named Andrew W. Mellon, a Pittsburgh businessman who had made hundreds of millions of dollars extracting aluminum and oil around the world, as secretary of the treasury.

Together Hughes, Hoover, and Mellon developed a foreign policy which would enable the United States to continue participation in the world's economic and political life while at the same time retaining a free hand in international relations. Although liberals had grown disillusioned with Wilson's compromises at Paris and thought that the United States should withdraw from world politics, the new Republican leaders had few Stillusions to lose. They did not believe that their country could escape an active role. But the script would not be the one which Wilson had written. Instead of preaching, the United States would join in the competition for the resources. Instead of using the League of Nations as the balance wheel of international relations, Americans would stand apart from the general organization, remaining free to make whatever bargains with other countries they found advantageous at the moment.

Three Republican administrations of the 1920s all followed a foreign policy of "conservative internationalism," inspired by Henry Cabot Lodge, who doubted that the Great War signified a departure in world history. "Wars always happen," he snorted, and the one just finished was no worse than any of the others that had occurred over the centuries. For Lodge, the alliance system of the past generation was the natural way that nations assured their own safety. The League was only a new sort of alliance, one which the United States could safely avoid. Lodge would, however, have the United States participate in world politics—especially economic affairs.

As the war ended, Lodge, Hoover, and Mellon joined with prominent bankers of the house of Morgan or the Rockefeller-backed Chase National Bank and important exporters in the National Foreign Trade Council to replace British merchants as the world's premier trader. "Political and business leaders" decided to "build an international commercial system which would allow American business to topple and replace British business interests," as Carl Parrini puts it in *Heir to Empire* (1969). By 1918, the Wilson administration had signed the Webb-Pomerene Act permitting American firms to divide foreign markets among themselves, something previously forbidden by antitrust laws. Foreign banking received another boost with the 1919 signing of the Edge Act, a law which encouraged American banks to create joint subsidiaries to lend money abroad. During the war the United States had gone from a debtor to a creditor nation as private firms and the United States Treasury had loaned money to the allies. The British and French governments had borrowed in America after demanding that private citizens turn in their overseas holdings to the government. As a result, Europeans no longer enjoyed the wide advantage over Americans in ownership of business in Latin America, Asia, or the Middle East.

Americans in the twenties wanted to narrow the gap some more while Europeans desperately tried to claw their way back to economic prominence. Hoover took the lead as secretary of commerce in making the United States compete with Europeans. He sent out a corps of commercial attachés whose job was to return information about the chances for American businesses, look for foreign firms which might like to trade with the United States, and spot changing markets where the Americans could introduce new products. Almost as soon as the first commercial attachés took up their posts in 1921, Hoover received complaints from foreign competitors and from the Department of State. Europeans resented being hustled out of overseas opportunities, and the professional diplomats of the Department of State watched in horror as their chance to direct foreign policy seemed to slip away.

Career Foreign Service officers of the diplomatic and consular corps bitterly resented having to share their authority with Hoover's new corps. Led by the chief of the consular bureau, Wilbur J. Carr, and the undersecretary of state, Joseph C. Grew of the diplomatic branch, the diplomats and consuls headed off the Commerce Department's attempt to direct the foreign economic policy of the government by complaining to Secretary of State Hughes. In 1923, Hoover agreed that all business conducted overseas would be channeled through the ambassador who reported to the secretary of state. In July 1924, career Foreign Service officers won another, more important, battle in the war to capture control over foreign policy when Congress passed the Rogers Act, combining the diplomatic and consular branches into a single foreign service. Diplomats, who came from privileged families, received less than $2,500 for work they thought was important but which the public scorned as "cookie pushing." Consuls, on the other hand, came from a wider cross-section of the population and earned a living wage of $5,000 to $8,000 a year. Members of Congress rarely ridiculed them. The newly amalgamated Foreign Service of the Rogers Act gave the diplomats the opportunity to earn as much as the consuls while holding out the promise to the consuls of doing some of the political reporting diplomats had always jealously guarded as their own. Diplomats also hoped that enough new recruits would make a career of the Foreign Service that within twenty years all ambassadorial appointments would come from the ranks of the career Foreign Service. Over the next five years Grew as undersecretary of state outmaneuvered Carr and prevented any of the former consuls from rising to the top of the new Foreign Service. But the leaders of the former diplomatic branch had less luck in reversing the deeply embedded suspicions that their profession attracted amiable young men who looked for government sponsorship for an indolent life of sipping tea. The new Foreign Service never became the major source of foreign policy advice or the place presidents looked for potential ambassadors.

The commercial expansionists went beyond the search for new business opportunities abroad to an assault on European trade barriers. At the end of the war, all industrial nations, including the United States, erected intimidating tariff laws against the competition. The American contribution, the Fordney-McCumber Tariff of 1922, reversed Wilson's movement toward lower trade barriers as a response to Commerce Secretary Hoover's warning that "the time has arrived when we require either disarmament or defense" in the "trade war" with Europe. He took the lead in demanding that American firms receive an opportunity equal to those of the imperial nations to extract the raw materials necessary for the automobile age. The world war had shown the importance of motorized vehicles, and now the race was on for rubber and petroleum. Hoover successfully beat back a British plan, drafted by James Stevenson, a Colonial Office functionary, to maintain high prices for rubber coming from Malaya and keep the companies who made

up the Rubber Association of America from sharing in this lucrative business. Throughout his tenure at the Commerce Department, Hoover threatened to block the import of Malayan rubber into the United States until the
American firms got their way, and in 1928 the British abandoned the Stevenson Plan.

OIL DIPLOMACY IN THE MIDDLE EAST

After the war, petroleum began to assume the important role it had later
in the century. American oil firms sought the help of the State and Commerce departments in their competition with the British. "Blood may have
been thicker than water during the war," writes John De Novo, the author
of the standard work *American Interests and Politics in the Middle East,
1900–1939,* "but thinner than oil once the war was over." The Standard Oil
Company of New York (Socony) started the process in 1919 and 1920 by insisting that it receive equal treatment with British firms in the former Ottoman territory of Palestine, now a British mandate. The British put up a
mild fight but did not press the issue since Palestine did not seem like a
promising place to drill for oil. Mesopotamia, modern-day Iraq, appeared to
be a more likely source of the precious fluid, and Hughes and Hoover led
an assault on British privileges there. In May 1920, Britain and France secretly agreed at a conference in San Remo, Italy, to close the door to all outside companies in Iraq. Wilson's last secretary of state, Bainbridge Colby,
made ineffectual protests, but it remained for the new Republican administration to attempt to force the Open Door policy upon the government of
Iraq. Tedious negotiations among representatives of American firms, the
State Department, the Commerce Department, the governments of Britain
and Iraq, and European oil companies took seven years. Finally, in July 1928,
the Americans, incorporated as the Near Eastern Development Corporation,
won the right to a 23.75 percent share of the Turkish Petroleum Company's
concession in Iraq. It seemed on the surface that Hoover had vindicated the
Open Door and ushered Americans through it to a share of the riches of
Baghdad, but the diplomacy of imperialism was always a dangerous game.
Unable to confront the Americans directly, the British worked behind the
scenes with the government of Iraq to void the sublease arrangements of the
Turkish Petroleum Company, which changed its name to the Iraq Petroleum
Company. By 1931, when the first oil in any appreciable amount was pumped
out of the Iraqi sands, the government there had given the Iraq Petroleum
Company, dominated by the British, exclusive rights to future discoveries.
No new American firms not associated with the IPC could produce oil in
Iraq. The Open Door policy "had been of no practical use in placing addi-
tional American companies in Iraq," writes De Novo.

Visions of oil fortunes also helped create the first but not last American encounter with the hostile face of nationalism in Persia, or Iran. As a nextdoor neighbor of Iraq, and sharing its geological formations, Iran seemed an ideal place for petroleum exploration, and Americans were welcome for a time. Perhaps the main advantage the Americans had was that they were not British, since the new ruler of Iran, Shah Reza Pahlevi, like most of his countrymen, deeply resented the encroachments on Iran made by Britain and Russia at the end of the nineteenth and beginning of the twentieth centuries. The shah appointed an American, Arthur C. Millspaugh, who had once been the economic adviser of the Department of State, to supervise the chaotic finances of the Iranian government. He was supposed to reorganize tax collections, supervise the customs, and most important, drum up American loans for projects in Iran.

Millspaugh arrived in 1922 and had a brief honeymoon before things went sour two years later. His American way of doing business clashed with the customs of the bazaar merchants, and his staff made no effort to accommodate the Shi'ite Muslim religious sensibilities of the Iranians. The American viceconsul in Tehran, Robert W. Imbrie, infuriated a crowd when he tried to photograph a religious celebration on July 18, 1924, and the participants took time from their rites to club him to death. A representative of the Sinclair Oil Company used Imbrie's murder as an excuse to end his company's agreement to pump oil out of Iran's desert and transport it across the Soviet Union. In fact, the company withdrew because its owner, Harry Sinclair, no longer could make good on his promise to the Soviet Union to influence Secretary of the Interior Albert Fall and Attorney General Harry Daugherty to grant American recognition of the Soviet government. All three men stood accused in the Teapot Dome scandal, an attempt to swindle the American government out of vast, profitable oil lands in Wyoming. Newspapers in Iran also claimed that Sinclair had bribed influential Persians to achieve his oil concession. Millspaugh, for his part, remained in Iran for another three years. Relations between him and Reza Pahlevi were never the same, however, with the latter saying, "There can be only one shah in Persia." Still, Millspaugh was not through with the country, and he returned during the Second World War, from 1943 to 1945, to lay the foundations for even greater American involvement in the Iranian economy.

OVERSEAS LOANS AND GERMAN REPARATIONS

While Hoover and Hughes tried to get equality of commercial opportunity for the United States, their counterpart in the Treasury Department, Andrew Mellon, attempted to direct the lending of money overseas by American banks. He knew that investment by American bankers overseas had dramatic foreign policy implications, and now that American banks could compete equally with their British counterparts, Mellon realized that American foreign economic policy might follow the path of European imperialism in the late nineteenth century. British overseas investors had induced their government to help them recover debts in Egypt in 1880 and in Chile in the 1890s. Mellon did not want the same thing to happen in the United States without officials knowing beforehand where Wall Street sent its cash.

In 1922, the Treasury Department drafted a set of rules governing overseas loans. The State Department immediately became alarmed at what the assistant secretary of state, Leland Harrison, saw as poaching on its territory, and Harrison grumbled that any regulations of overseas capital meant that the government would be offering protection to its bankers. Finally, the two departments compromised on a set of rules for the major American banks, requiring them to notify the State Department of any projected overseas loans. The department would check with officials at the Treasury to see if the loans violated any of the following provisions: no loans to countries in arrears to the United States; no loans for armaments; no loans to governments not recognized by the United States; and no loans to foreign monopolies maintaining high prices against Americans. Loans had to pay for themselves. If the project did not fall into one of these categories, then the State Department would simply write back that it had "no objection" to the loan. At the State Department, Charles Evans Hughes hoped that no banker would read a guarantee into these chilly words. Otherwise he feared that the United States government might someday be called upon to back its foreign bond holders.

Another international economic matter which complicated American foreign policy during the twenties was the related question of reparation and debt. At the Paris Peace Conference, the victors had not set a final figure for Germany to pay, agreeing instead that Germany bore the full responsibility for the war, but that the exact amount it would pay would be determined by a reparations commission. This body met in 1920, but Americans stayed away because the United States had opted out of the Versailles Treaty.

The commission assessed Germany five billion gold marks a year, with payments made every six months in gold. This system lasted for only two years. The German government refused to raise taxes to pay for the reparations bill, preferring to print money instead. The inevitable happened in 1922 and 1923 as an unprecedented inflation swept the country. Bread cost two million marks, and the savings of an entire middle class were wiped out. In January 1923, the German government suspended its payments of reparations to the victors, and the French retaliated by sending troops to occupy the Ruhr industrial area. With the occupation, Germany seemed on the verge of collapse, and many Europeans feared a revival of bolshevism. The British, ostensibly allied to France, thought the invasion a blunder, for they believed that Paris wanted to provoke a new war which none of the powers could afford.

Americans watched these upheavals from the sidelines, and Henry Cabot Lodge, for one, thought that the occupation of the Ruhr proved that the United States had been wise to steer clear of an alliance with the French at the end of the war. But Americans could not ignore a threat to their entry into Europe's economy. As long as Germany did not pay its reparations to the British and the French, these governments would not keep up the payments on their debts to the United States. Some American bankers such as Thomas Lamont and Norman Davis, an undersecretary of the treasury under Wilson, thought that 1923 would be a good time to start fresh and forgive the debts owed to the United States, but most bankers and businessmen who led foreign trading operations disagreed with such a radical proposal. They believed that debts should be repaid, albeit at a lower rate. European treasury officials and private American businessmen joined the State Department in selecting Charles G. Dawes, a Midwestern Republican banker, to head a commission to revise the amount owed by Germany for reparations. In March, the Dawes Plan became official. Germany's payments were scaled down to 2.5 billion marks over the next fifty years, and French troops left the Ruhr. Almost immediately, the German economy stabilized and took off like a rocket. In the next five years, Germany's exports tripled, people went back to work, and the country again became the foundry of Europe. German diplomacy also revived in the wake of the Dawes Plan as Foreign Minister, later Chancellor, Gustav Stresemann negotiated the Locarno Treaty with Britain and France, formally acknowledging the western borders set by the Versailles Treaty. The same year, 1925, Germany joined the League of Nations.

Part of the German recovery was fueled by a massive injection of American loans. Ironically, bankers who had been shy of shipping money to the victors because they had debts to the United States felt no such compunction about funding the German revival. Over the next five years, American banks sent $2 billion to Germany. The Germans used some of the money to build new plants but more went to meet the reparations payment to the European governments, which in turn sent money back to the United States in fulfillment of the war debts. Old Wilsonians such as Norman Davis complained that this system made no economic sense, but in the era of "Coolidge prosperity," these warnings had no impact.

TWENTIES REFLECTIONS ON INTERNATIONAL RELATIONS

While the government pursued its policy of independent internationalism, the remnants of the old Wilsonians continued to study international relations. The former president died in 1924, embittered by a betrayal of his hopes for a reformed world, but his supporters remained active. They established the Woodrow Wilson Foundation upon the death of their hero. One of the aims of this charitable organization was to generate ideas of world peace. Some of Wilson's old admirers drew a different lesson from the defeat of the Treaty of Versailles. Like Senator Lodge, such disillusioned Wilsonians as Walter Lippmann reasoned that the American public was not ready for another grand crusade.

Lippmann turned his back on foreign affairs in the twenties and devoted his time to exploring the bases of modern American politics. What he found did not encourage his faith in his fellow citizens. In three books—*Public Opinion, The Phantom Public,* and *A Preface to Morals* (1922, 1925, 1929)—he reached the self-righteous conclusion that the American electorate was too ignorant, too fickle, and too emotional to be trusted with the great issues of foreign affairs.

Not all old Wilsonians reacted as glumly as Lippmann. Some tried to keep the faith by encouraging the study and public discussion of world affairs. In 1921, about sixty of the foremost internationalists from the worlds of banking, law, trade, journalism, and the academy, led by Democrat John Davis and Republican George W. Wickersham, set up the Council on Foreign Relations in New York. It began publishing the journal *Foreign Affairs* the next year. At its monthly meetings and in the pages of its magazine, the council tried to maintain American interest in world politics while at the same time opposing the influence of "isolationists."

Universities also took up the study of international affairs in the twenties. At Harvard, Columbia, Yale, and state universities such as Illinois, Kentucky, and Indiana, courses arose in international relations. Some of them had the practical purpose of training functionaries for the Foreign Service or the Commerce Department, and some of these programs sent their graduates into overseas business ventures. More scholarly interest in international relations also grew. The major theme attracting the attention of writers on world politics was the current affairs question of the causes and aftermath of the Great War. As soon as the Paris Peace Conference branded the Germans the aggressors in the world war, scholars began questioning that judgment.

In Germany after 1919, an academic industry dedicated to the "war guilt question" sprang up. German historians concluded that the imperial government had been no more, and maybe less, to blame for the opening of the war in 1914 than had the French and the Russians. American historians such as Harry Elmer Barnes, Charles Beard, Sidney Bradshaw Fay, and Bernadotte Schmitt took up the same theme. In numerous books and articles in the popular press, the professors reversed the charges against Germany. The kaiser's court had been no more to blame than the allies. Of course Woodrow Wilson had said as much during the period of neutrality, but the revisionist historians went beyond a description of European politics on the eve of the world war to condemn America for fighting it. There were obvious implications for foreign policy of this new understanding of the recent past. If the European nations could not be trusted, American diplomats always were outwitted by the Europeans. Consequently, the United States was best advised to pursue an independent foreign policy.

IMMIGRATION, NATIVISM, AND FOREIGN RELATIONS

"A nation of immigrants" is the proud celebration of contemporary American multiethnic society. Everyone's ancestors did come from someplace else (although the original ancestors of American Indians may have made the trek ten thousand years ago and the forebears of black Americans made highly unwilling immigrants). But life has never been easy for newcomers to the United States. Mostly poor, they worked for little, and the availability of a large supply of submissive laborers helped spark the awesome economic expansion of industrial America in the late nineteenth century. Since the earliest days of the republic, however, antiimmigrant "nativists" have railed against the religion, politics, racial physiognomy, language, hygiene, intelligence, work habits, and culture of new arrivals. Before the Civil War, a political party, the American or Know Nothing party, attacked Irish Catholic arrivals. After 1865, bigots lynched Italians in New Orleans and killed scores of Chinese in Rock Spring, Wyoming.

Most significantly, perhaps, a movement emerged for legislation restricting or eliminating immigration. Chinese were the first to be excluded, in 1885. In the aftermath of the First World War, a nativist Congress passed immigration laws in 1921 and 1924 setting quotas on the number of immigrants each country could send to the United States. Quotas were based upon the proportion of that country's descendants in the total United States population in 1910 (for the 1921 law) and 1890 (for the 1924 revision). Britain and Germany, homelands of many of the White Anglo-Saxon Protestants (WASPs) who urged restriction, had huge, unfilled quotas in excess of sixty thousand per year while the mostly Catholic or Jewish immigrants from Southern and Eastern Europe scrambled for space in quotas under five thousand. The rest of the world fared worse, with countries receiving token allotments of one hundred. The Japanese, who had voluntarily stopped emigration under terms of the gentlemen's agreement of 1907, saw that accord abruptly terminated and discovered themselves excluded, like the Chinese they despised.

Not surprisingly, the discriminatory quota system caused difficulties in American relations with foreign governments which felt they had been unjustly singled out. Japanese politicians saw the abrogation of the gentlemen's agreement as further proof that the Caucasian nations never would treat them as equals. In Italy, as well, the new Fascist government of Benito Mussolini considered immigration restriction an affront.

THE WASHINGTON CONFERENCE, CHINESE NATIONALISM, AND PEACE PLANS

One legacy of Wilson's diplomacy was the movement to reduce armaments. The president had believed that the arms race between Britain and Germany had helped bring about the world war. Republicans close to Theodore Roosevelt were not as worried about arms races leading to war as Wilson had been, but they also wished to reduce arms. They noticed how expensive it was to provide a modern armed force. The naval building program of the United States had cost $1.5 billion since 1915. The Harding administration's economic policies rested upon a commitment to reduce taxes; Secretary of the Treasury Mellon worried about a naval construction program which would cause the government to continue the tax rates of the world war. There were also strategic reasons for the United States to advocate arms control or disarmament measures. The world war had seen the United States Navy grow from the fourth largest in the world to a fleet which rivaled the British, the greatest ever to sail. Along with the British, the United States was the only one of the great naval powers which maintained a fleet in both the Atlantic and Pacific oceans. Now that the United States had arrived as a naval power, it was a good time to call a halt to the naval arms race. Otherwise the competitors might try to overtake the American navy.

The same fears of excessive naval spending also sent shivers down the spines of finance ministers in each of the major naval powers—Great Britain, Japan, France, and Italy. All of them except Japan had suffered economically during the world war, and they could not afford to continue a naval arms race. For Europeans, the fear of Germany's navy had been eliminated. The British, French, and Italians had been allied during the Great War and saw no need to continue a naval rivalry with one another.

A naval race could easily arise in the Pacific, however, where Japan wanted to preserve gains made in the war. Japan, an ally of Britain since 1902, fretted that the treaty would not be renewed in 1921. With Germany disarmed, London no longer needed a naval partner, and Australia and New Zealand anticipated Japanese expansion to the south. The two Anglo-Saxon island states resented the Japanese taking over the German islands in the Pacific.

Secretary of State Charles Evans Hughes at the Washington Naval Conference flanked
by British foreign secretary Arthur Balfour (l.) and French foreign minister Aristide
Briand (r.). *(Wide World Photos)*

In 1920, Britain informed Tokyo that the alliance would not be renewed for
another twenty years.

One benefit of the Japanese treaty had been to assure Great Britain that
its naval interests would be protected in the seas around China. Now that it
no longer would have Japan on its side, Britain might have to bear the cost
of building ships for the Far East. Another issue was the future of China.
While the Chinese had objected mightily to the Shandong settlement at the
Paris Peace Conference, nothing had been done to protect them from Japan.

These interrelated questions of the naval balance and the future of China
became the subject of an international conference on the Far East and naval
disarmament which opened in Washington in November 1921. The United
States agreed to host the gathering of ten powers because Hughes convinced
Harding that it was a good time to demonstrate that despite rejection of membership in the League, Americans still had an interest in world affairs. Furthermore, the United States wanted to preserve some stability in the Far East.
If Japan's ambitions in China and the South Pacific were not checked, the
American stake in the Philippines, Guam, and Samoa could be threatened.

Most of the delegates who reached Washington that fall believed that the
conference would engage in tired rhetoric and solve nothing. Hughes had

other ideas. He astonished the diplomats and naval experts who met in November with an opening speech calling for the scrapping of two hundred thousand tons of capital ships built during the war. He proposed that after these vessels had been destroyed, rough equality should exist between the navies of Great Britain and the United States with other nations trailing behind. Under the plan, Japan would have a navy 60 percent as strong as that of the United States or Great Britain. Since, however, Japan used its fleet only in the western Pacific while the Anglo-Saxon powers sent their ships everywhere, the Japanese actually would be the premier naval power in their home waters. The conference continued until February 1922 with naval experts from each country pressing their political leaders to make certain that national interests were advanced over those of the other participants. Still, once Hughes suggested the reduction of the size of navies, most of the politicians present heaved sighs of relief. No longer would they have to borrow from already strained financial institutions to create navies.

In February 1922, three treaties ended the Washington Conference. The first, the Five Power Agreement, set the relative naval strengths of the United States, Great Britain, Japan, France, and Italy. The ratio among the powers was fixed at 5:5:3:1.67:1.67. The United States, Japan, Britain, and France signed another pact in which they agreed to respect one another's holdings in the Pacific. Finally came a Nine Power Treaty in which all of the states with interests in the Far East sanctioned the territorial integrity of China.

Almost forgotten in the bargaining over navies and borders were dramatic social changes within China. The republic created in 1911 persisted after the death of Sun Yat-sen in 1925. New leaders contended for preeminence but agreed on a central theme of the revolution, that the imperial powers had demoralized and humiliated China, and that all of them should go. One nationalist, Jiang Jieshi (Chiang Kai-shek), educated by American missionaries, assumed leadership. Jiang, like other nationalists, hoped to rid China of foreign leaseholds, end the degrading practices of extraterritoriality, and regain autonomy in foreign policy. American diplomacy ignored Jiang and the list of nationalist grievances against the outside powers, as the United States tacitly assumed that Japan dominated China. Stung by the American rebuff, Jiang for his part formed a temporary alliance in 1926 with the Soviet Union, another unhappy power left outside the Washington treaty system. The Chinese Nationalist party, or Kuomintang, belonged to the Communist International for three years while leaders of the International in Moscow ordered the small Chinese Communist party (CCP) to submit to Jiang's leadership. Surprised Chinese Communist officials meekly obeyed until April 1927 when Jiang suddenly ordered the massacre of thousands of CCP members and sympathizers. Over the next twenty years, Nationalists and Communists waged an intermittent civil war, with the United States becoming increasingly involved on the Nationalist side after Japan invaded China in 1937. Throughout the nearly fifty years of relations between the United States and Jiang Jieshi, which lasted until his death in 1977, each side distrusted the good faith, honesty, and competence of the other.

The naval limitations treaty proved the first step in the movement for international disarmament, but Wilsonians also placed importance upon the reduction of land armies. In fact, since most European wars had begun on the continent, a way had to be found to reduce the size of standing armies. Among the advocates of paring armies was a professor of international relations at Columbia University, James T. Shotwell, who had been with the American delegation at the Paris Peace Conference and, unlike many of the others who had been there, had not been disillusioned. In the twenties, he strove to continue Wilson's ideals of disarmament. One of his many essays on the subject of international reform won a prize offered by Edward Bok, the editor of the *Saturday Evening Post,* for the best plan to end war. Shotwell's single-minded but unworkable solution called for a declaration making war illegal. The way to end war was to declare it unlawful.

Remarkably enough, Shotwell's plan became the official policy of the United States government in 1927. Unlike the Columbia professor, who truly believed in his puerile scheme, officials in the American government who advocated peace reform acted from more cynical assumptions. What happened was this: In 1927, the French foreign minister, Aristide Briand, approached American Ambassador Myron T. Herrick with a request for a mutual defense agreement. The French had pestered successive American governments since 1917 with demands for a formal alliance. Each time the United States diplomats had put the French off with pleas that some international or collective agreement could substitute for a formal alliance. Once the United States had refused to join the League of Nations, the French complained that the security offered by the transatlantic ally had diminished. When the French tried again in 1927, Undersecretary of State William Castle thought of a way to end once and for all these constant demands. Why not change the proposal for a FrancoAmerican alliance into a general program, open to all the nations of the world, declaring war illegal along the lines of Shotwell's plan? The pact then would not commit the United States any more than any other nation to the security of France, and both powers would appear to have taken a forthright stand in favor of peace. Castle sold this hare-brained scheme to Secretary of State Frank B. Kellogg, a former senator from Minnesota who had taken over from Hughes in 1925. Consequently, in August 1928, Kellogg went to Paris to sign an agreement with French Foreign Minister Briand. The two powers invited every other nation of the world to join in the self-denial of the use of force, and all but five of them did. Later historians took a gloomy view of the proceedings. It was "an illusion and a deception" according to Robert Ferrell, who wrote a detailed history, *Peace in Their Time* (1952), from the sour perspective of someone who had experienced how little the pact had done to prevent the Second World War.

The Coolidge administration also pressed ahead with plans for disarmament. Although the Washington Conference of 1921–1922 had set limits on the size of the battleships and aircraft carrier fleets of the major powers, it said nothing about smaller ships. The naval powers had taken advantage of this loophole to compete in the smaller categories. Americans had stayed out of the race between Japan and Great Britain for budgetary reasons. In early 1927, the Coolidge administration called a new conference to expand the naval agreement. Meetings took place in Geneva, the home of the League of Nations, from June 20 to August 4. Nothing was accomplished. The United States, Britain, and Japan were the only nations represented. France refused to attend because it resented having been classed with Italy at the Washington Conference, and the Italians would not come if the French stayed home. Britain and Japan, which were there, refused to halt their cruiser rivalry. By the time the conference broke up in August, European newspapers were filled with accounts of the American president's "insufficient preparation," a polite way of saying that Coolidge did not know what he was doing. While Europeans clucked over the Americans' ignorance, Congress joined the arms race on the seas. A few weeks before the Coolidge administration left office in March 1929, the lawmakers passed a bill giving the United States fifteen heavy cruisers and an aircraft carrier.

Herbert Hoover succeeded Coolidge as president. While he did not think that war was necessarily evil, he did believe it was always expensive. In October 1929, two weeks before the stock market crashed, sending the world economy into the greatest depression in modern history, Hoover met with the new British prime minister, Ramsay MacDonald, in a Maryland mountain retreat, Rapidan. MacDonald, the first leader of the Labour party ever to serve as prime minister of Britain, also had a vaguely pacifist past. He had opposed Britain's entry into the world war, and as prime minister he wanted to end the arms race to divert funds to creating a welfare state. The old pacifist who wanted to fund unemployment insurance and the apostle of rugged individualism found they had much in common as they sat on a log under the crisp fall skies. They decided to convene another disarmament conference in London in January 1930.

Delegates met on January 21, 1930, as the world began its slide into depression. All governments present recognized that the best place to cut costs was in naval expenditures. The conference extended the Washington limits to the lighter categories of ships. America, Britain, and Japan agreed to limit all of their navies at the 5:5:3 ratio. Italy and France also signed the agreement at the end of discussions in April. At that time, the two European states could not agree exactly what the ratio between them should be, but they said they would resolve their disputes in the next two years. They did not.

Disarmament attracted sporadic attention in the thirties, but the Depression eliminated it as a major topic. In February 1932, the League of Nations sponsored another general disarmament meeting, in Geneva. Despite the League's endorsement, the United States attended. Herbert Hoover even offered another American plan for the scrapping of one-third of all arms. No one responded favorably, however, and the talks dragged on inconsequentially through 1932. When Adolf Hitler came to power in Germany in January 1933, the first thing he did was begin to rebuild the German armed forces. In 1934, the Geneva meetings adjourned temporarily, and they were never held again. The next year, 1935, the London naval conference reconvened to try to stop a new arms race in the Pacific. The rise of a new German navy made the outlook for success exceptionally bleak, and these talks, too, accomplished nothing.

THE UNITED STATES AND LATIN AMERICA

While the American attitude toward Europe, the Middle East, and Asia was that the United States should be the equal of the European powers, the policy in the Western Hemisphere was to keep the United States on top. The United States preserved its influence under cover through direct investment, its control of the Panama Canal, the sanctification of the Monroe Doctrine, and, where necessary, the direct intervention of troops. By 1929, United States citizens had doubled their pre–world war investment in Latin America from $1.26 to $3.52 billion. Americans owned railroads, electric utilities, oil, bananas, and sugar. The United Fruit and Standard Fruit companies accounted for most of the revenue of Honduras, and United States firms benefited from more than half of Venezuela's oil production. From the world war to the Great Depression, American exports to Latin America tripled in value and accounted for 20 percent of all goods shipped abroad. While the United States economic role in the hemisphere grew, that of the Europeans, and especially the British, slipped.

The United States government maintained troops in Haiti, the Dominican Republic, and Nicaragua. Americans controlled Cuban politics, and on several occasions came close to again coming to blows with Mexico. The way in which the United States resolved each of these episodes indicated the contempt Yankees had for their Spanish- and Portuguese-speaking neighbors and their desire to dominate the affairs of the hemisphere.

The United States had occupied the Dominican Republic in 1915 as part of the Wilson administration's campaign to teach the Latin American republics to elect good men. By the time of the election of 1920, many people wanted to end the occupation. The Republican platform of that year called for withdrawal because it cost too much to maintain a force in the island; once the Harding administration took office, liberals called on it to make good its promise. The marines who occupied the Dominican Republic and ran the customs house had imposed a rough order there. A national guard, trained by the Americans, kept matters quiet. In 1924, therefore, the Coolidge administration carried out the 1920 pledge to withdraw.

In part, the removal of forces from the Dominican Republic was designed to steal the thunder of the Progressives. Faced with the prospect of another four years of the Coolidge administration, some of the old liberals organized a new political party in 1924. Calling themselves Progressives, they nominated Sen. Robert LaFollette of Wisconsin to run for president. Their platform demanded an end to Yankee intervention in the affairs of Latin America as LaFollette maintained the opposition to an aggressive American foreign policy he had begun when he opposed the entry of the United States in the world war. LaFollette received only eight electoral votes in the 1924 election, but he outpolled the hapless conservative Democratic nominee, John W. Davis, in California, and 1.5 million Progressive voters indicated that some citizens doubted the wisdom of dominating the Western Hemisphere.

Among LaFollette's supporters was William E. Borah of Idaho, who became the chairman of the Senate Committee on Foreign Relations at the death of Lodge in 1925. Borah, the old Irreconcilable, waged a steady campaign against the interventionist policies of the United States in Central America. Nowhere was he more persistent than in his condemnation of American policy in Nicaragua. Partly in response to Borah's objections, the United States withdrew the marines from Nicaragua in 1925 but sent them back in 1926 during the war between the conservative church supporters led by Juan Sacassa and the liberal anticlerical party led by Emiliano Chamorro. As had happened in 1911 when the United States had first intervened in Nicaragua, the continuation of the war threatened the stability of the country and the property of Americans there, so the marines went back in 1926. They were followed shortly thereafter by a special representative of the president, Henry L. Stimson, former secretary of war under President William Howard Taft. Stimson had gone into the private practice of law in the 1920s and was amassing a large fortune. He saw himself as a selfless public servant who came off the street (Wall Street) to offer his skills to a beleaguered president. With the aid of the five thousand troops patrolling Managua, Nicaragua's capital, Stimson managed to arrange a tenuous peace between the liberals and the conservatives. This pact, the Peace of Tititapa, held with the American troops in place until 1934. As they patrolled Managua, the American marines trained a *guardia civil* to take their place. One young sergeant in that guard, Anastasio Somoza, took control of the country when the Americans left in 1934.

Yankees on guard in Haiti.
(National Archives)

He and his family retained power until 1979. Somoza's first official act was to invite the leader of the guerrillas, Augusto Sandino, to the capital at Managua for peace talks. When he arrived, the civil guard killed him.

The United States also ruled Haiti directly from 1915 to 1934. When Franklin D. Roosevelt became president in 1933, he boasted that he had single-handedly written the Haitian Constitution in 1918 while serving as assistant secretary of the navy. Roosevelt then proceeded to withdraw the marines in 1934, reasoning that they had created a friendly government. In the nineteen years the marines ran Haiti, they built roads, bridges, hospitals, and power plants, created another local army (the *Garde d'Haiti*), and carried with them their own racial prejudices. None of the improvements did much good for the Haitians, who remained the poorest people in the Western Hemisphere. One history of the country summarizes the place as the *Politics of Squalor.* American marines treated the Haitians little better than slaves. The ambitious road-building program was completed with a forced draft of labor. In 1919, many Haitians rebelled against being dragooned into chain gangs, and marines responded by killing nearly two thousand of them. The Americans also introduced racial segregation to Haiti and favored the mulatto elite over the blacker part of the population.

Throughout the twenties, the United States ruled Haiti with compliant local presidents. When the Depression began in 1929, the prices for Haitian coffee exports slumped and the public of Haiti grew fed up with colonial rule. Strikes and protest marches swept across the country, and the United States responded with an inquiry chaired by the former governor general of the Philippines, W. Cameron Forbes. The next year, 1930, Forbes's commission reported that the Americans had failed "to understand the social problems of Haiti." They recommended training more Haitians for local authority and the eventual withdrawal of the American forces from the island. Hoover's administration, desperately looking for ways to cut expenses, eagerly embraced the suggestion and Roosevelt finished the job in 1934. The Haitians celebrated a festival of Second Independence when the Americans left, but economic conditions did not improve with their own leaders.

ACCOMMODATING THE MEXICAN REVOLUTION

Mexico, richer, larger, and closer to the United States than Nicaragua or Haiti, presented special problems in the period of Republican ascendancy. The Wilson administration's unhappy experience of direct military intervention left an ashen taste in the mouths of many Americans. The United States granted de facto recognition to the country in 1917, but a bitter legacy remained. That same year Mexico adopted a new constitution, part of which sent shock waves through the community of foreign investors. Article 27 affirmed that all "land and waters" and all subsoil minerals belonged to the Mexican nation. American mining and petroleum companies immediately began to experience heavy taxes.

In 1921, Harding's new Republican administration asserted that the Mexican Constitution violated the principles of compensation in international law, and claimed that American firms were entitled to "prompt, adequate and effective compensation." In 1923, a more conservative president, Alvaro Obregón, negotiated the Bucerelli agreements with the United States. In exchange for formal recognition, Mexico acknowledged the right of ownership of American oil companies which had acquired lands before 1917. At the time, the Americans owned over half of the subsoil petroleum rights in Mexico. In 1925, Mexico lurched to the left with the election of Plutarco Calles, who believed that the Bucerelli agreements had sold out national interests. The Mexican Congress repudiated the granting of foreign ownership to oil companies. Instead, the Americans had a lease of only fifty years. American oil companies complained loudly in Washington, begging for another intervention.

But Mexico was not Nicaragua, and the Coolidge administration felt pressure from liberals not to intervene militarily. In 1927, the president sent an old college friend, Dwight Morrow, as ambassador to Mexico. No one could accuse Morrow of neglecting the interests of international financiers, as he was a partner in the J. P. Morgan banking concern. Morrow believed that the long-term interests of American bankers and investors required that Mexican pride be assuaged. Himself a masterful conciliator, he astonished the Mexicans by learning a few words of Spanish. A romance between his daughter and Charles Lindbergh, the "Lone Eagle" whose solo flight of the Atlantic in April 1927 had made the front pages in Mexico City, helped win the hearts of the Mexican leadership. In 1928, Morrow worked out a compromise under which Americans retained lands acquired before 1917 but leased those properties obtained afterwards. This agreement continued in force until 1938, when another strongly nationalist Mexican president, Lázaro Cárdenas, expropriated the property of all foreign oil companies. But it was a pyrrhic victory because the major producers there refused to handle the Mexicans' own oil. As a result, Mexico did not again become a major producer until the 1970s, when world demand for petroleum forced the international firms to buy its oil.

THE RETREAT FROM INTERVENTION

Understandably, United States dominance of Latin America created a reaction. Latin Americans themselves complained that the United States had become the "New Rome." By the time the Western Hemisphere republics assembled for their triennial conference at Havana in 1928, the Latin American delegates were in no mood to allow the United States to set the agenda as it had in the past. The Havana meeting took place in the shadow of the American troops landing at Nicaragua.

To head off denunciations of Washington's policy, the United States sent the most prestigious delegation to the conference. President Calvin Coolidge went to Havana to address the opening meeting, and Charles Evans Hughes headed the American contingent. Even the former secretary of state could not stanch the flow of criticism. The delegate from El Salvador introduced a resolution opposing the right of any state "to intervene in the internal affairs of another." Diplomats from Mexico and Argentina, two large republics which resented North American actions, backed nonintervention. Hughes first attempted to have the resolution suppressed, studied, or tabled for the next meeting. Finally, however, he had to defend American high-handedness, claiming that "we simply wish peace, order and stability and the recognition of honest rights properly acquired." Silence greeted his comments, but Hughes did manage to prevent the adoption of an anti–United States resolution.

The message of the Havana Conference was clear: the United States had to do something to mollify its neighbors. In the Hoover administration, the

United States repudiated the Roosevelt Corollary to the Monroe Doctrine while retaining the same informal control over the affairs of Latin America. The chief legal officer of the State Department, J. Reuben Clark, spent much of 1929 investigating the basis in international law for unilateral intervention. In 1930 he presented his memorandum on the Monroe Doctrine, which held that the right of intervention in the affairs of the Western Hemisphere advocated by the Roosevelt Corollary was not a logical or legal derivative of the Monroe Doctrine. While the Clark Memorandum stated that Theodore Roosevelt had erred in resting intervention on the Monroe Doctrine, Clark did not suggest that the United States would never again interfere in the internal affairs of the Western Hemisphere. Instead, the Hoover administration would begin a policy, followed by Franklin Roosevelt's administration and every subsequent presidency, of securing the agreement of the other Western Hemisphere states whenever the United States found it convenient to meddle. Franklin Roosevelt called his overtures to Latin America the "Good Neighbor policy." Harry Truman extended the doctrine of containment of communism to the Western Hemisphere. John F. Kennedy had the Alliance for Progress. Ronald Reagan pressed the Caribbean Basin Initiative and fought revolution in El Salvador and Nicaragua. But throughout it all, the Latins themselves continued to resent the overbearing manner of the Colossus of the North.

ASSESSING REPUBLICAN FOREIGN POLICY

When Americans came to reflect upon the Republican ascendancy of the twenties in the era of the New Deal and the Second World War, they found little to like. The twenties seemed a blotted decade in which frightened nativists slammed shut the door to refugees from Eastern Europe with the immigration laws of 1921 and 1924; leaders ignored social ills; hypocrisy flowed with the gin brewed in defiance of Prohibition; and President Coolidge complacently took four-hour naps each afternoon. From the perspective of American commitment to a new international organization after 1945, the diplomacy of the twenties represented, in the words of historian Manfred Jonas, an expression of a mean-spirited "isolationist impulse."

An almost inevitable swing of the historiographical pendulum took place as writers began to doubt the wisdom of the foreign policy undertaken by the Democratic Franklin D. Roosevelt from 1933 to 1945. If FDR's conduct had not been above reproach, perhaps his Republican predecessors had not made such a mess of things. William A. Williams set the boundaries of the debate in *The Tragedy of American Diplomacy* when he argued that the supposed "isolationism" of the twenties was a "legend" put forward by internationalist historians bemused by FDR's successes. Williams took the Republicans of the twenties seriously and insisted that they valued American participation in foreign affairs. Their concentration on the expansion of American commerce and demand that the door be opened to the United States in Latin America represented a clever strategy to assume the role of an exhausted Great Britain. A few years later, in 1967, Joan Hoff Wilson presented a subtle rehabilitation of the twenties diplomacy in *American Business and Foreign Policy, 1920–1933*. Arguing that business did not speak with a single voice, and that large and small manufacturers, exporters, and banks were often at one another's throats, Wilson discovered that business interests never turned their back upon foreign affairs. Their ideas were not frivolous, and they were united at least in a belief that the United States had to participate in foreign affairs.

By the 1980s, historians no longer spoke of the twenties as an isolationist period. Criticism of the Republican administrations did not take Harding, Coolidge, Hughes, Hoover, and Mellon to task for ignoring legitimate interests overseas. Instead, the debate followed the lines of the 1924 presidential election, with left-wing critics such as Jules Benjamin taking the Progressive position in *The United States and Cuba* (1974). Others thought that conservative internationalism made sense. William C. Widenor's *Henry Cabot Lodge and the Search for American Foreign Policy* (1980) presents a spirited defense of the Senate Foreign Relations Committee chairman's assessment of America's true interests in world politics.

No historian could erase all of the negative images of the Harding, Coolidge and Hoover years, as these three presidents present such convenient targets for the lampoonist. But the twenties also seemed to fit more neatly into the general course of the rise of American power in the twentieth century. Sometimes because of presidential action, but more often despite it, the United States continued in the "prosperity decade" to scramble for a position of equality with the world powers of Europe. As those powers nursed their wounds from the Great War, an assertive America moved them aside.

CHAPTER EIGHT

The Diplomacy of Depression, 1930–1939

The Great Depression represented the most searing episode in modern economic history, and only the notorious bloodthirstiness of the twentieth century prevents identifying it also as the most important event in modern international relations. Nonetheless, it runs a strong second to the wars that have devastated the world. It affected every aspect of American life, leaving what Caroline Bird calls a "hidden wound" on the minds of the generation that lived through it. Politically, it altered the balance of the two big parties, making the Democrats the majority for the next half-century. The New Deal began, and the Second World War completed, the process of enlarging the federal government and magnifying the power of the president to the point where he seemed to act at will in international affairs.

HOOVER CONFRONTS DEPRESSION

The Depression casts a giant shadow over the foreign policies of the Hoover and Roosevelt administrations. Herbert Hoover, who moved into the White House on March 4, 1929, with the hopes of applying the managerial skills of the "great engineer" to the problems of international relations, soon found himself grappling with an economic crisis no one understood and which he could do nothing to improve. As was the case in Britain and France, international affairs took a back seat to finding a way out of the sickening slump which threatened an end to world trade, an end to profits, and an end to work.

Hoover's secretary of state, Henry L. Stimson, came to his job beautifully equipped, having served as secretary of war under Taft and going on to lead troops in the Great War, make a fortune during the twenties, and mediate the civil war in Nicaragua. In his four years as the chief foreign policy adviser to the government, Stimson came to despise his boss. Despite a forbidding exterior and a reputation for smugness, Stimson was carefree compared to Hoover, who anguished over the economic crisis. Hoover wanted his cabinet members in his office every morning at seven, and Stimson, having worked hard for years, preferred not to arrive before ten. Once they got there, the president required them all to get into sweatsuits and shove a medicine ball into one another's ample stomachs. Afterward, they took breakfast together while Hoover's hounds climbed over them. Stimson, at sixty-three, had had enough exercise in his lifetime, and complained that the cabinet meeting with Hoover was "like sitting in a bath of ink." Worst of all, Stimson recalled, no matter how much attention Hoover gave to the Depression, things got worse.

Although the Depression had been sparked by the crash in the New York Stock Exchange on October 29, 1929, Hoover looked to international solutions to worldwide distress. The value of international trade spiraled downward from $2.858 billion in 1929 to $2.327 billion in 1930 to $1.668 billion in 1931 to $1.122 billion in 1932. American policy contributed to the commercial slump when Congress passed the Smoot-Hawley Tariff in 1930, raising rates to their highest level in history and effectively closing the United States market to Japan. Protectionist sentiment swept other countries too, as all European nations and Japan erected their own trade walls to shield endangered domestic industries.

An even darker economic cloud loomed over the future of international debts. American bankers had embarked on a frenzy of lending in the five years after 1924, and no project, no matter how unlikely to make money, escaped the interest of eager bankers. "The underwriters' margins in handling these loans was generous; the public took them up with enthusiasm; competition for the business was keen," writes John Kenneth Galbraith in *The Great Crash* (1955). Countries obliged to repay these loans could make gold shipments to the United States (which could not last long), export goods to America (a course blocked by the high tariff), or they could borrow more money at even higher rates of interest to repay the first loans. Once American banks ran out of money in 1930, foreign countries no longer could pyramid loans, and the house of cards of international finance collapsed in a roar of defaults.

European governments also threatened to stop payment on their public war debts to the United States. As had been the case in the Ruhr crisis of 1923, the United States received nothing until Germany sent reparations to the allies. The German economy, in turn, had been badly shaken by the suspension of American loans and the high United States tariff. Germany attempted to revive its domestic economy in the spring of 1931 by establishing a common market, or customs union, with the independent state of Austria. But the French government immediately howled that this plan violated the Versailles Treaty's prohibition of a union, or *Anschluss,* between Germany and Austria. The French believed that the common market was the first step toward unification of the two states. With fears of German nationalism a staple of French politics, the government scuttled the *Anschluss.*

The reaction in Austria was the June 1931 collapse of the largest bank in Vienna, the *Creditanstalt,* and a financial panic ensued. Germany suspended payments on reparations to the Allies and also threatened to stop installments of its world war debts to the United States. Hoover feared that an outright default by the Allies would enrage nationalist members of Congress who might retaliate with even higher trade restrictions against Britain and France. He hoped to buy time, let the Depression reach bottom, and then encourage Europeans to make good on the war debts. He therefore advocated a moratorium to last for a year and a half on the debts owed by the Allies to the United States; the Allies were not going to pay anyway, so he put the best possible face on a bad situation. On June 21, Hoover declared the moratorium. "Hoover's announcement, promising an end to the deteriorating international financial situation, was probably the high moment of his presidency. Millions of Americans received the news with acclaim," reports historian Robert Ferrell in *American Diplomacy in the Great Depression* (1957).

The public's relief passed quickly as the moratorium did little to stop the economic slide. By September, British unemployment reached a sickening 25 percent of the work force, and the Labour party government of Ramsay MacDonald fell in an angry dispute with the Bank of England. William Montague, the bank's president, threatened the prime minister that the bank would no longer maintain the value of the pound in relation to gold if the government continued to pay unemployed workers. Faced with an ultimatum, MacDonald abandoned his Labour principles and joined with the Conservative party to form a national government committed to slashing the budget. This move did not stop the Bank of England from taking Britain off the gold standard anyway.

THE MANCHURIAN CRISIS

News of the fall of the British Labour government reached Washington on September 16, 1931. The president hosted a dinner that evening for Stimson, Secretary of Commerce Robert P. Lamont, and Treasury Secretary Mellon. The four men sweltered in 95-degree heat, and the disconsolate Hoover could say nothing to lift his guests' spirits. All of them woefully agreed that the United States Treasury and Federal Reserve Board had no money to help bail out Great Britain, and they selected Stimson to bear the bad news to the British embassy on his way home.

While the American government confessed its financial impotence, an event took place twelve thousand miles across the Pacific Ocean which contributed to the paralysis of American foreign policy. In Manchuria, the northernmost province of China, a small war broke out between Japan and China. For the remainder of the Hoover administration, the president and his secretary of state had to cope with a conflict which threatened to engage the United States and upset the stability established by the Washington treaty system. Both China and Japan had suffered from the high American and European tariffs erected to stop the Depression. Leaders of the Japanese army, which had been stationed in North China since the beginning of the century, saw the Depression as an opportunity to find a market for Japanese goods there without having to fear retaliation from the Europeans and Americans. Consequently, on the night of September 18, 1931, Japanese troops staged an incident on the South Manchuria Railway's main line a few miles north of the town of Mukden. They blew up a short section of railroad track, accused the Chinese of having set the explosion, and used the affair as an excuse for a military expedition against China in Manchuria.

Japanese troops patrolling occupied Manchuria, 1932.
(National Archives)

Over the next month, Japan waged war on China while the world watched. No Western government could afford to stop the Japanese by force since war in the midst of Depression simply would cost too much. The League of Nations assembled in October 1931 and decided to send a commission of inquiry to China. British Lord Lytton headed this commission, which literally took a slow boat to China, arriving early in 1932. While the Lytton Commission dithered, Japan attacked the southern Chinese city of Shanghai. Secretary Stimson, flushed with indignation, concluded that the United States would act on its own if the League stood by. He drew upon the moralism of Woodrow Wilson and Williams Jennings Bryan to declare that the United States would not recognize any territorial changes brought about through the use of force. The so-called Stimson Doctrine of Nonrecognition was made public in a letter the secretary of state sent to Senator Borah, chairman of the Committee on Foreign Relations, on February 23, 1932. In it Stimson referred to the Open Door policy and the Nine Power Treaty of 1922. He told Borah that he was waiting for other powers to join in nonrecognition "which, as has been shown by history in the past, will eventually lead to restoration to China of rights and titles of which she may have been deprived."

Stimson wanted to go beyond nonrecognition to threaten actual military force against Japan. He knew that he would be bluffing but thought that Japan might back off if all the Washington treaty powers bluffed together. Yet Hoover refused to go along, rejecting an empty warning as unworthy of the United States and unlikely to fool Japan. Abandoned by his chief, Stimson sulked. Over the next twenty years, Hoover and Stimson engaged in a public row over whether the nonrecognition doctrine properly should be named after the secretary of state or the president. It hardly mattered, though, if it was called the Hoover Doctrine, the Stimson Doctrine, or the Hoover-Stimson Doctrine. Japan remained in Manchuria, renamed Manchukuo, until 1945.

EARLY NEW DEAL DIPLOMACY

Foreign policy issues had little to do with the election of 1932, in which people were preoccupied with the economic crisis, but a sharp observer could detect differences on international relations between Hoover and his Democratic rival, Franklin D. Roosevelt. At every stop in the campaign, Roosevelt blamed Hoover for the Depression and accused him of doing nothing to make it go away. The Democrat suggested that the president's concentration on the international origins of the economic calamity was a way of lifting blame from his shoulders: if the Depression truly was worldwide in scope, then the United States could do little on its own to get out of it. Roosevelt signaled other shifts away from his earlier commitment to Wilsonian internationalism. As a condition for his support in the general election, the influential newspaper editor William Randolph Hearst demanded and received assurances that FDR drop his long-standing support for American membership in the League of Nations. When Roosevelt won a landslide victory of 22,800,000 votes to Hoover's 15,750,000, no one knew the exact shape of his government's policies. Since the campaign had been fought and won on the domestic issue of the Depression, it was clear that the new president would devote the bulk of his attention to recovery from the slump. Diplomacy would not occupy his mind, and if he decided to adopt a nationalistic economic policy, the rest of the world would have to take a back seat.

The 1932 election was the last one in which the interregnum between the casting of the votes and the assumption of office lasted a full four months, from November to March. Never did the period seem longer or the results more catastrophic. The economy reached rock bottom in those five months. Thousands of banks closed while hundreds of thousands of people lost their jobs. Hoover bitterly resented the charge of cruelty, insensitivity, and blundering Roosevelt had thrown at him in the fall. The relations between the two men got worse in the winter as Hoover begged Roosevelt to support ongoing foreign economic policies by endorsing the moratorium on debt and agreeing to attend an international economic conference. But Roosevelt wanted to keep a free hand to avoid blame for any failures in his predecessor's policies and had no power until March 4. He said nothing about the moratorium, which was allowed to lapse in December 1932. As for the international economic conference, Hoover did coax a commitment to attend, but nothing more came from the president-elect, who refused to say what the United States would do once it got to the conference scheduled to open in London in June.

Roosevelt did not say because he did not know. He wanted time to experiment with the domestic economy, and some of his advisers, notably Raymond Moley, a Columbia University economist who headed the "Brain Trust," and George Peek, an agricultural economist, thought that experiments could be best conducted in isolation from the world's political and economic troubles. When Roosevelt stood on the steps of the Capitol on March 4, 1933, and proclaimed that "the only thing we have to fear is fear itself," he started the New Deal, but he did not start a new diplomacy.

Roosevelt's choice for secretary of state was a sixty-one-year-old courtly senator from Tennessee, Cordell Hull, who had spent the previous twenty years in Congress advancing the cause of world peace through tariff reform. He believed, along with the liberal reformers of the nineteenth century, that the cause of war was trade dislocations. He thought that if all nations could trade freely with one another, their economies would become so interdependent that they could not risk going to war. As secretary of state, he pressed a Reciprocal Trade Agreements Act which would cut American tariffs in response to similar cuts by the other nations of the world, but on other matters Hull had little expertise, interest, or comment.

Despite the president's hints that the Depression had to be beaten at home before the United States could turn to international relations, he had committed the United States to participate in the international economic conference in London that would be held from June 12 to July 24. Sixty-four nations were supposed to fix a value for one another's currencies. After the British and several other European nations abandoned the gold standard, the rate of exchange fluctuated wildly. Any business intending to ship goods to another country had trouble knowing what to charge because no one knew what payment in foreign currency, say British pounds, would mean in terms of one's own money, say dollars. Many merchants simply refused to trade, and the Depression got worse. The London Conference was also supposed to reduce trade barriers and maybe even eliminate the war debts owed by the Europeans to the United States. Roosevelt sent a high-level delegation headed by Hull and the chairman of the Senate Committee on Foreign Relations, a toughtalking, hard-drinking Democrat from Nevada, Key Pittman. As befitted a senator for a silver-mining state, Pittman had no interest in resurrecting the gold standard, preferring instead silver-based money which would raise the price of that metal. Moreover, in June 1933 Prohibition was still the law of the land. Pittman arrived in London like a man released from prison and headed to the nearest legal liquor store. At one point, an astonished member of the American delegation fled in horror as the senator, stark naked and holding a bottle of whiskey in one hand and a knife in the other, chased him down the corridor of their hotel shouting that he should support the monetization of silver.

While Pittman enjoyed himself, Hull laid on the table a plan for across-the-board tariff reductions. The British replied by saying that trade revival had to be accompanied by currency stabilization. Hull warred with Pittman, so the matter was referred to the president, who dispatched Raymond Moley to end the bickering. The conference did nothing while Moley took a leisurely seven-day liner trip to London. Newspapers headlined this expedition with "MOLEY, MOLEY, MOLEY, HOLY MOLEY." They should have restrained their enthusiasm, though, for shortly after Moley arrived, Roosevelt "torpedoed" the conference with a famous "bombshell" telegram of July 3. He announced, "The sound internal economic system of a nation is a greater factor in its well being than the price of its currency." Any plan for a fixing of the value of the dollar in relation to the currency of other nations would have to wait until a majority of nations had recovered economically, could "produce balanced budgets," and could live within their means. With these bows to nationalism and economic orthodoxy, the London economic conference ended in disarray. Two years later, in 1935, the central banks of Great Britain, France, and the United States worked out an informal arrangement to fix the values of their currencies. Yet nothing was done to create a general international agreement on currency stabilization until the Bretton Woods Conference of 1944 set up the International Monetary Fund. The failure of the London Conference signaled a retreat from international economic cooperation on the part of the United States.

Over the next few years, Secretary of State Hull managed to get the president's support for his plan of tariff reduction. In 1934, Congress passed a Reciprocal Trade Agreements Act which enabled the president to cut tariffs by as much as 50 percent. Hull wanted the president to use this immediately and across the board. Economic nationalists in the administration, however, thought that the United States should get something in return for its willingness to reduce its imports. George Peek called Hull's plan "unilateral economic disarmament." While Hull favored multilateralism, a plan where all nations would reduce their tariffs at once, the nationalists preferred bilateral agreements, and their view prevailed. In the years before the United States entered the Second World War, the State Department negotiated thirty agreements with other nations, mostly those in the Western Hemisphere, effectively tying their trade ever closer to the United States. The State and Treasury departments even went so far as to threaten the nations of Ecuador, Peru, Chile, and Argentina with limitations on their imports to the United States should they reduce their tariffs to other nations.

THE GOOD NEIGHBOR POLICY

In his inaugural address, Roosevelt announced that "in our relations with the western hemisphere, we shall be guided by the principle of the good neighbor." In actuality, New Dealers followed the outlines of policy set down by Herbert Hoover: the United States maintained control where it could over the Western Hemisphere but avoided the use of force. It would use persuasion and economic pressure to get the Latin American governments themselves to follow American leadership.

The United States would not, however, renounce the use of force for all time. At the seventh Pan-American Conference, held in Montevideo, Uruguay, in 1933, the resolution barring intervention again was presented. For the first time, the United States voted for such a resolution. Secretary of State Hull attached an important proviso, however. He said that the United States reserved its right to intervene "by the law of nations as generally recognized and accepted." Three years later, at the Buenos Aires Conference, the United States went further and voted for an unequivocal renunciation of the use of force. Nonetheless, the Americans did not abandon the right to apply political or economic pressure throughout the hemisphere.

The first test of the Good Neighbor policy came early in the Roosevelt administration in its relations with Cuba. The United States had retained the right of intervention there through the Platt Amendment of 1902 (Sen. Orville H. Platt, R. Conn.). Throughout the twenties, Americans had run the economy of the island with investments topping $1.5 billion in 1929. Americans controlled the treasury and tax collection and increased the size of the Cuban army. Gerardo Machado, an avowed admirer of Italy's Fascist *Duce* Benito Mussolini, served as Cuban president from 1924 to 1933. In 1929, the economy of Cuba began to unravel with a crash in the price of sugar. Strikes and protest erupted which Machado quelled by jailing or murdering leftists, labor union leaders, and student activists. Edward Guggenheim, the American ambassador in Cuba, unsuccessfully attempted to calm Machado.

When Roosevelt came to power, he sent a close friend from his Groton schooldays, Sumner Welles, to Cuba as ambassador. Later Welles became the undersecretary of state and was actually the president's confidant in the department. When Welles reached Cuba, he concluded that Machado had to go but that the United States could not use its own troops to evict him. To have done so immediately on taking office would give the lie to the Good Neighbor policy. Instead, while American warships steamed off the coast, Welles conspired with the old politicians, looking for one of them to take power. Faced with the Americans' hostility, a general strike, and a student uprising, Machado fled the country in August. Welles's handpicked president, Carlos Manuel de Céspedes, had no control over events. Less than a month after he assumed office, a group of army sergeants led by Sgt. Fulgencio Batista helped a liberal professor, Ramón Grau San Martín, take over the presidency.

Grau had long opposed the Machado government, which had forced him into exile, and the Platt Amendment. Soon after his elevation to the presidency, Grau abrogated the amendment, which gave the United States the right to intervene in the nation's internal affairs. He also suspended payment of loans to New York's Chase National Bank and began the expropriation of American-held plantations. Welles could not stand the independence and nationalism of Grau, nor could the military leaders who had helped him seize power. The fledgling Cuban Communist party, on the other hand, thought Grau too moderate. At one point that fall, Welles had asked Secretary Hull to approve sending troops to evict their hand-chosen president. The secretary thought that would not be very neighborly and opted instead for a convoy of warships. Welles spoke to Batista, who with the support of the army seemed to be the major power in Cuba. The ambassador returned to the United States in December, and in January 1934, Batista led a coup against Grau, who left the country for Mexico.

Early in the "era of Batista," the United States abrogated the Platt Amendment, lowered the sugar tariff under the Reciprocal Trade Agreement Act, and granted Cuba loans through the Export-Import Bank. The United States also backed Batista's rule, either personally as president or through strong men, until his ouster by Fidel Castro's revolutionaries in 1959. In return for these favors, the United States was given the rights to a naval base at Guantanamo Bay on the south coast of Cuba.

While the United States ruled Cuba directly or indirectly into the thirties, it reached an accommodation with the nationalists in Mexico. As had been the case in the Coolidge administration, a conciliatory ambassador was able to smooth the rough relations caused by Mexico's insistence on its rights to control its own mineral and petroleum wealth. Mexico's size, population, and militant nationalism prohibited the United States from seeking a military solution, although many would have wished it. In 1938 another strongly nationalist president came to power in Mexico. Lázaro Cárdenas abrogated the deal worked out by Dwight Morrow and declared that all of Mexico's mineral wealth belonged to its citizens. United States oil company executives fulminated, refused to sell Mexico the equipment to drill for oil, and boycotted Mexican products in the American market.

FDR's ambassador to Mexico, Josephus Daniels, had as secretary of the navy in 1914 sent the marines to Vera Cruz. As ambassador, he seemed bent on repairing that wrong, and he became every bit as effective as Dwight Morrow had been. A soft-spoken North Carolinian who neither smoked, drank, nor swore, he had been preaching the gospel of the Good Neighbor since he arrived in Mexico in 1933. When faced with the expropriation of American oil properties, Daniels took a softer line than his boss in Washington, Cordell Hull.

The secretary of state prepared a stinging telegram on expropriation which Daniels refused to deliver. Hull contemplated sending the marines until his ambassador told him this would violate the Good Neighbor policy. At one point, Hull ordered Daniels home, and the envoy ignored the request. Daniels had the support of the president who believed that the United States needed Mexico's friendship in the coming global confrontation with Nazi Germany. Accordingly, Roosevelt allowed Daniels to accept the principle that Mexico owned the subsoil mineral rights. The Mexican government agreed to compensate the American firms which had been expropriated, and the United States provided Mexico with a credit of $30 million under the Export-Import Bank.

RECOGNITION OF THE SOVIET UNION

Since the Bolshevik Revolution of 1917, the United States had refused to extend diplomatic recognition to the Soviet Union. In the Wilson administration, officials expected that the Communist government would quickly be replaced by another more favorable to the United States. During the Republican years, each administration thought that the Soviet Union was an outlaw state committed to the export of revolution throughout the world. Only the independent-minded chairman of the Senate Foreign Relations Committee, William Borah, kept up a steady campaign to send diplomatic representatives to Moscow. Secretary of State Frank Kellogg expressed the conventional view in 1926 when he blamed the Soviet Union for sending arms to Nicaragua via Mexico. In the twenties, the American government claimed that the repudiation of the czar's world war debts to the United States prevented recognition.

When Roosevelt took office, however, conditions had changed. Depression caused business to look at every country of the world, no matter how unlikely, as a possible outlet for American goods. Henry Ford, who had built car factories in the Soviet Union in the early twenties, wanted to go back. So did Gerard Swope, the president of the General Electric Company, and several other business leaders urged diplomatic recognition as a way of opening trade. There were strategic reasons as well. One of the principal China experts in the State Department, Stanley Kuhl Hornbeck, had been frightened for years about the rise of Japanese power at the expense of China. For a short time in the mid-twenties, the Soviet Union had been allied with the Chinese, but relations had broken down in 1927. Hornbeck wanted to use the Soviet Union as a counter to Japan, but to do so there had to be some sort of official relations between the United States and the Soviets.

The government in Moscow also wanted to end its long period of diplomatic isolation. The rise of the Nazi party to power in Germany had shocked the Soviets. Before Hitler became chancellor on January 30, 1933, the international Communist movement denied a Nazi threat. The German Communist party had waged bitter street battles with the Nazis, but the German Communists had not sought to ally with any of the "democratic" parties to stop the Nazi seizure of the state. On the eve of the Nazis' ascendancy, German Communists were foolish enough to predict "after Hitler, us." Instead, Communists were thrown into concentration camps, their party outlawed, and Nazi foreign policy spokesmen called the Soviet Union the enemy. Consequently, Soviet leader Josef Stalin switched course, tried to find allies among the democratic nations of the West, and told Western Communists to create "popular fronts" with non-Communist "progressive parties." In 1934, the Soviet Union joined the League of Nations, where its representative, Maxim Litvinov, became the foremost spokesman for collective security against Germany's military revival.

Before the Soviet Union joined the League, it opened diplomatic relations with the United States. Roosevelt used a special envoy, not a State Department official, to begin the conversations. The president wanted to keep the discussions secret, and he had no respect for the professional Foreign Service officers, calling them "effete" gentlemen who "wear handkerchiefs in their sleeves." They reminded the president too much of the frivolous golden youth he had grown up with. His special representative was none other than William C. Bullitt, a rich man who had gone to Harvard a few years after the president and a few years before his fracas with Woodrow Wilson over the the Bolshevik regime. Bullitt approached Boris Skvirsky, the principal Soviet representative in the United States, in early October 1933, offering an invitation from Roosevelt to a Soviet official to come to the United States. Skvirsky asked, "Does this mean recognition?" and Bullitt parried, "What more can you expect than to have your representative sit down with the president of the United States?"

The Soviets were pleased to send their foreign minister, Litvinov, to the United States for talks from November 8 to 16, 1933. Roosevelt used his legendary charm on the Soviet envoy. As became his custom later in his presidency, Roosevelt leaked to the press how his bonhomie worked wonders, this time in embarrassing Litvinov into allowing religious freedom for Americans living in the Soviet Union. He told his cabinet that he had toyed with the Soviet envoy: "You know Max, your good old father and mother, pious Jewish people, always said their prayers. I know that they must have taught you to say your prayers." Roosevelt continued with his tale in the cabinet meeting: "Max [Litvinov] blustered and puffed and said all kinds of things, laughed and was very embarrassed, but I had him." Roosevelt won from Litvinov the agreement that Americans in the Soviet Union could have religious freedom; this disarmed the criticism of the Catholic press in the United States. He extracted a pledge that the Soviet Union would pay from $70 to $150 million in war debts; this warmed the hearts of bankers. Businessmen were encouraged to believe that a vast market awaited them, and friends of China thought that finally a bulwark had been established against the Japanese.

These hopes proved illusory over the next five years. The Soviets did not allow freedom of religion. They did not repay the debts. Business and trade with the Russians went nowhere. And the Japanese continued their assault in the Far East. The enthusiasm for the Soviet regime of Bullitt, the first American ambassador to the Soviet Union, turned to equally unbalanced anticommunism within two years. He left in 1935 to become ambassador to France, leaving behind a staff of experts, led by George F. Kennan, most of whom grew disgusted with and frightened by the purges of old Bolsheviks which consolidated Stalin's rule. The Foreign Service experts on the Soviet Union thereupon began a campaign inside the State Department to alert politicians to the threat of communism.

NEUTRALITY

Robert Dallek, who has written the major study of FDR's diplomacy, *Franklin D. Roosevelt and American Foreign Policy* (1979), describes "his prevailing inclination to move slowly in foreign affairs." Only when the president could be certain of "an unequivocal popular consensus" behind him would he take a strong position, Dallek asserts. In the first Roosevelt administration, there seemed to be general agreement that the United States should steer clear of Europe's problems. The memory of the recent past and a fear of repeating unhappy experiences dominated policy. In the twenties, Americans were already suspicious of the motives of entry into the world war. With the onset of the Depression and the election of Roosevelt, the conservative internationalism of the Republican twenties became an object of scorn. Liberals came to believe that recent foreign affairs had served the interests of international bankers and investors, two especially reviled groups in 1933. When Richard Whitney, the vice-president of the New York Stock Exchange, went to jail in 1934 for swindling thousands of small investors, his disgrace highlighted the hypocrisy of the business community. These suspicions combined with the economic nationalism of the early New Deal to make a forward foreign policy seem the work of selfish, old-fashioned diplomats.

Americans reflected worldwide trends in their rejection of the Versailles Treaty and the policy of collective security. In Britain, liberals who had had such high hopes for the success of Wilsonianism had come to believe that the world war had been a mistake. W. H. Dawson's *Germany Under the Treaty* (1932) and Lord Birkenhead's *Turning Points in History* (1929) joined John Maynard Keynes's *Economic Consequences of the Peace* (1920) in creating a widespread agreement that Germany had been mistreated by the Treaty of Versailles. The British Labour party, having broken with Ramsay MacDonald in 1931, turned its back on international questions to concentrate its attention on complaints about the government's fumbling attempts to handle the Depression. Once the Conservatives came back to power in 1935, under the premiership of Stanley Baldwin, they too hoped to appease the German ambitions. Some prominent conservatives, such as Lady Astor, Lord Halifax, Neville Henderson, or Frank Ashton-Gwatkin, found virtues in the Nazi government. Some Tories, terrified of revolution, liked the Nazis' anticommunism; others hated Jews and saw nothing wrong with Hitler's anti-Semitic ravings; and still others thought that Germany was a fertile market. Similar feelings arose in France in the midst of the Depression. Except for a brief interlude in 1936 and 1937 when a popular front government of liberals, socialists, and Communists, headed by a Jewish politician, Léon Blum, was in power, France in the thirties had little stomach for a confrontation with Germany. Bled white by the world war, which had cost France alone one and a half million lives, no government in the Depression wanted to spend money for weapons against Germany.

In the United States, the revulsion at the memory of the world war took the form of neutrality laws designed to prevent Americans again being sucked into a war. Four such laws passed Congress: in 1935, 1936, 1937, and 1939. The first came as a result of hearings held by a Senate Select Committee in 1934. Senator Gerald Nye, a Progressive Republican from North Dakota, chaired a committee especially empowered to look into charges raised in the book *Merchants of Death* (1934) that the United States had been gulled into fighting the war by an unholy alliance of bankers and munitions manufacturers. Dorothy Detzer, the head of the Women's International League for Peace and Freedom, had approached Sen. George Norris, a Progressive Republican from Nebraska, who favored an investigation. Norris asked Nye to assemble a committee, which met in late 1934 and early 1935. Nye's committee heard from businessmen, historians, and diplomats and concluded that the United States had not truly been neutral in the years before 1917. America could only have avoided conflict, the committee decided, by avoiding financial dealing with embattled countries.

The researches of the Nye Committee became more than an academic enterprise in 1935. Fascist Italy under Benito Mussolini looked for a way to restore the glory of the Roman empire. He found it in East Africa where, from the end of 1934 until the fall of 1935, Italy made demand after demand on Ethiopia. Finally, Italy attacked Ethiopia on October 3, 1935. Alarms ran through European capitals, where politicians feared that the attack on Ethiopia signaled a crisis as grave as the one which had touched off the world war.

The answer of the Nye Committee to these new tensions was to draft new laws with three provisions—a ban on travel by Americans to a war zone (to avoid another *Lusitania* incident), a ban on loans by Americans to belligerents, and most important of all, an impartial embargo on arms to belligerents. Roosevelt spoke up for the authority to impose a discriminatory embargo, that is, one which would let him declare one nation an aggressor and embargo weapons only to that one. But Nye and his supporters would have none of a discriminatory embargo, and they filibustered against it on the Senate floor. At one point, frantic members of the Committee on Foreign Relations found their leader, Chairman Key Pittman, barely sober enough to stand. Doses of coffee revived him enough to come to the Senate floor and announce that the president would agree to a bill which had an impartial arms embargo. Both houses of Congress passed the bill, and on August 31, 1935, President Roosevelt signed the Neutrality Law. When signing, Roosevelt did warn, however, that the impartial arms embargo "might have exactly the opposite effect from that which was intended. In other words, the inflexible provisions might drag us into war instead of keeping us out."

The next year, 1936, Congress passed a second neutrality law which simply extended the first for another year. In 1937, lawmakers had to contend with another European crisis—the civil war in Spain—when they sought to make the neutrality law permanent. The Spanish Republic, proclaimed in 1931, was led by liberals and moderate socialists. In July 1936, Gen. Francisco Franco, the commander of Spanish forces in North Africa, led an uprising against the Republic. Fascist Italy and Nazi Germany quickly came to Franco's aid with troops and weapons. A few months later, the Soviet Union enlisted on the side of the Republic with smaller amounts of military aid. The British led an international movement to stay neutral in the fighting. Foreign Secretary Anthony Eden convinced the French, who had an agreement to aid the Spanish Republic, to stay out. Britain also wanted the United States to remain neutral, and President Roosevelt was happy to oblige. American opinion was deeply divided over the Spanish civil war with liberals and leftists supporting the Republic and conservatives and the bulk of the Catholic hierarchy backing Franco. Roosevelt had no wish to alarm Catholics or British diplomats, so he invoked the neutrality act to keep Americans from backing either side.

Crises in European politics seemed to come with increasing frequency; either they would lead to war, or they would become endemic. Whatever happened, advocates of neutrality wanted to find a way for Americans to continue to reap the benefits of trade with contentious and warring Europe while at the same time avoiding the risk of involvement in war. The next addition to the neutrality law was the brainchild of Bernard Baruch, a South Carolina selfstyled adviser to presidents who had made millions in stock market "bucket shops," establishments in which customers bet on the price of common stock they happened not to own. Baruch, who had been the head of the War Industries Board during the Great War, believed that the threat of neutrality came from American ships being sunk. Ban shipping in a war zone, and there would be no chance of war. How then could Americans continue their trade? The answer: "Get the belligerents to pay for the goods beforehand and ship them home themselves." He expressed this cash-and-carry principle this way: "We will ship to any belligerent anything except lethal weapons, but the terms are '*cash on the barrel head and come and get it.*' " Roosevelt favored this plan because he knew that it subtly shifted the balance in favor of Great Britain, a state whose foreign policy he approved, and away from Germany. The British had the merchant marine which the Germans lacked. Advocates of strict neutrality such as Nye preferred a total embargo, but they thought that the cashand-carry provision was the best they could get through Congress. Thus, on May 1, 1937, Roosevelt signed a permanent Neutrality Act. Under its provisions, whenever the president declared that a state of war existed anywhere in the world, he had to place three major restrictions on Americans—an arms embargo, a prohibition of loans, and a prohibition of travel on belligerent ships. It was also up to him to place all trade with belligerents on a cash-andcarry basis. The main provisions of the act were permanent, but the cash-andcarry feature was due to expire in May 1939. Robert Divine describes the Neutrality Act of 1937 in *The Reluctant Belligerent* (1965, 1979) as "a compromise that reflected the contradictory desire of the American people to remain economically in the world and politically out of it."

THE SECOND SINO-JAPANESE WAR, 1937–1939

On July 7, 1937, war broke out again between Japan and China, and Japanese troops attacked north of Beijing in an effort to extend Japan's domination of China's economy. The war continued until the final defeat of Japan in 1945; it involved the United States and, most important, hastened the revolution which swept the Communists to power in 1949. American voices began calling immediately for an international condemnation of the Japanese. Henry L. Stimson, who had hoped for a stronger policy against Japan when he was secretary of state, led a movement for a boycott of Japanese goods, and the State Department's chief China hand, Assistant Secretary of State Stanley Hornbeck, also wanted a strong American stance in support of China. On the other side, however, American diplomats stationed in Tokyo, led by Ambassador Joseph C. Grew, who held the post from 1931 to 1941, thought that any American criticism of Japan would further inflame the Japanese against China.

Like Hoover before him, Roosevelt did not wish to risk war with Japan over China. He dismissed a trade embargo on Japan as unworkable in the midst of the Great Depression. At one point, on October 5, 1937, he delivered a speech in Chicago which seemed to condemn Japan as he called for a "quarantine" of aggressors, including Italy for its attack on Ethiopia, Germany for its violations of the Versailles Treaty, and Japan for its war on China. Reaction to the quarantine speech in the American press was surprisingly favorable. Even the *Chicago Tribune,* a staunch foe of any American involvement in *European* quarrels, said the prospect of economic and financial steps against Japan "would not lead to war." Having launched his trial balloon and not seen it explode, Roosevelt went no further in the direction of sanctions. He refused to believe that the public would actually support American military action in China, and consequently did no more. His suspicions that few Americans wanted to be involved in an Asian war seemed confirmed the next month. On December 12, 1937, Japanese planes bombed an American naval gunboat, the *Panay,* patrolling the Chang Jiang (Yangtze) River in China on behalf of the Socony-Vacuum Oil Company. Instead of calling for a punitive reaction against Japan, Arizona senator Henry Ashurst voiced the views of most Americans when he answered that "none of my" colleagues would vote for war with Japan. Indiana congressman Louis Ludlow took the opportunity to gain floor action on a constitutional amendment requiring a national referendum before declaring war. Peace groups wondered what an American gunboat had been doing in China helping Socony-Vacuum. They expressed a widespread sentiment that the government had no business bailing out businessmen who worked in dangerous regions and called for the withdrawal of the American navy from China. When Japan apologized and offered to pay for damages on Christmas day, the furor subsided. For the next two years, American policy in the Far Eastern crisis was to give public lip service to the idea of the Open Door, to give private military and economic aid to Jiang Jieshi (Chiang Kaishek) and to maintain a precarious peace with Japan, but in 1940 and 1941 American policy toward Japan became more hostile (see Chapter Nine).

AMERICA: HITLER'S SILENT ACCOMPLICE?

After the Second World War broke out in September 1939, *appeasement* became a dirty word, and the Munich Conference of September 1938 came to symbolize everything that was wrong with the foreign policy of the allies before the Second World War. Appeasement suggested naiveté, weakness, and wishful thinking. Neville Chamberlain, the British prime minister who orchestrated the Munich Conference on Czechoslovakia, became a pathetic figure of fun. Opponents of the abandonment of the Czechs for a time even refused to carry umbrellas because of the association with the prime minister, who carried one off the plane from Germany when he proclaimed, "This is the second time in our lifetime that a British prime minister has returned from Germany with peace and honor. I believe it is peace for our time." In 1938, however, the appeasement of Germany's "legitimate" desires to rectify the Versailles Treaty was seen as "a self-confident creed . . . both utopian and practical," writes historian Martin Gilbert in *The Roots of Appeasement* (1966). The policy "sought to satisfy legitimate national aspirations without fomenting aggressive, destructive nationalism."

Adolf Hitler receives the adulation of jubilant Nazis at a party rally.
(National Archives)

Since taking power in 1933, Hitler had systematically gone about reversing the judgment of the Versailles Treaty. In 1935, he began rearming the German military; in 1936, he established military bases in the Rhineland in violation of the treaty. In the fall of 1936, he provided an air force and tanks to fight on the side of Franco in Spain; in March 1938, he annexed Austria to Germany. All the while he denounced the Western democracies, Bolsheviks in the Soviet Union, and Jews everywhere, claiming that they were responsible for all the world's woes. Promising to restore Germany to its rightful place in the sun, he claimed that only Communists, Jews outside of Germany, and a few professional German-haters and militarists wanted to wage war on the Nazis. In Great Britain, for example, Winston Churchill led an isolated fringe group of conservatives who called for British rearmament, but Churchill's views were ignored when they were not considered radical and at war with reality.

In summer of 1938, a new crisis arose in central Europe. Hitler tried to join the Germans living in Czechoslovakia to the Reich, just as he had done with Austria. This time, however, Czech prime minister Eduard Beneš was more fiercely opposed than the Austrians had been, and war threatened to erupt late that summer. The Czechs had a security treaty with France and another with the Soviet Union and believed that they could resist the Germans. At this point Britain, also allied with France, stepped in to look for a peaceful solution. Prime Minister Chamberlain traveled twice to visit Hitler in his mountain retreat near Munich. At the second of these meetings, the French also participated. Significantly, the Czechs, whose fate was being decided, and the Soviets, who were willing to fight the Germans, were not invited. The Munich agreement awarded one-third of Czechoslovakia to Germany in return for a promise not to take the rest. Later a hapless Czech President Emil Hácha was chased around a table by German foreign minister Joachim von Ribbentrop until the dejected Czech signed away his country. But Chamberlain returned home with his umbrella. Less than six months later, in March 1939, Germany finished the job, annexed the rest of Czechoslovakia, and killed British hopes that Germany's leader was a traditional politician whose aims could be appeased. The Roosevelt administration reacted with pleasure to the Munich agreement. The president sent Chamberlain a two-word cable, "GOOD MAN," when he learned that the conference had averted war. Still in the Depression—the economy had taken another nose-dive in 1937–1938—the Roosevelt administration had no desire to confront the Germans directly.

Nor did the administration do anything to aid the most direct victims of nazism—Jews forced to flee their homes. American immigration policy remained hostile to Jewish refugees in the 1930s. The quotas passed in 1921 and 1924 had excluded Eastern European Jews as of "low racial quality." One American diplomat in the twenties suggested that the Jews who applied for visas to enter the United States gave his office "a smell no zoo could equal." The Roosevelt administration did nothing to lift barriers to immigration. Foreign Service officers retained their animosity to Jews after Hitler rose to power. In 1935, Germany passed the notorious Nuremberg racial laws, making it virtually impossible for Jews to make a living in the Reich. Thousands of them left Germany in the wake of these laws. More followed after November 1938, when a wave of violence against Jews swept over Germany. Throughout this period, the United States resisted the idea of allowing more into the United States than would be permitted under the quota for Germany. In early 1939, a ship laden with refugees was forced out of Havana harbor in Cuba, where the authorities would not let it land. No other safe haven beckoned, and it had to go back to Germany.

No international action occurred to ease the plight of the refugees. A conference at Evian-sur-les-Bains, a comfortable resort town in central France, took place in 1938. The nations of Europe and Latin America, along with the United States, met to decide if any could accept more Jewish refugees. All agreed that because of the Depression their economies simply were too strained to make room for any more of the victims of nazism. The conference ended with a pious declaration that the German government should stop the persecutions.

This apparent underestimation of the dangers posed by the rise of German power set off a mild flurry of controversy among historians although it never became as heated as the arguments over American entry into the First World War. In the palmy days of consensus that American participation in the Second World War made sense, the complaint arose that the United States had become, in Robert Divine's words, a "silent accomplice" of Hitler's grand design for world conquest. Roosevelt, who became "the soldier of freedom," in political scientist James MacGregor Burns's estimate, during the Second World War, was viewed as having been too cautious in the thirties. According to some historians, by not raising the alarm, Roosevelt actually encouraged Hitler to go further than he might otherwise have done. Written in the midst of the Cold War competition with Russia, the complaints about Roosevelt's apparent reluctance to get too far in front of the public justified confrontations with Russia. As doubts emerged about the Cold War, some New Left historians resurrected old criticisms of American diplomacy in the thirties. One of them, Patrick Hearden, presents a different picture of Roosevelt than that he feared leaving public opinion behind. In *Roosevelt Confronts Hitler* (1987), he argues that the president opposed nazism in order to establish a Pax Americana of United States commercial dominion. While admitting that Roosevelt was "genuinely concerned about the plight of the Jews," Hearden states that ethical concerns did not move the administration.

WAR IN EUROPE: SEPTEMBER 1939

The desperate illusion that the Munich Conference would promote peace in Europe was shattered early in 1939 when Germany annexed the rest of Czechoslovakia. That summer a crisis erupted over control of the German-speaking city of Danzig, the port which gave Poland access to the sea. Danzig was a "free city" under League of Nations supervision, and the residents were Germans who sympathized with the Nazi government in Berlin. They demanded the right to attach themselves to Germany and Hitler backed them, threatening Poland with war unless it relented.

The Western powers, Britain and France, had realized with the conquest of Czechoslovakia that Hitler's word could not be trusted. Besides, the Poles had a history of fighting quixotic wars which they had no chance of winning and, unlike the Czechs, were likely to oppose the Germans without allies. Therefore, British and French diplomats gloomily concluded that war was likely in the summer of 1939.

London and Paris clung vainly to the hope that the Soviet Union or the United States might force the Germans to back down. Britain and France conducted desultory talks with the Soviets in July. But reactionary Western officers did not have their hearts in these conversations, and the envoys took weeks getting to Moscow. A suspicious Josef Stalin, mindful of his exclusion from the Munich negotiations, feared being sucked into a losing battle with Hitler. He dropped his Jewish foreign minister, Maxim Litvinov, who advocated collective security, and responded to Nazi overtures. Hitler's foreign minister, Joachim von Ribbentrop, flew to Moscow on August 22. The next day he and his Soviet counterpart, Vyacheslav Molotov, Litvinov's replacement, stunned the world with the announcement that their governments had signed a nonaggression pact.

Official Washington reaction to the crisis over Danzig and the Nazi-Soviet Pact was measured even though war seemed likely. Roosevelt did press Congress to lift the arms embargo required by the neutrality acts. The president preferred to allow belligerents to buy arms if they could pay cash and carry them away. Roosevelt retreated, however, in the face of a certain filibuster by senators who feared an arms trade would make the United States a quasibelligerent. The president was stirred to action by the Nazi-Soviet Pact. Upon learning of the agreement on August 23, he telegraphed the king of Italy, asking him to intercede between Germany and Poland. The next day he sent similar messages pleading for restraint to Hitler and Polish president Ignacy Moscicki. None of Roosevelt's messages worked, of course. On August 25, Great Britain signed a formal alliance with Poland. Exactly one week later, on September 1, Hitler attacked Poland. Two days afterward, the British and the French invoked their alliance with the Poles and declared war on Germany. The Second World War had begun. Unlike the First World War, no crowds plunged into the streets in any of the capitals of the belligerents. None had recovered from the first war, and most believed that the second would be even more brutal.

CHAPTER NINE

The Politics of Coalition Warfare, 1939–1945

Contemporary American foreign policy came alive during the Second World War. In 1940, Henry Luce, the inventor of *Time* magazine, proclaimed that "America is already the intellectual, scientific and artistic capital of the world." He assured the public that the world had entered "the American century" in which "we have that indefinable, unmistakable sign of leadership—prestige." Directors of American foreign policy from the president to the lowliest Foreign Service officer, army lieutenant, or congressman shared the view that their country would be the premier power in the world once the war ended.

NEUTRALITY, AGAIN

People who called themselves internationalists in the thirties filled the two years between the outbreak of war in Europe in 1939 and the American entry in December 1941 with calls for military aid to France and Britain and preparedness for war. Later, advocates of aid to the Allies saw the two prewar years as a test of the moral fiber of Americans: would they assume their "rightful role" in world politics? For others, who called themselves noninterventionists in the thirties, the two years after 1939 bore a striking and sad similarity to the period between the outbreak of war in 1914 and the American declaration of war in 1917. Leading noninterventionists like historian Charles Beard, air hero Charles Lindbergh, and Sen. Robert Taft insisted that the United States recapitulated the mistakes of earlier neutrality and grimly predicted the coming of a garrison state bereft of democracy and civil rights.

Both internationalists and noninterventionists organized politically to mold government policy and change public opinion. Barely two weeks after the outbreak of war in September, Walter Mallory, executive director of the Council on Foreign Relations, one of the foremost internationalist bodies, dropped in on Assistant Secretary of State George Messersmith to see how the council could be useful to the government. They worked out a deal for the New York organization to draw up a series of plans for the postwar world since State Department functionaries were too busy with day-to-day affairs to devote time to long-term planning. The council obliged by creating the War and Peace Studies project, a research network of over three hundred academics, journalists, diplomats, and military officers who drafted plans for American political, strategic, and economic dominance of the postwar world. Other advocates of American participation in the European war acted more publicly. Encouraged by the president and Secretary of the Interior Harold Ickes, William Alanson White, a well-known liberal Republican newspaper editor from Emporia, Kansas, organized the Committee to Defend America by Aiding the Allies in June 1940.

The White Committee came to life as the Roosevelt administration sought to undermine the appeal of a group born in the late spring of 1940 to keep the United States out of war. The America First Committee, the brainchild of Robert B. Woods, an heir to the Sears Roebuck fortune, included as prominent members Charles Lindbergh, Yale professor of international law Edward Borchard, and Sen. Burton K. Wheeler of Montana.

While the White Committee debated the America Firsters, accusing them of a cowardly refusal to admit that Germany threatened America, the Roosevelt administration was busy blackening the reputations of those who opposed aid to the allies. The president had Ickes and the director of the Federal Bureau of Investigation, J. Edgar Hoover, launch a whispering campaign against the leaders of America First, suggesting that they took their orders from Berlin. The FBI followed members of America First, opened their mail, and concocted phony letters to prove they had the best interests of the Nazis at heart. By the fall of 1941, the campaign against America First had been successful, and public opinion polls showed that over 40 percent of the American people were willing to fight. The attacks on America First also helped set a pattern of presidential accusations that opponents lacked patriotism. Roosevelt honestly perceived a threat to the United States in 1940 and 1941, but later presidents used the vilification of opponents in lesser causes. By the early 1970s, the meaning of the phrase *national security* had expanded to the point where the two words came to symbolize the abuses known as Watergate.

While Roosevelt himself wanted the United States to fight the war on the side of Britain and France, he feared leaving public opinion too far behind.

Remembering how the initial enthusiasm for Woodrow Wilson's program in war and peace had evaporated in the hard reality of the war, he wanted assurances that if the United States were to fight in the Second World War, the public would stay the course. He preferred to lead the public slowly to appreciate that the United States had to fight the war for self-interest, not for any grand program of international reform.

In the process, Roosevelt exaggerated the threat to create a popular consensus for war. He began in the fall of 1939 when he tried once more to revise the neutrality laws. This time he succeeded in eliminating the arms embargo in favor of the ability to sell arms on a cash-and-carry basis. He disingenuously suggested that the arming of the Allies would work to keep the United States out of the war, but he did not pretend that the end to the embargo gave equal access to all the belligerents. "Cash and carry" aided the British and French who had the merchant marine, navy, and money to buy while the Germans were effectively frozen out of the American arms trade. Making no secret of his sympathies for the Allies, Roosevelt offered no admonition to Americans to be neutral in thought as well as deed. Throughout the winter of 1939–1940, Americans shipped over $50 million in arms to Britain and France.

WAR IN EUROPE

The president's warm feeling for Britain and France came partly from memory of his experiences as assistant secretary of the navy during the First World War. He had visited the front in 1917, spoken to government officials, and come home convinced that Germans fought with cruel, heartless tenacity. Americans who had been to Germany after Hitler's rise to power in 1933 saw with their own eyes Storm Troopers beating Jews, Nazi bonfires of books, and hate-filled faces of participants at the annual rallies of Hitler's followers in the Bavarian town of Nuremberg. Austrians and Czechs had gotten an unforgettable taste of life under Nazi rule in 1938 and 1939, and in September 1939 the world learned how Hitler's armies fought.

The *Wehrmacht* (war machine) moved hundreds of thousands of infantrymen behind thousands of tanks and under the cover of fighter bombers which seemed to emerge out of nowhere to terrify the enemy. This *Blitzkrieg* (lightning war) surprised military experts who expected any new combat would resemble the trench warfare of 1914–1918. Poland was crushed within six weeks, and the Nazis continued a brutal campaign of terror against Jews, local Communists and socialists, and anyone connected with the old Polish government. Treating the Poles as *Untermenschen* (subhumans), commando squads of the SS (special security army) stripped, beat, and bludgeoned to death thousands of Poles in the autumn. This was only a foretaste of the systematic murder of five million Poles (including three million Jews) begun in 1941. Germany installed the sadist Hans Frank as military governor to extract as much labor as he could from the Poles. While Germany perfected new sorts of tyranny in the western two-thirds of Poland, the Soviet Union occupied the eastern part of the country under the terms of the Nazi-Soviet Pact of late August. Thousands of Jews and leftists received a temporary safe haven from the Russians.

Although Britain and France had declared war in support of Poland, they sent no troops and did not attack Germany in the fall and winter of 1939–1940. Hitler, contentedly digesting Poland, believed the Allies incapable of fighting, and Germans suggested that *Blitzkrieg* had turned to *Sitzkrieg* (sitdown war). Domestic opponents of the British government who urged action against Hitler charged that diplomats and generals throughout Western Europe fought a "phony war."

The United States shipped over $50 million in arms to Britain and France from October 1939 to April 1940, but the primary target of American diplomacy was not Germany, but the Soviet Union, which sent its army against neighboring Finland in December. Roosevelt promised arms to the Finns, the one country to have fully repaid its First World War debts. The British government, baffled at ways to fight Hitler but eager to do battle somewhere, drew up unworkable plans to ship a division across frozen Norway to Finland. The League of Nations, unable to do anything about the spread of nazism, responded to the Russo-Finnish winter war by expelling the Soviet Union. This was the only time in its history that the League evicted a nation for violating the covenant's prohibition of aggression. Japan, Italy, and Germany, each of which had sent its armies against other countries in the thirties, had all left before the international organization could throw them out.

In 1940, Germany and Italy created an alliance of their own as a ghastly mockery of the League. Mussolini called it the Rome-Berlin Axis because the world would now revolve around the Nazi and Fascist states. A new German *Blitzkrieg* exploded the phony war in April. Panzer tanks and Stuka dive bombers led one million of the best-armed foot soldiers the world had ever seen across Denmark, Norway, Holland, and Belgium. All these countries capitulated within six weeks. In London, Neville Chamberlain reluctantly resigned in the face of a revolt by fellow Conservatives, one of whom stood up in the House of Commons, wagged his finger at the prime minister, and bellowed words spoken three hundred years before by Oliver Cromwell, "You have sat too long in this place. In the name of God, go." Winston Churchill, for years regarded as an irritating romantic, in love with the empire, the monarch, and the products of the Uppmann Cigar Company, took over a coalition of the Conservative, Labour, and Liberal parties in May.

Churchill's warnings about the danger of German rearmament seemed vindicated by his elevation to prime minister, but he could do nothing to prevent the German army from rolling over France in early June. As the *Wehrmacht* surrounded the French troops, Churchill flew several times across the channel to encourage continued resistance. He went before the microphones of the British Broadcasting Corporation to offer France "indissoluble union" with Great Britain if only Paris would not surrender to Hitler. French president Eduard Daladier, shocked by the German success at outflanking the supposedly unbreachable Maginot Line of defense, wanted no part of Great Britain. Most French people were bewildered by the collapse of their army, resented the dramatic escape of the two-hundred-thousand-member British Expeditionary Force across the channel from the beach at Dunkirk, and thought the Germans invincible. The government fled Paris in front of tens of thousands of terrified refugees who clogged the roads to the south and west away from the approaching Nazis. Marshal Henri Pétain, a hero from the First World War, took over. The government surrendered on June 22. A jubilant Adolf Hitler accepted France's capitulation in the same railroad car the Allies had used to host the German officers who signed the armistice on November 11, 1918. The Nazi leader emerged smiling from the car, danced a jig for reporters, and then made his only visit to Paris where he sped through the deserted streets to look down on Napoleon's tomb to remind the world that Europe had a new conqueror.

Now Britain stood alone expecting an imminent invasion. Exhilarated Britons compared themselves favorably to the French as they listened on the radio to the distinctive gravelly voice of their new prime minister promising "blood, toil, tears, and sweat"; they thrilled at the sight of his short, stubby form, arm upraised in the V-for-victory sign, and went about filling sandbags, sewing burn dressings, and encouraging their neighbors to keep the blackout. Camaraderie, defiance, and determination were not enough, however, as the British were desperate for American weapons by the summer of 1940.

AID FOR BRITAIN

In August, Roosevelt readied a plan for temporary relief to Britain with a gift of fifty obsolete destroyers in return for bases for the American navy in Britishowned Caribbean islands. Winston Churchill hoped for more direct aid, but he was mollified by Roosevelt's assurance that the destroyers-for-bases swap meant the death of official American neutrality. Encouraged to believe that the "English-speaking peoples" were now "somewhat mixed up together," Churchill could say that their friendship was "like the Mississippi, it just keeps rolling along."

Roosevelt also shook up his cabinet in the summer of 1940, turning his back on New Deal domestic reforms as he recruited important Republicans to fill key military assignments. On June 19, he named Henry Stimson and Frank Knox, two of the best-known pro-Allied Republicans, as secretary of war and secretary of the navy, respectively. Stimson, a former secretary of war for Taft and secretary of state for Hoover, seventy-two years old at the time of his appointment, favored repeal of all neutrality laws and enactment of compulsory military training. Knox, the Republican vice-presidential candidate in 1936, was even more fervent in his support of Britain, urging an army of one million Americans, the largest air force in the world, and the immediate shipment of hundreds of planes to Britain.

Later that summer, Roosevelt moved to make a reality of the larger army. On August 2, he swung his support behind the moribund bill creating a Selective Service system to draft young men into the military. Roosevelt's announcement that he was "distinctly in favor" of the draft encouraged Congress to pass the law in September. The draft would last for one year and included a provision that conscripts would serve only in the Western Hemisphere. Despite these qualifications designed to quiet the anxieties of peace societies and "Silver Star Mothers" (women whose sons had died in the last war) who had flooded the Congress with mail opposing the draft, FDR's advocacy of Selective Service left little doubt that the president believed war was likely in the next year.

Roosevelt did nothing further publicly to aid the Allies before the election of 1940. He looked forward to an unprecedented third term when he disappointed the hopes of his vice-president of eight years, John Nance Garner of Texas, and received the Democrats' nomination. The Republicans, frustrated at having twice unsuccessfully run well-known officeholders against FDR, chose a newcomer to politics, Wendell Willkie of Indiana, who came from the "moderate" wing of the Republican party which supported the British in the war. During the campaign, neither Roosevelt nor Willkie spoke of their true feelings about the need for the United States to come to the aid of Britain, and both promised peace. Willkie supported the destroyers-for-bases deal and the conscription law. Yet in the heat of the campaign, he blurted out, "If you elect me president, I will never send American boys to fight in any European war." FDR replied in kind on October 30 when he promised American mothers, "I have said this before and I shall say it again and again and again: Your boys are not going to be sent into any foreign wars." That was enough for the public; Roosevelt was reelected on November 5 with 55 percent of the popular vote. His margin of victory had declined since 1936, and a majority of people questioned by Gallup said they would have voted for Willkie had it not been for the war. Congress too was less heavily Democratic than the one elected in 1938, but FDR's fellow Democrats still enjoyed a margin.

Now that his authority had been renewed, Roosevelt returned to the problem of Britain. By December, the British had exhausted their foreign currency reserves and could no longer pay cash for American arms. The neutrality laws and the Johnson Act of 1934 prevented floating private loans, but in a fireside chat on December 29, Roosevelt told the public that the United States should become "the great arsenal of democracy." When Congress convened the first week of January 1941, he let the senators and representatives know that the United States stood for Four Freedoms—freedom of speech, freedom of worship, freedom from want, and freedom from fear. He then explained that the United States would protect these freedoms by aiding the British and asked Congress to enact a "lend-lease" law. The bill proposing Lend-Lease, called H.R. (House Resolution) 1776, authorized the president to "lease, lend, or otherwise dispose of," to any country whose defense was vital to the United States, arms and supplies up to the astonishing amount for the time of $7 billion.

Noninterventionists immediately saw that their carefully constructed system of neutrality was about to come crashing down, and they railed against Lend-Lease. Democratic senator Burton K. Wheeler of Montana compared the proposal to an early New Deal program, the Agricultural Adjustment Administration, which had ordered farmers to plow under their crops to raise prices. "The lend-lease-give program is the New Deal Triple A foreign policy; it will plow under every fourth American boy," Wheeler charged. A stung Roosevelt used his outrage to vilify the noninterventionists, and he told a press conference that Wheeler's remark was "the most dastardly, unpatriotic thing that has ever been said. Quote me on that. That really is the rottenest thing that has been said in public life in my generation."

But the opposition kept at it. Testifying before a Senate committee, historian Charles A. Beard pleaded against enacting a law which was certain to lead the United States to war. He begged the senators to "preserve one stronghold of order and sanity even against the gates of hell." But this was the view of a minority. Internationalists made equally fervid appeals to pass LendLease as a means of keeping the United States out of war. Finally, in mid-February, Wendell Willkie, the titular head of the Republican party, endorsed the law, making it a bipartisan issue. Both houses of Congress passed the bill, the House by a vote of 317 to 71 and the Senate by a margin of 60 to 31, and on March 11, the president signed Lend-Lease. Within a month, Congress appropriated the $7 billion Roosevelt requested for aid to Britain and its allies.

CONFRONTATION WITH GERMANY

Even as Congress debated Lend-Lease, the United States moved toward a military confrontation with Germany. From January 29 to March 27, high-ranking representatives of the British and American Chiefs of Staff met secretly in Washington to coordinate military strategy in the event of American entry into the war. The talks set a pattern which continued throughout the war. The two sides never saw eye to eye as the British clung to an empire the larger, richer, and more powerful Americans tried to pry loose. Whatever their political squabbles, the Chiefs of Staff did settle a military question, adopting the suggestion of the American chief of naval operations, Harold R. Stark, that in event of war with both Japan and Germany, the United States and its allies would fight against Germany first. When the talks ended on March 27, the two sides had adopted a plan, "ABC-1," under which they ratified Stark's ideas.

While these secret conversations went forward, Roosevelt tested the public's appetite for the American navy to escort the ships carrying weapons to Britain. On March 15, he made a cryptic remark in a radio address in which he said he would maintain "a bridge of ships" to Britain. Two days later, the Committee to Defend America by Aiding the Allies, the William A. White Committee, came out in favor of convoys. In his press conference of March 18, FDR was noncommittal about convoys, and at the end of the month, two noninterventionist members of Congress, Sen. Charles Tobey of New Hampshire and Rep. Harry Sauthoff of Wisconsin, introduced a joint Senate-House resolution against convoys. The resolutions never came up for formal votes, but enough opposition was expressed to convoys to give Roosevelt pause. Over the next month, he distinguished between "patrols" and "convoys." He admitted the navy conducted patrols but denied that convoys were part of the American operation. There was the same difference between a convoy and a patrol, he told his press conference on April 25, as between a cow and a horse. "If one looks at a cow and calls it a horse that is all right with the president, but that does not make a cow a horse."

Instead of publicly acknowledging that the navy was convoying American ships, Roosevelt moved stealthily to bring the American navy into the war zone. On April 9, an agreement was reached with the Danish foreign minister placing Greenland inside the American "sphere of cooperative hemisphere defense." Three months later, on July 7, the United States made a similar pledge to Iceland, placing that island, five hundred miles northwest of Britain, officially in the Western Hemisphere. The United States received the right to station its destroyers in naval bases in Iceland from which they escorted American ships bearing Lend-Lease aid to Britain.

The German reaction was predictable, and maybe slower in coming than FDR had hoped for and expected. When the Nazis began attacking American destroyers, Roosevelt used the incidents as reasons formally to convoy vessels bound for Britain. The first German episode occurred on September 4, when a U-boat fired torpedoes at the American destroyer *Greer*. Roosevelt indignantly announced in a radio broadcast of September 11 that the ship had been innocently engaged in carrying passengers and mail to Iceland when "she was then and there attacked by a submarine. . . . I tell you the blunt fact that the German submarine fired first upon this American destroyer without warning and with deliberate design to sink her." He then said that he had responded by ordering the navy to "sink on sight" hostile submarines, and that the navy was now indeed convoying merchant ships.

The facts of the *Greer* case made the navy less the innocent victim of German aggression than Roosevelt had implied. The destroyer had actually received radio word from a British warplane of the presence of a German submarine. The *Greer* had then given chase for the next three and one-half hours, radioing the position of the U-boat to the British plane. The warplane had joined the hunt, during which it dropped four depth charges that missed the submarine. The German boat fired a torpedo which crossed the American vessel about one hundred yards behind. The destroyer responded with eight more depth charges, each of which missed; the submarine replied with another erring torpedo. The chase continued for a few more minutes with the destroyer dropping more depth charges. Finally, the American ship gave up and went on to Iceland.

A more serious incident involving an American destroyer and a German U-boat took place a month later, on the night of October 16–17. A German submarine fired a torpedo which hit the American destroyer *Kearney*, severely damaging it and killing eleven sailors. "America has been attacked," Roosevelt said on the radio on the evening of October 17. He neglected to mention that the *Kearney*, like the *Greer*, had been stalking the submarine and dropping depth charges when it had been torpedoed. Three days later, a U-boat sank the tanker *Salinas*, and the same night the Germans torpedoed and sank the American destroyer *Reuben James*, with the loss of ninety-six sailors.

By November 1941, the United States was involved in an undeclared war with Germany. Beginning with the destroyers-for-bases deal and continuing with Lend-Lease and the extension of the hemisphere zone of defense eastward to Iceland, Roosevelt had aligned America's security with the British while publicly maintaining that these measures were defensive. When the conscription law came up for renewal in July 1941, Roosevelt asked that draftees serve for the duration of the war and requested the authority to send them any place in the world. Extension of Selective Service aroused more passion than the first law, as many congressmen said they had been deceived by a president who no longer would promise to keep conscripts out of harm's way. The America First Committee denounced extending Selective Service as an inevitable step toward war. The issue remained in doubt until the House of Representatives passed the extension by a single vote in mid-September.

THE FIRST SUMMIT

In the midst of these military moves, Roosevelt started a political friendship with British prime minister Churchill. They kept in touch nearly every day by telephone and cable until Roosevelt's death in April 1945. Churchill flattered Roosevelt before the United States entered the war. In their secret telegrams, Churchill addressed him as "Former Naval Person" (referring to the president's stint as assistant secretary of the navy during the First World War). Roosevelt replied in kind, addressing Churchill as "First Sea Lord." The PM spoke of a "special relationship" which bound the "English-speaking peoples." Had he wanted to acknowledge some unpleasant facts, Churchill might have noticed that he used these terms of political endearment more than did the president. Churchill played the courtier because he lacked more forceful ways of compelling the Americans to see things Britain's way. Roosevelt recognized early on that the age of British domination of world politics had passed, to be replaced by a Pax Americana. While happy to have the British support American schemes for a new world order. Roosevelt carefully avoided any commitment to restore Britain to its former position of influence. The British were to recognize American superiority, and if they did not, Roosevelt would use any means at his disposal to force them to.

This pattern became apparent in August 1941 when the two leaders met for the first time on two warships, the *Augusta* and the *Prince of Wales,* in Placentia Bay off the coast of Newfoundland, Canada. Both knew that the United States would someday join the war, and both hoped to create a warm relationship of mutual trust. Each recalled how Woodrow Wilson's hectoring of the Europeans during World War I had wrecked his chances to reform world politics.

The "first summit" lasted from August 9 to August 12, during which the two leaders took up the progress of the war, American participation, and what the postwar world should look like. On June 22, 1941, Hitler had attacked the Soviet Union, and Stalin had responded by obtaining an alliance with the British and sending a mission to the United States which received a promise of a billion dollars in Lend-Lease supplies. Roosevelt and Churchill agreed at the conference to continue the pipeline of supplies to Stalin, thinking that Hitler had made a major mistake in tackling Russia.

They also hammered out a set of principles to use in the war against the Germans. While Roosevelt would make no public declaration that the United States would enter the war, believing that public opinion still would not support him, he did endorse Churchill's suggestion of a joint communiqué, called the Atlantic Charter, which explained the two leaders' vision of the postwar world. They banned "aggression" and upheld the Four Freedoms.

Franklin Roosevelt and Winston Churchill at the Atlantic Conference,
August 1941. *(National Archives)*

But they had more trouble resolving differences over the future of the British empire and the establishment of a new general international organization to replace the League of Nations. The call for "the right for all peoples to choose the form of government under which they will live" brought forth a disclaimer from Churchill, who denied "that the natives of Nigeria or East Africa could by a majority vote choose the form of government under which they live." Leo Amery, an extremely conservative British member of Parliament, decried the charter's "meaningless platitudes and dangerous ambiguities" and concluded that the self-determination clause "was inserted as a reassurance that we are not out to democratize countries that prefer a different form of government." Sir James Grigg, Churchill's former private secretary and now permanent undersecretary of war, brushed aside the anticolonial provision as "great poppycock."

Roosevelt shocked Churchill with a proposal for a new economic order ending the trading preferences Britain and other colonial powers enjoyed with their colonies. The president followed Secretary of State Hull's advice that the way to create American domination of the world's trade after the war was to break the stranglehold of the colonial powers, and he insisted on the end to imperial preference. Churchill was willing to include a statement about ending unfair trade relations so long as it was understood that the United States and Britain applied these provisions primarily to Germany and Japan and left the British system intact. In the final public version of the Atlantic Charter, postwar free trade became a vaguely worded hope. The future of the British empire remained a constant irritant, as the Americans pressed for more commercial access against a determined, but ultimately unsuccessful, British effort to keep them out.

Roosevelt objected when the talk turned to the general international organization. He recollected how the controversy around the League of Nations had sparked a major reaction against Woodrow Wilson's internationalism. He avoided a specific pledge to join a new organization "because of the suspicions and opposition that such a statement . . . would create in the United States." He even encouraged the PM to think that he favored a joint Anglo-American peace force rather than a new universal organization to keep the peace. They then generated a statement pledging the freedom of the seas and the disarmament of aggressor nations "pending the establishment of a wider and permanent system of general security."

On August 14, two days after the meeting ended, the Atlantic Charter was made public. Noninterventionists howled that Roosevelt had had no right to meet with Churchill, and they were certain the two men had struck a private deal to bring the United States into the war. Had they known what Churchill said to the war cabinet upon his return to England, they would have had their worst fears confirmed. The prime minister assured his colleagues that "the president had said he would wage war, but not declare it." Roosevelt, he predicted, "would become more and more provocative . . . he would look for an 'incident' which would justify him in opening hostilities." That, of course, was precisely what Roosevelt looked for in the Atlantic in the fall, but he found his "incident" in the Pacific.

AMERICA'S ASIAN WAR

"For a long time I have believed that our best entrance into the war would be by way of Japan," Secretary of the Interior Harold Ickes confided to his diary in October 1941. Roosevelt, however, moved slowly. For example, he had refrained from cutting off Japan's oil supply, as Ickes urged, because "I simply have not got enough navy to go round, and every little episode in the Pacific means fewer ships in the Atlantic." At the Placentia Bay conference, Churchill tried to get Roosevelt to issue a warning to Japan, but the president refused, saying again that he doubted that public opinion would support a public declaration of opposition to Japan. Roosevelt did, however, believe that the United States had to do something to stop further Japanese advances in China, South Asia, and the Pacific islands.

Japan had waged continuous warfare against China since 1937. The United States had done little publicly to stop the onslaught after Roosevelt had withdrawn from his quarantine speech of October 1937. Secretly, however, the administration had actively encouraged Chinese resistance to Japan. In 1939, Secretary of the Treasury Henry Morgenthau elaborated a scheme to send the Chinese government of Jiang Jieshi (Chiang Kai-shek) an air force bearing Chinese markings but flown by American pilots. At one point in 1940, Morgenthau, Gen. Claire Chennault, and Chinese foreign minister T. V. Soong suggested that these planes take off from Chinese bases and bomb the Japanese, who presumably would know that the United States had supplied the planes and pilots and back away from more war against China. The need to supply Britain with arms stopped this plan, but its serious consideration showed how far the United States would go to stop Japan.

In mid-1940, while the administration's attention was fixed on Europe after the collapse of France, the appointment of the militantly anti-Japanese Henry Stimson as secretary of war signaled opposition to Japan. Stimson, who had led the anti-Japanese boycott movement, continued to call for a firm resistance to Japan.

Japan formally aligned itself with Italy and Germany in the Tripartite Pact of September 1940. The next summer, Tokyo continued its southward march. For the past decade, Japanese expansion had rested on the assumption that the island nation was overcrowded and needed an outlet for its surplus products which the rest of the world could not provide. Europe, in the midst of war, held no prospect of becoming a reliable trading partner for Japan. While the United States might have filled the role, the jeers of friends of China disqualified America as a safe market. Furthermore, the Japanese were smitten with the hope of creating a new economic order, a "Greater Asia Co-Prosperity Sphere" accessible to their goods and emigrants, to replace the dying European empires in Asia. By carefully playing upon anti-European nationalism in South Asia, Japanese planners thought they might generate local support for their economic domination of the region. Japan promised a modest development of South Asia, just enough so Indochina, South China, Malaya, and Indonesia might exchange their raw materials for Japan's finished products. While the remainder of Asia would become a subordinate "little brother," Japanese publicists argued that the rest of the Eastern Hemisphere had more to gain from voluntarily cooperating with a nonwhite Asian empire than from maintaining ties to Europeans who had purposely kept them poor. Japan airily dismissed as utopian dreams nationalist calls for Asian freedom from both European colonialism and Japanese commercial hegemony. Such independence created "chaos" and would upset the "natural hierarchy" of international relations. The model for Japan's grandiose plans for Asia was United States dominance of the economic and political life of Central America and the Caribbean, and Japanese diplomats likened their Co-Prosperity Sphere to the Monroe Doctrine. Washington's complaints about Japanese expansion only seemed to confirm the worst racial suspicions of the Japanese that the white nations of Europe and North America resented the economic, political, and military accomplishments of a successful Asian competitor.

In the summer of 1941, Tokyo faced an impasse in its four-year-old war with China. Although Japan controlled all of the coast, one-third of the territory, and 40 percent of the population of China, the Chinese would not formally surrender. The Nationalists led by Jiang Jieshi and the Communists under Mao Zedong had even patched together an uneasy truce in their civil war in the interests of ridding their homeland of invaders. Unable to win decisively in China, Japanese generals proposed widening the war to China's neighbors in the hopes of further isolating Jiang and forcing him to give in. Natural resources from the rest of Asia (rubber and oil in the south or coal in the vast Siberian wilderness of the north) would help run Japan's industries and armed forces, so Japan's government, led by Prime Minister Hideki Tojo, had to choose between a strike north against the Soviet Union or south against the British, French, and Dutch colonies.

Eventually, the government settled on the southern route in the fall of 1941; complicated relations with the Soviet Union, Europe, and the United States molded its choice. In 1940, Japan and the Soviet Union had signed a nonaggression pact, a mutual pledge not to attack each other, and the Japanese did not wish to break it even after the Germans invaded Russia in June 1941. Japan already had adequate if not abundant supplies of coal, so the booty of Siberia seemed less alluring than the riches available in Indochina, Malaya, New Guinea, and Indonesia. With France and Holland humiliated and occupied by Germany, neither could keep its grip on its Asian colonies, French Indochina (Vietnam, Laos, and Cambodia), or the Dutch East Indies (Indonesia and half of New Guinea). Britain, holding its breath for an expected invasion across the channel, could hardly defend Malaya or its half of New Guinea. In July 1941, Japan took the first step in its southern march by taking over control of French Indochina.

A confusing and provocative American policy encouraged Japanese expansionists to strike before the United States could muster an effective military force. In July, Roosevelt finally threw a bone to the pro-Chinese boycotters and slapped an embargo of trade on Japan, freezing its assets in American banks and barring its access to American petroleum and scrap iron vital to a mechanized army and navy. Roosevelt balanced this threat with the promise of friendlier relations if the two countries could come to terms over the future of China. Rather than break all ties, the president preferred "to slip the noose around Japan's neck and give it a jerk now and then," Ickes reported. Secretary of State Hull spent the fall pressing Japan to accept a cease-fire in the Chinese war. In late November, Japanese ambassador Kichisaburo Nomura learned to his horror that Hull wanted nothing less than the complete evacuation of all the Chinese territory, including the puppet state of Manchukuo (Manchuria), it had seized since 1931. Nomura, a former admiral who still had friends in the navy, told Tokyo that Hull's insistence on withdrawal represented an ultimatum and proof that the American government plotted war against Japan. Stimson watched the failure of the Hull-Nomura talks and noted in his diary the president's whispered warning "that we are likely to be attacked, perhaps by next Monday." The secretary of war decided that "the question was how we should maneuver them into firing the first shot without allowing too much danger to ourselves."

Japan had been readying just such an attack against American possessions in the Philippines, Guam, and Hawaii ever since the freeze order. On September 6, the war cabinet agreed to complete preparations for war against the United States, Great Britain, and the Netherlands. One planner predicted that "it would be well-nigh impossible to expect the surrender of the United States," but he hoped that initial successes might condition Americans to accept a secure Japanese sphere of influence in the Pacific. The naval chief of staff rallied his colleagues with the homely advice that "one cannot obtain a tiger's cub unless he braves a tiger's den." Prime Minister Tojo tried to cheer up a doubting emperor with the reminder that "sometimes a man has to jump with his eyes closed." The chief of naval operations likened Japan's condition to that of a seriously ill patient who could "find a way to life out of a seemingly fatal situation" with a drastic operation. While the generals and admirals knew that an attack on the United States would mean war, they reasoned the way the German high command had in the winter of 1916–1917.

As negotiations stalled in Washington, plans went forward in Japan for a dramatic surprise attack throughout Southeast Asia and Hawaii. A carrier force destined for Pearl Harbor in Hawaii secretly set sail from Japan on December 2, and on Sunday morning, December 7, the admiralty radioed EAST WIND RAIN, the signal to bomb the American fleet. At 7:55 Hawaiian time, a wave of 170 Japanese planes struck the American fleet. Another wave of 190 planes took part in the two-hour-long raid which sunk 7 battleships, killed 2,403 Americans and wounded another 1,178, and destroyed or put out of commission most of the army and navy planes parked on the runways of the island of Oahu. Simultaneously with the attack on Pearl Harbor, the Japanese army launched invasions of the American-held Philippines and British-owned Malaya and Singapore.

Roosevelt went before Congress the next morning to denounce the "dastardly" attack, predicted that December 7 would live as a "day of infamy" in history, and asked for a declaration of war. Stunned noninterventionists were left speechless, and the war resolution passed both houses with only one dissenting vote, that of Montana congresswoman Jeanette Rankin, who had also cast a ballot against the First World War. Three days later, Hitler, invoking his alliance with Japan, declared war on the United States to the great relief of Roosevelt who wanted to be sure that the United States fought Germany as well as Japan.

A furious controversy about Roosevelt's complicity in the Japanese attack erupted immediately and continued unchanged for a generation. Revisionist historians of the entry into the First First World—Harry Elmer Barnes, Charles Beard, and Charles Tansill—charged that the president knew of Japan's plan, baited the Japanese into implementing it, and refrained from warning the defenders of Pearl Harbor, all in the interests of maneuvering the United States into war with Germany by the "back door." Critics pointed to the American practice of deciphering Japanese secret cables for the previous decade and asserted that knowledge of the attack was available to FDR had he chosen to use it. Roosevelt had told Churchill that when America entered the fray, there would be none of the idealistic talk about a "war to end war" which had led to such disillusionment after 1918. The United States would fight in the forties to defend itself, and the attack on Pearl Harbor was the most dramatic demonstration that the Republic was in peril. The America First Committee disbanded in a flurry of apologies, and red-faced noninterventionist congressmen publicly recanted their views in humiliating speeches which called to mind the confessions wrung from the old Bolsheviks during the Moscow purge trials of 1935–1938. From these tantalizing hints, revisionists concluded that Roosevelt had secretly maneuvered the Japanese into administering the kind of shock to the American public he had been unable to find over the previous two years.

Such damning charges naturally touched a tender nerve among the president's admirers, who hastened to his defense. Historians from Basil Rauch, who wrote *Roosevelt: From Munich to Pearl Harbor* (1950), to Herbert Feis, who weighed in with *The Road to Pearl Harbor* (1950), to Gordon Prange, who contributed the most thorough account of Japanese and American actions in *At Dawn We Slept* (1981), to Robert Dallek, who produced the standard synthesis of work on New Deal diplomacy in *Franklin D. Roosevelt and American Foreign Policy* (1979), all deny the particulars of the revisionists' indictment. A specialized study by political scientist Roberta Wohlstetter, *Pearl Harbor: Warning and Decision* (1962), absolves Roosevelt of the most serious charge, that of withholding warning from the naval commander at Hawaii, while detecting flaws in the way the government evaluated intelligence reports. Wohlstetter concludes that the decoded Japanese messages never made much of an impression on officials, who had trouble separating worthwhile information from the ocean of "noise" emanating from the broken codes. Not expecting an attack on Hawaii (they believed Japan might strike further west in the Philippines and Malaya), the administration simply ignored the warnings about the attack on Pearl Harbor.

COALITION WARFARE

However bizarre the idea that Roosevelt conspired with the Japanese, the president was nonetheless relieved to end the anxiety over when the United States would join the fight. He enjoyed a suspension of partisan dissent, at least in the beginning, as the Republican national chairman pledged his support. The president went on the radio two days after the attack on Pearl Harbor to rally the public with the announcement that "every man and woman and child is a partner in the most tremendous undertaking of our American history." No one was happier that the United States no longer stood on the sidelines than Prime Minister Churchill. His immediate thought was "so we had won after all!" He telephoned Roosevelt on the afternoon of December 7. FDR remarked, "We are both in the same boat now," to which Churchill replied, "That certainly simplifies things." The two leaders arranged for Churchill to come to Washington over Christmas to produce a strategy for waging war and producing a peace settlement.

The White House Conference of December 1941–January 1942, code named ARCADIA, was supposed to eliminate the friction which had made life miserable during the First World War. Instead of the United States issuing orders for the rest of the world to follow, jointly developed principles would be in order. Instead of the president remaining aloof, he would make friends with other wartime leaders. But instead of the American military following strategies laid down by the Europeans, United States admirals and generals would tell the Allies how to fight the war.

In practice, Churchill and Roosevelt discovered that they could reach easier agreements on military questions than on political arrangements. Despite the shock of Pearl Harbor, Roosevelt, a committed Atlanticist, never wavered from Adm. Harold Stark's plan of winning the war in Europe before going after Japan. Roosevelt's inclinations were strengthened by the nearly unanimous view of the American generals that the German army was a more formidable foe than Japan. If the Germans lost, Japan would fall, but if the Allies knocked Japan out of the war, Germany would still remain a fighting force. Concentration on Europe first also promised political and personal advantages for the president as Asia had traditionally attracted more attention from Republicans than Democrats. Midwestern isolationist papers such as the *Chicago Tribune,* never friendly to Roosevelt, urged that war be conducted against Japan and Germany be ignored. The president thought there was nothing to gain by following the *Tribune*'s advice. Moreover, if Roosevelt wanted the public to maintain an interest in the active American foreign policy after the war, the United States had to look to Europe. Finally, an Asia-first strategy would mean that General Douglas MacArthur, the imperious commander of the American forces in the Philippines, would take over the direction of the war. Roosevelt could not stand MacArthur, a vain

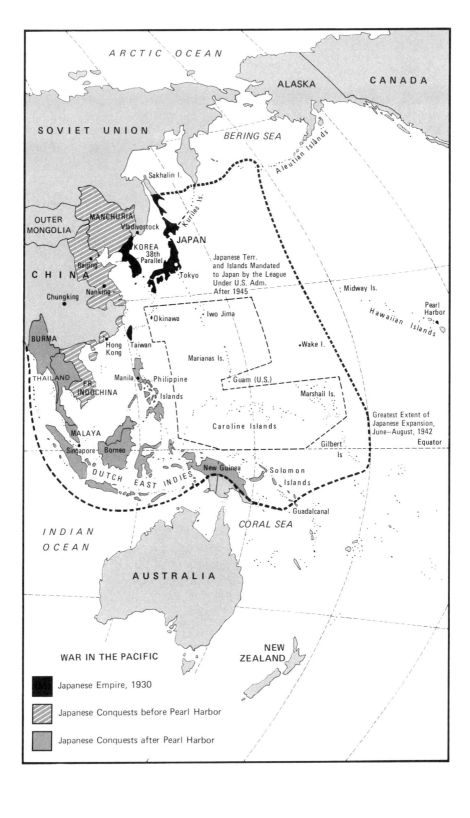

ARCTIC OCEAN

ALASKA   CANADA

SOVIET UNION   BERING SEA

Aleutian Islands

Sakhalin I.

OUTER
MONGOLIA   MANCHURIA
              Vladivostock
                        JAPAN
              KOREA
              38th
              Parallel
CHINA   Tokyo
Beijing
Chungking Nanking

              Okinawa   Iwo Jima

BURMA
          Hong   Taiwan
          Kong
THAILAND
     FR.   Marianas Is.
     INDOCHINA   Manila Philippine
                         Islands

     MALAYA
Singapore Borneo
       DUTCH EAST INDIES
                              New Guinea

INDIAN
OCEAN

                    AUSTRALIA

Midway Is.

Hawaiian Islands

Pearl
Harbor

Wake I.

Guam (U.S.)

Marshall Is.

Caroline Islands

Greatest Extent of
Japanese Expansion,
June–August, 1942
                    Equator

Gilbert
Is

Solomon
Islands

Guadalcanal

CORAL SEA

Japanese Terr.
and Islands Mandated
to Japan by the League
Under U.S. Adm.
After 1945

Kuriles Is.

NEW
ZEALAND

WAR IN THE PACIFIC

Japanese Empire, 1930

Japanese Conquests before Pearl Harbor

Japanese Conquests after Pearl Harbor

authoritarian who wanted someday to be president. FDR did not relish the idea of having such a potential rival in charge of the major American offensive.

At ARCADIA, Roosevelt and Churchill quickly agreed that the European war would take precedence, but they differed on what kind of attack to mount on Germany. The chief of the American staff, George C. Marshall, favored a second front on the continent as quickly as possible, but Churchill, with memories of the carnage of the First World War fresh in his mind, demurred. He offered an invasion of North Africa in which the British and the United States could test their forces but not suffer large casualties, hoping all the while that the Soviet Union would bear the brunt of fighting the Germans. Over the next year, the most nettlesome question among the Soviets, British, and Americans was when and where the Western powers would open a second front against Germany.

Roosevelt and Churchill also parted company over the political goals to be pursued after the war. Seeking an accommodation with his major ally, Roosevelt urged Churchill to commit himself to an open trading system once the war ended, but the prime minister would not drop his fears for the future of the British empire. Just as he had during his meetings the previous August off the coast of Newfoundland, he turned down the Americans' invitation to make specific pledges about a free trading system after the war. The two leaders merely issued a vaguely worded Declaration of the United Nations on January 1, and they invited all of the countries fighting the Axis to join the alliance (the United Nations) and pledge themselves to continue until the Axis powers were defeated.

The war in the Pacific went badly for the United States and Britain in early 1942. By March, the Japanese completed their conquest of the Philippines, Malaya, and Singapore while increasing their hold on China. In June, however, one of the largest naval engagements in history took place near the island of Midway. In three days of aerial warfare, United States navy planes destroyed a Japanese fleet and stopped further Japanese expansion across the Pacific. After the battle, the United States could contain Tokyo and wait for the day in which Germany was defeated.

Combat in Europe also turned in late 1942, as the Germans suffered setbacks in Russia and North Africa. The Nazis had gained against the Russians in their summer offensive, aiming at the oilfields of the Caucasus Mountains, but in November the Red Army counterattacked, surrounding the over one million German troops at the Volga River city of Stalingrad on November 26. At that point, the German army lost its invincible reputation, although two and one-half years of hard fighting remained.

At the same time, a joint Anglo-American force invaded North Africa, sweeping the Germans out of Morocco, Tunisia, Libya, and Algeria within two months. The first American encounter with Germany demonstrated some of the political difficulties of coalition warfare. The United States commander, Dwight David Eisenhower, fearful that the untried American troops would do badly against German veterans, allowed local French authorities to continue in power in return for helping the Allies. Unfortunately, the head of the French military, Gen. Jean Darlan, represented the collaborationist government of Vichy France and had close ties to the Nazis. The "Darlan deal" angered American liberals and the Free French forces led by a former tank commander, Col. Charles de Gaulle, who denounced Eisenhower for helping a "traitor." But President Roosevelt supported the arrangement since he shared Eisenhower's apprehensions about the quality of the American troops. Moreover, Roosevelt had no use for de Gaulle, whom he considered a sort of French MacArthur and a self-important potential dictator. The British, who had sheltered de Gaulle in 1940, had more tolerance for the commander of the Free French than did the Americans, and British officials begged Eisenhower to let de Gaulle take over in North Africa. Yet the American commander would not break his word to Darlan. A serious rift in the alliance was avoided only by accident in late December when a Free French supporter shot and killed Darlan. The new French leader, Gen. Henri Giraud, had fewer connections to the Germans and shared power with de Gaulle, who grudgingly accepted him.

PLANNING FOR THE POSTWAR ERA

The complicated relationship between the British, Americans, and Free French was followed by other more important imbroglios among the United Nations. While formally allied against Germany, the United States, Britain, and the Soviet Union each looked forward to ending the war in a way that would boost its own position in the postwar world. Roosevelt kept a tight rein over foreign policy during the war, relying upon personal advisers Sumner Welles (1933–1943) and Harry Hopkins (1943–1945) to get across his ideas for American domination of postwar diplomacy. The State Department, unable to do much about daily diplomacy, slipped into producing grand plans for the future which never got read. In poor health and fed up with being ignored by Roosevelt, Hull resigned in 1944. His successor, Edward Stettinius, formerly the president of United States Steel, tall, solid, and handsome, made up in white-haired dignity what he lacked in knowledge of foreign affairs.

While the secretaries of state were shunted to the sidelines, a variety of other government bureaus competed to set the postwar policies of the United States. The armed forces, under the leadership of Henry Stimson, developed a clear set of plans for the postwar world. So did the Treasury under Henry

Morgenthau, who pressed proposals for international monetary reform shelved since the London economic conference of 1933. All of the plans tried to ensure American leadership of a stable, predictable postwar world.

In January 1943, Roosevelt met Churchill at Casablanca in recently liberated North Africa. They decided that the United Nations would insist upon an unconditional surrender from the Germans, Italians, and Japan and that none of the Allies would sign a separate peace with the Axis powers. Churchill was unhappy with unconditional surrender, fretting that the plan took away a potential bargaining tool with the Germans, but accepted it as a way of buying Soviet friendship without opening a second front in Europe. In the 1950s, as well, Hanson W. Baldwin, the chief military correspondent for the *New York Times*, described unconditional surrender as "one of the great mistakes of the war." Both Churchill and Baldwin thought that unconditional surrender meant that United States government officials neglected the postwar period for the immediate goal of beating the Axis. Critics took pains to blame Roosevelt and his principal advisers for nonchalantly closing their eyes to the opening chasm between the Anglo-Saxon powers and the Soviet Union.

Nothing could be further from the truth. Planning for the postwar period paid considerable attention to the shape of Soviet-American relations. According to the optimistic assessments of State, War, and Treasury after the war, the Soviet Union, like every other power, would cheerfully acknowledge American leadership after beating the Axis. Roosevelt believed that the needs of the Soviet Union for reconstruction aid would be so great that Stalin would beg Washington for loans and credits. The president also thought that his own easy charm could make Soviet leaders support the American viewpoint. The president consciously wooed Stalin by telegram and in the two meetings they had at Tehran in November 1943 and at Yalta in early February 1945. At both these conferences, Roosevelt befriended the Soviet leader, made jokes at Churchill's expense, and positioned the United States between Great Britain and Russia.

From 1943 on, the United States worked out a plan for the future of Germany. Having twice experienced a German threat to the security of the Western powers, some of Roosevelt's advisers wanted to render Germany incapable of again waging an aggressive war. Treasury Secretary Henry Morgenthau believed that Germany should be split into at least five different nations, each one of which would be stripped of its industrial capabilities. The Morgenthau plan won acceptance from the White House before a meeting with Churchill at Ottawa, Canada, in August 1944. The prime minister, however, thought that the dismemberment of Germany would leave a vacuum in central Europe—one which the Soviet Union might rush to fill. The American military leadership supported the British position, with Stim-

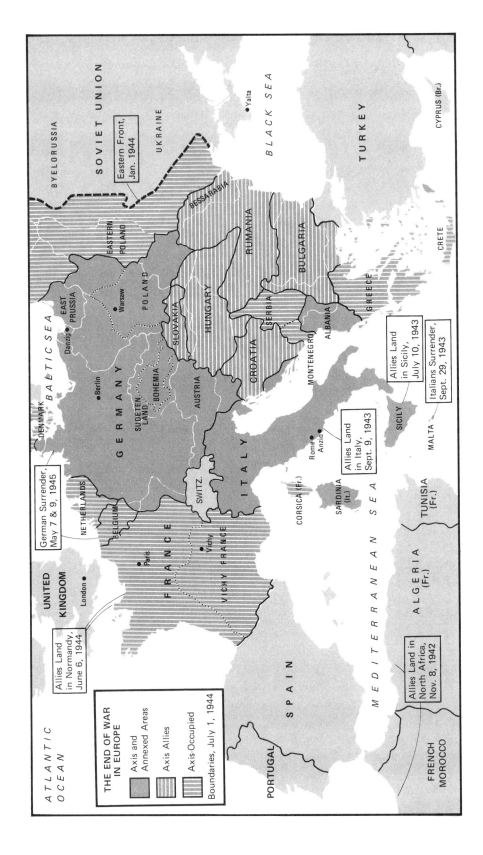

THE END OF WAR
IN EUROPE

Axis and
Annexed Areas

Axis Allies

Axis-Occupied

Boundaries, July 1, 1944

ATLANTIC
OCEAN

SOVIET UNION

BYELORUSSIA

UKRAINE

Eastern Front,
Jan. 1944

Yalta

BLACK SEA

TURKEY

CYPRUS (Br.)

BALTIC SEA

EASTERN
POLAND

BESSARABIA

RUMANIA

BULGARIA

CRETE

EAST
PRUSSIA

Danzig

POLAND

Warsaw

SLOVAKIA

HUNGARY

SERBIA

ALBANIA

GREECE

DENMARK

Berlin

GERMANY

SUDETEN-
LAND

BOHEMIA

AUSTRIA

CROATIA

MONTENEGRO

Allies Land
in Sicily,
July 10, 1943

Italians Surrender,
Sept. 29, 1943

German Surrender,
May 7 & 9, 1945

SWITZ.

ITALY

SICILY

MALTA

NETHERLANDS

BELGIUM

Rome

Anzio

Allies Land
in Italy,
Sept. 9, 1943

UNITED
KINGDOM

London

FRANCE

Paris

Vichy

VICHY FRANCE

CORSICA (Fr.)

SARDINIA
(It.)

MEDITERRANEAN SEA

TUNISIA
(Fr.)

Allies Land
in Normandy,
June 6, 1944

SPAIN

ALGERIA
(Fr.)

Allies Land in
North Africa,
Nov. 8, 1942

PORTUGAL

FRENCH
MOROCCO

son and Marshall, chairman of the Joint Chiefs of Staff, distressed at the cost of occupying a Germany which no longer was the engine of central Europe. A permanent American presence might be called for. Marshall opted for a quick transition of Germany back into regular membership in the European community. To break up Germany smacked of the kind of vengeance imposed after the First World War, and it might inhibit a potential market for American goods.

THE HOME FRONT

The memory of the First World War affected domestic policy as well after December 1941. The government resumed control over production, prices, and wages. Business executives joined labor leaders on the War Resources Board, the War Labor Board, the War Production Board, the Office of Production Management, and the Office of Price Administration—all of which were designed to coordinate production and assure labor peace. In return for government guarantees of full employment and price stability, the American Federation of Labor and the Congress of Industrial Organizations agreed to forgo strikes throughout the war. Acquiescence was not universal as John L. Lewis, head of the United Mine Workers and one of the founders of the CIO, a longtime foe of FDR, called his men out of the coal mines in early 1944. Threat of government takeover of the pits brought an end to the walkout but left a bitter legacy.

While inviting labor into the government, FDR acknowledged that the war signaled the end of efforts at liberal reform as he shifted from "Dr. New Deal" to "Dr. Win the War." Scores more business executives flocked to Washington, often serving as "dollar a year men" to award war contracts to plants only beginning to emerge from the Depression. Congress decreed that 25 percent of the value of all contracts go to businesses worth less than $2 million, but investigations by oversight committees revealed that many major firms like General Motors, Ford, or General Electric had surreptitiously acquired orders slated for small businesses.

While Republicans might privately take heart at the New Deal's demise, they did not make up as much electoral ground as their predecessors did in the 1918 mid-term election. They voiced few complaints over FDR's internationalist foreign policy. The president retained an uncanny knack for mollifying defeated foes, and he enlisted the 1940 GOP nominee, Wendell Willkie, in the campaign for public support. Willkie returned from a round-the-world trip in 1943 to publish *One World,* a book whose title expressed his and the president's expectations for the future. The 1942 congressional elections drew the lowest voter turnout, 43 percent, in modern history. The GOP narrowed the gap in the House of Representatives to 221 Democrats against 211 Republicans while Senate Democrats held a 57-to-38 majority. In 1944, Roosevelt, concealing his failing health, ran for a fourth term. Immense popularity among soldiers offset his ebbing appeal in traditional Republican strongholds of the Midwest to enable him to defeat New York governor Thomas Dewey with 53 percent of the popular vote, his lowest margin.

For vice-president he dropped Henry A. Wallace, whose outspoken liberalism annoyed conservative Southern Democrats. FDR coyly played with several potential vice-presidential candidates, including Wallace, liberal Supreme Court justice William O. Douglas, and conservative South Carolina senator James F. Byrnes, before settling on a safe choice, Missouri senator Harry Truman. An apparently colorless product of the Kansas City Democratic machine, Truman had been a quietly loyal New Dealer whose only claim to fame had been chairmanship of the Senate committee investigating the conduct of the war. The president seldom consulted with him during the fall campaign and virtually ignored him after the fourth inauguration on January 20, 1945.

The government engaged in an ugly reprise of the persecution of minorities which had besmirched domestic life during the First World War. This time Americans of Japanese descent suffered the most. Anti-Japanese hysteria swept across the west coast after Pearl Harbor as congressmen, state legislators, and mayors accused local Japanese citizens of espionage, sabotage, and sending radio messages to the imperial fleet supposedly standing offshore in preparation for an invasion. In January 1942, Roosevelt joined the posse when he signed an executive order arresting all Japanese-Americans and sending them to "relocation camps" scattered across the country from California to Arizona to Colorado to Louisiana. United States marshals pounded on the doors of some 110,000 men, women, and children, giving them seventy-two hours to close their shops and houses, collect one suitcase, and board buses and trains for the trip to the prisons which would be their homes for the next two years. The only escape was offered young men of military age who could join the armed forces for the war in Europe against Germany and Italy.

No similar actions were taken against Americans of German and Italian ancestry, and naturally, the Japanese-Americans affirmed their loyalty to the United States and resented their mistreatment. For a generation after the war they hoped for an official apology, but none came. Earl Warren, California's attorney general who had pressed for the deportation, became chief justice of the United States in 1954. As leader of a liberal court devoted to protecting civil liberties, he privately acknowledged "a great injustice against the Japanese." Most officials were unrepentant, though. A House subcommittee held hearings on the subject in the summer of 1982. Former Assistant Secretary of War John J. McCloy, then eighty-eight, proudly defended the relocation camps as "necessary in time of war."

Political dissenters fared better than the Japanese and probably better than their counterparts in the First World War. The nation had not grown more tolerant, but the fighting attracted broader support than the 1917–1918 involvement. Where Socialist party leaders had gone to jail for denouncing the earlier conscription law, the Communist party of the United States earnestly backed the campaign to defeat nazism and fascism once Germany attacked the Soviet Union. Party secretary Earl Browder proclaimed, "Communism is twentieth-century Americanism." Party members gleefully enlisted in the armed forces, while those who remained at home helped sell war bonds, collect burn dressings, and enforce blackouts. Many other former noninterventionists dropped their public dissent from official foreign policy in the aftermath of Pearl Harbor. While some shared the worries of gadfly historian Charles Beard that the war would "militarize" American society, most kept their doubts to themselves. Pacifists of military age who opposed all wars and refused service as noncombatants fared as poorly as the Japanese. Thousands went to jail.

REACTION TO THE HOLOCAUST

Opposition to Henry Morgenthau's plan for the dismemberment of Germany drew strength from a darker motive—anti-Semitism. Stimson and Marshall muttered that the treasury secretary was incapable of adopting an objective stance toward the problems of Germans because he was Jewish. Although Jews suffered the most from the Second World War and were the targets of the Nazi "final solution of the Jewish problem," the murder of all Jews in Europe, the United States did next to nothing to alleviate their plight. News of the death camps, which were killing thousands of Jews a day, reached Washington in 1942. Roosevelt received a continuous stream of impassioned pleas from Jewish leaders in the United States to do something about the death camps. One described the gas chamber at Auschwitz: "It holds 2,000. . . . When everybody is inside the heavy doors are closed. . . . After three minutes everybody in the chamber is dead." Rabbi Stephen C. Wise asked the president at least to state publicly that he knew of the Nazi extermination policy and warn the Nazi leaders that they would be held accountable for their campaign of murder. Other Jewish leaders begged the secretary of war to send airplanes to bomb the extermination camps. In both cases, Washington replied with bureaucratic evasions. The State Department did not change usual visa practices. The War Department refused to bomb the rail lines leading to the extermination camps. Assistant Secretary of War

McCloy said attacking the camps would be "impracticable, because it could be executed only by diversion of considerable air support." He told the World Jewish Congress that Allied attention to the Nazi atrocities "might provoke even more vindictive actions by the Germans." He did not indicate what more the Germans might do.

Roosevelt himself, while professing personal sympathy to the Jewish leaders, may have also believed that he risked losing general American support for the war effort if he made a special appeal for the Jews. According to public opinion polls, anti-Semitism reached a new high in the United States in 1945, with 55 percent of the population expressing anti-Jewish prejudices. Roosevelt, a consummate judge of public sentiment, thought that if he were to make a special plea for Jews, other Americans would no longer think the war was their fight.

ECONOMIC PLANS

Morgenthau had more success in drafting plans for a postwar international monetary order at the conference of the major economic powers which convened at Bretton Woods, New Hampshire, in August 1944. Significantly, the Soviet Union, skittish about being swallowed by a capitalist economy, sent no representatives to this meeting designed to breathe life into the proposals for a multilateral trading order at the end of the war. The British sent a large delegation in which John Maynard Keynes took the lead in pressing a plan for a new international currency. Morgenthau, for his part, would not go as far as Keynes in creating an international source of money, preferring instead that nations bow before American economic power and fix their money in terms of the dollar. This view prevailed in the new International Monetary Fund (IMF) created at Bretton Woods to assure that every nation's currency was freely convertible into that of every other potential trading partner. Backed with capital of $10 billion, half of which came from the United States, the IMF was supposed to lend money to nations which temporarily found themselves short of foreign reserves. In return for its loans, the IMF could demand changes in a borrower's economic and trade policies—insisting that it balance its budget, allow its citizens to hold foreign currency, permit convertibility of its currency into other money, and drop restrictive tariffs. At a time when the United States alone seemed in a good position to export goods, the IMF would help produce a congenial trading environment for American enterprise. Bretton Woods created a companion organization for the IMF in the International Bank for Reconstruction and Development, or World Bank, a multinational organization with power to finance longer-term programs than those covered by the IMF. The memory of abuses in private lending during the twenties combined with the fear that the needs for reconstruction af-

ter the Second World War would be more than could be met by private banks
to lay the ground for the government-sponsored World Bank.

THE FUTURE OF ASIA

American plans for the postwar Far East called for the replacement of the
Japanese empire with a stable and predictable region under the influence
of the United States and a China backed by America. The president detected
a "warlike" streak in the Japanese national character. He sustained a three-
year correspondence with an anthropologist at the Smithsonian Institution
about the advisability of "cross-breeding the Japanese" with "gentler" Pacific
islanders. More practically, FDR encouraged the ambitions of China's leader,
Jiang Jieshi.

Roosevelt had a soft spot in his heart for Generalissimo Jiang, despite dis-
couraging reports coming from his adviser in China, Joseph W. Stilwell. In
1943 and 1945, Gen. Stilwell concluded soon after his arrival in Chungking
that the Nationalist government was ridden with embezzlement and bribery
and commanded no popularity. He mocked Jiang to all who would listen as
"the peanut" and other epithets, some unprintable. By 1944, the complaints
of the Nationalists were so loud that Roosevelt had to replace Stilwell as adviser to Jiang. He chose as ambassador one of the most unsuitable envoys in
the twentieth century, Patrick C. Hurley. A former Republican governor from
Oklahoma, Hurley knew nothing about China but compensated with loud
rebel yells, slaps on the back, and viselike handshakes. The new ambassador
decided that Jiang was indeed the savior of his country and that his reputation had been blackened by disloyal Foreign Service officers tricked by the
Communists they had visited in their mountain headquarters in Yenan.

Roosevelt tolerated Hurley and may have shared his enthusiasm for the
generalissimo, but the president also acknowledged Jiang's corruption and
unpopularity. In a way, these deficiencies made the Chinese leader a more
pliable friend of the United States. Roosevelt thought that someday China
could become a great power like Britain or the Soviet Union; in the meantime, the Chinese depended upon Washington for aid and political guidance. With Japan out of the picture, America could run the affairs of the Far
East with the aid of the Chinese.

Roosevelt also looked forward to the end of the Dutch, French, and
British empires in Asia, which had discriminated against American products.
His scorn for colonialism strained Europeans nerves. When British colonial
secretary Oliver Stanley called at the White House late in the war, FDR
taunted him: "I do not want to be unkind or rude to the British, but in 1841,
when you acquired Hong Kong, you did not acquire it by purchase." An angry Stanley shot back, "Let me see, Mr. President, that was about the time

A haggard FDR flanked by Winston Churchill and Josef Stalin at Yalta, February 1945. *(National Archives)*

of the Mexican war, wasn't it?" FDR knew that the United States would have to bear the cost of restoring the economies of the imperial powers in Europe, and he shrank from the prospect of American aid being squandered on their Asian territories. Finally, American experts on colonial matters considered the independence of the Asian possessions a foregone conclusion, so why waste the time, energy, and money restoring the Europeans' colonies which soon would send them home?

The easiest colony to make independent was the Dutch outpost in the East Indies. The Netherlands, a minor power, occupied by the Germans and dependent upon the goodwill of the United States for its postwar recovery, could not hold Indonesia. The British and the French also could be persuaded to sacrifice the Dutch if they could maintain their hold on their own colonies. So in 1944 American policy was to evict the Dutch from Indonesia after the war, and this goal was accomplished in 1949.

The French in Indochina presented a more difficult case. Roosevelt, who could not abide General de Gaulle and thought the French decadent for their 1940 surrender to Germany, approved a plan in 1943 for placing French Indochina under the trusteeship of China at the war's end. The Free French objected and gained support from Britain, which hoped to restore its own power in the Far East. Stimson's War Department and American headquarters in the China-Burma-India theater also thought the eviction of the French from Indochina would make it harder to win the war against Japan. By the middle of 1944, Roosevelt retreated from his plan for a Chinese caretaker for Indochina, and at the Ottawa Conference in August, he gutted his trusteeship plan and accepted the French return under the condition that they promise eventual freedom for Indochina.

In the case of the British empire in the Far East, the United States pressured Churchill for an early independence for India. Since previous British governments had been willing to grant Indian independence, Churchill reluctantly went along. But the prime minister wanted to keep the remainder of the British empire intact. British experts on joint Anglo-American committees studying postwar problems fought a ferocious and ultimately successful rear guard action to keep their Asian possessions.

Americans continued their efforts to displace the British from the oil-rich regions of the Middle East. American petroleum engineers discovered vast reserves in the deserts of Arabia in the mid-thirties. By 1939, a consortium of American firms lifted nineteen thousand barrels of petroleum per day. Officers of the Arabian-American Oil Company (Aramco) worried that the British might reexert their traditional influence in Arabia once combat ended. A 1944 Office of Strategic Services report concurred the "century-old policy of regarding Arabia as a British sphere of influence" hindered American interest. Noting a "delicate balance" of oil supply and demand Interior

Secretary Harold Ickes fought for the creation of an American-financed Trans-Arabian Pipe (TAP) line. Churchill objected to Roosevelt that "the United States has a desire to deprive us of our oil assets in the Middle East." FDR did nothing to ease British anxieties.

YALTA

D-Day, June 6, 1944. Five hundred thousand American, British, French, Canadian, and other Allied troops successfully invaded northern France, and the end of the war was in sight. Churchill, Roosevelt, and Stalin agreed to meet at Yalta on the Crimean Sea in early February 1945 to decide what the future would look like. In ten days of hard bargaining, the Big Three agreed that Germany would pay some reparations, but not the entire cost of the war. They decided that the new international organization, the United Nations, would be a universal organization, but the major powers—the United States, Great Britain, the Soviet Union, France, and China—would be permanent members of the Security Council. Each of the great powers could veto any resolution of the body. They also seemed to agree on the future of Eastern Europe where the Soviet Union was guaranteed "friendly" governments on its borders. No end of problems were created by this provision, since the Soviet Union also agreed to permit "free elections" in Poland. In fact, the Yalta Conference left more issues unresolved than it settled. Roosevelt, however, had few reservations; he was sure that the personal bond between himself and the other leaders could smooth over the rough spots in the alliance. They would soon meet after Germany was defeated to tie up the loose ends of the war. Remembering the First World War experience, he favored a series of conferences at the end instead of one big peace meeting which all of the major wartime leaders would attend.

The one thing finally settled at Yalta concerned the war in the Far East. In return for a Soviet pledge to enter the war against Japan three months after the war in Europe ended, the Western powers made territorial concessions to the Soviets in Asia, granting them the southern half of Sakhalin Island from Japan and a return of the old Russian railroad in Manchuria. Stalin sweetened the deal when he concluded a treaty of friendship with the Nationalist Chinese and restrained the Communists from resuming the civil war.

TRUMAN BECOMES PRESIDENT

Roosevelt was a sick man at Yalta. His face grew gray, and his strength was gone. Nevertheless, he hardly expected to die within two months of his return. When news of his fatal stroke flashed across the world on April 12, Hitler rejoiced, thinking it a sign of divine intervention for the Nazi cause. Vice-President Harry S. Truman, a former haberdasher and Missouri senator chosen by Roosevelt as a safe, inoffensive running mate in 1944, told reporters that he felt "as if the sun, moon, and the stars," had just fallen on him and asked for their prayers. Untutored in foreign affairs, kept in the dark about the most important military secret of the war—the atomic bomb—Truman did not have Roosevelt's confidence that his personal conduct of diplomacy would preserve an effective anti-Axis coalition.

The new president determined to mask his uncertainties in international relations with displays of toughness and temper toward Allied diplomats who might take advantage of him. Barely a week in office, Truman met Soviet foreign minister Molotov in the White House and dressed him down for his government's hostility toward non-Communist politicians in liberated Poland. "I've never been talked to that way before in my life," Molotov complained when the new president finished his harangue. "Keep your agreements and you won't be talked to that way," Truman replied. The San Francisco meeting of the United Nations organization, which opened on April 24, saw more bad blood between the Soviets and the United States. The American assistant secretary of state for Latin America, Nelson Rockefeller, pressed for the admission of Argentina despite that government's Fascist inclinations. Surprised Soviet diplomats saw the invitation to the Latin American republic as a signal that the Americans would have their way in the postwar world.

ATOMIC DIPLOMACY

Two weeks later, on May 7, Germany surrendered, and the Big Three resolved to meet again in July at the former headquarters of the German general staff at Potsdam, outside Berlin. At that encounter, they intended to discuss the future of Europe and the war against Japan. Although Germany had collapsed, some military planners thought that the war in Asia might take another five years and require an invasion of the home islands of Japan.

The plans did not account for the dreadful power of a new superweapon, the atomic bomb. Produced by the Manhattan Project, the most expensive weapons-development program undertaken to that time, the atomic bomb represented three years of work by approximately one hundred twenty thousand people at a cost of $2 billion. American officials shared scientific information about atomic energy with their British counterparts, but they did not breathe a word to the Soviet Union. The first atomic test took place on July 16. As a light brighter than a thousand suns flashed across the desert sky, scientific director J. Robert Oppenheimer thought of a line from the *Bhagavad-Gita,* an Indian holy book: "I am become Death, Destroyer of Worlds." General Leslie Groves, Manhattan Project supervisor, described the event in a cable to Truman at Potsdam: "The test was successful beyond the most optimistic expectations of anyone. . . . I estimate the energy generated to be in excess of the equivalent of 15,000 to 20,000 tons of TNT." Stimson watched Truman read Groves's message and reported that "the president was tremendously pepped up by it."

Encouraged by a sense of American invincibility, Truman hardened his language toward Stalin. "I shall state frankly what I think," he told the Soviet leader. Churchill found him "emphatic and decisive . . . telling [the Soviets] as to certain demands that they absolutely could not have." At an informal break in the conversations, Truman mentioned to Stalin that the United States now possessed a weapon of "awesome destructiveness." The Soviet nonchalantly wished the Americans well against Japan. He probably knew of the Manhattan Project through surreptitious agents, resented Anglo-American attempts to keep atomic secrets, and feigned indifference to bluff the Americans. Had Truman hoped to use "atomic diplomacy" to force the Soviets to accept American suggestions, the remainder of the Potsdam Conference disabused him. Like Yalta, Potsdam left unresolved many major issues, including the future of occupied Germany, the amount of reparations to be paid to the Allies, and an agenda for a peace conference. Unlike Yalta, the leaders could not agree to meet again. They never did.

Afraid of settling every problem in a grand assembly on the pattern of the 1919 Paris Conference, Truman set his hopes on a series of more modest ministerial discussions. He authorized his newly appointed secretary of state, former South Carolina senator James F. Byrnes, who had been a rival for the 1944 vice-presidential nomination, to reach accommodations with suspicious coalition partners. Like Truman, Byrnes erroneously assumed that "the bomb assured ultimate success in negotiations."

On August 6, two weeks after the Potsdam Conference broke up in disarray, the United States Army Air Force B-29 *Enola Gay* dropped an atomic bomb, nicknamed "Little Boy," on the mid-sized Japanese industrial city of Hiroshima, instantly killing at least eighty thousand people. Later studies of the bombing record "that the whole city was ruined instantaneously." Survivors of the blast discovered "a heap of debris and corpses and a stunned mass of injured humanity." A grocer recalled a procession of thousands of injured people slowly leaving the site of the conflagration. "They held their arms bent and their skin . . . hung down . . . [they looked] like walking ghosts. They didn't look like people of this world." Another eyewitness observed people "so broken and confused that they moved and behaved like automatons."

The devastation at Hiroshima.
(National Archives)

The next day the Soviet Union made good its Yalta pledge and declared war on Japan as its armies crossed the border between Siberia and Manchuria. On the 9th another B-29 made the twenty-five-hundred mile flight from Saipan to detonate a plutonium-based bomb on Nagasaki, and more than sixty-thousand Japanese died. Emperor Hirohito now told his government that the war was lost and they had to move more quickly on the desultory surrender negotiations which had been stalled since June over the issue of whether Hirohito should retain his title. The government now dropped its request for reassurances, threw itself to the mercy of the Allies, and announced that it had accepted the principle of unconditional surrender. On September 2, a sad-faced Adm. Sadatoshi Tomioka climbed aboard the American battleship *Missouri* to sign a surrender document and place himself and his country at the mercy of Gen. Douglas MacArthur, who headed the Allied delegation.

EFFECTS OF THE WAR

So ended the most destructive war in history. Forty million soldiers and civilians were dead, and an additional ten million refugees wandered forlornly across Europe and Asia. Production had stopped in much of Western Europe, Germany, the Soviet Union, and Japan. Hitler's Thousand Year Reich lasted only twelve, but it managed to commit such crimes as to numb the imagination and be summarized in a single capitalized word: Holocaust. Japan failed in its bid to organize East Asia, and the atomic firestorms which highlighted the end of the Japanese empire also highlighted the dangers of the postwar world. Now humanity seemed nearly able to kill everyone on the planet.

The end of the war saw the United States finally become the world's foremost power, confirming what nationalist and internationalist thinkers had predicted, longed for, and fretted over. Unlike the end of the First World War, when Americans faced the prospect of sharing their newfound authority with European coalition partners who could not bring themselves to acknowledge their time had passed, American planners expected that other nations would beg for leadership from the New World. While the other belligerents had seen their cities bombed and plants leveled, the war enabled the United States to snap out of the Depression. At the beginning of 1940, over ten million American adults had no jobs; in 1945, there was a shortage of workers. The armed forces had fourteen million men and women in uniform, and an additional five million people had taken positions on the assembly lines producing the weapons for "the arsenal of democracy." While fearing a return to the breadlines, economic planners hoped that an open trading system would keep up high production. The war also continued the expansion of the federal government begun by the New Deal. The government spent more than $200 billion in each of the four war years, 1942–1945, nearly eight times more than it had spent before. More significant perhaps were the thousands of experts who flocked to the capital to wage war and prepare for peace. The State, War, Navy, and Treasury departments contended with each other and specially created agencies such as the Office of Strategic Service (the overseas espionage office), the Office of War Information (the propaganda service), the Office of Price Administration, and the War Production Board, whose functionaries hoped to continue their work in the peacetime era.

Franklin D. Roosevelt, who had presided over this untidy growth, no longer was alive to soothe hurt feelings in the United States or across the Atlantic with his bonhomie. Some historians, like Gar Alperovitz in *Atomic Diplomacy* (1965), argue that the change from Roosevelt to Truman caused many of the subsequent disappointments for American diplomacy. True, but the answer is not so simple. At the end of the war, Americans' hopes exceeded the ability of any nation to realize them. The real sense of obligation former coalition partners had to America could not mask equally strong feelings of envy and fear for the future.

CHAPTER TEN

The Early Cold War, 1945–1952

As Europeans poked through the rubble left by the Second World War, Americans interested in foreign affairs assumed that their former partners would continue to accept aid and guidance from Washington. But other nations, suspicious of American ambitions, wanting to regain their positions in world markets, and bearing old grudges, surprised old friends by not marching to Washington's drum. The Grand Alliance which had defeated Hitler fell apart in a chorus of charges of bad faith, and the new United Nations organization never restored the camaraderie of wartime.

By January 1947, and probably earlier, political leaders, diplomats, and publicists on both sides of the Atlantic knew that the United States and the Soviet Union were scrambling for advantages against each other in Europe and Asia. Two years later, the United States broke the traditional ban against permanent alliances and concluded its first peacetime military pact with ten European countries and Canada—the North Atlantic Treaty. Shortly afterward, the Soviet Union exploded an atomic bomb, and serious-minded Americans and Europeans trembled that a new world war, fought with atomic weapons, was about to break out between America and Russia. In June 1950, a different sort of war, directly involving the United States but not the Soviet Union, did erupt in Korea.

What caused the world of 1950 to look so different from the rosy predictions of the wartime Washington? Was it a failure of vision? The intractable problem that the future can never be known? The belligerence of the Soviets? The arrogance and ineptitude of American diplomacy? A combination of these? Or something else?

These questions divided politicians and citizens at the time, and they set historians at one another's throats for a generation afterward. The battle-fields ran between supporters of American foreign policy who argued that the Cold War came about because of Soviet imperialism, and critics, who laid much of the blame for postwar tension on American misconduct. The critics were divided among themselves. One conservative-minded observer, John Spanier, writing in *United States Foreign Policy* (1960), blames the Cold War on the ineptitude of Americans, who had underestimated what the United States would have to do to preserve its leadership. As America dal-lied, the Soviets prepared for power.

A more liberal critic of immediate postwar American foreign policy, Sen. J. William Fulbright (D., Ark.), pointed to the "arrogance of power." Armed with a monopoly on the atomic bomb, and leading the most powerful econ-omy in the world, Americans brushed aside the natural aspirations and fears of the Soviet Union and even the Western European nations. Their reac-tions were not what the Americans predicted; instead of supinely accepting the leadership offered by the United States, the rest of the world thumbed their noses at the upstarts.

A radical interpretation of American foreign policy after the Second World War went further. In *The Politics of War* (1968) and *The Limits of Power* (1972), Gabriel Kolko charges that it was the nature of the American capi-talistic economic and social system to expand. As the leading advocate of pri-vate ownership, America needed a stable, predictable world, eager for im-ports, to avert a resumption of the Depression. The United States wanted to put down nationalist movements around the world. Groups such as the Vi-etminh in Indochina or the Greek revolutionary movement threatened the open market system. No admirer of Stalin's brutal dictatorship, Kolko argues that the United States joined with the Soviet Union to put down the forces of revolutionary nationalism. Kolko explains that while the Soviet Union posed as a revolutionary state yearning for the victory of the Communist par-ties of the world, Josef Stalin often tacitly acquiesced in American plans to stop the forces of change. This accommodation did not satisfy Americans, who insisted on having their way. Consequently, the Cold War shaped East-West relations for the next two decades.

THE FIRST YEAR OF PEACE

President Truman came to office with little experience in foreign affairs and chose to rely on the advice of his cabinet and ambassador to Russia, Averell Harriman. Yet his newly appointed secretary of state, James F. Byrnes, re-sented Truman's accession to the presidency, believing that the Democrats should have selected him as their candidate. The secretary, unlike the president, expected good relations with Moscow.

The Soviets could not easily be mollified in the second half of 1945; they remembered Anglo-American mistreatment during the war. The United States and Britain had delayed opening a second front in Europe until 1944. An American OSS (Office of Strategic Services) official, Allen Dulles, had held secret surrender talks with the German commander in northern Italy in April 1945, generating fears among the suspicious Soviets that the Western powers might conclude a separate peace with the Germans. Most frightening of all, from Moscow's perspective, the Americans had kept the British informed of the Manhattan Project developing the atomic bomb but had not provided information to Moscow until Truman's nonchalant comment during a break in the Potsdam Conference. Josef Stalin and Vyacheslav Molotov worried that Britain and America would pay less attention to Soviet security needs now that Germany no longer posed a threat. American reliance on the monopoly of the atomic bomb to force the Soviets to see things Washington's way did nothing to allay Moscow's anxieties.

Byrnes failed dramatically to revive the coalition spirit in the fall and winter of 1945–1946. In September, he met with the British, Soviet, French, and Chinese foreign ministers in London to write peace treaties for Hungary, Bulgaria, Rumania, and Finland, all former allies of Germany. The Soviet Red Army had occupied the first three countries and part of Finland during the war, and Byrnes tried unsuccessfully to dislodge the Russians at the London Conference. Molotov refused to budge, despite, or perhaps because of, Byrnes's ostentatious references to American atomic weapons, which the Soviets did not yet possess. The five foreign ministers could not even agree on the wording of a communiqué to be released to the press.

Byrnes dropped "atomic diplomacy" when he went to Moscow for conversations with Molotov and Stalin in December. Despite the chilly Russian winter, the secretary of state thought he achieved more than had been accomplished in London. The Soviet leaders reiterated their determination to have friendly governments along their borders, but Stalin allowed that "perhaps the Bulgarian parliament could be advised to include some members of the loyal opposition in the new government" and suggested "it might be possible to . . . satisfy Mr. Byrnes" about Rumania. Byrnes perked up at these Soviet concessions, but the Russians remained firmly in charge in Eastern Europe. George Kennan, the second in command at the American embassy in Moscow, called the Bulgarian and Rumanian accommodations "fig leaves of democratic procedure to hide the nakedness of Stalinist dictatorship."

The president also was less hopeful than his secretary, and Truman resented Byrnes's habit of not keeping him more abreast of ongoing negotiations than could be learned from reading the newspapers. "It was more like

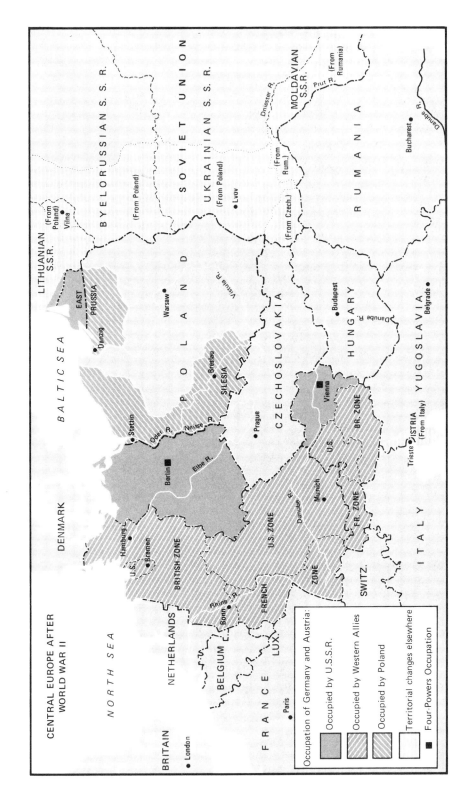

CENTRAL EUROPE AFTER
WORLD WAR II

NORTH SEA

BRITAIN

• London

BALTIC SEA

LITHUANIAN
S.S.R.

(From
Poland)
Vilna •

BYELORUSSIAN S.S.R.

SOVIET UNION

UKRAINIAN S.S.R.

(From Poland)

(From Poland)

Lvov •

Dniester R.

(From
Rum.)

Prut R.

(From
Rumania)

MOLDAVIAN
S.S.R.

Danube R.

Bucharest •

DENMARK

EAST
PRUSSIA

Danzig •

Stettin •

Oder R.

Neisse R.

Warsaw •

Vistula R.

P O L A N D

(From Czech.)

R U M A N I A

Breslau •

SILESIA

CZECHOSLOVAKIA

Prague •

H U N G A R Y

Budapest •

Danube R.

Belgrade •

Berlin ■

Elbe R.

Vienna ■

BR. ZONE

Y U G O S L A V I A

Hamburg •

U.S.

Bremen •

BRITISH ZONE

U.S. ZONE

Danube R.

Munich •

U.S.

FR. ZONE

Trieste •

ISTRIA
(From Italy)

NETHERLANDS

BELGIUM

Bonn •

Rhine R.

FRENCH
ZONE

ZONE

SWITZ.

I T A L Y

LUX.

F R A N C E

Paris •

Occupation of Germany and Austria:

Occupied by U.S.S.R.

Occupied by Western Allies

Occupied by Poland

Territorial changes elsewhere

■ Four-Powers Occupation

one partner in business telling the other that his business trip was progressing well and not to worry," Truman grumbled. The president got angrier when Byrnes made a radio report of his trip upon landing in Washington without first coming by the White House. When the secretary finally did present himself on the presidential yacht, he got a dressing down from Truman who rebuked him for letting the public know things "I had never heard of." The chief executive went on to say that he "would not tolerate such conduct." Relations between the president and secretary of state barely improved for the rest of 1946.

Truman had other things to worry about besides Byrnes. The economy was in a mess, but not because depression had returned, as many economists had predicted. Instead, consumers rushed to buy the houses, cars, refrigerators, shoes, and clothes they had wanted during the thirties but could not purchase because they lacked jobs and could not have during the war because of rationing. Prices shot up 18 percent in 1946 after Truman bowed to business pressure to disband the Office of Price Administration in the fall of 1945. Labor unions, freed of their no-strike pledge, stopped work in the steel, rail, and auto industries. Lacking FDR's charm, Truman had no rapport with labor leaders. He toyed with the idea of drafting strikers into the armed forces to make them work and even wrote out the text of a radio broadcast to veterans urging them to help him lynch union leaders. His aides persuaded him that such demagogy might not calm public passions, and he never delivered it.

Relations with the Soviet Union deteriorated further in 1946. On February 9, Stalin delivered a rare public speech in which he explained the fundamental incompatibility of communism and capitalism. The latter system, he stressed, needed war for raw materials and markets. The Second World War had only been the most recent in a chain of conflicts which could be broken only when the world's economy made the transformation to communism. Henry Luce's *Time* magazine concluded that the remarks were "the most warlike pronouncement uttered by any top-rank statesman since V-J Day."

Two weeks after Stalin's speech, George F. Kennan sent an eight-thousand-word "long telegram" to the State Department explaining why the Soviets behaved the way they did. The Soviets saw the world divided into hostile capitalist and communist camps between which there could be no peace. They held as an article of faith that capitalism would collapse under the weight of its internal contradictions and that socialism would replace it. The Soviet leaders clung to their revolutionary outlook because "Marxism is the fig leaf [this image covered a lot for Kennan] of their moral and intellectual respectability. Without it they would stand before history, at best, as only the last in that succession of cruel and wasteful Russian rulers." Unlike many diplomatic dispatches, this one actually was read by the president, who found it unlocked the mystery of Soviet foreign policy.

Poland became the most emotional point of contention between the Soviet Union and the United States. Where Roosevelt had favored any cosmetic agreement over the future of Poland which allayed the anxieties of the Polish-American community, Truman chose to interpret Soviet backing for a Communist-led government in Warsaw as proof that Stalin sought dominion over all of Eastern Europe. When the new Polish government persisted throughout 1946 in denouncing opposition groups as "neo-Fascist" and "Nazi collaborators," confiscated Church lands, nationalized industries, and refused to join the new International Monetary Fund and World Bank, United States diplomats, churchmen, and politicians ignored earlier promises that Moscow would have a friendly Poland on its border. The United States, seeing only that it was frozen out of Eastern Europe, spent the next five years making certain the Soviet Union would have nothing to say about events west of the Elbe River which separated the Soviet zone of occupied Germany from German territory held by American, British, and French forces.

Truman's animosity toward the Soviet Union neatly coincided with the opinions of the generals and diplomats in charge of the occupation of Germany. Nothing had come of the wartime plan for Great Britain, France, the Soviet Union, and the United States to administer Germany jointly. An Allied Control Commission met throughout 1945 and 1946, but the powers reached no agreement on German reparations, elimination of Nazi influences, or local governments. Often the French joined the Soviets in charging the Americans and British with softness toward former Nazi party members. But Gen. Lucius D. Clay, commander of United States forces in Germany, rejected all complaints. He preferred to believe that the Soviets sought Communist rule for all of Germany as a first step in their eventual subjugation of Western Europe. Convinced that Moscow looked toward displacing "bourgeois" governments, Clay toyed with the idea of a revived Germany blocking Russia's way.

Truman signaled his new toughness in September 1946 when he fired former vice-president Henry Wallace as secretary of commerce. A thorn in the side of conservatives for years, Wallace in 1946 took a gloomy view of the name-calling between Moscow and Washington. After brooding for six months, he delivered a speech on foreign affairs on September 12 before twenty thousand people assembled by the U.S.–Soviet Friendship Association in New York's Madison Square Garden. "The tougher we get, the tougher they will get," he predicted. He also denounced "namby-pamby pacifism" in the United States and criticized the Soviet Union for its repression and contempt for civil liberties.

His audience, mostly old popular fronters sympathetic to the Soviets, hissed and booed him for these remarks, but Byrnes had a different reaction. Attending a meeting of Soviet, European, and American foreign ministers, he thought that Wallace's criticism cut the ground from under him. Byrnes phoned Truman to insist upon Wallace's muzzling or his head. These demands put the president in a ticklish spot, for he had actually read and approved Wallace's speech before he delivered it. Feeling sorry for himself, Truman unburdened his grievances with the commerce secretary to his diary. "Wallace is a pacifist 100 per cent," he wrote. "He wants . . . to give Russia our atomic secrets and trust a bunch of adventurers in the Kremlin politburo. . . . The Reds, phonies and the 'parlor pinks' seem to be banded together and are becoming a national danger. I believe they are a sabotage front for Uncle Joe Stalin." On September 20, Truman sent Wallace a letter as illtempered as his diary entry, firing him from Commerce. Wallace returned the smoldering document to Truman rather than embarrass him before posterity, cleared out his desk, and departed. Byrnes's victory lasted barely three months. In early January 1947, it was the turn of the secretary of state to get in trouble with Truman. When he went to Moscow and made conciliatory sounds, Truman fired him somewhat more gracefully than he replaced Wallace.

The choice to follow Byrnes as secretary of state was General George C. Marshall, chief of staff during the Second World War. In December 1945, Truman had seen Marshall in China attempting to work out an accommodation between Communists and Nationalists. When he came home in January 1947, he said that no compromise was possible between the two sides in their ongoing civil war and that the Communists were bound to win. Marshall had a formidable reputation for integrity, and Truman chose him as someone immune from criticism.

THE TRUMAN DOCTRINE, CONTAINMENT, AND
THE MARSHALL PLAN

The Truman administration needed all the protection it could get. The new Republican Congress had been elected in 1946 by two insulting slogans: "To err is Truman," and "Had enough?" An incident in the eastern Mediterranean in early 1947 sparked a new approach to the Soviet Union. On February 21, the British government told the United States that it no longer would pay the upkeep on Greek and Turkish efforts at fighting domestic leftist uprisings. American officials had expected the financially strapped British to renege on their commitments to Greece and Turkey for some time, and they did not mind their leaving the Middle East to the United States. The British need for hard cash offered an opportunity for the United States to insist upon an end to their exclusive control over the "sterling bloc" as a quid pro quo for American aid. In return for an American loan of $2 billion, the British had to agree that the currencies of their dominions would be fully convertible into dollars.

Events in Greece and Turkey also presented the United States with an opportunity to outflank the Russians to the south. Although President Roosevelt had agreed to the British and Soviets sharing power in Greece, the Truman administration wanted to rid the country of the taint of communism. Americans had encouraged Britain to arm Greece's government in its civil war against the leftist National Liberation Front, known by its Greek initials EAM. Despite the fact that EAM had attracted 1.4 million, mostly non-Communist members in a country of 7.5 million people, the State Department considered the movement "not a 'friend' or ally of the USSR; it is an instrument of Soviet policy." The War Department's intelligence division decided that Russia's goal was "to gain complete control of Greece." Loy Henderson, a State Department Soviet expert, reported that "the Soviet Union seems determined to break down [Britain's] great dam [blocking] the flow of Russian power to the south." Now that the British seemed reluctant to maintain that dam, the United States eagerly offered direct aid to Greece.

The question was: How should the United States announce its commitment to Greece and Turkey? George F. Kennan, the chief of the newly established Policy Planning Staff of the Department of State, advised simple support of these two governments without enlarging the commitment into a global confrontation with the Soviet Union. But Kennan's moderate approach fell foul of Marshall and Truman, both of whom thought that the Greek and Turkish crisis presented the opportunity to throw down the gauntlet to Moscow.

On March 12, Truman went before Congress to ask for an aid package of $300 million for Greece and $100 million for Turkey to equip their armed forces for the job of chasing and killing Communist guerrillas. Assistant Secretary of State Will Clayton urged a militant speech, as "the United States will not take world leadership effectively unless the people of the United States are shocked into doing so." Informed by Republican senator Arthur Vandenberg that he had to "scare the hell out of the country," the president went beyond pleas to assist these two governments by promulgating a "Truman Doctrine," committing America to aid all governments facing domestic leftist insurrections. He rallied Democrats and drew clenched-teeth praise from most Republicans. The privately expressed doubts of George Kennan were joined by the public fears of Walter Lippmann, who dismissed the Truman Doctrine as a "vague global policy, which sounds like the tocsin of an ideological crusade" and "has no limits." Neither complaint made much of an impression.

Another Kennan-Lippmann controversy became public in the summer of 1947, resulting in two slogans—*containment* and *Cold War*—which described American policy for years. As an active Foreign Service officer, Kennan felt compelled to cloak his identity. Under the pseudonym "X," he published an article, "The Sources of Soviet Conduct," in *Foreign Affairs* in July. He zipped through three hundred years of Russian and thirty years of Soviet history to demonstrate that Moscow's foreign policy rested on three pillars—traditional Russian imperialism, revolutionary Communist ideology, and the paranoid suspicions of Josef Stalin, whom "X" considered deranged. Only the first of these sources—traditional Russian expansion—was likely to endure, as Kennan doubted that a nation could maintain Marxism for long or forever submit to the whims of a dictator. "We are going to continue for a long time to find the Russians difficult to deal with . . . but the United States has it in its power to increase enormously the strains under which Soviet power must operate," he asserted. While waiting for the Soviet Union to abandon communism and behave like any other state, the United States had to "contain" it in areas of Eastern Europe already under its control. Lippmann responded in a series of *New York Herald Tribune* columns critical of containment as a "strange monstrosity" doomed from the start. He predicted that the United States would have to engage in "recruiting, subsidizing, and supporting a heterogeneous array of satellites, clients, dependents, and puppets"; the result would be perpetual "Cold War" with the Soviet Union.

The Truman Doctrine formed only one part of a concentrated strategy, the second half of which was announced by Secretary of State Marshall to the graduating class of Harvard University on June 6. He invited European nations to step forward with requests for reconstruction assistance from the United States. A radical reversal stood behind this innocuous-sounding proposal: no longer did American planners believe, as they had in 1945, that the United Nations should coordinate aid. The economic situation in Europe appeared desperate, and British inability to fund Greece and Turkey represented only one example. American travelers to Europe in the winter of 1946–1947 reported dark cities, cold houses, closed factories, empty treasuries, and starving people badly in need of dollars, coal, and food. Russell C. Leffingwell, a banker with the house of Morgan, came back in April 1947 to predict an inevitable seizure of power by French, Italian, and German Communists unless the United States stepped in to revive the economies of Western Europe. Recovery there would encourage consumption from restarted American factories.

The fears of the post–World War I era returned, but this time the United States took the lead in crusading against revolution. The beauty of Marshall's plan was that it did not appear on the surface to be directed against the Soviet Union. The secretary of state never mentioned the dangers of communism or the Soviet Union, and he opened the program to all European nations. He knew, however, that the Soviet Union would reject the invitation as a transparent attempt to penetrate Eastern Europe with American commerce. The State Department expected the Soviets to prohibit their Communist-dominated governments of Eastern Europe from joining others in asking for aid. The onus for dividing Europe into two hostile camps would fall on Moscow, not Washington.

The division occurred in the summer of 1947. Western European nations assembled in August to draft a European Recovery Program, the formal title for the Marshall Plan. The Czech government, not thoroughly controlled by the Communist party, sent a representative, and the Poles tried to join. The Soviets quickly sent word that they believed participation by the Eastern European nations would marry their economies to the United States, and the Czechs and Poles retreated. The European Recovery Program took shape without any participation from the governments east of the Elbe River, and Marshall succeeded in launching reconstruction linking the fortunes of Western Europe firmly to the United States.

Congress approved the Marshall Plan in the summer of 1947. Republicans who might have objected to a program calling for $23 billion in economic aid had no qualms at all about endorsing a package designed to thwart the Soviet Union. Republicans from Arthur Vandenberg to the staunchly conservative William Jenner of Indiana, an enthusiastic member of the China Lobby (which opposed Truman's Asian policies), joined a chorus of Democrats in supporting the appropriations. Truman had cut the ground from under the resurgent Republican majority in the Congress but he paid the price by publicly announcing that the two superpowers were on a collision course. No longer did he or any other important figure in the administration harbor any more hopes that the United States and the Soviet Union could reach an agreement on the future of Europe.

DOMESTIC POLITICS AND THE COLD WAR

While the phrase *Cold War* became a cliché in mid-1947, the conflict between the United States and the Soviet Union had existed during the Second World War. It became obvious to the public in 1946 that the two former allies disagreed about every important issue in Europe and Asia. For the remainder of the Truman administration, the attitude of the public became central to the administration's conduct of foreign affairs. The Republican party, which had been a "loyal opposition in time of war," played a more complicated game after 1945. Sometimes it supported Truman in a proud display of bipartisanship while other times it threw noisy tantrums about the "subversives," "spies," and "security risks" it said penetrated the American government at the bidding of a Communist conspiracy directed by the Kremlin.

At the beginning of the postwar era, the most prominent Republican spokesman on foreign affairs was Sen. Arthur Vandenberg of Michigan, who had expressed typical Midwestern isolationist sentiments and distrust of Franklin Roosevelt before Pearl Harbor. The Truman administration changed his mind on one important aspect of internationalism, however, when it secured his support for the United Nations organization in May 1945. Over the next four years, Vandenberg, as the ranking minority member and then chairman of the Foreign Relations Committee, led his fellow Republicans in support of Truman's strong anti-Soviet stand in Europe. But the opposition had nothing good to say about the administration's response to events in Asia. The Chinese civil war between Nationalists and Communists resumed in early 1946, and American friends of Jiang Jieshi (Chiang Kai-shek)—conservative Republican members of Congress cheered on by Henry Luce's *Time* magazine and the *Chicago Tribune*—blamed Truman for weakening the Nationalists.

The administration tried to protect itself from criticism coming from anti-Communists by introducing its own program for exposing and eliminating "subversives" working for the government. In the process, Truman climbed on the back of a tiger and found it hard to dismount without Republican politicians accusing him of ignoring subversion. In July 1945, the Federal Bureau of Investigation announced it had arrested the editors of *Amerasia*, a small-circulation journal devoted to academic articles on United States–Asian relations, and charged them with possession of classified government documents. The FBI also detained John Stewart Service, an American Foreign Service officer home on leave from his post in China. Service, later cleared of the charges in the *Amerasia* case, became the first of several American experts on China charged with disloyalty when their only crime was accurately predicting the demise of the Nationalists. The furor over *Amerasia* passed in a few months, but the Truman administration used the case to commence a program of loyalty investigations of government employees early in 1947.

A Loyalty-Security Board began inquiring into the political beliefs of all federal workers, hearing secret testimony it was not required to share with the accused. The board never defined what loyalty was, but all government functionaries knew that past association with Communist or Communist-led organizations could cost them their jobs. The loyalty-security program struck fear in the hearts of old New Dealers, but it did little to quiet the Republican clamor for stricter measures. In the summer of 1947, the House Committee on Un-American Activities, now chaired by Republican J. Parnell Thomas of New Jersey, conducted investigations of the motion pictures industry in Hollywood. In four days of testimony, broadcast across the country by radio, the committee discovered little more proof of Communist influence than the ominous fact that smiles lit up the faces of Soviet children in the movie *Song of Russia.*

The Truman administration was happy to use the issue of the threat of domestic subversion as a way of generating public support for its foreign policy so long as it did not lose control of it to the opposition. By portraying a worldwide Communist conspiracy operating inside the United States, the administration hoped to frighten the public into support for a forward foreign policy.

REORGANIZING THE FOREIGN AFFAIRS APPARATUS

Congress also remodeled the foreign affairs apparatus in 1946 and 1947. Ever since the Second World War, experts had worried about the confused lines of authority in the foreign affairs bureaucracy. President Roosevelt, with his personal style and his reliance upon friends to conduct delicate negotiations abroad, had left the professionals in the State Department angry and humiliated. The armed services had engaged in bitter wrangling for turf, and the Office of Strategic Services—the espionage organization headed by a wealthy Republican, William J. "Wild Bill" Donovan—had been a virtually independent arm of the executive branch. Reformers thought that some order had to be brought to these fiercely competitive agencies. Members of each body wanted to preserve and expand their own authority at the expense of others. Truman and his advisers wanted to make certain that the president could dominate foreign affairs even if he did not have the political appeal of his popular predecessor.

Two laws tried to bring order to the conduct of foreign affairs. The first, the Foreign Service Reform Act of 1946, represented an attempt by professional diplomats to recapture the center stage in the making of foreign policy. Ignored by Roosevelt, career officials looked forward to a fairer deal from Truman. During the war, many officials from other agencies temporarily joined the State Department, and Foreign Service officers had served tours in Washington. The reforms of 1946 attempted to make these arrangements permanent by creating Foreign Service reserve officer classifications for officials who entered the service for short terms. It also merged the State Department and the Foreign Service into one single organization. Now diplomats and consuls would rotate back to headquarters in Washington between tours of duty. Time in the capital no longer would be considered a vacation or a punishment, as professionals learned about and helped formulate policies. The next year, 1947, the State Department set up a Policy Planning Staff, made up of Foreign Service officers instructed to provide insights into the future.

While the Department of State attempted to seize the initiative, leaders of other foreign affairs bureaus fought back. The most successful were the armed forces. After all, the army and navy had over a million men in uniform after demobilization but the State Department numbered two thousand. The Pentagon spent over $9 billion, and the appropriation for the State Department was under $40 million. Insofar as the United States affected world events, the Army and Navy departments were central.

During the war, military reformers had come to believe that the division of effort into a War Department and a Navy Department made little sense. The use of airplanes to bomb cities and battlefields had made military affairs more complicated. Pentagon advocates of air power encouraged congressional supporters who believed that a new age of warfare had begun with the explosion of the atomic bomb. Some members of Congress backed a new unified force amalgamating all three branches—army, navy, and air force—into a single service. Of course, generals and admirals of the traditional branches gulped in amazement at suggestions for them to give up their long-held commands. Their brethren who had served in the air forces of the army or navy also shunned a merger into a single service, predicting that a new air force would give them the opportunity to rise more quickly.

The National Security Act passed by Congress in late July 1947 compromised among these competing plans. On the military side, no unified single service was set up, and a separate air force was carved from the old army air corps. Yet the planners did create a new Defense Department, presided over by a civilian secretary, to coordinate the work of the army, navy, and air force. To preserve the civilian control over the military, no one could become secretary of defense who had been on active service with the military over the previous five years.

The National Security Act also dealt with the problems of extralegal, or covert, operations of the government. The Office of Strategic Services had been disbanded at the end of the war. A wide gulf had separated the upper echelons of the OSS, led by Donovan and peopled by mostly conservative Ivy Leaguers, and the lower-level analysts who tended to be political liberals. When the OSS was closed, liberals lost influence, but now that the Cold War had erupted, the administration reasoned that a new spy organization was needed. The National Security Act created a Central Intelligence Agency to place all spy activities under a single roof. Unstated in the act, but clear in the minds of its authors, was the notion that the CIA would be the arm of the government which would do those jobs too unsavory for the remaining branches.

The final provision of the National Security Act established a coordinating body, the National Security Council (NSC), headed by the president and including the chairman of the Joint Chiefs of Staff, the secretaries of state and defense, the vice-president and anyone else the president wanted to invite. Intended to eliminate the chronic squabbling among various foreign affairs and military bureaus, the early NSC had no permanent director nor any professional staff members. Truman used it to assess the shape of the world in the future. In 1950, it produced one of the most important memoranda since the Second World War—NSC-68—a prediction of the military requirements of the United States in the next five years. The paper called for a buildup of American conventional forces and the annual expenditure of $50 billion on defense, a rise of 300 percent. Yet the National Security Council did not come into its own as an independent agency until the Kennedy administration. Then other officials resented the national security adviser and members of the NSC staff. One of the characteristics of the 1960s, 1970s, and 1980s became unsporting wrestling between the NSC and the other shapers of foreign policy.

IMMIGRATION POLICY AFTER WORLD WAR II

After 1945, only minute policy changes took place in restrictive immigration policies. Anywhere from 750,000 to 1,500,000 displaced persons (DPs), victims of the Holocaust, languished in camps supervised by the United Nations. Relief agencies lobbied Congress for the special displaced persons laws finally passed in 1948 and 1950. Ironically, the first law assisted the oppressors—Nazi officers and collaborators—more than the victims. One lobbying group decried "the unashamed cynicism displayed in legislating ostensibly for the relief of those who suffered most from the last war, while actually locking the doors against them." In Congress, one bigot damned DPs as "the scum of the earth," and another characterized them as "bums, criminals, subversives, revolutionists, crackpots and human wreckage." Public outcry led to the removal of the most flagrant restrictions on DPs in 1950.

For the next thirty years, the displaced persons acts served as models for other efforts at admitting refugees from governments the United States opposed. The most generosity was shown to people fleeing Communist regimes. Congress made special provisions for anti-Communist Hungarians after the unsuccessful uprising of 1956, Cubans after the revolution of 1959, and Indochinese after the Communist victories in 1975. The national quota system as a whole, which had caused such resentment abroad, was scrapped in 1965 and replaced by an overall ceiling of four hundred thousand immigrants permitted annually. But the new law did not permanently settle immigration policy. Millions of noncitizens simply crossed the frontiers without official permission. By 1982, the Immigration and Naturalization Service (INS) estimated that as many as twelve million such "undocumented" aliens lived in the United States, where they took the worst jobs, found the poorest housing and lived in terror of being turned over to the authorities. At the same time, the government applied inconsistent standards to refugees entering the country. While welcoming those from Communist countries, it jailed and deported thousands from poor, dictatorial Haiti and strife-torn El Salvador. By the 1980s, with immigration barriers offering few restraints and some Americans bitterly resentful of the new arrivals, additional legislation was introduced. It provided amnesty to some undocumented aliens already in the country while imposing stiffer penalties on any future unfortunates who attempted to seek their fortunes in America without the blessing of the INS.

THE MIDDLE EAST

While relations with the Soviet Union in Europe dominated Truman's foreign policy, the administration also expanded its interests in the Middle East. The establishment of the Jewish state of Israel in the British mandate of Palestine in 1947 and 1948 set the stage for a dispute which has not been resolved to this day. Jewish settlers in Palestine had decided during the Second World War that they would fight simultaneously with the British against the Nazis and against the British for the establishment of a separate Jewish state. At a meeting of the World Zionist Congress at the Biltmore Hotel in New York in 1942, political representatives of the settlers agreed to seek immediate independence after the war, but British authorities continued their prewar practice of restricting the entry of Jews into the mandate. This prohibition of immigration was made all the worse by the memory of the destruction of six million Jews and the miserable sight of hundreds of thousands of death camp survivors and refugees languishing in displaced persons camps throughout Europe.

American policy during the war had been to encourage the Jews of the United States to believe that FDR supported the idea of their creating a Jewish state in Palestine. Truman continued to raise hopes in May 1946, when he backed the Jewish demand for the immediate admission of one hundred thousand Jews to the Holy Land. Then, spurred by a desire to remove an issue from the Republican opposition, Truman for the first time announced his support of the Jewish state in Palestine in early October, on Yom Kippur, the holiest day of the Jewish year. He had received word shortly before that the Jews of New York would desert the Democratic party for the Republicans in the upcoming congressional election unless he made some dramatic gesture, and that the Republican governor of the state, Thomas E. Dewey, the party's presidential candidate in 1944 and the front-runner for 1948, planned to make a statement favoring the admission of several hundred thousand European Jews to Palestine. Nativism also played a part in nudging Truman toward sympathizing with the plight of the Jewish victims of Hitler, as British foreign secretary Ernest Bevan, a visceral anti-Semite, projected some of his prejudices onto the president when he said Truman badgered Britain to admit more Jews into Palestine "because he did not want 100,000 Jews in New York."

In mid-1947, in response to American pressure as well as the Jewish revolt in Palestine which killed over one hundred British troops, the British government announced that it was abandoning its mandate by December 31 and turning the issue over to the United Nations, which established a Special Commission on Palestine. The commission traveled to the area to hear testimony from Arabs and Jews and recommended the partition of Palestine into two states—one Jewish and one Arab—to the General Assembly. The Jewish Agency accepted partition; the Arabs did not. On November 27, 1947, the General Assembly voted by a two-thirds majority to partition Palestine, with American ambassador Warren F. Austin joining the European and Latin American nations and the Soviet bloc in voting for the creation of Jewish and Arab states in mid-May 1948.

In the intervening six months, American policy underwent dramatic reversals. State Department experts on the Middle East had never been happy with the idea of Jewish aspirations. One diplomat called American support of Zionism "a major blunder in statesmanship; it might even threaten world security." Another offered a cold assessment of why the United States should support the Arab claims: "As for the emotions of the Arabs, I do not give a dried camel's hump. It is, however, important to the interests of this country that these fanatical and overwrought people do not injure our strategic interests through reprisals against our oil investments." Officials also predicted a bloodbath should the Jewish Agency go ahead with its plans to declare independence in the face of Arab hostility. In February 1948, the State Department presented a radical reversal of course to Ambassador Austin at UN headquarters at Lake Success, Long Island. Instead of a Jewish state, the United States would agree to act as trustee for all of Palestine. Austin dutifully presented this scheme to the Security Council, thinking it had the backing of Truman. Jewish leaders were astonished and depressed. Chaim Weizmann, longtime head of the world Zionist movement, in New York for the UN session, rushed to Washington to convince the president to reaffirm the American commitment to an independent Jewish state. Truman, fearing reprisal from Jewish voters in 1948, and convinced that the Jews needed a state of their own, explained that Austin did not speak for the administration. A chastened UN ambassador gamely accepted this presidential dressing down and reported that the United States accepted a new Jewish state.

On May 14, 1948, David Ben-Gurion, the head of the Jewish Agency, proclaimed the independence of the Jewish state of Israel. Five Arab nations im-

President Harry S. Truman (r.) and Secretary of State George C. Marshall take
a look at the Middle East. *(Harry S. Truman Presidential Library)*

mediately attacked and looked forward to pitching the Jews into the sea
within weeks. On the day of the declaration of independence, the Truman
administration, hoping to beat the Soviets to the punch, announced it had
extended de facto recognition. By the summer, the Israelis had beaten back
the invasion forces from Egypt, Jordan, and Syria, and negotiations opened
for an end to the war. The next year, 1949, saw an armistice between Israel
and its Arab neighbors. No peace treaties followed that agreement until the
Egyptian-Israeli Treaty, negotiated with the help of the United States, was
signed in March 1979.

American policy throughout this crisis demonstrated caution, hesitation,
and vacillation. Torn between a sense of relief that the British had left the
Middle East, a genuine concern for the Jewish victims of nazism, fear of the
power of Jewish voters, and an equally strong urge to please the Arab states,
the Truman administration sought to appease each of the quarreling parties. In the end, the British resented American moralizing, and the Arabs
distrusted American support of Israeli independence. The new government
of Israel was delighted, of course, that the United States had been the first

foreign power to extend recognition, but the Israelis tempered their grati-
tude with boasts that they had won the war with their own arms and military
prowess. For the next generation, American diplomats struggled with the
problem of reconciling fiercely competitive interests in the Middle East.

THE ELECTION OF 1948, THE BERLIN CRISIS,
AND THE CREATION OF NATO

Bipartisan agreement over foreign policy unraveled in the aftermath of the
presidential election of 1948. Republicans, believing that the inept Harry
Truman would be an easy target, expected to win handily, and practically
everyone else agreed. In early 1948, fearing a debacle at the polls, some liberal Democrats led by Eleanor Roosevelt sought out war hero Gen. Dwight
David Eisenhower to see if he would consent to run for president as a Democrat. The general refused, and the Democrats faced the gloomy prospect
of losing the presidency as well as the Congress. The Republicans, supremely
confident, chose New York governor Thomas E. Dewey, who had lost to
Franklin D. Roosevelt in 1944. Dewey spent much of his campaign assem-
bling his cabinet, so sure was he of victory. On foreign policy, he supported
the Truman administration's shrill confrontation with the Soviet Union in
Europe, and coming from the eastern internationalist wing of the party,
Dewey did not indulge in any baiting of the Democrats for the decline of
Jiang Jieshi in China.

The campaign took place in the midst of growing European tensions and
the revival of Republican charges of spies among the New Dealers. In September 1947 the Soviet Union, responding to the American and British introduction of a new form of currency in their zone of occupied Germany,
cut off land access by the Western powers to their zones of Berlin, officially
under the joint control of the Allies. The confrontation over Berlin represented the final episode in the ill will between East and West over the future
of Germany which had been building since the Potsdam Conference. Unable to reach agreement on reparations, the Allied Control Commission,
which was supposed to formulate policy for all the occupied zones of Germany, produced only an endless series of acrimonious meetings among representatives of the Soviet Union, Britain, France, and the United States. Many
of the confrontations pitted the three Western powers against the Soviet
Union, but there were also occasional outbursts of bad feeling between the
French and the two Anglo-Saxon powers. Britain and the United States consequently decided to combine their two areas of occupied Germany into a
single "Bizonia" capable of putting to good use the billions of dollars in reconstruction loans expected under the Marshall Plan.

The creation of Bizonia in mid-1947 persuaded the Soviet Union that the United States and Britain contemplated a revived German state, possibly armed and assuredly hostile to its eastern neighbors. The Soviets bided their time until the Western powers reformed the currency of their parts of Berlin without first securing the approval of the Allied Control Commission. Then Russian troops turned back all traffic, including soldiers, goods, and foods, bound from the Western zones of occupation to Berlin. The American commander in Germany, Gen. Lucius D. Clay, told Truman that the Russian move was the opening shot in the Third World War and asked for authority to enter Berlin by force. Cooler heads held the day in Washington, however, and Truman ordered Clay to organize cargo flights from the Western zones of Germany to Berlin. The airlift went forward for the next seven months, during which time the American diplomats acknowledged that Germany had been split in two. When the Soviets gave up their attempt to force the Western powers out of Berlin in late April 1949, the United States was not mollified and pressed its advantage over the Soviets by encouraging the creation of the Federal Republic of Germany. This new West German state, made up of British-American Bizonia, the French section, and the three Western sectors of Berlin, signaled the official end of the occupation and the fiction of Allied cooperation.

The Berlin airlift gave Truman a boost during his reelection campaign, but new charges about "spies" and "subversives" arose in the late summer and fall to shake the president's equanimity and alarm the remnants of the New Dealers. In August, the House Committee on Un-American Activities heard Whittaker Chambers, a former Communist, senior editor of *Time* and the translator of *Bambi* from German to English, testify that he had recruited into the Communist party Alger Hiss, in 1945 director of the State Department's Office of Special Political Affairs and then head of the Carnegie Endowment for International Peace. Hiss hotly denied party membership, said he had never met Chambers, and sued for libel. Committee members, loving the publicity, arranged a dramatic confrontation between Hiss and Chambers in a room at Manhattan's Roosevelt Hotel. Hiss repeated his denials under oath, making clear that he expected the committee to challenge the veracity of his tormentor, Chambers, whose story seemed preposterous. Throughout the fall, the committee dithered, not wishing to lose its star witness, but lacking evidence to proceed against Hiss. After the election killed Republican hopes, Chambers's greatest supporter on the committee, Richard M. Nixon, a second-term Republican representative from California, helped the *Time* editor publicize a far more damaging charge against Hiss. Not only had the former high State Department official been a member of the Communist party, Chambers now claimed, but he was also a spy who had passed secret State Department memoranda to Chambers to transfer to Soviet offi-

Alger Hiss (standing l.) confronts Whittaker Chambers (standing far r.) as Richard Nixon presides over the House Committee on Un-American Activities, August 1948. (*Wide World Photos*)

cials. To prove his charge, Chambers led Nixon and a posse of reporters to a pumpkin patch on his Maryland farm where he extracted from the hollowed-out orange vegetables several rolls of microfilms containing pictures of the documents Chambers claimed to have received from Hiss. The statute of limitations having expired for the crime of espionage (all the documents bore the dates 1937 or 1938), a New York grand jury indicted Hiss for perjury for denying under oath that he had been a Communist or knew Chambers.

The Hiss case threw the Truman administration into an uproar, with the president agreeing to a reporter's description of the charges as a Republican "red herring" dragged across the trail of the election. The U.S. attorney general looked into the possibility of indicting Chambers, not Hiss, for perjury, before the *Time* editor pulled the films from the pumpkins. Chambers's revelations unnerved Truman, who approved the indictment against Hiss. He was tried twice—the first trial ending in a hung jury—convicted in 1950, and sentenced to a five-year prison term. More than a former State Department official stood in the dock, though. As Alastair Cooke, a long-time American correspondent for the British Broadcasting Corporation, described it, the case put "a generation on trial." All former New Dealers who, like Hiss, had hoped for a continuation of goodwill between the United States and the Soviet Union, seemed accused. While he was on trial for acts committed in the late thirties, Hiss's enemies in the newspapers made much of his presence as a diplomat at the Yalta Conference in February 1945.

For the next several years, the Republican right spat out the words *Yalta* and *Hiss*. Liberals, many of whom now rushed to embrace the doctrine of containment and occupy what Arthur Schlesinger, Jr., dubbed "the vital center of politics," voiced feeble rejoinders to their right-wing tormentors. Some New Dealers stood by Hiss as an honorable man accused by a psychopath—Chambers—and framed by a guttersnipe—Nixon. Even as they defended Hiss's reputation, however, Democrats, who adopted a tough stance toward the Soviet Union, thought that the problem with Hiss's critics was not their militancy but their competence to conduct an effective confrontation with Moscow.

Truman's reelection surprised the political experts and infuriated Republicans who lost the presidency, Congress, and something else—the sense that they would be rewarded for their bipartisan support for the president's foreign affairs initiatives in Europe. GOP stalwarts again saw themselves forlornly pushing their noses against the window as Democrats ran things. In April, Truman submitted the North Atlantic Treaty to the Senate for ratification. Made up of twelve countries—the United States, Canada, Denmark, France, Iceland, Italy, Portugal, Norway, Great Britain, and the three Benelux nations—NATO was to be both a military and political alliance. Gen. Omar

Bradley, the chairman of the Joint Chiefs of Staff, told the Senate Foreign Relations Committee that the Western European countries had insisted upon NATO as a more effective defense against the Soviet Union than the United Nations. Dean Acheson, appointed secretary of state in January 1949, argued that NATO would do more than maintain a "balance of power" and would give the West a "preponderance of power" over the Soviet Union. Even with the alliance, however, the Soviets enjoyed superiority in conventional forces, which the United States outweighed with its monopoly of the atomic bomb. Acheson explained NATO's political importance to the senators. He considered it a demonstration to the Eastern Europeans of American concern for their welfare, thereby preventing a revival of "neutralism" or "appeasement" in Europe. Utah Republican senator Arthur Watkins opposed the pact as providing little additional military security for Western Europe. Watkins noted that the "constitutional processes" clause of the treaty required that each nation declare war in the legally defined manner, and he predicted that the Soviet Union could overrun Europe before the Congress declared war. Sen. Robert Taft, the Ohio Republican who had consistently opposed American participation in Europe's conflicts since the late thirties, added his voice to the opposition to NATO as a departure from traditional American avoidance of entangling alliances. But only eleven senators cast votes with Watkins and Taft, and the Senate ratified the treaty by a vote of eighty-two to thirteen in July. Upon signing the treaty, Truman sent Congress a Mutual Defense Assistance Act with a price tag of $1.5 billion for one year's worth of military equipment for Europe.

THE FAR EAST: CHINA, JAPAN, AND INDOCHINA

Having failed to dent Democratic successes in molding policy in Europe, Republicans scored heavily as they second-guessed Truman's confused responses to changing circumstances in Asia. By the middle of 1949, it was clear that the Communists led by Mao Zedong would win the Chinese civil war. Friends of Jiang Jieshi in the Republican party—William Knowland of California, Walter Judd of Minnesota, and Willian Jenner of Indiana—complained that Democrats had let the Communists win. Joined by Henry Luce, the China Lobby wondered aloud why the Truman administration had stopped supplying weapons to Jiang after the Marshall mission of 1946. So annoyed were the president and the new secretary of state, Dean Acheson, by this barrage of criticism that they responded by making public the record of American aid to China. Acheson, immaculate, tall, with an upturned mustache and well-appointed suits, was the son of the Episcopal bishop of Connecticut. Supercilious in his bearing, tone of voice, and even his face, he enraged former isolationist Republicans. One GOP congressman surveyed the secretary's clothes and bearing and wanted to shout, "Get out, get out. You're all that's been wrong with the United States for twenty years." For his part, the secretary had no respect for Congress, calling the conservatives "primitives" who knew nothing of foreign affairs but kept him away from his job by testifying before them.

In August 1949, the State Department sought to silence opponents by publishing a white paper on China—a two-volume edition of the diplomatic

The bearing that drove Republicans and nationalists wild. Dean Acheson testifies before the Foreign Relations Committee. *(Wide World Photos)*

correspondence between the United States and China over the previous generation. The documents indicated that the United States had done everything possible to aid the Nationalist government. If Jiang had lost the civil war, it was because of his own failings: his corruption, unpopularity, and reluctance to fight. In the end, the white paper concluded that the Chinese civil war had been lost by the Chinese Nationalists themselves. The volumes came equipped with a covering "letter of transmittal" produced by Assistant Secretary of State for Far Eastern Affairs Dean Rusk, in which he accused the Chinese Communists of being puppets of Moscow. Rusk looked forward to the day when the Chinese would free themselves of "foreign domination."

While his assistant secretary fretted about Moscow's long reach, Acheson looked for ways to open diplomatic relations with the new Chinese government in Beijing. The secretary of state thought that the United States and China should maintain their embassies, as he had received reports from Foreign Service officers serving in China that the Communists looked forward to demonstrating independence from the Soviets. Moreover, Acheson expected the Nationalists, who had escaped to Taiwan in the autumn of 1949, to become a drain on American resources with persistent demands for arms and money to apply to pointless assaults on the mainland. Acheson told the Senate Foreign Relations Committee that the government of Jiang would quickly succumb to the Communists. After "the dust settled," the United States and Beijing could resume diplomatic relations. In fact, the Korean War which started in June 1950 changed the picture.

On September 23, 1949, the president announced that a "nuclear explosion"—he carefully avoided uttering the dread words atomic bomb—had occurred earlier that month in the Soviet Union. This news sent shock waves through Washington and set off a search for a scapegoat. No one had predicted that the Soviet Union would be able to have a bomb so quickly, so it seemed that spies must have slipped atomic secrets to Russia. The arrest in 1950 of Julius and Ethel Rosenberg, one of whom, Julius, had worked on the Manhattan Project, added to the espionage furor.

The Soviet bomb also forced a revision in American strategic planning, which had rested since 1945 on a monopoly of what Bernard Baruch called "the winning weapon." In late 1949 and early 1950, officials of the departments of State and Defense and the National Security Council defined a new mode of competition. They completed their work before the new year, and it became official policy in April 1950 with the adoption of National Security Council Memorandum 68 (NSC-68). As previously mentioned, this document, largely the work of Paul Nitze of the State Department's Policy Planning Staff, predicted what the world would look like over the next five years. Asserting that the Soviets could not mount a military challenge before 1955, NSC-68 called for an extraordinary increase in the defense budget, from $13 billion to $50 billion a year, to maintain American superiority. To prepare the United States to wage a land war against the Soviet Union, the army had to be increased through a revived and expanded Selective Service system.

While NSC-68 did not foresee a major war for the next five years, small outbreaks were possible. Where would these wars occur? NATO's creation coincided with a relaxation of fears in Europe, so new conflict over Germany seemed remote. The Far East, however, was less tranquil. With the fall of Jiang's Nationalists, the United States looked for another nation to act as surrogate. Japan filled the bill. As early as 1947, the policy of occupation pursued in Japan had taken a "reverse course." No longer did the independent, arrogant Gen. Douglas MacArthur have a free hand in remolding Japanese society. Now Washington took an increased interest in Japan. Liberal plans for breaking up the giant Japanese trusts or *zaibatsu* were shelved in favor of revitalizing Japanese industry to trade with the remainder of Southeast Asia. Such trade would reduce the subsidy from the United States to Japan and prevent the Japanese from coming to terms with the Soviet Union.

Indochina, where the French had fought a guerrilla war since 1946, also attracted American attention in early 1950. Immediately after the Second World War, the United States had helped the French return to power in Indochina. For the first two years of the insurrection against the French, the United States had not taken an active interest. Then, after Jiang's collapse, American policy shifted as Washington saw the French standing in the way of a Communist sweep of Southeast Asia. In February 1950, the Truman administration agreed to send $18 million in military aid to fight the war against the Vietminh nationalists in Indochina.

WAR IN KOREA

The last place in Asia where Americans became interested in 1950 was Korea. At the end of the Second World War, the Americans had occupied the southern half of the country while Soviet troops took over north of the Thirty-Eighth Parallel. According to the Yalta accords, this division would end with the eventual unification of Korea. But the same divisions between Communist and non-Communist governments which had arisen in Eastern Europe also became the rule in Korea. North Korea set up a People's Republic led by Kim Il Sung while South Korea became the Republic of Korea led by Syngman Rhee.

The United States substantially reduced its Korean military mission in 1949. General MacArthur wanted troops in Japan, and military planners believed the South Korean armed forces could resist an attack. In early 1950, the Korean issue became embroiled in the partisan wranglings over the "loss"

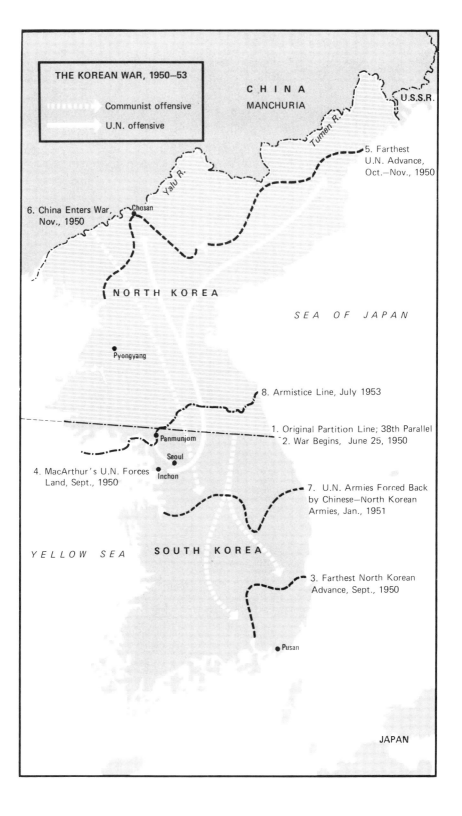

THE KOREAN WAR, 1950–53

⟶ Communist offensive

⟶ U.N. offensive

CHINA
MANCHURIA

Tumen R.

U.S.S.R.

5. Farthest
U.N. Advance,
Oct.–Nov., 1950

Yalu R.

6. China Enters War,
Nov., 1950

Chosan

NORTH KOREA

SEA OF JAPAN

Pyongyang

8. Armistice Line, July 1953

1. Original Partition Line; 38th Parallel
2. War Begins, June 25, 1950

Panmunjom

Seoul

4. MacArthur's U.N. Forces
Land, Sept., 1950

Inchon

7. U.N. Armies Forced Back
by Chinese–North Korean
Armies, Jan., 1951

YELLOW SEA

SOUTH KOREA

3. Farthest North Korean
Advance, Sept., 1950

Pusan

JAPAN

of China. Congressional Republicans held up a bill to aid Korea until the Truman administration agreed to supply weapons to the Nationalists in Taiwan. Dean Acheson also commented on the situation in Korea at an address to the National Press Club on January 13. He admitted that the United States had drawn a "strategic defense perimeter" in the Pacific which ran from Japan through Taiwan, through the Ryukyu Islands, to the Philippines. He did not include Korea because the Joint Chiefs of Staff denied its military value. The generals, led by MacArthur, believed that a major buildup of American troops on the mainland of Asia would divert resources from where they were needed—Japan. Acheson acknowledged, however, that an assault against Korea would be met with a UN response.

That attack came unexpectedly on June 25, 1950. At dawn, about one hundred ten thousand North Korean soldiers crossed the Thirty-Eighth Parallel and immediately overpowered the South Korean forces. Within fortyeight hours, General MacArthur flew to the battlefield to assess the chances of the South Koreans. Truman returned to Washington from his home in Independence, Missouri, convened a meeting of his principal advisers, and decided that the United States would commit troops to fighting the North Koreans. On Tuesday, June 27, the United Nations Security Council, fortunate in having Russia absent as a protest against the refusal to seat or recognize legitimacy of the mainland Chinese government, adopted an Americansponsored resolution to send forces to Korea.

American newspapers widely applauded Truman's decision to fight in Korea. From the independent *New York Times*, to the Republican *New York Herald Tribune*, to the old isolationist *Chicago Tribune*, to the liberal *Christian Science Monitor* came editorial support. Republicans who had attacked the administration for neglecting Asia hopped on board. Sen. William Knowland of California thanked Truman for drawing a "line" in the Far East. He said that Truman "should have the overwhelming support of all Americans regardless of their partisan affiliations." Republican senators Leverett Saltonstall of Massachusetts, H. Alexander Smith of New Jersey, Wayne Morse of Oregon, and Henry Cabot Lodge also praised Truman's decision to send troops. The war also made the defense expenditures proposed by NSC-68 politically feasible.

Widespread public fervor for the war lasted until December. In mid-September, General MacArthur led the American troops on an amphibious invasion of the Korean peninsula at Inchon near the capital of Seoul. Within days, Americans and Koreans had recaptured Seoul and forced the North Koreans to retreat. MacArthur's forces did not stop, however, at the Thirty-Eighth Parallel. They pressed north to eradicate Communist rule throughout Korea.

Gen. Douglas MacArthur strikes a pose on the Korean battlefield.
(National Archives)

In October, Truman flew to Wake Island in the Pacific to consult with MacArthur about the future of the war. The general treated the president as his inferior while assuring him that there was no danger of Chinese intervention if the Americans went north. The president, buoyed by American military accomplishments, gave the general the go-ahead.

The United States and South Korean forces overcame North Korean resistance in October and November, and near Thanksgiving they had nearly reached the Chinese border. In Beijing, the Communist party panicked. What if the Americans crossed the Yalu River, the border between Korea and Manchuria? Zhou Enlai, the Chinese premier, sent word through the Indian government that China would not accept an American army on its borders. In Washington, the administration ignored the warning.

Then, on November 27, a Chinese army of four hundred thousand men attacked the American forces in North Korea. A rout ensued, and by Christmas the Americans stood south of the Thirty-Eighth Parallel again. The initial Chinese victory came so fast that Truman wondered whether the United States should use the atomic bomb on China. This offhand remark sent a frightened British prime minister, Clement Attlee, scurrying to Washington to warn against using the winning weapon. Truman hastily withdrew the threat.

In early 1951, with the American forces back in South Korea, one of the most dramatic confrontations between civil and military authority in American history occurred. Truman fired MacArthur. The general had been a thorn in the flesh for years. MacArthur spoke to reporters when told to keep quiet, tried for the Republican presidential nomination in 1948, and sent longwinded telegrams to veterans' groups outlining his own personal foreign policy for the Far East. The general provoked a "cold fury" in Truman, who concluded that "there were times when he was . . . I think out of his head and didn't know what he was doing." The president told MacArthur to clear all public statements with Washington, but the general continued to press for air force attacks on China. He wrote Joseph Martin, the House minority leader, supporting the use of Nationalist Chinese troops against the mainland and insisting, "We must win." Martin released the letter. Truman exploded, "If what MacArthur had proposed had happened . . . we would have wound up being at war not only with Red China but with Russia too and . . . it might have meant the destruction of a good part of the world." Knowing that there would be some public uproar but determined that MacArthur had to go, Truman called in Gen. Omar Bradley and told him, "The son of a bitch isn't going to resign on me. *I want him fired.*" On April 3, the White House press secretary read a statement relieving MacArthur of his command.

At first, Truman seemed to have miscalculated the warrior's grip on the public imagination. He returned to a hero's welcome in San Francisco, and millions crowded downtown Manhattan for the largest New York ticker-tape parade since Charles Lindbergh's triumphal processional in 1927. Republicans blamed Truman for betraying the troops. Sen. Joseph McCarthy, the junior Republican from Wisconsin, and Joseph Martin called for impeachment proceedings against the president and Dean Acheson. Other senators invited MacArthur to Washington to testify before the Foreign Relations and Armed Services committees about how the president had forbidden him to win. He addressed a joint session of Congress, leaving not a dry eye when he finished with "Old soldiers never die, they just fade away." A popular song,

"Old Soldiers Never Die," played over the radio within two weeks. Truman did not attend the speech, "and there wasn't any law that I knew of that could make me listen to it" on radio or watch it on television. He summarized his reaction to it in a brisk two-word Anglo-Saxon expletive and later remembered that "I knew that once all the hullabaloo died down, people would see what he was."

Truman predicted a six-week uproar over MacArthur, and that was about how long the spotlight focused on the aging general. His testimony to congressional hearings dragged through May with newspapers devoting less and less space to it. He retired to a $130-dollar-a-day suite at New York's Waldorf Astoria to await a call to the Republican presidential nomination in 1952. Much to his surprise, no one asked him to run.

THE ELECTION OF 1952

As MacArthur's star faded, other Republicans kept alive the issue of the Democrats' overseas failures. The opposition rallied around Senator McCarthy's year-old charges, made before a partisan Wheeling, West Virginia, audience in February 1950, that he held in his hands a list of 57 or 205 (he kept changing the number) Communists in the Department of State. His accusations had not made news until the Korean War began. Then he used his chairmanship of the Investigations unit of the Senate Committee on Government Operations to vilify Foreign Service officers who had been in China, demand to know "who lost China," and stress that the Democrats had presided over "twenty years of treason." He threatened to make the 1952 election a referendum on his remarkable accusation that some Democrats and professional diplomats had served Moscow's interests.

Another Republican, who had a chance at the 1952 nomination, Robert Taft, also denounced the administration's foreign policy. Taft criticized the way Truman conducted diplomacy as well as what he did. Writing in *A Foreign Policy for America* (1951), Taft charged that Truman's "moral position" in the Korean War was unassailable, "but he did not recognize the implications of what he had started." The senator resented that the president had not asked for a declaration of war in Korea. He thought that Truman had violated the Constitution and arrogated far too much power to the White House. These were the same criticisms which isolationists had leveled at President Roosevelt before the Second World War. Taft believed that the United States should defend itself and wage unrelenting war against the Soviet Union in the Far East. He opposed, however, the alliances which Truman had developed. He expressed the traditional American view of foreign policy as something intermittent to be abandoned in peacetime. According to Taft, the policy of containment spelled a recipe for continuous American involvement in foreign wars.

Buffeted by these complaints, the Truman administration watched morosely as the public grew to detest the stalemated war in Korea. Talks opened with the North Koreans in mid-1951, but they seemed to go nowhere. Unresolved issues included the future of prisoners of war and whether Korea would be unified.

In early March 1952, Truman lost the New Hampshire primary election to Tennessee senator Estes Kefauver. He announced that he would not run again for president. The last year was a sad time for his administration. Acheson had to testify continuously before Congress, and he lost his cool reserve in the face of hostile questions from Republicans who smelled blood. At one point, he took a "swing" at Nebraska's Kenneth Wherry. The secretary felt the sting of Senator Nixon's assault on "Dean Acheson's cowardly college of Communist containment."

The Republicans, not wishing to be denied the White House again, turned their back on the conservative Taft and embraced the hero of World War II, Gen. Dwight David Eisenhower. Ike had finally become a Republican, and he wrested the nomination from the Ohio senator with the help of the eastern internationalist wing of the party. He defeated Taft but he mended fences with his rival shortly thereafter by appointing a conservative New York lawyer, John Foster Dulles, as the principal Republican spokesman for foreign affairs. He also kept his lines open to the strident critics of Truman, selecting California's junior senator, Richard Nixon, as his vice-presidential nominee. He also chose not to repudiate Senator McCarthy for his denunciation of Gen. George C. Marshall as "an agent of the Communist conspiracy."

He clinched the election when he promised to "go to Korea" if elected. His Democratic opponent, Adlai Stevenson, governor of Illinois, could only lamely promise that if the voters chose him, he too would visit the fighting. A general made more sense on the battlefield. Public weariness with "K_1C_2" (Korea, communism, and corruption), a sense that the Democrats were tired and the Republicans deserved a chance, and happy memories of smiling Ike leading the invasion of Europe in 1944 gave the former general a landslide victory, with over 55 percent of the vote. He called it a "mandate for change."

CHAPTER ELEVEN

Eisenhower's New Look,
1953–1960

President Dwight Eisenhower's principal speechwriter, Emmet John Hughes, described the new president's advisers as "bound and united . . . in a few elemental convictions. . . . All of them believed the national government to be languishing in a state of decay and disorder, calling for swift remedy. They thought the world menace of communism had been so idly abetted by American irresolution that some show of resolution—spiced with some specific, but not too costly, show of force—would change matters considerably." The president himself vowed to clean up "the mess in Washington" left by twenty years of rule by Democrats.

These hopes bore few fruits. After eight years in office, Eisenhower left with a warning that a "military-industrial complex" had ruined the American economy and distorted its diplomacy. His administration did little to alter the basic approach to foreign affairs of the Truman administration. The United States continued a policy of containment of communism and confrontation with the Soviet Union. The Cold War got no worse, but it got no better either. America stopped fighting in Korea but only postponed a full-scale war in Southeast Asia. Relations with China remained frozen. The ongoing tension in the Middle East proved impervious to American mediation. The rest of the world took on new importance. By the end of the decade, independence movements had swept the European powers out of Africa and Asia, catching the United States unaware. A revolution succeeded in Cuba to Washington's consternation. Throughout it all, Ike expanded the use of covert operations, toppling unfriendly governments in Iran in 1953 and in Guatemala in 1954 and propping up weak ones like South Vietnam after 1956.

ASSEMBLING THE TEAM

Eisenhower selected as secretary of state John Foster Dulles, a New York lawyer with Sullivan and Cromwell and one-time Republican senator, a foremost Republican spokesman on foreign affairs, and a member of the right wing. Dulles, a sour-tempered, mean-spirited self-promoter, savored apocalyptic statements about the future. He claimed that Soviet Communists believed "that human beings are somewhat superior animals . . . and that the best kind of world is that world which is organized as a well-managed farm is organized, where certain animals are taken out to pasture, and they are fed and brought back and milked, and they are given a barn over their heads." Contemporary observers claimed that he dominated foreign policy. Sherman Adams, Ike's chief of staff, categorically asserted that "Eisenhower gave Dulles a free hand and wide responsibility in conducting foreign policy." Later observers were not so sure. In a major rehabilitation of Eisenhower's foreign policy reputation, historian Robert Divine wrote in 1981, "Eisenhower used Dulles." The president, serenely self-confident in his own grasp of foreign affairs, employed a secretary of state as a spokesman and lightning rod. Dulles protected Eisenhower from conservative Republicans who had vowed to "lib-

President Dwight D. Eisenhower (l.) confers with Secretary of State John Foster Dulles.
(Dwight D. Eisenhower Presidential Library)

erate" Eastern Europe from the grasp of the Soviet Union. The president remembered how Acheson had exhausted himself testifying before congressional committees. Ike gave Congress a secretary of state so militant in his rhetoric that it would be appeased.

Dulles went a long way toward satisfying the most vulgar of congressional critics, Sen. Joseph McCarthy, who had called for a purge of "comsymps" (Communist sympathizers) from the State Department. Throughout the first eighteen months of the new administration, McCarthy leaked word to favored newspaper reporters about sedition within the Foreign Service. Dulles, who did not credit lurid tales himself, offered no public protection to beleaguered Foreign Service officers. Instead, he helped the senator's cause with the appointment of Scott McCleod, an admirer of McCarthy, to the post of inspector general for personnel. McCleod conducted his own secret security investigations in which accused officials could not examine the evidence against them. The inspector general ordered the firing of three highly qualified professional diplomats who had served in China in the forties: John Paton Davies, John Stewart Service, and John Carter Vincent. Their crime was to have exposed the ineptitude and corruption of Jiang Jieshi's (Chiang Kai-shek) government and predicted its fall to the better-organized Communists. For years afterward, fear gripped Foreign Service officers as they wondered what controversial statements in their dispatches later would be used against them. Rarely outspoken in the best of times, they became almost invisible in the fifties.

For secretary of defense, Eisenhower selected Charles E. "Engine Charlie" Wilson, the president of the General Motors Corporation. During his confirmation hearing, a senator asked Wilson if he foresaw any conflicts of interest between government service and his career as head of the world's largest industrial corporation. He replied, "What's good for the country is good for General Motors and vice versa." Wilson entered the government vowing to cut the budget and get "more bang for the buck." As Senator Taft argued during the 1952 campaign, the United States faced bankruptcy if it did not slash its taxes and budget and eliminate the deficit. Secretary of the Treasury George Humphrey ageed that the voters of 1952 had instructed the new government to reduce the budget, including the defense expenditures. How could this be done while still following a tough stance against the Russians?

THE NEW LOOK IN DEFENSE

The Eisenhower administration developed a "New Look" as a military posture to reconcile the competing claims of the military for more money and the Treasury Department for smaller deficits. The New Look required the

Defense Department to reduce the size of conventional forces and rely upon nuclear weapons to terrify the Soviet Union into accommodation. The air force, with its heavy bombers, would win the race for more defense expenditures, while the army, especially the infantry branch, was cut from twenty to fourteen divisions, a slash of five hundred thousand men. Eisenhower, a former commander of the army, believed that he alone could make such severe cuts in the size of the defense establishment. No one could accuse an old war hero of being indifferent to the needs of the military.

John Foster Dulles gave his own interpretation of the New Look in a publicly aired speech before the Council on Foreign Relations in New York on January 12, 1954. He announced that in the future the United States would no longer be bound to use conventional arms to fight the Soviet Union. Instead, he proclaimed a policy of "massive retaliatory power" to halt aggression. Simply put, the United States now threatened to use the most awesome weapons in its arsenal against the cities of the Soviet Union in cases such as the war in Korea. Massive retaliation ignited a firestorm of protest. Editorialists in the *New York Times* and Walter Lippmann in the *New York Herald Tribune* accused Dulles of going to the "brink of war" to threaten the Soviets. But the president refused to join the debate. He told reporters that Dulles was "merely stating what, to my mind, is a fundamental truth." Later, he informed a March 17, 1954, press conference that the beauty of the policy of massive retaliation was its purposeful vagueness. No one "would undertake to say exactly what we would do under all that variety of circumstances."

A NEW ASIA POLICY

The new administration had its first chance to demonstrate its differences from Truman in Asian affairs. Eisenhower moved quickly to end the deadlock in Korea with a combination of negotiations and threats to use the atomic bomb. Peace talks, begun in 1951, had been stalled over the issue of North Korean prisoners of war. The North Korean government wanted them repatriated while the government of South Korea asserted that the prisoners wanted to remain in the South. In June, South Korean president Syngman Rhee broke the deadlock himself by releasing the prisoners in the South. Some Americans also wanted to stay in North Korea, which caused great embarrassment to the United States. Still, with the end of the prisoners issue, an American negotiator, Adm. C. Turner Joy, worked out an armistice arrangement with his Chinese and North Korean counterparts. The final agreement, signed at the border at Panmunjon in early July 1953, called for a division of Korea at approximately the same lines which had existed in June 1950—the Thirty-Eighth Parallel. The partition would not be permanent, however, as the two Koreas promised to open talks aimed at unification. United States forces under the auspices of the United Nations remained until an agreement could be worked out to send them home. A demilitarized zone five kilometers wide separated the two parts of Korea until reunification.

With the war settled, the first real test of the doctrine of massive retaliation came in Indochina in 1954. The civil war raging in Indochina since 1946 had attracted increasing American attention. In May 1950, the Truman administration had begun the process of paying for the French war effort. The same spring, National Security Council Memorandum 64 described Indochina as vital to the United States. Three years later, in August 1953, the NSC warned that "the loss of Indochina would be critical to the security of the United States." The council urged full support for the French war effort because "any negotiated settlement would mean the eventual loss to communism not only of Indochina but of the whole of Southeast Asia."

Encouraged by American backing, the French adopted the Navarre Plan, a creation of the new commander in Indochina, Gen. Henri Navarre. He proposed an army of five hundred fifty thousand French and Vietnamese troops to launch an offensive against the Vietminh. The United States would pay $385 million for the operation. Secretary of State Dulles assured a press conference that the Navarre Plan would "break the back of organized Communist aggression" by the end of the 1955 fighting campaign. A month later, in January 1954, Navarre forced a showdown with the Vietminh by trying to hold Dienbienphu, a Vietnamese outpost near Vietnam's borders with China and Laos. Dienbienphu, a major crossroads in a deep valley, was not a natural fortress. Twelve thousand French troops were surrounded by the Vietminh and several divisions of Chinese Communist troops who had been relieved by the end of the Korean War. In March, a panicky French government sent the chief of staff, Gen. Paul Ely, to Washington to ask for more aid. His American counterpart, Adm. Arthur Radford, was more forthcoming than Ely could have dreamed. The admiral offered an American air raid against the Vietminh attackers. Radford proposed a plan, code-named VULTURE, in which sixty American bombers based in the Philippines aided by one hundred fifty carrierbased fighters would attack the Communists. This massive air raid, possibly including tactical nuclear weapons, would break the siege and rescue the French from certain defeat. Vice-President Richard Nixon enthusiastically backed the suggestion for possible use of atomic weapons to lift the siege.

VULTURE never flew. President Eisenhower scrapped it in April. He believed that Indochina was either a "domino," the fall of which would set in motion a chain reaction, or a "cork in the bottle" containing communism. But he also had little faith in the French. He decided that they had badly mishandled the affairs of Indochina by clinging to their imperial role. More-over, Eisenhower would not act without support from the British and the United States Congress. British prime minister Winston Churchill refused to give his country's assent to an international force to rescue the French, and congressional leaders in the United States proved unwilling to engage in an-other Asian land war. Senate minority leader, Democrat Lyndon Johnson of Texas, railed against "sending American GI's into the mud and muck of In-dochina on a bloodletting spree." Massachusetts senator John F. Kennedy proclaimed that an American war in Indochina would be "dangerous, futile and selfdestructive."

On May 8, the French garrison at Dienbienphu surrendered to the Vi-etminh forces under Gen. Nguyen Giap. A new French Socialist government under Prime Minister Pierre Mendès-France came to power in June vowing to end the war in one month. France agreed to open negotiations with the Vietminh and the British, Soviets, and Chinese at Geneva to end the war. American policy was ambiguous in late May. Eisenhower briefly approved a Joint Chiefs of Staff plan for "employing atomic weapons, whenever advan-tageous . . . against those military targets in China" in case the Chinese en-tered the war. Eisenhower was careful, however, to link his acceptance of the plan to European support. He told Robert Cutler, his national security ad-viser, that "unilateral action by the United States in a case of this kind would destroy us. . . . If we intervened alone in this case we would be expected to intervene alone in other parts of the world."

Instead of dropping bombs, the United States reluctantly allowed the Geneva Conference to proceed with Britain and the Soviet Union acting as cosponsors. The Soviets and the Chinese applied pressure to the Vietminh to accept a division of Vietnam at the Seventeenth Parallel, even though the Communist forces controlled two-thirds of the country. The Chinese and So-viets reasoned that it was only a matter of time before Ho Chi Minh's forces completed their unification of the country. Faced with a lack of support from his two principal allies, Ho agreed to withdraw. He expected elections to be held within two years, and these polls would give his forces complete con-trol of the entire country. The United States never signed these accords. Dulles only announced that the United States would support "free elections supervised by the United Nations."

Shortly thereafter, the United States began a program of direct aid to the government of South Vietnam. In late September and early October 1954, Dulles said that American aid would go directly to the government of South Vietnam and not through the French. America would not permit the French to maintain their "protected preferential market," and Japan could not now sell directly to South Vietnam. In November, an American military mission headed by Gen. J. Lawton Collins came to Saigon to help train the

South Vietnam President Ngo Dinh Diem arrives at the Saigon cathedral with
Bishop Nguyen Van Binh. *(Wide World Photos)*

South Vietnamese army. That fall the United States also brought Ngo Dinh
Diem, exiled at the Maryknoll mission's headquarters in Ossining, New York,
to Saigon to take over the government of South Vietnam over the strenuous
objections of the French.

The next summer, the French evacuated South Vietnam, and President
Diem announced that he would not hold the elections called for in the
Geneva accord. The United States supported this decision, arguing that
Diem's government had not signed the Geneva agreement. More to the
point, Dulles thought that Diem would have a difficult time defeating Ho in
any election. Subsequently, the United States continued to arm and supply
the government of Vietnam.

Americans were everywhere in South Vietnam from 1956 to 1960. Military men helped create the Army of the Republic of South Vietnam (ARVN).
Col. Edward Lansdale arrived in Saigon to apply lessons learned in the Philippines war against Communists. He soon recruited an army of secret agents
to harass, arrest, and kill revolutionaries. The United States embassy in Saigon
housed university and government law enforcement experts who instructed

local policemen in controlling crowds, checking passports, and interrogating suspicious characters. Economic assistance officers scurried into the countryside to tell bewildered villagers how to increase crop yields, pay their landlords, and open their ears for antigovernment remarks.

Immediately after the Geneva agreements temporarily split Indochina, Eisenhower faced a flare-up of fighting between the Communist and Nationalist Chinese. On the morning of September 3, 1954, Communist artillery on the mainland began shelling Nationalist positions on the offshore island of Quemoy. Two American soldiers died in the assault, and the Eisenhower administration found itself in the midst of a dilemma.

During the campaign of 1952, Republicans had complained that the Truman administration had hamstrung Jiang Jieshi in his campaign to recapture control of China. They resented the Democrats' sending the Seventh Fleet to the Formosa Strait for the purpose of preventing Jiang from invading China while the Korean War went on. Vowing to "unleash Jiang Jieshi," the Eisenhower administration had removed the fleet in 1953. In August 1954, Chinese Communist foreign minister Zhou Enlai renewed the pledge to liberate Taiwan from the Nationalists. Eisenhower responded by remarking that "any invasion of Taiwan would have to run over the Seventh Fleet," which now returned to protect the Nationalists. But the islands of Quemoy and Matsu, a few miles off the coast of the mainland and directly opposite its port city of Amoy, were a different matter. They had always been a part of mainland China, and American moves to resist the Communists there might seem to be a direct assault on the mainland.

Eisenhower resisted calls from the Joint Chiefs of Staff to bomb the mainland. He sent Dulles to Taiwan to restrain Jiang. The secretary of state worked out a defense treaty with the Nationalists under which the United States pledged to defend Taiwan. In return, the Nationalists agreed not to use force against the mainland without first consulting the United States. By signing a defense treaty with the Nationalists, Eisenhower wrecked what chances remained for a rapprochement with the Communists. At the same time, the defense pact was Ike's payment to the right wing of the Republican party, which had demanded that the administration blockade the entire coast of China.

In mid-January 1955, the crisis in the Formosa Strait reached a new height when the Communists attacked the Tachen Islands, about two hundred miles northwest of Taiwan. Ike's military advisers told him that the Tachens were not vital to the security of Taiwan. Consequently, he helped the Nationalists evacuate them while asking Congress for a joint resolution authorizing the use of force to protect the island of Taiwan and the nearby Pescadores chain. Congress passed a resolution at the end of January, leaving vague whether the United States had made a commitment to defend the offshore islands of Quemoy and Matsu as well as Taiwan itself.

A little over a month later, Secretary of State Dulles returned from a trip to Asia to announce that the situation in the Formosa Strait was worse than he had realized. He told a Washington news conference on March 10 that he feared a Communist attack on Quemoy and Matsu as a prelude to an invasion of Taiwan. The secretary then touched off a major war scare by remarking, "If we defend Quemoy and Matsu we'll have to use atomic weapons." Two days later, on March 12, Dulles informed reporters of "clean" nuclear weapons "of precision which can utterly destroy military targets without endangering unrelated civilian centers." His aides checked with the Pentagon and found that such weapons did not exist and that the smallest nuclear attack on China would cost a minimum of twelve million civilian lives. Eisenhower heightened the war tension with a remark to the press on March 15. He said that he saw "no reason why [tactical nuclear weapons] should not be used exactly as you would use a bullet or anything else." Over the next week, hawks rallied to the president. Gen. James Van Fleet, the former commander of the Eighth Army in Korea, advocated sending more American troops to Quemoy and Matsu. If the Communists continued their shelling, the Americans should "shoot back with atomic weapons." Doves were less certain. Majority Leader Lyndon Johnson feared an "irresponsible adventure." Former Democratic presidential candidate Adlai Stevenson infuriated Eisenhower when he accused him of "risking a third world war for the defense of these little islands."

With war fever running high, Eisenhower had to backtrack. His press secretary, James Hagerty, advised him to duck questions about the nuclear warning to China at his March 23 press conference. "Don't worry, Jim, . . . I'll just confuse them." The president then told a reporter who asked about the use of atomic bombs to defend Quemoy that he could not make any predictions. "Every war is going to astonish you in the way it occurred, and in the way it is carried out." Eisenhower thereby managed to warn the Chinese without at the same time saying what he would do. Ike's critics accused him of bringing the country to the brink of war and allowing his secretary of state to get out of hand. His supporters make a novel defense. According to Robert Divine, "The beauty of Eisenhower's policy is that to this day no one can be sure whether or not he would have responded militarily to an invasion of the offshore islands, and whether he would have used nuclear weapons."

COVERT OPERATIONS: IRAN AND GUATEMALA

Eisenhower and Dulles's threat to use atomic weapons in Asia was part of a careful strategy of public diplomacy. At the same time, the United States moved secretly to pursue its goals in international affairs. The Central Intelligence Agency conducted these operations in Iran and in Guatemala.

The American involvement with Iran represented one aspect of American petroleum policy in the Middle East. Since the 1940s, American petroleum companies had become active in the Persian Gulf, a region traditionally the preserve of the British, French, and Dutch corporations. During the Truman administration, the government developed a deliberate policy of noninterference in the international activities of the oil companies. In 1950, the State Department came up with a "golden gimmick" to lessen the tax burden on the four American companies—Standard of California, Texaco, Mobil, and Esso (later Exxon)—which made up Aramco (Arabian American Oil Company). Under Acheson's plan, Aramco could deduct the amount of royalty it paid to the Saudi Arabian government from its United States income taxes. The State Department then informed Saudi Arabia that the $50 million it received from the oil companies really would have been foreign aid from the United States. In this way, the government of the United States could offer aid to Saudi Arabia without annoying supporters of Israel who would not like to see the United States underwrite the Saudi monarchy.

The Eisenhower administration inherited this free rein for the oil companies. It saw the policy tested first in Iran in 1953. Two years earlier, Dr. Mohammed Mossadeq had become Iran's prime minister. An enthusiastic opponent of foreign domination of Iran's wealth, Mossadeq had nationalized the holdings of the Anglo-Iranian oil company. The international oil companies had responded with a boycott of Iranian oil. American firms active in the Persian Gulf and Saudi Arabia happily cooperated with the boycott, for it made their own holdings in other countries more valuable. Faced with the united hostility of the international oil companies, the Iranian government considered turning to the Soviet Union. On May 28, the prime minister cabled Eisenhower that the boycott of the international oil companies might force him to turn to the Soviet Union for aid. Eisenhower waited until July to reply. When he did, he refused to provide any aid, and he warned Iran that it should undertake a "reasonable settlement" with the British.

As a nationalist, Mossadeq distrusted all outside powers' attempts to control Iran's source of wealth, oil, and its territory. Soviet troops had occupied his country from 1942 to 1946 when they had withdrawn under threats from the United States. Washington had looked on sourly as London and Moscow agreed in 1942 jointly to control Iran's foreign policy until the war ended. The arrangement seemed to revive the old Anglo-Russian condominium in the Persian Gulf, and American oilmen resented a British grab of Iran's vast petroleum reserves. As the Cold War spread in 1946, the United States used its majority in the United Nations to force Soviet troops to return home from Iran. While Tehran feared their eventual return, the grip of foreign oil companies seemed a more pressing problem.

Throughout these maneuvers, Shah Mohammed Reza Pahlevi, the official head of state, remained quiet. Installed by the British in 1941, he replaced his father, Reza Pahlevi, who had dallied with the Nazis in hopes of evicting the British. During the war, Britain and the Soviet Union curbed the monarch's powers. Once foreign troops left, he agreed to a constitutional monarchy. The hostility of Prime Minister Mossadeq to Britain and his adoption of Soviet rhetoric, however, offered the shah his chance to gain absolute power. His personal interests coincided temporarily with those of American oil executives and diplomats who wanted for reasons of their own to take over Britain's place in the confrontation with Russia in the Persian Gulf.

Privately, Eisenhower moved to overthrow the government of Iran. He authorized the CIA to carry out a coup against the government and restore the power of the shah. Kermit Roosevelt, grandson of President Theodore Roosevelt and a veteran of the World War II spy agency the OSS, became the organizer of the coup on the scene. Arriving in Tehran in early August, he found Gen. Fazollah Zahedi eager to lead the operation with the approval of the shah. Roosevelt then recruited a mob made up of circus performers—weight lifters and trapeze artists—and army and police NCOs dressed in civilian clothes who took to the streets in antigovernment demonstrations. An enraged prime minister, seeing the hand of a figurehead shah behind the scenes, moved to arrest the monarch, who fled to Rome. Then Roosevelt conducted a "James Bond–type" operation in which the army staged an assault on the Parliament, arrested the prime minister, and installed Zahedi in his place. In Washington, Eisenhower publicly congratulated Zahedi and the shah on September 5, and announced that the United States would offer $45 million to the new government. He secretly awarded the National Security Medal to Kermit Roosevelt.

Among the great winners in the American-sponsored coup were United States oil companies. Eisenhower, having done well with one president's grandson, chose another's son, Herbert Hoover, Jr., as the negotiator between Tehran and the British oil companies. Hoover had earlier advised Iran on its dealings with the British oil companies, and he knew that the shah would lose support of his subjects if he simply restored the old contracts. Furthermore, as an old American oilman, Hoover saw an opportunity for American firms in the oilfields. At first, the American firms demurred. Their own holdings in the Persian Gulf and Saudi Arabia had done well when the major companies had refused to handle Iranian crude oil. Nonetheless, Hoover asked them to "serve the national interest" and move into Iran. They agreed if the American government promised to exempt them from antitrust actions for acting together in Iran. The president himself told Attorney General Herbert Brownell that "the enforcement of the anti-trust laws of the United States against the Western oil companies operating in the Near East may be deemed secondary to the national security interest."

Hoover then assembled a new consortium of Western companies to distribute Iranian oil. The negotiations took a year; the Iranian Parliament ratified the final terms in October 1954. Under the agreement, the Iranian National Oil Company retained control of the oilfields and refineries while the consortium of eight Western companies purchased the oil and agreed to distribute it. Anglo-Iranian Oil, the old British company, received a 40-percent share of the new consortium; the five American companies also got 40 percent, and the remaining 20 percent was divided between a Dutch and a French company. Faced with a glut of oil from the Middle East, the Western firms secretly agreed to limit the amount of oil they would buy from Iran. The Eisenhower administration's oil policy in the Iranian crisis enhanced the power of American firms. As of 1954, the United States stood poised to supplant the British as the major Western power active in the Middle East.

The Eisenhower administration used a similar covert technique to overthrow the government of the Central American country of Guatemala in 1954. That nation experienced a nationalist-liberal revolution in 1944. The new administration, made up of middle-class army officers and urban intellectuals, wanted an end to the large plantations which dominated the country's agriculture. They also called for a more democratic government with regular elections. These were duly held and Juan José Arevalo took office as the first freely elected presidenct since 1821. Arevalo began a program of political, labor, and land reforms. Calling his policy "spiritual socialism," he pushed a new constitution guaranteeing political rights and laws allowing agricultural laborers to form unions and strike. Limited by the Constitution to a term of six years, Arevalo supported Jacobo Arbenz Guzmán, his defense minister, in the 1950 election. One of Arbenz's conservative opponents, Francisco Javier Araña, met an assassin's bullet in July 1949, leaving only Miguel Ydígoras Fuentes, a fierce reactionary, as a conservative candidate. Arbenz won an overwhelming victory in 1950, and his government enacted an agrarian reform law which expropriated idle land and gave it to the poorest of the peasants.

The Eisenhower administration decided to rid Guatemala of Arbenz shortly after his government took over four hundred thousand acres of unused land owned by the Boston-based United Fruit Company. *La Fruitera*, as it was called in Latin America, profited handsomely from concessions granted earlier by conservative governments. It paid few taxes, had protection from competition, charged what it wanted for its port facilities, sent all of its profits back home, and was permitted to expand its operations at will. UFCO paid an intermittent wage of $1.36 a day for seasonal work. Laborers purchased company-supplied medical care, bought necessities at a company store, and rented cramped but clean living quarters from their employer. As they walked to the outhouses, they could peer over the high wire fence separating them from the opulent single-family homes, swimming pools, and golf courses of their North American bosses.

State Department officials joined publicity agents for United Fruit in asserting that Arbenz was a Communist and an agent of the Kremlin. The American ambassador to Guatemala, John Peurifoy, told a House committee, "I spent six hours with him one evening, and he talked like a Communist, and if he is not one, Mr. Chairman, he will do until one comes along." The United Fruit Company launched a campaign to channel this fear of communism into sympathy for its cause. It sponsored junkets to Guatemala for reporters, editors, and publishers. Well aware that the American government probably would not intervene by force solely to stop expropriation, United Fruit's public relations counsel, Edward Bernays, emphasized the supposed international Communist conspiracy. On May 3, 1954, the *New York Times* editorialized that the "constant harassment here [in Guatemala] to which the company [United Fruit] now is being subjected is largely a Communist tactic."

In the summer of 1953, Eisenhower authorized the CIA to develop a plan to overthrow the Arbenz government. Code-named PBSUCCESS, the operation established a field headquarters at Opa Locka, Florida, near Miami. The project cost between $5 million and $7 million, which was used to pay about one hundred Americans and an equal number of mercenaries recruited from Guatemala and neighboring Central American nations. These men received military training while other CIA operatives cast about for a suitable Guatemalan figurehead for the invasion. The CIA's experts rejected defeated presidential candidate Ydígoras Fuentes as too reactionary and finally settled on forty-year-old Carlos Enrique Castillo Armas, a military man who had trained at the United States Army School at Fort Leavenworth, Kansas. The CIA provided Armas with money, a radio station in neighboring Nicaragua, and an "army" made up of the mercenaries trained in Florida.

Certain that the United States was conspiring with the dictator of Nicaragua, Anastasio Somoza, to overthrow him, Arbenz sought military aid from Communist countries. The Kremlin, sensing an opportunity to embarrass the Americans in their own hemisphere, authorized the Skoda works in Czechoslovakia to send weapons to Guatemala. The Swedish freighter *Alfhem*, carrying nineteen hundred tons of small arms and light artillery, reached Puerto Barritos, Guatemala, on May 15. The CIA knew the shipment was on the way, and its arrival determined the date of Castillo Armas's uprising. The arms shipment drew denunciations from officials in Washington. Senate Foreign Relations Committee chairman Alexander Wiley (R., Wis.) insisted that it represented "part of the master plan of world communism," and President Eisenhower snapped that nineteen hundred tons went beyond "any legitimate, normal requirements of the Guatemalan armed forces." CIA director Allen Dulles assured the National Security Council that the arms shipment demonstrated Soviet contempt for the Monroe Doctrine and an intention to establish a military base in the Western Hemisphere.

On June 18, 1954, Castillo Armas's "army" of 1,950 men crossed the Honduran border into Guatemala. They settled down in a religious shrine six miles from the border and confidently awaited the collapse of Arbenz. The Guatemalan president believed the propaganda broadcasts of the Voice of Liberation radio stations. His nerves cracked as he envisioned Castillo Armas leading an effective fighting force backed by United States troops. The CIA had never intended to commit American forces, predicting that Arbenz would not fight. The clandestine radio stations broadcast an appeal by a liquor-laden defector from the Guatemalan air force for his fellow pilots to follow his lead and join Castillo Armas's forces. Faced with the imminent defection of his army, Arbenz considered arming the peasantry. The prospect of an armed popular militia gave the final push to the army officers, who saw their traditional privileges eliminated. The chiefs of the armed forces deserted Arbenz and demanded his resignation. On June 27, the president complied, fled the country, and left power to Castillo Armas. Guatemala slipped again into dictatorship. The lands of the United Fruit Company were restored. In Washington, the astonishing ease of the CIA's victory in Guatemala boosted the reputation of the agency and laid the groundwork for a later clandestine operation against Cuba in April 1961.

RELATIONS WITH THE SOVIET UNION

While the Cold War became a global conflict during the Eisenhower administration, relations with the Soviet Union remained the central issue. On March 5, 1953, barely six weeks after Ike took office, Josef Stalin died. His replacement as premier, Georgi Malenkov, departed from Stalin's foreign policy by seeking a relaxation of tension with the United States. Locked in a power struggle with the secretary of the Communist party, Nikita Khrushchev, Malenkov wished to concentrate on internal political problems. He hoped that a bid to end the Cold War would encourage the Western European allies to reduce their reliance upon the United States. In April, he called for the opening of talks between East and West on reducing forces in Europe.

The initial response to Malenkov's peace initiative was hesitant and confused. No one in the State Department wanted to incur the wrath of Senator McCarthy. Secretary of State Dulles, clinging to a belief in an "irreconcilable conflict" between "Godless communism" and the West, was loath to respond favorably to Malenkov's offer. Eisenhower offered the formal answer to the Soviet premier's new tactics on April 16 when he admitted that detente could come if the Soviets ended Communist revolts in Malaya and Indochina, allowed "a free and united Germany with a government based on free and secret elections," "free choice" of governments in Eastern Europe, and a treaty restoring Austrian independence." Dulles testified before the Senate Foreign Relations Committee the next day. The *New York Times* headlined his remarks "DULLES BIDS SOVIETS COOPERATE OR FACE VAST WEST ARMING."

This belligerent approach drew fire from a surprising source, the old antiCommunist and opponent of appeasement Winston Churchill, who on May 11 called for a "summit conference" for world leaders to solve problems. A call from Churchill, the most respected leader in the Western alliance, profoundly unnerved officials in Washington. Senate majority leader William Knowland assumed that Churchill favored a "Far Eastern Munich." Eisenhower himself had explained why the official reaction was cool. In words that bewildered reporters, he muttered, "The world happened to be round and it had no end and he didn't see how you could discuss the problems, the great basic problems of today, which were so largely philosophical in character, without thinking in global terms." Whatever the president had in mind, the result was that no meeting with the Soviet leaders took place before 1955.

In the meantime, the arms race between the atomic powers became more heated. The United States pressed forward with the development of the "superweapon," the thermonuclear hydrogen bomb, despite the misgivings of J. Robert Oppenheimer, the scientist who headed the research project which created the atomic bomb. Oppenheimer lost his security clearance for his refusal to be "enthusiastic" about the hydrogen bomb, a charge which provoked *Washington Post* cartoonist Herbert Block to produce a drawing of a workman entering a scientist's office and replacing the sign urging "Think" with one demanding "Enthuse." On March 1, 1954, the Atomic Energy Commission detonated an H-bomb at Bikini Atoll in the South Pacific. Twenty-three Japanese fishermen aboard the *Lucky Dragon* had the bad luck to be trolling about eighty miles from the blast. They all suffered radiation poisoning, and one of them died shortly thereafter. Their plight awakened the world to the dangers of radioactive fallout. Atomic Energy Commission chairman Lewis Strauss compounded the problem by saying that fallout was not much of a problem since most of it fell in the direct vicinity of a blast. And how big might that blast be? reporters asked. "An H-bomb can be made as— large enough to take out a city . . . to destroy a city."

By the fall of 1954, the Soviets had exploded their own H-bomb, eliminating the hopes of Americans to enjoy a few more years of nuclear superiority. The Eisenhower administration now responded to the growing international pressure for a summit conference with the Soviet leaders. The Russians announced in April that they were willing to sign a peace treaty for Austria, something they had resisted since 1945. The former wartime allies quickly signed an agreement creating a neutral Austria in May. Later that month, the Soviet delegate to the UN Disarmament Conference presented a new plan to end the arms race. The Soviet proposal moved closer to Western plans for reduction of conventional forces as well as nuclear arms. The ground was now prepared for a summit conference of the heads of government of the Western alliance and the Soviet Union.

Eisenhower met with the new Soviet leaders, Prime Minister Nikolai Bulganin, who had replaced Malenkov, and Party Secretary Nikita Khrushchev, the third week of July 1955 in Geneva, Switzerland. The president came equipped with a plan for mutual aerial inspection of Western and Soviet nuclear facilities. This "Open Skies" proposal emerged from a committee of arms experts headed by presidential assistant Nelson Rockefeller. Secretary of State Dulles objected to the plan since it seemed to depart from his hard line. The president told Dulles he would not announce Open Skies before the conference, but he annoyed the secretary of state by raising the hopes of the public before his departure for Geneva. In a nationally televised speech before he left, Eisenhower predicted that the summit conference would "change the spirit which has characterized the intergovernmental relationship of the world during the past ten years."

Relations were cool between the Soviet Union and the United States at the opening of the conference. Bulganin and Khrushchev refused to budge on the issue of the reunification of Germany. On the fourth day of the conference, Eisenhower showed the Open Skies proposal to British prime minister Anthony Eden, who immediately gave his approval. He then presented it theatrically to the entire assembly. Taking off his glasses and speaking directly to the Soviet leaders, he proposed regular and frequent aerial inspections of American military facilities in return for the same privilege from the Soviets. A thunderstorm dramatically punctuated the president's performance; as soon as he finished speaking, lightning flashed and the lights went out in the room.

The British and the French predictably voiced approval of the American plan. The Soviets, finding themselves upstaged, seemed nonplussed. They made no public response to Open Skies, but that evening Khrushchev drew Eisenhower aside at a cocktail party that ended the day's session. The translator, American ambassador to the Soviet Union Charles Bohlen, recalled the Soviet leader asking Eisenhower "whom was he trying to fool?" Khrushchev called Open Skies a "very transparent espionage device." Eisenhower seemed to agree since the Russians already knew the locations of most

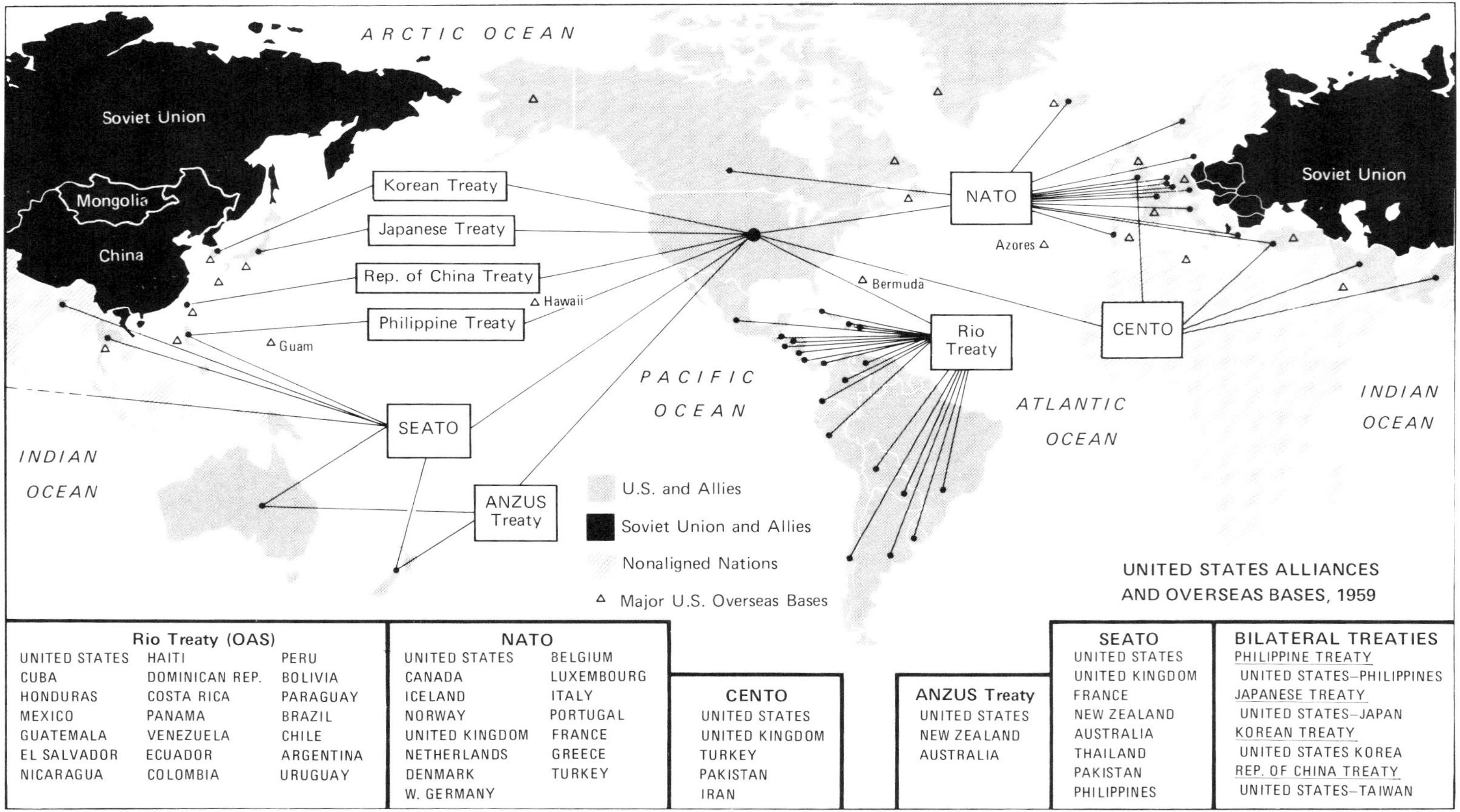
ARCTIC OCEAN
Soviet Union
Mongolia
China
Korean Treaty
Japanese Treaty
Rep. of China Treaty
Philippine Treaty
Hawaii
Guam
SEATO
ANZUS Treaty
INDIAN OCEAN
PACIFIC OCEAN
NATO
Azores
Bermuda
Rio Treaty
CENTO
Soviet Union
ATLANTIC OCEAN
INDIAN OCEAN
U.S. and Allies
Soviet Union and Allies
Nonaligned Nations
Major U.S. Overseas Bases
UNITED STATES ALLIANCES
AND OVERSEAS BASES, 1959
Rio Treaty (OAS)
UNITED STATES
CUBA
HONDURAS
MEXICO
GUATEMALA
EL SALVADOR
NICARAGUA
HAITI
DOMINICAN REP.
COSTA RICA
PANAMA
VENEZUELA
ECUADOR
COLOMBIA
PERU
BOLIVIA
PARAGUAY
BRAZIL
CHILE
ARGENTINA
URUGUAY
NATO
UNITED STATES
CANADA
ICELAND
NORWAY
UNITED KINGDOM
NETHERLANDS
DENMARK
W. GERMANY
BELGIUM
LUXEMBOURG
ITALY
PORTUGAL
FRANCE
GREECE
TURKEY
CENTO
UNITED STATES
UNITED KINGDOM
TURKEY
PAKISTAN
IRAN
ANZUS Treaty
UNITED STATES
NEW ZEALAND
AUSTRALIA
SEATO
UNITED STATES
UNITED KINGDOM
FRANCE
NEW ZEALAND
AUSTRALIA
THAILAND
PAKISTAN
PHILIPPINES
BILATERAL TREATIES
PHILIPPINE TREATY
UNITED STATES–PHILIPPINES
JAPANESE TREATY
UNITED STATES–JAPAN
KOREAN TREATY
UNITED STATES KOREA
REP. OF CHINA TREATY
UNITED STATES–TAIWAN

American military facilities. He told Nelson Rockefeller that "mutual agreements for such overflights would undoubtedly benefit us more than the Russians, because we know very little about their installations." Ten years later, Eisenhower told an interviewer who asked about Open Skies, "We knew the Soviets wouldn't accept it. We were sure of that." The Geneva Conference ended with no agreements on the major issues of the future of Germany or disarmament. East and West did conclude a cultural exchange agreement, and newspapers wrote of a "spirit of Geneva" which reduced the tensions over the arms race.

The new spirit survived barely a year after the conference. In February 1956, Khrushchev, having banished Bulganin, consolidated his hold on the party apparatus with a speech before the Twentieth Congress of the Communist Party denouncing the crimes of Josef Stalin. Despite attempts to keep the address secret, news leaked to Eastern Europe where reformers hoped that the Soviets would permit a relaxation of repression. In June, riots erupted in Poland, where opponents of the regime demanded the ouster of Stalinists. A reformer, Wladislaw Gomulka, took power pledging an end to some of the excesses of the secret police. In the fall, Khrushchev thought he had gone too far, and he told Gomulka to rein the reforms. Instead, the Polish leader threatened to call out the Polish public. Khrushchev backed down, a retreat which encouraged anti-Communists in Hungary. Students took to the streets in Budapest on October 23, demanding the replacement of long-time Stalinist Erno Gëro with Imre Nagy. When the secret police sought to crush the demonstrations, workers struck. The Soviets sought to stem the tide by agreeing to the exchange of Nagy for Gëro, but the crowd no longer could be mollified. They demanded the removal of Soviet troops, which was done on October 28. Three days later, in the midst of an Anglo-French-Israeli attack on Egypt, the Soviet leaders reversed themselves. The new Hungarian government had withdrawn from the Warsaw Pact on October 29; that was too grave a threat to Soviet control over its Eastern European empire. As the Anglo-French army moved toward the Suez Canal on November 4–5, Russian tanks crushed the Hungarian uprising.

American reaction appeared hesitant and confused. After bombastically calling for the "liberation" of Eastern Europe in the campaign of 1952, Republicans did nothing to help the Hungarians. The United States probably encouraged the Hungarians to make a futile gesture of defiance with the broadcasts emanating from American Radio Free Europe headquartered in Munich. At the height of the crisis, on November 3, John Foster Dulles, who had gone to the "brink of war" with the Soviets, underwent emergency surgery on the stomach cancer which eventually killed him in 1959.

All of this activity, or handwringing, took place in the midst of the presidential election of 1956. Eisenhower had delayed announcing his candidacy until early 1956. He had suffered a heart attack in mid-1955, and Democrats were encouraged that the genial, grandfatherly Ike would step aside for the sharp-tongued and not especially popular Richard M. Nixon. The prospect of a Nixon bid for the White House alarmed Republican regulars who thought that Ike was the only choice to continue Republican rule. For their part, the Democrats again chose Adlai Stevenson. Foreign policy played a small but important part in the campaign of 1956. Ike ran on his record of ending the war in Korea and the nascent spirit of Geneva. Stevenson opposed him from both the left and the right. On the more liberal side, the Democratic candidate called for disarmament, an end to the testing of atomic weapons, and study of the possible end to the draft. With the crisis in the Middle East and Hungary at full boil, Stevenson accurately pointed out that the Eisenhower administration had been slow to recognize "a vast new upheaval in the balance of world power." At the same time, Stevenson attacked from more nationalist assumptions, reviving old Cold War rhetoric. He faulted Ike for letting half of Indochina "become a new Communist satellite," and he contrasted Harry Truman's toughness with the Soviets with Ike's neglect of "great opportunities to exploit weaknesses in the Communist ranks and advance the cause of peace." Whatever Stevenson said was to little avail. A popular president running against an opponent with little difference to offer except style, he defeated Stevenson with 57 percent of the vote.

SUEZ AND LEBANON

Another of America's gloomy encounters with revolutionary nationalism occurred in the Suez crisis of 1956. Four years earlier, the corrupt and inept Egyptian monarchy of King Farouk had been toppled in an army coup led by Col. Gamal Nasser. The rebels had been angry and humiliated at the defeat inflicted on the Arabs by the Israelis in 1948. Israeli military superiority over Egypt continued after the coup as the Israelis launched an attack across the border into the Gaza Strip in 1955. Nasser wanted arms to rebuild his defenses. The Western nations proved unwilling to supply them, so in September 1955, Egypt concluded an agreement with Czechoslovakia to supply tanks and artillery.

At this point, Dulles became interested in bidding for Nasser's friendship with American financial support for the planned Aswan Dam. This project would stop the waters of the lower Nile, providing electric power for all of Egypt, open new land for cultivation, and demonstrate to the world that Egypt had entered the world of electric modernity. In December, the United States and Great Britain agreed in principle to help finance the Aswan project. In February 1956, Nasser reached an agreement with Eugene Black, the president of the World Bank, for funds from America, Britain, and the bank.

Nasser then formally requested $100 million in aid from the United States. He heard nothing for the next five months.

In the meantime, Dulles changed his attitude toward Nasser. The Czech arms deal was followed in April by a military alliance with Saudi Arabia, Syria, and Yemen, the obvious target of which was Israel. In May, Nasser dropped his diplomatic relations with Jiang Jieshi and recognized the government in Beijing. An outraged China Lobby allied with Southern congressmen from cotton-producing states who feared the Aswan Dam would depress cotton prices to block the American support for the project. Dulles reasoned that he could teach Nasser a lesson if he withdrew American support for the Aswan Dam. Ignoring a warning from Eugene Black that "all hell might break loose" if he reneged on his promise, Dulles on July 19 bluntly declared that the United States would not send money to Egypt for the project.

One week later, Nasser struck back by nationalizing the British-owned Universal Suez Canal Company. The Egyptian leader promised to keep the canal open to all former users of the waterway, but the British and French did not believe him. Nearly all of Europe's oil came through the canal, and the Europeans feared that an intense nationalist such as Nasser might interrupt this flow. Dulles tried to reduce tensions between the Europeans and Egyptians with a solution which pleased neither side. He proposed a users' association to manage the canal. Nasser did not want to share power with the foreigners, and the Europeans distrusted any Egyptian control. At the end of July, the British foreign minister let Dulles know that the Europeans would move militarily against Egypt if the crisis were not resolved quickly.

By October, Egypt still operated the canal on its own, and the British and the French secretly adopted a plan to go to war. They coordinated their strategy with the government of Israel, which believed that the European anger at Nasser was the perfect cover by which they could rid themselves of the irritating foe. In mid-October, Israeli prime minister David Ben-Gurion flew secretly to an airfield outside of Paris where he reached an agreement with the British and French governments for a joint assault on Egypt. The Israeli army crossed the frontier into the Sinai Desert on October 29, and the next day the British and French announced that they would join the war "to protect the Suez Canal," already closed by sunken vessels. French and British paratroopers landed in the zone on November 1 and demanded that the Egyptian and Israeli forces withdraw to a zone five miles on either side of the waterway.

The Anglo-French statement of protection for free passage through Suez fooled no one. Opposition parties in France and Britain raised a howl, and the British Parliament erupted in shouts. The assault failed in its underlying purpose of evicting Nasser. It could not keep the ships moving, and the Western alliance underwent its greatest strain. In Washington, Dulles, who heartily disliked British prime minister Eden, thought the British had purposely misled him. The United States joined with the Soviet Union in condemning the Western powers and Israel at the United Nations, where the General Assembly voted a resolution demanding a cease-fire. This alignment between the Americans and the Soviets came at an especially embarrassing juncture, for the Soviet tanks were at that moment crushing the counterrevolution in the streets of Budapest.

With the sinking of ships in Suez, Europe lost access to Middle Eastern oil. Dulles thereupon pressed Latin American nations not to send petroleum to Britain and France as long as they remained in Egypt. In December, the Europeans caved in to American pressure and announced their withdrawal from Egypt. American-European relations were badly shaken, and the French especially rethought their policy toward Arab nationalism. Instead of trying to overcome nationalists like Nasser, the French moved over the next few years to make an accommodation with them.

So did the Americans. In January 1957, Eisenhower asked Congress for a resolution endorsing the president's use of force in the Middle East "to block Communist aggression." This so-called Eisenhower Doctrine required Congress to yield its traditional warmaking power to the president, and friends of Israel in the Senate complained that the president sacrificed support for the Jewish state by posing as the protector of anti-Communist Arab nations. Still, Ike, like Truman before him, chose to use the fear of the Soviet Union to gain his foreign policy objectives; the Eisenhower Doctrine sailed through the Democratic-controlled House and Senate in March. That same month, the administration also terrified Israel into withdrawing fully from the Sinai Desert and Gaza Strip captured from Egypt the previous November. In return for a pledge of a United Nations buffer force in the Sinai and UN control over Sharm el Sheik, the point controlling the access to Israel's Red Sea port of Eilat, Israel agreed to leave the Sinai. Lurking behind the UN proposals was an American threat to embargo the millions of dollars American Jews sent in aid to Israel.

The Eisenhower Doctrine received its major test in mid-1958. In the spring, Nasser formed a United Arab Republic of Egypt, Syria, and Yemen. Two months later, on July 14, a nationalist coup occurred in Iraq, where Gen. Abdel Karim Kassim toppled the monarchy. Kassim's first move was to announce the opening of talks with Nasser about joining the UAR.

Iraq was important for its oil, but its location made it inaccessible to American pressure. Dulles wanted to demonstrate American power in the Middle East, and he found a convenient arena in Lebanon. On the day news of the Kassim coup reached Washington, the United States received a request from the president of Lebanon, Camille Chamoun, a Maronite Christian, for help in Lebanon's civil war. Eisenhower immediately ordered fourteen thousand American soldiers to Lebanon to quell what was portrayed as a threat and as a "Communist-inspired" coup d'état. Sunbathers on the beaches of Beirut, Lebanon's capital, watched in astonishment as a division of combat-clad marines waded ashore looking for Communists. This large force had its effect on the new government in Iraq and on Nasser in Egypt. Over the next few months, Iraq assured Western oil companies that their properties were safe, and Kassim dropped his bid for membership in the UAR. Nasser as well had to back down after flying to Moscow in the midst of the crisis and learning that the Soviet Union would not move beyond verbal support.

SOCIAL CONFORMITY IN THE COLD WAR

Consensus over foreign policy from 1945 to 1960 was bought at the cost of enforced silence and social conformity. A "silent generation" of college students looked forward to quiet suburban houses and unchallenging, secure and well-paid jobs in large, anonymous organizations. Political issues of war and peace and capitalism, socialism, and communism seemed curiously old-fashioned. One sociologist, Daniel Bell, himself a former radical in the thirties, noted an "end of ideology." Nowadays, he claimed, all political questions could be easily resolved through good public administration.

Some social critics lamented the blandness of the times. David Reisman, a Harvard sociologist, noted in his 1950 study *The Lonely Crowd* that the American national character had been transformed from the rugged individualism of "inner-directed," self-confident sorts to a mindless, timid herd of "other-directed" conformists. William H. Whyte, the editor of Henry Luce's *Fortune* magazine, decried the sheeplike behavior of modern managers who had recruited a phalanx of fearful "organization men" to take over large corporations. John Kenneth Galbraith, a liberal economist at Harvard, attracted wide public comment with his 1958 study *The Affluent Society,* in which he worried about America's "private affluence and public squalor." Reisman, Whyte, and Galbraith represented the limits of acceptable dissent in the fifties. But other, outside voices also spoke even if respectable opinion paid little attention. As in the twenties, some of the most pungent criticism came from poets. Where the "lost generation" of expatriates excoriated American culture from Paris cafés, "beatnik" poets, wearing black turtleneck sweaters, goatees, and berets, settled into coffeehouses in New York, San Francisco, and Denver to listen to jazz, smoke marijuana, and read their works. One of the best known of the beats, then and later, was Allen Ginsberg. In one 1956 poem he howled, "I saw the best minds of my generation destroyed by madness." In another, more directly political effort, called "America," he mocked "the impression I get from looking at the television set":

America you don't really want to go to war.
America it's them bad Russians
Them Russians them Russians and them Chinamen. And them Russians.
The Russia wants to eat us alive. The Russia's power mad. She wants to
    take our cars from our garages.
Her wants to grab Chicago. Her needs a Red Readers' Digest . . . That no
    good.

No one took Ginsberg seriously. Ten years later, many "responsible" people sounded just like beat poets.

THE REVIVAL OF FEAR, 1957–1960

The second Eisenhower administration saw a revival of the fear of the Soviet Union. Opposition Democrats, searching for an issue for the 1960 election, seized upon the supposed growth in Soviet military power. They decried decline in American "prestige" in Latin America, Asia, and Africa, and they accused the Eisenhower administration of a weak and vacillating response to the inevitable changes in world politics.

The renewed concern over Soviet might began on October 4, 1957, when the Soviets launched the world's first space satellite, called *Sputnik*. American education experts were stunned at what they saw as proof of Soviet technological superiority. They also saw an opportunity to boost American spending on technical education in the wake of *Sputnik*. An alliance of educators, defense contractors, and Democrats in Congress passed the National Defense Education Act in 1958. It called for the spending of $5 billion on higher education in the sciences, foreign languages, and humanities over the next few years to counter a perceived threat from the Russians.

American defense planning underwent one of its periodic reversals in the second Eisenhower administration. Army generals had resented Ike's cutback on their service in favor of air power and nuclear weapons. In 1959, retired general Maxwell Taylor published a scathing indictment of the Republican defense posture, *The Uncertain Trumpet*. Taylor charged that the reduction in size of the conventional armed forces made it impossible for the United States to fight any war but a nuclear one. He predicted that the next wars the United States would encounter would be small "brush-fire" encounters, not in Europe, but in Asia, the Middle East, Africa, and Latin America. He warned that the decline of the European empires meant the United States would soon find itself fighting wars of "national liberation" against nationalist forces, sometimes sympathetic to the Communists, in Asia, Africa, and Latin America. The army had to be enlarged and a new strategy of "counterinsurgency" developed to fight such wars.

While Taylor advocated a revival of interest in nonnuclear weapons, nongovernmental strategists took another look at the policy of massive retaliation. The obvious flaws of this approach—its inflexibility and its consequent lack of believability—led civilian students of conflict to search for other means of nuclear warfare. One of them, Henry Kissinger, published *Nuclear Weapons and Foreign Policy* in 1957, arguing that massive retaliation by itself was not enough. These fears were increased with *Sputnik* because it now appeared that the Soviet Union had the capacity to hit the United States with atomic bombs mounted on top of missiles.

Democratic candidates for the presidential nomination of 1960, led by Missouri's Stuart Symington, a former secretary of the air force and an expert on air power, insisted that the Eisenhower administration increase its spending for missiles as well as for everything else. By the middle of 1959, Democrats accused Eisenhower of wholesale neglect of national defense. Reluctant to choose the cheapest among a variety of weapons systems or strategies, Democrats assured the public that the wealthy United States could afford any weapons its scientists could invent and that Ike's stinginess could imperil the nation.

In the middle of 1958, an episode in Latin America gave the opposition the chance to complain about the decline in American "prestige" abroad. Vice-President Nixon, never one of the opposition's favorite politicians, had his motorcade stoned and spat upon when he traveled to Venezuela and Peru. To the Democrats, this rough treatment at the hands of local student leftists proved that the administration lacked the ability to put the American case before the non-European world.

Nineteen fifty-nine seemed to prove the critics' complaints that the rest of the world rudely intruded on American foreign policy. On the first day of the year, a nationalist revolution in Cuba led by Fidel Castro sent Fulgencio Batista fleeing from Havana to Miami. Batista, the real power in Cuba since 1934, had close ties to the American government as well as to organized crime within the United States. Havana had become a haven for gamblers, drug dealers, and prostitutes. Immediately on seizing power, Castro commenced executions of Batista's henchmen, closed down the gambling casinos, and threatened expropriation of American sugar holdings. Initially, liberals in the United States were pleased at Castro's victory over what they considered a disgraceful dictatorship. In a whirlwind trip to the United States in April, Castro addressed a huge audience at Harvard's Soldiers' Field, but he received a chilly reception from Eisenhower. By the end of the year, many liberal Democrats had stopped praising Castro's government and pointed instead to the prominence of Communists in it. They accused the Eisenhower administration of weaknesses and, just as the Republicans had done a decade earlier in the case of China, muttered about the "loss" of Cuba to the Communists. Isolated radicals continued to present Cuba's case. C. Wright Mills, a sociologist at Columbia, returned from the island in August 1960 to fire off *Listen, Yankee!,* an angry indictment of American misbehavior in the Caribbean. Yet his demand "Hands off Cuba!" and his plea "for a completely new United States approach to the problems of the hungry world" fell into a lake of indifference.

John Foster Dulles died in April 1959, leaving the conduct of foreign relations completely in Ike's hands. A new secretary of state, Christian Herter, a member of the Republican internationalist establishment, never sought the limelight the way Dulles had. Eisenhower sought to use his last eighteen months in office to undertake a series of personal visits around the globe to create a peaceful world. He thought that relations with the Soviet Union might be improved and the arms race ended. To this end, he invited Nikita Khrushchev to the United States for a visit in September 1959. Khrushchev had consolidated his power in the Soviet Union in 1958. He had quickly announced that the deadlock over a split Germany, which had persisted since the close of the Second World War, must end. On November 10, 1958, he demanded that the United States and its Western allies withdraw one hundred thousand troops from West Berlin, make the former German capital a "free city," and negotiate access to it with the East German government. By the time Khrushchev reached the United States the following September, he had dropped that demand, and he spent his time touring an Iowa corn farm and unsuccessfully seeking admission to the newly opened Disneyland. Eisenhower and Khrushchev's meeting at Camp David did not resolve their differences, but they agreed to another summit in Europe the following spring. After the meeting of all the major powers, Eisenhower planned to travel to the Soviet Union.

Ike's return visit never occurred. On May 1, 1960, on the eve of the summit conference in Paris, the Soviet Union shot down an American espionage plane flying seventy thousand feet above Soviet territory. The CIA pilot of this U-2 plane, Francis Gary Powers, safely parachuted but was captured. These flights had been going on from bases in Turkey for the previous two years. The president first denied that the United States was conducting aerial spying on the Soviets and then admitted it, saying that national security demanded such overflights. He refused to apologize, and the Soviet leader cancelled his visit. This was not the only trip the president had to erase from his schedule. A visit to Japan was blocked when rioting students made a visit by the president appear unsafe.

Khrushchev and Eisenhower never met again, but the Soviet prime minister did come to the United States in the fall of 1960 to attend the United Nations General Assembly. Fidel Castro came as well, got evicted from the Waldorf Astoria for keeping chickens in his room, and moved to Harlem's

Happy times at the UN. Nikita Khrushchev embraces Fidel Castro, October 1960, as Americans believe their worst nightmares have come true.
(Wide World Photos)

Hotel Theresa where he addressed a crowd from a balcony. Khrushchev, wearing an impish grin for most of the session, drove American television viewers wild with rage when he took off a shoe and banged the table in carefully planned anger.

Khrushchev's visit took place in the midst of the presidential election in 1960. Democrats tried to create the public impression of a bumbling, sleepy, remote president who had never taken charge of the foreign affairs bureaucracy. Washington senator Henry Jackson invited academic foreign affairs experts, many of whom had served in previous Democratic administrations, to tell what was wrong with Ike's organization of foreign relations. For two weeks in the spring of 1960, Democratic senators nodded sagely in agreement to attacks on the Republicans' National Security Council as ignorant, slow, "only reactive," unable to plan, and insufficiently "tough-minded."

Democrats chose the youngest man ever to run for the presidency, Massachusetts senator John F. Kennedy. He campaigned on a platform of waging the Cold War with more "vigor" than the Republicans. The Republicans were led by a man almost as young as Kennedy, the forty-seven-year-old vice-president, Nixon. Each candidate outbid the other in his anti-Soviet militance. Kennedy ran on more defense, more missiles, a larger army, and more action in Latin America and Africa. Cuba and Fidel Castro became his bête noire. Nixon, recalling his seven-hour shouting match with Nikita Khrushchev in a model American kitchen in 1959, reminded voters that he actually had the experience of "standing up to the Russians." In foreign policy, the election of 1960 replayed 1952 with the parties reversed. Democratic outs charged that the Republican ins had squandered opportunities and predicted that if given the chance they would vanquish the Soviet Union. For their part, Republicans asked the country to rely upon the experience of their leaders in actually waging Cold War.

Eisenhower himself played little part in the election. When asked to explain what Nixon had done to help in his administration, he begged, "Give me a week and I'll explain it." After Kennedy won by the narrow margin of one hundred twelve thousand votes, Eisenhower delivered a famous speech warning against an excessive militarization of the Cold War. He explained that the United States was in the grip of a "military-industrial complex" which might distort the country's democratic institutions. That speech, like so much of Ike's foreign policy, was long on promise but short on performance. Coming to the office to end containment, he expanded it with "liberation." He missed opportunities to deal with a post-Stalinist Russia. Europe remained a divided and armed camp. The United States maintained an outmoded China policy and ignored nationalism in the Middle East, Africa, and Latin America. But the United States avoided foreign combat for eight years. The same could not be said for the following decade, which saw Americans engage in their longest, most divisive, and most futile war.

CHAPTER TWELVE

Globalism Triumphant, 1961–1968

American hopes to shape world events soared to their highest levels in the sixties before sinking in the mud of Vietnam. Exuberant, energetic, vigorous representatives of the United States appeared in the remotest regions of the world carrying the message that the American styles of government, economic system, and social values should sweep all alternatives. Convinced of the rightness of their cause, the evils of communism, and the poorer nations' longing for guidance, the Kennedy and Johnson administrations waged Cold War heedless of the consequences or costs.

Harry Truman's containment policy seemed too defensive, Secretary of State John Foster Dulles's "brinkmanship" too blustery, and Ike's appeals to end the arms race too defeatist for the Democrats who took over in January 1961. They put into practice global theories developed in government service, academic offices, and private research organizations. The results surprised them and nearly tore the country apart as the "consensus" of foreign policy, imposed on the public after the Second World War, collapsed. From Africa to the Caribbean to Vietnam, Americans learned hard lessons of the cost of global competition with communism. They confronted each other in angry street clashes by the end of the Johnson administration. For both those who continued to believe in an American anti-Communist mission and those who preferred an end to foreign interventions, the optimism of 1961 seemed only a memory in 1969. The mood of government officials, the general public, and foreign observers soured as people around the world discovered the limits of American power.

KENNEDY IN POWER

John F. Kennedy took Washington by storm in January 1961. Arthur Schlesinger, Jr., a historian who served on his staff, seemed awestruck by his style and grace under pressure (a phrase borrowed from Ernest Hemingway), and thrilled to be part of history in the making. He gushed that "never had men seemed so charming or girls so pretty" as during the Kennedy years. The thousand-day administration came to be called Camelot, after King Arthur's mythical court where weather was perfect, no one argued, and everyone had a good time. Kennedy filled the White House with "intellectuals"— artists, musicians, actors, writers and professors. The president cultivated a sense of youthful activity which he thought stood in sharp contrast to the lethargy of his seventy-year-old predecessor. Where Ike had relaxed with a leisurely game of golf, the forty-three-year-old Kennedy, who loved golf, kept this passion quiet and brought guests to one of his several homes for rough games of touch football.

This desire to take command and demonstrate a contrast to his predecessor also dominated Kennedy's foreign policy. The president set the tone in an inaugural address memorable principally for its nationalistic call for intervention around the world. The country was prepared "to pay any price, bear any burden, meet any hardship, support any friend, oppose any foe to assure the survival and success of liberty."

Unlike Eisenhower, Kennedy chose to concentrate foreign policy in the White House instead of sharing it with his secretary of state. For that office he selected Dean Rusk, the assistant secretary under Truman who urged an uncompromising policy toward China before the Korean War. Not a friend or long-time supporter of Kennedy, Rusk had spent the fifties as president of the Rockefeller Foundation. He had good connections with the foreign policy establishment, which respected him as a man who knew when to keep his peace. Rusk rarely asserted himself in the councils of the new administration, preferring to sit impassively, "Buddha-like," while members of the White House staff discussed the issues.

His secretary of state reduced in influence, Kennedy relied upon the advice of a group of "action intellectuals" in the augmented National Security Council, the White House, State Department, and Defense Department. For the previous decade, academic entrepreneurs had told each other, government officials, and the public that the Cold War was too important to be left to politicians, diplomats, and generals. In Cambridge, New York, and Berkeley, a tightly knit group of political scientists, military strategists, and "development" economists created theories they hoped to apply to the endless competition with the Soviet Union. They took pride in their "hard-headed realism," their "tough-mindedness," and their "lack of sentimentality" while ignoring C. Wright Mills's scornful dismissal of them as "crackpot realists."

For national security adviser, the president chose McGeorge Bundy, former dean of the faculty at Harvard, a liberal Republican, and the son of a major aide of Secretary of State Henry L. Stimson. Bundy's brother William, the son-in-law of former secretary of state Dean Acheson, served as assistant secretary for international security affairs in the State Department. Another academic, MIT professor of economic history Walt Whitman Rostow, became the head of the Policy Planning Staff of the State Department. Earlier, Rostow had written an influential study, *Stages of Economic Growth,* the subtitle of which, *A Non-Communist Manifesto,* explained how professors could wage Cold War among the world's poor. The Kennedy administration proved some of Rostow's notions about how the "development" of the poorer countries could be brought about. Probably the most dazzling of the new group of advisers was the secretary of defense, Robert S. McNamara. Like Ike's first secretary of defense, Charles Wilson, McNamara had been president of an automobile company, Ford. Unlike Wilson, McNamara fancied himself a thinker. He had been a professor, and a member of the United States Air Force Strategic Bombing Survey at the end of the Second World War, and he was a man more comfortable in the company of scholars, artists, and journalists than with the blunt businessmen of the car industry. He had been at Ford only one year and was bored by it when the president asked him, a nominal Republican, to join his administration. He leapt at the chance to apply the most up-to-date sort of management to the work of the Defense Department. Phrases such as *systems analysis, operations research,* and *cost-benefit ratio* peppered McNamara's conversation. The secretary, with his slicked-back hair and rimless spectacles, gesturing with a pointer to a collection of charts, became a familiar figure testifying on Capitol Hill. Members of Congress were dazzled with his brilliance, command of the subject, and mastery of the defense establishment.

All of these advisers and Kennedy himself had served as junior officers during the Second World War, and in the manner of lieutenants everywhere, they had believed they could run the war better. The fact that the supreme commander during the Second World War had been General Eisenhower intensified their desire to show their toughness. The academics among them resented the crude charges of Sen. Joseph McCarthy that many professors had either supported communism or failed to take a vigilant stand in the Cold War. From their offices at Harvard and MIT, professors had come to believe that Eisenhower had failed to understand recent changes in the world. The principal area of conflict with the Russians had shifted from Europe to nationalist movements in Asia, Africa, and Latin America. Kennedy himself as a senator had been bored by domestic matters, thinking that a statesman must follow the action and make his mark in international affairs.

WAGING COLD WAR IN LATIN AMERICA

Latin America was the first place in which the Kennedy administration tried to set a new tone. On March 13, Kennedy announced the Alliance for Progress with the Latin nations. Kennedy would add $20 billion in foreign aid for the hemisphere over the next ten years. However, bureaucratic infighting and corruption in Latin America limited the effectiveness of the alliance over the next five years. The Peace Corps, made up of idealistic young men and women—recently graduated from college and without gainful employment—who would go abroad to teach and perform technical service, would pay special attention to Latin America. At the same time, the Pentagon and the CIA increased the training of Latin American police and paramilitary outfits in order to help them fight guerrilla wars. The Pentagon set up a Jungle Warfare School in the Panama Canal Zone and at Fort Bragg, North Carolina, to train Latin American units. The Agency for International Development brought some five hundred Latin American policemen to the Canal Zone school to learn how to infiltrate leftist groups and control the crowds of the type which had taunted Vice-President Nixon on his trip to South America in 1958.

The alliance and the training of police was designed to prevent the rise of another Castro-like nationalist revolution in Cuba. But what to do about the revolutionary government in Cuba itself? The Eisenhower administration had broken diplomatic relations with Castro in January 1960. Throughout the election campaign, Kennedy had accused the Republicans of doing nothing about Castro, and he threatened some sort of an invasion if he were elected. Nixon, an old anti-Communist and Red baiter par excellence, found himself in the uncomfortable position of opposing military action as a violation of international law, even though he knew that the CIA had plans underway to attack Cuba. Nixon suspected that Kennedy knew of these proposals and had mentioned them for the rankest sort of political advantage, knowing Nixon could not reveal or discuss the operation.

Whether or not he learned of them before the election, Kennedy was briefed by CIA director Allen Dulles on the agency's scheme to train Cuban exiles in Florida and Central America and then ferry them into Cuba. Some of the same CIA men who had plotted the Guatemalan adventure in 1954 thought that an invasion of Cuba would be accomplished as easily. In January 1961, the new president gave his approval for the CIA to continue with the planned April invasion. JFK even convinced the *New York Times* not to

Cuba's Fidel Castro denounces the United States.
(Wide World Photos)

publish a report of the impending operation, arguing that to do so would compromise the "national interest." On April 17, a force of about sixteen hundred guerrillas landed at the Bay of Pigs in southern Cuba. The CIA's director of operations, Richard Bissell, had assured Kennedy that this force would encourage a general rising of the Cuban population against Castro. Even if there were not an immediate rush to the anti-Communist colors, the invaders could withdraw to the mountains, which Bissell said were nearby. In fact, the poorly supplied and inadequately prepared force landed in a swamp with no mountains for miles. No uprising greeted them, as Castro was popular in the whole island and nowhere more so than the Bay of Pigs, where he frequently went on holiday. Within forty-eight hours of their landing, the brigade was captured by the Cuban army. Kennedy admitted responsibility but then fired Allen Dulles as head of the CIA. Over the next year, the United States ransomed the invaders with $10 million in medical supplies.

Undaunted, the CIA spent the next eighteen months trying to embarrass, confuse, or murder Castro. The agency planned to drop depilitating powder into his shoes to make his beard fall out. Strategists suggested slipping him a cigar laced with LSD, offering him a pen with a poison tip, or blowing his legs off with exploding clamshells while he snorkled in the blue Caribbean. Five times the agency approached underworld figures, eager to regain control of prostitution, gambling, and narcotics in Havana, about sending a gunman to shoot the Cuban leader. The Cuban people became targets of Operation MONGOOSE, developed by Edward Lansdale, the former head of covert activities in Saigon. He suggested sending a submarine to the shore where it would illuminate the night sky with incendiary shells to convince the peasantry of the imminent Second Coming of Christ. E. Howard Hunt, who helped plan the overthrow of the Arbenz government in Guatemala in 1954 and later recruited the Watergate burglars in 1972, undertook a series of nighttime commando raids on the beaches. They managed only to rally the Cuban public to the revolution and encourage Castro to ask Moscow for military aid.

KHRUSHCHEV AND THE GERMAN QUESTION

The public rallied to Kennedy's support after the Bay of Pigs disaster. This customary rise in the polls in the face of adversity did little to bolster the president's self-confidence, however. He wanted some way to prove his grasp of foreign affairs, and he thought he found it in a confrontation with Soviet premier Khrushchev at a summit meeting in Vienna. The Soviet leader again wanted a solution to the question of the division of Germany and Berlin. When the two leaders met in Vienna in May 1961, Kennedy was unyielding on the question of German reunification and believed that the Soviet chairman considered him a weak, inexperienced youngster.

The Berlin crisis in 1961 culminated a series of East-West confrontations arising from the two nations' inability to reach agreement on Germany's future after 1945. Even after presiding over the birth of the Federal Republic of Germany (FRG) in 1949, the United States insisted upon reunification of Germany into a single, presumably non-Communist, state. No Western nation extended diplomatic recognition to the Democratic Republic of Germany (DRG), created as a Soviet response. Instead, the NATO countries persisted in calling the DRG an illegitimate creature of the Soviet Union and argued that having its capital in the Soviet-occupied sector of East Berlin violated the Yalta and Potsdam agreements. The FRG tried to ostracize its East German counterpart by breaking diplomatic relations with any non-Communist nation bold enough to open an embassy in East Germany. After Stalin's death, successive Soviet governments urged a general European security conference to settle the German question, but the West refused, fearing recognition of the DRG and the end of the illusion of reunification.

Kennedy returned from Vienna in a somber mood and soon asked Congress for an increase in the defense budget of $3.25 billion. In words not heard since the days when John Foster Dulles had spoken of going to the brink of war, Kennedy said, "We do not want to fight, but we have fought before. And others in earlier times have made the same dangerous mistake of assuming that the West was too selfish and too soft and too divided to resist invasions of freedom in other lands." Relations with the Soviets plunged throughout the summer. On July 25, Kennedy called up the reserves to protect Western access to Berlin. When asked if he thought that the call-up was fair, he replied, "Life is unfair." The Communist response to this saber-rattling caught Washington by surprise. On the night of August 13, the Soviet government erected a heavily guarded wall between East and West Berlin. The drain of refugees, which had reached one hundred thousand in the previous year, abruptly stopped. Khrushchev dropped plans to sign his own peace treaty with the East Germans since the wall effectively sealed the eastern zone from the western. Kennedy's show of force had done nothing to prevent the final division of Germany. The United States protested the wall, and the president later made a highly publicized visit to the divided city to proclaim "*Ich bin ein Berliner* (I am a Berliner)." But the wall remained, a testimony to a failure of imagination on the part of American diplomats.

THE CONGO

As if to provide a test of the theories of the academic foreign affairs specialists, events on the periphery consumed the attention of the Kennedy administration for the next year. In Central Africa, the United States participated in some shabby intrigues in the newly independent state of the Congo (later called Zaire). This former Belgian colony had gained its independence in mid-1959, when the former colonial rulers abruptly left. Unprepared for independence, with fewer than two hundred college-educated people in the country, the Congo quickly became a battleground for several tribal and political factions. Patrice Lumumba, leader of the ardent nationalist faction, became the prime minister. The Belgians hated Lumumba, hoping a puppet leader would invite them back to run the mines and profit from the country's immense mineral wealth. As a civil war broke out in the Congo, the United Nations sent a peacekeeping force to separate the armies of the Lumumba government and the Belgian secessionists in the mineral-rich southern province of Katanga, led by Moise Tshombe. The United States gave lip service to supporting the UN force but actually favored secession. The CIA saw Lumumba as a Moscow puppet since he had received training in the Soviet capital. If Katanga seceded, the gold, diamonds, and uranium of the area would stay under Western control. In January 1961, Lumumba was assassinated with the help of the CIA. The civil war dragged on for another year, but eventually a pro-Western government under the lead of

Joseph Kasavubu took power. For the rest of the sixties, rumors were rife in Africa about the American complicity in the murder of Lumumba. The Kasavubu government soon became dependent upon the West for financial support and was wracked by a series of civil wars and secessions. The American attempt to use the United Nations as an instrument in the Cold War also caused other African nations to suspect the motives of the Kennedy administration.

THE CUBAN MISSILE CRISIS AND ITS AFTERMATH

According to the foreign policy experts of the Kennedy administration, the best thing a government official could do was called *crisis management*. Their criticism of Ike's handling of foreign affairs concerned his desire to avoid conflict; they welcomed it, hoping to prove their toughness. They met their severest test in October 1962 in the controversy with the Soviet Union over missiles in Cuba. Kennedy's reputation as a steely leader, able to overcome foes with his careful assessment of a situation, rests on his handling of the Cuban missile crisis. Critics, however, accused him of endangering the safety of the world by a display of *machismo*. Bertrand Russell, the philosopher and pacifist, charged that Kennedy during the Cuban missile crisis blithely risked the death of one hundred million people to prove his nerves.

Soviet intermediate range ballistic missiles (IRBMs) in Cuba assaulted American pride more than they threatened the physical security of the United States. Based ninety miles from the southernmost tip of Florida, the weapons could reach targets in the eastern and central United States in fewer than eight minutes, cutting the already minuscule reaction time of twenty-five minutes after the launch of intercontinental ballistic missiles (ICBMs) based in the Soviet Union or the United States. But America had for years pointed its own IRBMs at Soviet targets from bases in neighboring Turkey. A Soviet base in Cuba seemed to reply in kind to the American strategy of ringing the Soviet Union with troops and weapons. But retaliation for Western encirclement may not have been uppermost in Khrushchev's mind. Moscow moved at the urging of frantic pleas from Cuban president Fidel Castro to do something about the CIA's continuing clandestine war against his person and his government.

The crisis took place in the midst of the congressional election of 1962, in which the Republicans expected to make the typical gains of the opposition party in nonpresidential elections. New York senator Kenneth Keating raised the alarm in September, publicizing reports of anti-Castro Cuban exiles in Miami that the Soviet Union had installed offensive nuclear armed missiles in Cuba. The Kennedy administration's initial reaction to Keating's charge was to cry political foul. They accused him of warmongering to gain advantage for the Republicans, and they said that the CIA had no evidence of Soviet missiles in Cuba. Kennedy also issued a warning against the Soviets in September. U-2 flights in August had revealed Soviet construction of a missile site, but CIA director John McCone was honeymooning on the French Riviera and could not be reached to confirm the data.

In early October, with McCone back in Washington, the CIA presented Kennedy with evidence that the Soviet Union had indeed constructed a missile base. With the election barely three weeks away and new Republican calls for action, Kennedy convened his leading foreign policy advisers. They secretly met in a side office of the State Department so as not to attract attention of the press. Former secretary of state Dean Acheson, Chairman of the Joint Chiefs of Staff Maxwell Taylor and Air Force Chief Curtis LeMay urged an immediate air strike against the missiles. The president's brother, Attorney General Robert Kennedy, supported the position of Undersecretary of State George Ball, who recommended a blockade of Cuba. Ball thought that if the blockade failed, an attack could always be ordered later, and Robert Kennedy opposed a Pearl Harbor–type preemptive strike. The president, he recalled, did "not want to be known as another Tojo." Secretary of State Dean Rusk kept silent, resenting having to share the limelight with other advisers. The president held his own views during the meetings, not wishing to inhibit discussion. Students of the Cuban missile crisis such as Graham Allison (*The Essence of Decision* [1969]) and Irving Janis (*Victims of Groupthink* [1972]) award the president high marks for the way he listened to all the advice before deciding on the blockade. In later years, decision makers attempted to emulate the president's leaving open of options in the Cuban missile crisis.

On Monday, October 22, Kennedy publicly announced the presence of the Soviet missiles in Cuba. He imposed a blockade of the island to prevent the Soviet Union from arming the missiles with atomic warheads. He gave the Soviets no deadline but made it clear that the missiles themselves had to be withdrawn. Two days later, a blockade line went up, and Soviet naval ships en route to Cuba were turned away. On Friday the 26th, sailors from the U.S. destroyer *Joseph P. Kennedy* boarded a Soviet-chartered freighter bound for Cuba. Then, on October 28, Kennedy announced that the Soviet Union had agreed to crate up its weapons. Kennedy's supporters exulted, and the world drew back from the brink of nuclear war. Secretary Rusk summarized his feelings with a cowboy metaphor when he recalled that "we were eyeball to eyeball, and the other fellow blinked." As a result of the confrontation, the United States and the Soviet Union set up a direct teletype link, the "hot line," to use in the case of crises. The United States promised not to invade Cuba and intimated that it would withdraw its outmoded missiles from Turkey. This last pledge came easily, since at the beginning of the crisis Kennedy had not known that the United States had these weapons stationed near the Soviet border.

Not surprisingly, Castro was furious at the Soviet betrayal. He refused to see Moscow's special envoy who came to Havana to explain the benefits of the deal. The Soviets, unwilling to confront superior U.S. military power, saw merits in the American pledge not to attack Cuba, but Castro expected the secret war to continue, as it did until the assassination of President Kennedy in November 1963. Nor would the furious Cuban leader publicly agree to renounce support for revolutionary activity in the Western Hemisphere. Khrushchev had his own problems with his Politburo colleagues, who squirmed in embarrassment at their chairman's humiliation at the hands of the Americans. They resolved to remove him at the earliest opportunity, which occurred two years later, in 1964. They embarked upon a rearmament program to match the American naval and air superiority which had forced their surrender.

The European allies had publicly given their support to the United States during the crisis. Even France's president, Charles de Gaulle, long a critic of the United States for its arrogance and reluctance to consult with Europeans, had told roving ambassador Averell Harriman of his full support during the height of the tensions. Privately, however, Europeans expressed grave misgivings about the way the United States had behaved in October. De Gaulle, most notably, saw the episode as proof that the United States would act in its own interests. Even as he reassured Harriman, de Gaulle worried that Washington's unilateral actions meant that Europeans had to watch impotently from the sidelines. De Gaulle decided that the best way for France to assert itself in international affairs was to build its own *force de frappe* of atomic weapons. Later, in 1966, France withdrew its armed forces from the unified command of the NATO alliance. British reaction to the Cuban missile crisis was more muted but the results were the same: Britain was shown to be the idle bystander to great events.

British prime minister Harold Macmillan prided himself on his friendship with the new president. Both liked fine English suits, admired cool understatement, and discussed the books published by the prime minister's family publishing house. Kennedy had spent time in England when his father was ambassador in the late thirties. Both leaders liked to speak of the special relationship binding their two nations. While chancellor of the exchequer during the fifties, Macmillan had acknowledged the superiority of American power but explained that "Britain would play Greece to America's Rome." In other words, the worldly British, with their vast experience in international affairs, could teach the bumptious Americans how to behave. In December 1962, Macmillan met Kennedy at Nassau in the Bahamas and learned a stinging lesson in power politics. The British wanted the United States to supply their armed forces with an air-launched ballistic missile, the Skybolt, to deliver their own nuclear forces. Secretary of Defense McNamara thought that Skybolt cost too much and could not deliver a weapon, and believed that the British should not have an independent nuclear force anyway. Kennedy agreed that the British should join an American-sponsored multinational force, a group of ships made up of the navies of all the NATO allies with the United States command having final say over the use of these weapons. Hidden beneath the rhetoric of cooperation between the allies lurked the need to get the Germans involved in nuclear defense. No European power wanted West Germany to have nuclear weapons on its own, but the United States defense planners recognized that Germany was the most robust power in Europe. The British meekly accepted the demise of Skybolt and agreed to join the multinational organization. The prime minister had trouble, however, convincing his countrymen that the special relationship with the United States did much good. The comedy group "Beyond the Fringe" had audiences howling over a skit showing the new British deterrent force consisting of a man carrying a stepladder to the Berlin Wall, climbing it, and hurling a suitcase containing an atomic bomb into East Berlin.

THE TEST BAN

While Kennedy moved on one front to bring the powerful West German army into the nuclear arms race, the administration also sought to reduce nuclear competition. During the fifties, private groups in the United States such as the Committee for a Sane Nuclear Policy (SANE) and well-known scientists led by chemist Linus Pauling and physicist Edward V. Condon had complained about the effects of radioactive fallout on people's health. One radioactive isotope, Strontium 90, which was discovered in cow's milk, was found to cause a rise in cancer. While the Atomic Energy Commission sought to minimize fears during the fifties, its own scientists admitted to a congressional hearing in 1956 that "any quantity of radioactive fallout is undesirable."

Pressure mounted during the Kennedy administration for a ban on testing nuclear weapons in the atmosphere after the Soviet Union exploded a bomb of fifty megatons and threatened to explode one of one hundred in late 1961. The United States responded with atmospheric explosions of its own hydrogen bombs in 1962, setting off thirty-three shots that year. By the beginning of 1963, public alarm over the health dangers of radiation worried officials. Furthermore, arms experts in the Defense Department assured the president that nothing could be learned from atmospheric testing which could not also be discovered from explosions set off in underground caverns. Kennedy had established an Arms Control and Disarmament Agency in the State Department in 1961 with the purpose of organizing efforts at reducing the arms race. The agency had opened talks but accomplished little in the first two years of his administration, so the possibility of a test ban seemed to present a way of making use of it.

In the spring of 1963, the United States and the Soviet Union negotiated seriously to stop testing atomic weapons in the atmosphere. Both sides realized the potential health hazards, and both recognized that their arms programs would not suffer if they switched to subterranean experiments. In mid-June, they concluded a treaty banning future tests in the atmosphere. Either country could abrogate the treaty by giving one year's notice. Both agreed to continue the search for a complete ban on atomic explosions and to confer on reducing nuclear arms in general. Over the next decade, hundreds of meetings took place at disarmament conferences in Vienna, but the hopes of 1963 for an expansion of the first agreement into a real sort of disarmament proved illusory. The United States tried to maintain its superiority over the Soviet Union, which in turn hoped to narrow the gap between the two powers.

SOUTHEAST ASIA

By the summer of 1963, the Kennedy administration was spending an increasing amount of time wrestling with the war in South Vietnam. In 1961 and 1962, American interest in Indochina had focused on Laos, where a civil war raged between a right wing general, Phoumi Nosavan; a neutralist prince, Souvanna Phouma; and a Communist prince, Souphanou-vong. At various times confused Americans provided aid to all three. In the spring of 1962, a new Geneva conference had opened co-chaired by France and Britain. This time the United States, as full participant, and the parties had agreed to neutralize Laos. The Kennedy administration heaved a sigh of relief that the Communists had not won the war and was gladdened that the United States would not fight in as remote a place as Laos.

While Laos drew the headlines in 1961 and 1962, the civil war grew in South Vietnam. As a senator, Kennedy had been a member of the American Committee for a Free Vietnam, which had boosted the reputation of President Ngo Dinh Diem. Upon taking office, one of the first briefings the president had received concerned the new insurgency of the remnants of the Vietminh in South Vietnam. His newly appointed chairman of the Joints Chiefs of Staff, Gen. Maxwell Taylor, believed that Vietnam would be an excellent place to test new counterinsurgency fighters, the special forces called Green

Berets. President Kennedy himself went down to Fort Bragg, North Carolina, in 1961 to see a display of firepower and watch a demonstration of snake-eating and tree-swinging by a contingent of Green Berets.

In 1962, the Defense Department sent a team of advisers into the field with the South Vietnamese army, the ARVN, to live off the land with it as it rooted out the insurgents. Other advisers from the Agency for International Development or the State Department went into the countryside to build an "infrastructure" of social institutions, in the words of the academic special-ists who planned their tours. Michigan State University continued its train-ing of the police force of South Vietnam, and other universities sent spe-cialists in "nation-building" into the countryside to assist the process.

By the middle of 1963, the United States had over ten thousand troops stationed in Vietnam, and the fiction that they were engaged only in "advis-ing" no longer carried weight. In June, the public's attention was riveted by a Buddhist monk in Saigon who poured gasoline over his body and set him-self on fire. This self-immolation climaxed a series of demonstrations by the Buddhists, some 80 percent of South Vietnam's population, who deeply re-sented the control exercised by the Catholic 10 percent who backed Diem. While Americans watched the public burning in horrified fascination, Madame Nhu, the sister-in-law of the president and wife of the head of the South's secret police force, accused American television reporters of having staged the suicide. She charged that the Buddhists were Communists and cruelly joked that she would "supply the mustard for the monks' next bar-becue."

For Kennedy and his advisers, the Buddhist rebellion suggested that the Diem government no longer had the confidence of the country and was un-likely to quell the insurrection. That summer, another five thousand Amer-ican soliders disembarked in Vietnam while the American government looked for alternatives to Diem. In August, Kennedy appointed an old po-litical rival, Henry Cabot Lodge, the grandson of the Republican opponent of Woodrow Wilson and the Republican vice-presidential candidate in 1960, as ambassador to South Vietnam. Hoping to enlist Republicans into a bi-partisan agreement on Vietnam, Kennedy saw Lodge as shoring up his po-sition with the opposition. Immediately on arrival in Saigon, Lodge learned from the CIA chief in South Vietnam that the ARVN's top generals no longer had confidence in Diem's leadership. Along with his brother, the Vietnamese president seemed more interested in siphoning American aid than waging war. The army itself was a shambles which fled at the first sign of the enemy. To American diplomats, the complaints about Diem seemed depressingly like those voiced in China against the corruption of Jiang Jieshi (Chiang Kai-shek) before 1949. CIA operatives in Saigon thought that the replacement of Diem with a group of less corrupt military men could improve the morale of the troops and lead to a suppression of the insurrection. Lodge forwarded these hopes and fears to Washington with a recommendation that the United States provide tacit support for a coup against Diem. Lodge's proposal found favor in the White House, where National Security Adviser McGeorge Bundy reasoned that nobody could be worse than Diem.

Word went back to Saigon in September that the American government would approve a change in leadership. On November 1, the plotters, led by Gen. Duong Van Minh, toppled Diem's government, seizing the president and his brother. Both were taken to the outskirts of Saigon and executed. Kennedy expressed surprise that the two men had been killed, and historians still argue over whether the CIA had ordered or knew about the plans to eliminate the Vietnamese president. Whether the actual directive received approval from the American embassy in Saigon is less important than the fact that the United States ambassador and the national security adviser had decided that the government of Vietnam had to be replaced.

On November 22, 1963, barely three weeks after Diem's murder, John F. Kennedy himself was gunned down in Dallas. A week before his death, he expressed misgivings about the American buildup, likening it to an alcoholic "who takes a drink. The effect wears off, and you have to take another one." Protectors of the president's memory took heart from such remarks and a casual comment to a political aide, Kenneth O'Donnell, about withdrawing from Vietnam after the presidential election of 1964. In fact, the president never mentioned quitting the war to his foreign affairs advisers. If he doubted, his glum premonitions were the fleeting sort which might assail any politician when the outcome of events cannot be known. In 1963, Kennedy decided to give the doctrine of counterinsurgency another chance in Vietnam. The possible gains from a demonstration of American toughness, the ability to win a war of national liberation, and the avoidance of the charge that another Democratic administration had "lost" a country to communism far outweighed any costs. For all of their "tough-minded realism," the president and his advisers indulged in the most insipid sort of wishful thinking.

The horror of the president's death and the nostalgic longing for his cheerful good nature created a small industry of laudatory books about his brief tenure in office. Theodore Sorensen, his principal speechwriter, lamented in his biography that Kennedy "had only begun, he was given so little time." The Cuban missile crisis became a source of studies showing how to make decisions under pressure. Even obvious disasters like the Bay of Pigs invasion won points for showing how the president could learn from his mistakes. Vietnam became seen as part of emerging knowledge about the limits of American power. Nevertheless, Kennedy's administration did not fulfill its promise. In the disillusionment which set in with the disaster of Vietnam, other observers took a hard look at the Kennedy foreign policy. Richard Walton produced a biting assessment, *Cold War and Counter Revolu-*

tion (1972), which concludes that "the president moved back, not ahead as he promised." He increased the tensions of the Cold War, brought the world the closest it had come to nuclear holocaust in the Cuban missile crisis, let the allies know that they were unimportant, and began the escalation of the Vietnam War. Walton condemns Kennedy as a "Cold Warrior and Counter Revolutionary. Cuba, Berlin, Vietnam—these are his monuments."

LYNDON JOHNSON TAKES CHARGE 1963–1964

Lyndon Johnson never wanted to be vice-president; few people do. He had taken the job when Kennedy asked at the 1960 convention because he saw no way of continuing as an effective majority leader of the Senate if he turned it down. A great bear of a man, Johnson seemed to shrink physically as he went through the ceremonial duties of the vice-presidency. He never gained admission to the inner circle of Kennedy's advisers, who shunned him as a rude Texan given to telling dirty jokes and emitting uncouth noises. Johnson delighted in the opportunity to escape from Washington as a goodwill ambassador. He went around the world as if campaigning for office. Europe, Latin America, the Indian subcontinent, and Indochina all got the Johnson "treatment." He astonished a Pakistani camel driver with a hug and an invitation to visit his ranch on the Pedernales River in Texas. In Vietnam, he called President Diem the "George Washington of Southeast Asia."

Johnson had deep insecurities about his own grasp of international relations which he covered with bravura and by twitting "experts." During a vicepresidential visit to West Berlin, a worried Foreign Service officer went on at great length about German affairs and then asked, "Is there anything else?" Johnson fixed him with a withering gaze and said, "Yeah, tuck in your shirt." Once he became president, he poked fun at the "Harvards" who had advised Kennedy while at the same time relying on their advice. Robert McNamara particularly won his heart with his "stacomb on his hair and his flow charts." Johnson had strong, sometimes unprintable views on the foreign leaders he met. After a dinner with the king of Norway, he whispered to an aide, "That's the dumbest king I ever met. I didn't know they made kings that dumb."

For all of his defensiveness, Johnson appreciated the delicacy of his position as an unelected president. Kennedy supporters thought him nearly a usurper, and he wanted to calm their nerves by following the policies of the fallen hero to the letter. Despite his mockery of "Harvards," be begged them to remain at the White House. The Bundys, McNamara, and Rostow all stayed for the first eighteen months. In domestic affairs, where Johnson's grasp was keen, he soon surpassed Kennedy's record. Nineteen sixty-four and 1965 saw Johnson extract from Congress the greatest series of social reform programs since the New Deal and civil rights acts since Reconstruction. In foreign affairs, Johnson decided to figure out precisely what his predecessor would have done and continue along the same lines.

VIETNAM AND THE ELECTION OF 1964

In Vietnam, that meant continuing the role of the American advisers in hopes that the new military government could do a better job than Diem. In January, Gen. Nguyen Khan seized power in another coup, but the new government soon proved just as ineffective as earlier ones. ARVN troops showed no greater willingness to fight, and the attempts at "nation-building" went nowhere. In the summer of 1964 the American navy began accompanying South Vietnamese patrol boats as they traveled north of the Seventeenth Parallel to attack the northern coast. For General Khan, these patrols were the prelude of a "march north" to carry the war into North Vietnam. Throughout the summer, American ships heavily laden with super secret electronic gear monitored North Vietnamese communications while the South Vietnamese gunboats raided the coast. Sometimes the American ships came within three miles of the North. On the night of August 2, three North Vietnamese vessels fired at one of the American destroyers, the *Maddox*, engaged in espionage in the Gulf of Tonkin. The damage was a bullet hole one inch in diameter, and the *Maddox* could not hit any of its attackers with its return fire. When the president learned of the response, he upbraided his red-faced admirals with "You've got a whole fleet and all those airplanes, and you can't even sink three little old PT boats." The navy sent another destroyer, the *C. Turner Joy*, to continue to show the flag in the Tonkin Gulf, and two nights later sonar operators on the second ship reported that torpedoes had been fired from North Vietnamese boats. The night was stormy, the sonar operators inexperienced, the whole crew jittery, and the navy expected an attack. No physical evidence of an assault was found, and the "return" fire from the *C. Turner Joy* hit nothing. Johnson expressed his doubts of a report of a second attack saying, "For all I know our navy might have been shooting at whales out there."

It hardly mattered what actually had happened in the Tonkin Gulf, for the Johnson administration wanted a reason for some dramatic gesture against both North Vietnam and the conservative Republican presidential candidate, Arizona senator Barry Goldwater, who accused Johnson of meekness in the war. As soon as news of the incident with the *C. Turner Joy* reached Washington, Defense Secretary McNamara ordered an air strike against North Vietnam's coast. As the planes were in the air, McNamara announced the American attack and Johnson sent to Congress the text of a resolution offering support from the House and Senate for the "defense of American forces in Southeast Asia." The National Security Council had prepared the text of a "general or permissive" resolution two months before, in June, and

the approach of the Democratic National Convention the third week in August made the timing right. The chairman of the Senate Committee on Foreign Relations, J. William Fulbright of Arkansas, who later became one of
the harshest critics of the war in Vietnam, led the debate for the Gulf of
Tonkin Resolution. He later apologized to the two senators who voted against
it, Wayne Morse of Oregon and Ernest Gruening of Alaska, saying it was "the
dumbest thing I've ever done." At the time, Morse and Gruening were pil-
loried in the press for their criticism, *Newsweek* magazine calling them "gad-
flies" and "lightweights." The resolution passed the House without a single
no vote, without hearings, and with only one hour of debate. For the next
six years, until Congress repealed it in 1970, the Gulf of Tonkin Resolution
became the legal basis presidents Johnson and Richard M. Nixon used for
the American war in Vietnam.

The air strike and resolution caused Johnson's popularity to shoot up in
public opinion polls which showed him defeating Senator Goldwater with
over 60 percent of the vote. The election campaign of 1964 saw Johnson accusing Goldwater of being a "trigger-happy" menace who would let American field commanders use atomic bombs without consulting the president.
A Johnson television ad, used once, showed a little girl picking petals from
a flower, counting down from ten to one as the scene shifted to an atomic
bomb–caused mushroom cloud. On Vietnam, the president's supporters accused Goldwater of favoring a buildup of hundreds of thousands of American troops and favoring a war against North Vietnam which would inevitably
bring China and the Soviet Union into a fight with the United States. Goldwater offered an inviting target with his offhand remarks on how to conduct
military operations in Vietnam, "I would turn to my Joint Chiefs of Staff and
say, 'Fellows, we made the decision to win; now it's your problem.' "

Liberals swallowed their misgivings about Johnson's personality and his
conduct of the war because of their fear of Goldwater, and they enlisted in
LBJ's reelection campaign. Several public figures who later became active opponents of the war in Vietnam—Dr. Benjamin Spock, David McReynolds of
the Socialist party, and Prof. H. Stuart Hughes of Harvard—signed public appeals to "go part of the way with LBJ." On election day, Johnson overwhelmed
Goldwater with 60 percent of the vote, carrying forty-four of the fifty states.
Johnson could claim that he represented general agreement, both foreign
and domestic, and that he had been chosen "president of all the people."

ESCALATION AND THE COLLAPSE OF THE COLD WAR
CONSENSUS, 1965–1968

The election of 1964 represented the high-water mark of the consensus which
had dominated discussion of international relations since 1945. Over the

next three years, Americans lost their unquestioning faith in the president's right to conduct foreign affairs as he saw fit; they began to doubt his word; and eventually they would not let him show his face on a college campus. The specter of communism and the "loss" of another country to radicals no longer could elicit fear. Where once academic experts had drawn up plans to wage wars of counterinsurgency, now professors denounced America's war as "genocidal" and drew unflattering comparisons between American behavior in Vietnam and Nazi conduct in Europe. The works of historians critical of the course of American foreign policy found a new respectful audience. William Appleman Williams's *Tragedy of American Diplomacy,* published to negative reviews in 1959, became a standard of a new school of revisionist writers. David Horowitz called the United States *The Free World Colossus* (1965), and Ronald Steel told the story of the *Pax Americana* (1967) which had ruled the world since 1945. Richard Barnet searched for *The Roots of War* (1972) and found them in the way Americans had sought to run the world to their liking. College campuses erupted into violent riots fueled by student disgust with the war and fear of the military draft. By 1967, hundreds of thousands of mostly young Americans took to the streets in demonstrations attacking American foreign policy in Vietnam and around the globe. Even Congress, which had offered its support for nearly every presidential departure in foreign affairs for twenty years, proved balky. It questioned Johnson's assumptions about world politics and threatened to develop a foreign policy of its own.

All of these changes took place while the number of American troops in Vietnam grew from fifty thousand in early 1965 to five hundred thirty-five thousand in early 1968 and while American planes dropped three million tons of bombs on North and South Vietnam. The air war eventually ignited more explosions than Allied planes set off in Europe and Japan during the Second World War. The bombing of the North began in February 1965 after North Vietnamese commandos attacked the marine garrison stationed at Pleiku in South Vietnam. Again, Washington used a North Vietnamese attack as a justification for military action long in the planning. McGeorge Bundy muttered, "Pleikus are like streetcars; there's one every ten minutes." In early 1965, the Joint Chiefs of Staff had told President Johnson that the South Vietnamese army could not be expected to defend itself for at least another year. They recommended a commitment of U.S. combat troops and bombing of the North to lift morale in Saigon and stem the flow of supplies to the South. Johnson approved the ROLLING THUNDER bombing of the North in late January, but he stipulated that he personally would select the targets for the American planes. The president feared Chinese intervention if the planes came too close to the border, and he had small respect for the mental capacity of his air force commanders. "The generals only know two words—bomb and spend," he complained to a visitor.

North Vietnam's Ho Chi Minh.
(Wide World Photos)

Johnson continued his habit of giving the generals some but not all of what they wanted throughout the next three years as the United States "escalated" the war. The term *escalation* itself originated with academic strategists in the Office of Operations Research of the Pentagon, and it meant that a gradual increase in force would "exceed the enemy's threshold of pain." Presumably the North Vietnamese would quit before the Americans. Secretary of Defense McNamara, an ardent believer in these theories at the beginning, returned from Vietnam in 1965 and 1966 with reports that he could "see the light at the end of the tunnel" and victory was "just around the corner." President Johnson used earthier language as he sent a group of GIs off to the war with the command that they come back and "nail the coonskin to the barn door."

In April 1965, the president outlined his war aims at a speech at Johns Hopkins University, one of the last times he could safely appear before an audience of college students. He offered to negotiate with the North Vietnamese about their withdrawal of troops from the South. He held out the prospect of more bombing and more American troops if they refused and promised a "TVA [Tennessee Valley Authority] for the Mekong Delta and North Vietnam" should they accept. Ho Chi Minh, observing the United States had simply taken over from the French as the major imperial power, flatly refused to negotiate while the United States bombed North Vietnam. The American proposal seemed especially impudent to him as it was the United States which fought ten thousand miles away from home while the North Vietnamese sent soldiers south to take part in a "civil war." Ho's position, constant throughout the war, was that the United States should stop bombing and withdraw its troops and then negotiations could begin.

The Johns Hopkins speech boosted Johnson's standing in the polls, but it drew ominous warnings from domestic critics. Walter Lippmann, now seventy-five, saw it on television and was dismayed that the president ignored his advice to call an unconditional halt to the bombing. He predicted the United States courted disaster in Southeast Asia because Johnson had "not taken to heart the historic fact that the role of the white man as a ruler in Asia" had ended in 1945. Senator Fulbright started his journey into opposition by complaining that the Johns Hopkins speech offered nothing new.

INTERVENTION IN THE DOMINICAN REPUBLIC

These qualms grew with another American military operation in April 1965: the invasion of the Dominican Republic to stop a "Communist-inspired" coup there. The Dominican Republic emerged from thirty years of despotism when Rafael Trujillo, the dictator of the country since 1931, was assassinated in 1961. The Kennedy administration had sent a naval squadron to the republic to prevent the return to power of the dictator's son, Ramfis, and in December 1962, the reformers elected Juan Bosch president with over 60 percent of the vote. Bosch lasted only ten months before he was ousted by an army coup which installed Donald Reid Cabral as the head of a conservative junta. The new Johnson administration disdained Bosch as a "poet and dilettante" and esteemed Reid Cabral, just as his junta lost support from both the army and businessmen. When Reid Cabral announced his decision to run in the presidential election of 1965, the opposition groaned, and the United States extended a loan of $5 million to the unpopular government.

Faced with an unfair election, the supporters of deposed President Bosch staged a coup of their own on April 24. Four days later, after word from Ambassador John Barlow Martin that fifty-eight (or fifty-three) "identified Communist or Castroite leaders" were in the rebel force, the United States dispatched thirty-three thousand marines and army troops to crush the rebellion. Johnson announced that "we don't intend to sit here in our rocking chair with our hands folded and let the Communists set up any governments in the Western Hemisphere." Newspaper reporters accompanying the troops believed that the embassy's list of subversives was spurious, and they gave wide publicity to Bosch's complaint that "this was a democratic revolution smashed by the leading democracy of the world." The Johnson administration coaxed a reluctant vote of support for its operations from the Organization of American States. Privately, diplomats from other Western Hemisphere countries indicated that United States actions demonstrated the Yankees' contempt for their southern neighbors. Had these officials heard Johnson's comments on the regional organization—"The OAS can't pour piss out of a boot if the instructions were written on the heel"—they would have had their worst fears confirmed. Foreign Relations Committee Chairman Fulbright exploded that "the whole affair . . . has been characterized by a lack of candor." An aide later explained that the chairman "realized that if LBJ was lying to him about the Dominican Republic, he might be doing the same about Vietnam."

RIDING THE TIGER IN VIETNAM

Over the next year, the Arkansas Democrat broke with the administration over the endless war in Southeast Asia. In early 1966, he denounced the "arrogance of power" of American diplomacy since the Second World War. Mocking the nightmares of American strategists, he reported that "certain pledges must be repeated every day lest the whole world go to rack and ruin—e.g., we will never go back on a commitment no matter how unwise." He nudged the committee into probing the extent and purpose of participation in the war in Vietnam. In the midst of two weeks of televised hearings, Secretary of State Rusk explained that the United States found itself in "the process of preventing the expansion and extension of Communist domination by the use of force against the weaker nations on the perimeter of Communist power." He lectured the committee that "the war in Vietnam is as much an act of outside aggression as though the Hanoi regime had sent an army across the seventeenth parallel rather than infiltrated armed forces by stealth." Fulbright seemed unmoved, and a plaintive Rusk asked, "Senator is it not just possible that there is something wrong with them [the North Vietnamese]." The chairman replied, "Yes, there is something wrong with them. . . . They are primitive, poor people who have been fighting for twenty years and I don't understand myself why they continue to fight, but they do." Some members of the foreign policy establishment who testified before the

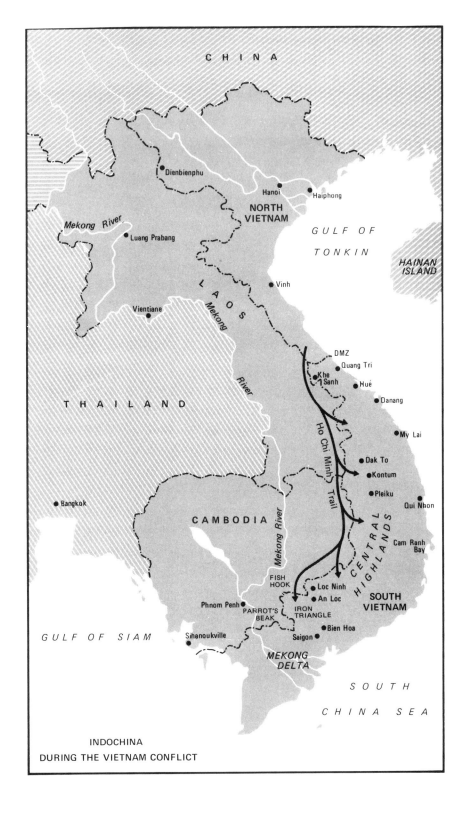

INDOCHINA
DURING THE VIETNAM CONFLICT

committee—former diplomat George Kennan, the father of containment; former army general James Gavin; and "realist" professor of international relations Hans J. Morgenthau,—agreed with Fulbright. They thought that the United States diverted precious resources from Europe, the proper focus of diplomatic attention, by waging a fruitless, costly, unwinnable war in Southeast Asia. These misgivings provoked President Johnson's denunciation of "Nervous Nellies . . . who become frustrated and bothered and break ranks under the strain and turn on their leaders, their own country and their fighting men."

The heaviest buildup in American forces in Vietnam occurred after July 1965 when Johnson accepted his generals' request for more ground troops. For the next three years, the Pentagon dropped the fiction that United States personnel served as "advisers" to the army of South Vietnam. It became America's war, fought by draftees who quickly learned to despise all Vietnamese, both friend and foe. The city of Saigon became an American outpost, resembling any town adjacent to a base. Brothels, bars, and opium dens catering to Americans sprang up, and the metropolis grew to a population of over 1.5 million. Some of the new immigrants came to work for the Americans, and others fled in terror from the war in the countryside. The Americans may not have welcomed them in town, but they were delighted to have them leave the land. The new American commander in Vietnam, Gen. William C. Westmoreland, favored a strategy of "search and destroy" in which the American troops scoured the countryside looking for the enemy and killing them. The fewer friendly Vietnamese the better, and the Americans cleared "free-fire zones" in which anything which moved was fair game. In a war without traditional front lines or regular enemy units, the "body count" became the means of measuring progress. Secretary of Defense McNamara required numbers from commanders to judge the success of the war. From the lowliest lieutenant to the colonels and generals, the number of dead on the other side was exaggerated until it appeared that the United States was slaughtering three hundred thousand Vietnamese a year.

These reports convinced the secretary of defense until the middle of 1967, when he noticed that the North Vietnamese had no trouble replacing their losses in the South even though commanders had told him that more men were being killed than could be drafted. At the same time, McNamara was wracked with doubts about the morality of the bombing campaign in the North and the South. He asked an assistant, Leslie Gelb, to compile a documentary history of the American involvement in the war. *The Pentagon Papers,* which emerged from this study, concluded that the United States leaders since Roosevelt had deceived the public into supporting an unwinnable war. In the fall, McNamara, ashamed of his participation in the war, convinced that it could not be won, asked Johnson for another job. LBJ, furious at his defection, let him become president of the World Bank. Few doubts assailed the president. His principal concerns in the war were not to lose, not to allow the Chinese or Soviets to intervene, and to keep the public behind him. He hoped to maintain popular support by making the fighting as painless as possible. Despite repeated pleas from the Pentagon, Johnson refused to call up reserves. While nearly two million draftees went into combat, they served a tour of twelve months rather than for the duration of the war. Even as the cost of the war soared to $50 billion per year, Johnson refused a plea by his chief economic advisers to raise taxes to pay for it or ask Congress to curb spending for the war on poverty. Instead, the administration paid for the war with public borrowing, causing inflation to rise in the United States to from less than 3 to about 5 percent a year and flooding Europe with unwanted dollars.

INTERNATIONAL REPERCUSSIONS

Allied governments did little to help as they watched the economic and political results of the war in Vietnam with a combination of horror and some secret delight at America's discomfiture. The United States persuaded no Europeans to join the war effort as it had in the Korean War. Small contingents from South Korea, the Philippines, Australia, and New Zealand, all handsomely paid by the United States, joined the fight. The Koreans especially acquired a reputation for fierceness bordering on savagery in combat. But the European nations criticized the United States on several fronts. German chancellor Ludwig Erhard, a former finance minister, believed the United States was exporting inflation. French president Charles de Gaulle voiced the harshest criticism when he predicted in a 1966 speech in the Phnom Penh, Cambodia, soccer stadium that "there is no chance that the peoples of Asia will subject themselves to the law of the foreigner who comes from the other shore of the Pacific, whatever his intentions, however powerful his weapons." Back in Paris, he blasted the "bombing of a very small people by a very large one" and condemned American actions as "unjust . . . detestable war, since it leads a great nation to ravage a small one." He offered to arrange a swift cease-fire and American withdrawal.

Dean Rusk shrugged off de Gaulle's proposals to mediate as the sour grapes of the leader of a country which had lost in Vietnam and wanted the Americans to suffer a similar humiliation. But Americans had a harder time responding to other concerns often voiced in Europe during the Vietnam years: namely, the war had diverted American attention from other, more important, world events. This objection seemed borne out when a war erupted between Israel and three of its Arab neighbors—Egypt, Jordan, and

Syria—in June 1967. In May, President Gamal Nasser of Egypt evicted the United Nations force from the Sinai Peninsula and closed the Strait of Tiran to ships bound to and from the southern Israeli port of Eilat. The United States, which had become a major supplier of arms to Israel in the Kennedy administration, tried to arrange an international force of warships to test the Egyptian guns at Sharm el-Sheik, which blocked the straits of Tiran. To the chagrin of Johnson, Rusk, and McNamara, none of the fifty states approached was willing to join the United States in challenging the blockade. At the end of May, Johnson begged Israeli foreign minister Abba Eban for more time to reach a peaceful settlement. His government waited two weeks, but when it became apparent that the United States could not force Nasser to back down, Israeli warplanes struck at dawn on June 5, destroying Egypt's air force on the ground. The war lasted only six days, with Israel humiliating the combined armies of Egypt, Jordan, and Syria. Israel captured the Sinai Peninsula from Egypt, the West Bank of the Jordan River and eastern Jerusalem from Jordan, and the Golan Heights from Syria. Israeli bombers sank ships in the Suez Canal the first morning of the war, thereby closing that waterway for the next seven years. European powers were furious that their supply of oil would now have to make the ten-thousand-mile trip around Africa, but the United States found some comfort in the canal's blockage: now the Soviet ships had a longer voyage on the way to carrying supplies to Vietnam.

In the aftermath of the Six Day War, Soviet prime minister Alexei Kosygin came to New York to attend a special session of the United Nations. While in America, the Soviet leader met President Johnson for their only conference at the small college town of Glassboro, New Jersey. Johnson wanted Soviet help in pressuring the North Vietnamese to negotiate with the Americans. The Soviet leader was noncommittal, but Johnson at least came away with the relieved sense that Kosygin desperately wanted to avoid a direct military confrontation with the United States in Vietnam. The two men also agreed to do more to limit the race in strategic arms between the superpowers.

INTELLIGENCE: SERVANT OR MASTER OF FOREIGN POLICY?

As the foreign policy consensus collapsed under the weight of the Vietnam War, Americans took a hard look at clandestine activities by their intelligence operations—the Central Intelligence Agency, the Federal Bureau of Investigation, the Defense Intelligence Agency, and the National Security Agency. Reports surfaced in 1967 that the CIA had funneled funds to foreign political parties, labor unions, newspapers, and publishers. In violation of its 1947 charter, the agency spied on American citizens in the United States, opening their mail, tapping their telephones, and tracing their friends. The CIA had secretly paid the bills of the liberal anti-Communist National Student Association from 1951 to 1966 and provided subventions for publishing books on international affairs which subtly supported the American point of view. The CIA also plotted the assassination of foreign leaders, hatched a coup in Iran in 1953, invaded Guatemala in 1954, planned the Bay of Pigs invasion in 1960–1961, "destabilized" the socialist governments of Chile after 1970 and Nicaragua after 1980, and helped scores of anti-Communist governments crush domestic rebellions and undermine opposition parties. More than $5 billion yearly went to the various intelligence operations, but the appropriations were hidden in innocuous-sounding programs in the Defense, State, Commerce, Treasury, and Agriculture department budgets. Few members of Congress beyond a trusted inner circle knew how much money went for intelligence.

Fierce battles raged within the intelligence community itself. While the 1947 National Security Act supposedly centralized information-gathering under the authority of the director of central intelligence, the CIA never managed to keep the field to itself. The FBI under the leadership of the prickly, maybe paranoid, J. Edgar Hoover, its only director before 1971, resented the CIA. Hoover despised its use of non-Communist liberals and socialists in foreign countries to achieve its ends. Suspecting that the well-connected Ivy Leaguers the CIA recruited as its operatives harbored liberal sentiments of their own, Hoover forbade the FBI agents from sharing information with their counterparts in the CIA. The FBI persisted in its own domestic espionage activities, code-named COINTELPRO (Counter-Intelligence Program), under which it infiltrated the American Communist party, the Socialist Workers party, the Students for a Democratic Society, the Black Panthers, and other dissident groups.

The CIA also encountered competition from intelligence operations in the armed forces, the State Department, and the National Security Agency. During the Vietnam War, the CIA consistently presented accurately pessimistic estimates of the chances for success. Alarmed generals, admirals, and diplomats ordered their own departments to prepare more cheerful forecasts. The National Security Agency, created in 1946 as a code-breaking operation, soon exceeded that technical function. After the United States began launching communications spy satellites, the NSA could intercept and decipher telephone conversations around the globe. "We know what Brezhnev says to his chauffeur," boasted one official. Instead of providing the raw data to the CIA for analysis, the NSA acquired its own staff of specialists to explain what the messages meant.

During the 1975 congressional investigations of covert intelligence activities, Frank Church, chairman of the Senate subcommittee, charged that the CIA had become a "rogue elephant," plunging uncontrolled into a steamy jungle of deception, assassination, and counterrevolution. The charge that intelligence agents had become the masters rather than the servants of foreign policy is too simple. Political leaders often welcomed the "deniability" offered by entrusting "dirty tricks" to secret agents. Because they were outside the scrutiny of press, public, or Congress, covert operations permitted officials to avoid the second-guessing of democracy, which makes life harder to people at the top. Moreover, the confusion within the intelligence community mirrored the competition in more visible parts of the foreign policy bureaucracy. Intelligence agencies had the same type of parochial interests that the other offices pursued in the decades that the United States had global interests. The CIA, NSA, DIA, and FBI have been no more the servants or masters of foreign policy than other groups. All have been part of the vast, untidy apparatus which has projected American power.

JOHNSON'S FALL

Lyndon B. Johnson lost ground politically in 1967. He no longer spoke about being "president of all the people" and retreated to "I'm the only president you've got." While he met with Kosygin, a National Conference for New Politics opened in Chicago, hoping to form the first left-wing political party in America in twenty years. Martin Luther King, the most prominent of the nation's black civil rights advocates, opposed the war in Vietnam as needlessly causing the death of black draftees and called on Johnson to step down. In November, as many as one hundred thousand demonstrators marched on the Pentagon to hear calls for immediate American withdrawal from Vietnam. Rejecting pleas for "moderation," "responsible debate," and "negotiated settlements," speakers told the crowd "the only thing to negotiate is the route American troops use out of Vietnam." While some demonstrators listened to the speeches, others followed the lead of poet Allen Ginsberg in attempting to levitate the Pentagon through mystical incantations. Others, like Norman Mailer, participated in mass arrests to emphasize opposition to the war. Calls went out throughout the antiwar movement to make the transition "from dissent to resistance."

Conventional politicians also looked for ways to "dump Johnson." Allard Lowenstein, a moderate antiwar activist, persuaded Sen. Eugene McCarthy of Minnesota to challenge Johnson for the Democratic nomination in the primary elections upcoming in the spring of 1968. Robert F. Kennedy, elected to the Senate from New York in 1964, had come out against the war in 1966, and he waited for the right opportunity to enter the fray against Johnson. Another dissident Democrat, Gov. George C. Wallace of Alabama, expecting to capitalize on the "white backlash" to the civil rights movement and the public weariness with the small progress in Indochina, announced his candidacy. Among Republicans, Richard Nixon, Nelson Rockefeller, George Romney, and Ronald Reagan all hoped to run against "Lyndon Johnson's war." While the Republican contenders said little about what they would do differently, they all agreed that Johnson had mishandled affairs.

The last hope the administration had of persuading the public that the war could be won vanished when the North Vietnamese launched the Tet (New Year's) offensive on January 31, 1968. In two weeks of fighting, the North Vietnamese captured eight provincial capitals, blew up the wall surrounding the United States embassy in Saigon, and held the grounds for several hours. American television viewers saw the police chief of Saigon put a bullet through the head of a Vietcong suspect, and they heard an American officer proclaim the awful words "We had to destroy the village in order to save it." A month after the Americans beat back the offensive, Lt. William Calley led a company which gunned down over two hundred infirm men and women and small children in the hamlet of My Lai. No calming remarks

The most famous photograph of the Vietnam War. South Vietnamese national police chief Gen. Nguyen Ngoc Loan executes a Vietcong suspect on a Saigon street in the midst of the Tet offensive, February 1, 1968. After the fall of Vietnam, General Loan fled to the United States where he became a pizza chef.
(Wide World Photos)

from General Westmoreland about having crushed the Tet offensive could change the public's disgust with the endless bloodshed.

By March, Johnson was severely shaken. Senator McCarthy nearly defeated him in the New Hampshire primary, which caused a wavering Robert Kennedy formally to enter the race. The president knew that Kennedy would defeat him in the Wisconsin primary. Johnson's newly appointed secretary of defense, Clark Clifford, supported by a group of "wise men" led by the former secretary of state, Dean Acheson, let him know that they believed the war could not be won. Having only hardliners like Rusk and Walt Whitman Rostow behind him, Johnson reluctantly turned down General Westmoreland's request for two hundred six thousand additional troops. On March 31, the president shocked the public by announcing his withdrawal from the presidential race so he could devote himself full time to negotiating a settlement. He stopped the bombing north of the Nineteenth Parallel in an effort to open peace talks in Paris.

Things got worse before they got better. Several American cities erupted in flames after Martin Luther King was murdered on April 4. Johnson called up thousands of regular army troops to suppress the insurrection in Washington. Two months later, another assassin shot Robert Kennedy, shocking the world and stripping antiwar Democrats of the only dissenter who had a chance of gaining the party's presidential nomination. When the Democratic convention met in Chicago in August, Vice-President Hubert Humphrey, the president's choice, became the nominee in the midst of massive antiwar demonstrations. Six thousand troops joined hundreds of Chicago police in clubbing antiwar activists who chanted, "The streets belong to the people" and "The whole world is watching" while trying to march on the convention hall. President Johnson, fearful of the chorus of boos which would greet his appearance (despite Chicago mayor Richard Daley's packing the gallery with loyal sanitation collectors), did not come to the convention.

The Democrats emerged from Chicago in such disarray that even the resurrection of Richard Nixon as the Republican nominee could not unite them. Liberals thought Nixon had committed political suicide when he lost the governorship of California in 1962 and told reporters, "You won't have Nixon to kick around any more." Now there was a "new Nixon," the foremost Republican statesman on foreign policy, who would take the high road while his running mate, Maryland governor Spiro Agnew, pictured Humphrey as soft on communism.

Nixon won in November by a mere five hundred thousand votes, a margin nearly as small as the one by which he had lost to John Kennedy in 1960. Many antiwar Democrats decided to support Humphrey at the last minute, after he announced that he would suspend all bombing of the North to get peace talks started. A few days before the election, actual discussions between

the United States and North Vietnam did open in Paris after the diplomats resolved a months-long dispute over the shape of the negotiating table. More voters probably wanted to escalate the war than wanted withdrawal. George Wallace received eight million votes as an independent running on a prowar platform with former air force general Curtis LeMay, who expressed the wish to "bomb them [the North Vietnamese] into the stone age."

Nixon's own proposals for ending the Vietnam War were even more obscure. During the campaign, he indicated that he had a secret plan which would assure "peace with honor" but to reveal it publicly would ruin Johnson's chances of ending the conflict. Privately, he doubted that the war could be won. A month after the election, he chose Henry Kissinger, a Harvard political science professor who formerly had been foreign policy adviser to Nelson Rockefeller, to be the head of the National Security Council. Nixon and Kissinger together spent the next four years looking for ways to conclude America's war in Vietnam and silence the voices challenging the assumptions on which American foreign policy had rested since 1945.

Lyndon Johnson departed Washington a broken man on January 20, 1969. His leadership in the most controversial war in American history coincided with the end of the era of American dominance of world politics. As the Europeans had learned to their discomfort in the aftermath of World War II, losing an empire leaves a bitter taste.

CHAPTER THIRTEEN

The Cold War Takes a Holiday, 1969–1976

Richard Nixon had no secret plan for ending the war in Vietnam, but he knew what he did not like. The war had wrecked Johnson's ability to act freely in foreign affairs, and the new president wanted to restore the authority of the White House. A man who did not inspire affection, Nixon shrank from confronting the sort of angry demonstrations which had made life miserable for Lyndon Johnson. Nor was the president's personal popularity the only thing threatened. The bewilderment of the Europeans with the American preoccupation in Vietnam meant that the United States no longer could count on subservience from former clients. For example, French president Charles de Gaulle assured fellow Europeans that the war in Vietnam hastened the day when "the Americans would no longer have any reason to stay on this side of the ocean."

The excessive commitment of American power in Vietnam prevented the United States from responding to other changes in the world balance. For years, Americans had denied the split between the Soviet Union and China, and Secretary of State Dean Rusk explained that the United States fought in Vietnam to meet the threat of "a billion Chinese armed with nuclear weapons." By 1969, however, with China convulsed in a "Great Proletarian Cultural Revolution," American diplomats no longer ignored the fact that the People's Republic went its own way. American and Soviet influence seemed to ebb in the rest of the world too. This "diffusion of power," as Johnson's undersecretary of state Eugene Rostow called it, reflected the changes in the world's economy. No longer did the United States sit alone as the world's only wealthy country, as it had at the end of the Second World War. There was nothing Nixon could do to restore American economic dominance, but he reasoned that extrication from Vietnam would provide greater maneuverability in a competitive world.

ASSERTING CONTROL OF FOREIGN POLICY

Nixon's first object in the Vietnam War was to silence domestic and foreign critics. Then, perhaps, government could govern without having to answer opponents it could never satisfy. Nixon's style of making foreign policy—his dramatic reversals, his reliance on trusted staff members, and his sanctimony—helped lower the rhetoric over Vietnam. His collaboration with National Security Adviser Henry Kissinger set the tone. They complemented each other, secretly directing relations with other nations while one of Nixon's oldest friends in political life, William P. Rogers, made the public appearances as secretary of state from 1969 to 1973. Rogers had been the man Nixon turned to when Eisenhower had wanted to drop him from the 1952 ticket as a result of the controversy over the "secret fund" provided by Nixon's business friends. Rogers had listened patiently as the vice-presidential candidate practiced his speech pledging his family attachment to their dog, Checkers. Throughout the remainder of the Eisenhower administration, Rogers remained one of the few men who liked Nixon and still retained his own sense of decency. His reward for befriending Nixon was appointment to the premier spot in the cabinet, where he suffered the indignity of being kept in the dark on important issues. Kissinger, who bested Rogers in the bureaucratic wars and could afford to appear generous, recalled that "Rogers was in fact far more able than he was pictured; he had a shrewd analytical mind and outstanding common sense."

With Rogers put forward to give an impression of well-intentioned honesty, Nixon and Kissinger went about their own work of creating an "illusion of peace," as former *New York Times* reporter Tad Szulc described it. Nixon's reliance on Kissinger rested on more than both men's enthusiasm for manipulation and secrecy. Both acknowledged the problems of bureaucratic rivalry which had plagued American foreign policy for half a century. They realized that the National Security Act of 1947 had built a framework for presidential control over foreign policy, but it had not eliminated interagency warfare. Things had gotten worse in the sixties when the Pentagon under Robert McNamara assumed an increasing share of the business of foreign policy. Kissinger proposed to Nixon to make the National Security Council "the principal forum for issues requiring interagency coordination, especially where presidential decisions of a middle or long range are involved." On the first day of the new administration, Kissinger seized control of the planning function for the National Security Council by demanding in the president's name that all policy papers receive clearance from him and his staff. He bombarded the State, Defense, and Treasury departments with requests for information. He set up special working groups to coordinate policies on Vietnam, southern Africa, and the Middle East.

LIQUIDATING VIETNAM

Nixon also took a visible part in setting a new course. In May 1969, he met South Vietnamese president Nguyen Thieu on the island of Midway to discuss the future of the war. Nixon told Thieu that American troops no longer could be as obtrusive in the war, that American forces had to be withdrawn with the South Vietnamese soldiers doing more of the fighting. So began the disengagement of American ground troops, a process as awkward as the new word *Vietnamization* Nixon invented to describe it. While the United States gradually reduced the troop level from five hundred thirty-five thousand to four hundred thousand over the next year and American casualties fell from over three hundred men to under one hundred men killed a week, the air war increased. In 1969 and 1970, the United States dropped tons of bombs on battlefields in South and North Vietnam up to the Nineteenth Parallel and in Cambodia. From Midway Island the president flew to Guam where he promised a new "Nixon Doctrine" designed to limit American engagement in future wars. The United States would use small nations as surrogates, he asserted. America would provide the arms, advisers, and financing for other countries to wage guerrilla or conventional wars against domestic insurgents or foreign enemies.

Despite its promise of reducing American participation in overseas conflicts, the Nixon Doctrine changed little in the way the United States dealt with other lands. First, the president indicated that the United States would move to this new strategy only after the war in Vietnam ended. Moreover, the United States had modestly increased its sale of weapons throughout the sixties, but these activities mushroomed 150 percent in the early seventies. In 1970, the United States exported $1.8 billion worth of arms. That figure rose to $4.3 billion in 1973 and then skyrocketed to $11 billion in 1974 and $15.2 billion in 1976. While fewer Americans fought wars, the level of violence rose. Some regions, notably the Middle East, developed voracious appetites for sophisticated, deadly equipment. By 1977, the nations from the Mediterranean to the Persian Gulf absorbed 39 percent of all military sales, more than the purchases of the NATO and Warsaw Pact countries combined. These tools of destruction brought greater insecurity, not peace, to the region. A major war broke out between Israel and the Arab states in 1973, and the region was in flames again at the end of the decade.

The negotiations to end the war in Vietnam proceeded along two tracks. The public conversations begun a week before the 1968 election by the Johnson administration continued in Paris with Philip Habib, a career Foreign Service officer, leading an American delegation in endless hours of fruitless conversation with the National Liberation Front contingent headed by Madame Nguyen Thi Binh. While these talks failed to hasten the coming of peace, they did explain to the world that it was talking with, and listening to, an exasperating foe. The North Vietnamese insisted that the diplomats resolve the military question of when the United States would withdraw its troops and stop the bombing. In reply, Americans linked the military and political sides of the war. The United States was willing to withdraw troops, but only if the North Vietnamese did the same. Each time Nixon took to the air to announce withdrawal of more troops, American negotiators hoped to obtain North Vietnamese consent to a political deal. Instead, the adamant North Vietnamese stayed put, and with each reduction in the size of the United States army in South Vietnam, American leverage over the future of Indochina diminished.

While the public talks went nowhere, Kissinger began in August 1969 a series of secret negotiations with Xuan Thuy, the principal representative from the North Vietnamese delegation. The national security adviser would fly from Washington to unnamed airbases in France or West Germany and be whisked to private retreats on the outskirts of Paris. There, in villas owned by members of the Communist party of France, where priceless Picassos hung on the walls, the national security adviser and Thuy spoke privately. At one point in the conversation, an enterprising reporter learned of Kissinger's presence, but the West German government put out a cover story that the plane carrying the American to Paris actually bore a mistress of French president George Pompidou. The national security adviser appeared more flexible in private than did the official team. He suggested that the United States was heartily sick of the war, but America could not leave immediately for fear of alienating President Thieu and being seen as weak. He indicated to Xuan Thuy, however, that the Americans would be willing to separate the military and political issues in the war if the North showed similar willingness to hold back in its eventual takeover of the South. Xuan Thuy did not encourage Kissinger in the early days of their conversations, but the American could be as menacing as he could be generous.

The United States signaled the North Vietnamese that it would enlarge the air war while it reduced the troop level. In April 1969, Nixon ordered the secret bombing of Cambodia, a traditional neutral which had managed to stay out of the war for the previous five years. Led by Prince Norodom Sihanouk, the Cambodians had allowed the North Vietnamese to use their territory as staging areas for the war in the South. American generals had wanted for years to cross the border into Sihanouk's country and eliminate what they thought was a secret command headquarters for the National Liberation Front. Lyndon Johnson had always resisted the expansion of the war beyond Vietnam, but Nixon and Kissinger believed that a "sideshow" in Cambodia would keep the generals happy while the United States brought troops home. If the prince did not complain about the bombing, which was to be kept secret, then it would indicate that the Cambodians actually supported the Americans. The North and South Vietnamese would also know about the attacks, but news would be withheld from the press and public. Even the men who flew the giant B-52s were under the misconception that they dropped their bombs in South Vietnam. Whenever there was a special order for the MENU bombing, the code name for the operation, enlisted men secretly adjusted the coordinates on the airplanes' computers without the pilots' knowledge so they woud fly over Cambodia. When the *New York Times* broke the story in April, a brief flurry of public opposition arose. Nixon and Kissinger offered bland assurances that the Cambodians did not object and continued with the bombing.

Prince Sihanouk, chief of state of Cambodia since 1945, never found favor with official Washington which found him too fond of good wine, fast cars, and France, where he had spent much of his life. A proud nationalist who worried that the United States, Vietnam, and China each had designs on his land, the prince had tried, not always successfully, to stay aloof from the war in Vietnam. He closed his eyes to North Vietnamese troops in his land while at the same time uttering no protest when American B-52s bombed them. He drew the line, however, at American or South Vietnamese ground troops on Cambodian soil. But an ambitious anti-Communist army general, Lon Nol, had fewer qualms about inviting outsiders. When Sihanouk made his yearly visit to the French Riviera in March 1970, the general deposed the prince and made himself prime minister. In Washington, Kissinger and Nixon cheered the news of a more complaisant Cambodia which would actively join the war against North Vietnam.

The cavalier disregard of the public's objections continued in the fall when the antiwar movement tried once again to end the fighting. A broad coalition ranging from moderate Republicans to revolutionary supporters of the Vietcong scheduled a demonstration in Washington for the weekend of November 14. A week before the march, which drew close to half a million people, Nixon announced the withdrawal of an additional seventy-five thousand troops. He also called upon the "great silent majority" of the American public to support him in the war. On the day of the demonstration itself, buses ringed the White House to prevent any of the demonstrators from getting too close to the president, who, his aides announced, spent the afternoon watching television as the Notre Dame football team defeated Michigan State. The November demonstration was the high water mark for massive, peaceful marches on the nation's capital. Seemingly having no effect on the administration's policies, and with the large public happy that the troops were being withdrawn, the antiwar movement cast about for new techniques. Activists on college campuses suggested that student strikes occur each month, with the duration increasing.

The antiwar movement got another chance in May 1970, when the Nixon administration became convinced that the bombing of Cambodia had done little good and that an invasion was necessary. On the evening of April 30, Nixon took to the airwaves with the announcement that American and South Vietnamese troops had crossed the border to find the "headquarters of the North Vietnamese." Campuses erupted across the country. National guardsmen, summoned by Ohio governor James A. Rhodes to Kent State University, killed four and wounded twenty-two students attending a rally called to get the militia off the campus. In mourning, stunned undergraduates across the country refused to attend classes. Rhodes lost a close primary the next week, hundreds of television reporters descended on the town of Kent, and novelist James A. Michener produced a six-hundred-page book on the incident. The public paid much less attention when Mississippi national guardsmen shot and killed two student antiwar protestors at Jackson State College, a black institution, the week after the massacre at Kent.

President Nixon offered no condolences to the families of the slain demonstrators, but he did ask his chauffeur to drive him to the Lincoln Memorial on the night of May 7 to talk about the war to some of the thousands of college students who had flocked to Washington to express their outrage. Senators John Sherman Cooper, a Kentucky Republican, and Frank Church, an Idaho Democrat, angry at the widening war, introduced legislation repealing the Gulf of Tonkin Resolution. Several members of Kissinger's staff submitted resignations, while the national security adviser himself confronted angry Harvard students and professors. "They were as wrong as they were passionate," he recalled. He told them he had restrained Nixon from even more forceful acts and begged his former colleagues for patience, but he concluded he "would get no help" from his old colleagues. Eager to demonstrate his loyal support for the Cambodian operation, Kissinger thereupon authorized the Federal Bureau of Investigation to install taps on the telephones of aides suspected of speaking to reporters. The taps revealed little. Nixon later explained to White House Counsel John Dean at the height of the Watergate scandal, "Lake and Halperin [two staff members under surveillance], they're both bad. But the taps were too. They never helped us. Just gobs and gobs of material: gossip and bullshitting."

The invasion proved a fiasco. The Americans and South Vietnamese found no headquarters because none existed. Nixon shortly thereafter announced that the troops would leave Cambodia by June 30, thereby eliminating the small hope that the mission made military sense. In Cambodia, the results of the invasion were worse. With Sihanouk deposed, a long-smoldering civil war erupted in full flame between the Cambodian Communists, or Khmer Rouge, and Lon Nol's government. Both sides used boys as young as twelve as soldiers. These untrained, frightened youths, imbued by officers with implacable hatred of the other side, engaged in murderous assaults. The better-led Khmer Rouge conducted some of the worst atrocities of the Indochina war. After their victory in April 1975, they forced hundreds of thousands of Cambodian city dwellers to leave their homes and live off the land. A total social breakdown ensued, and as many as three million innocent people, nearly 40 percent of the population, were starved to death by the new government. The unhappy country's troubles continued for years. In 1979, the new Communist government of Vietnam invaded Cambodia and installed a less brutal regime, but one which was a virtual puppet of Hanoi. Prince Sihanouk, now living in Beijing as a guest of the Chinese government and bitterly opposed to Vietnam, made another of his startling shifts of alliances and backed the remnants of the Khmer Rouge, despite their having murdered several of his children. The United States too decided that anything, including the odious Khmer Rouge, was preferable to Vietnamese domination of Cambodia. After 1979, American representatives at the United Nations continued to vote for the seating of the vestiges of the Khmer Rouge in the General Assembly. Prince Sihanouk, whom Washington had airily dismissed, returned for a triumphal American tour in 1981, in which private church and relief groups publicly promised aid and public officials privately expressed their understanding and support for his attempts to regain his throne with the aid of the butchers of his kingdom.

The American army began to disintegrate as troop withdrawals mounted. No soldier wanted to be the last man killed in action. Platoons refused to go on patrol, officers were murdered by their own men, and marijuana smoking increased. The absurdity of the wartime experience increased the disillusionment. As a disgraceful character in the antiwar novel *Dog Soldiers* put it, "When elephants are hunted by armed men in helicopters, the only solution is to get high." Interracial hatred mounted, as black soldiers believed they bore the brunt of the fighting and dying, and race riots broke out on navy vessels. In the midst of this, the massacre at My Lai came to light, and Lt. William J. Calley stood trial for murder. Although a court-martial convicted Calley in 1971 and sentenced him to a prison term of fifteen years, Nixon spoke out in favor of reducing the sentence. The president hoped to align himself with the prowar segment of the population who thought that Calley had been unfairly accused by the antiwar movement.

A year after the invasion of Cambodia hastened the destruction of that country, the United States helped the Vietnamese army move into another neutral neighbor, Laos, in May 1971. American television viewers saw the reality of Vietnamization as the Vietnamese troops scrambled for cover instead of fighting. The invasion turned into a rout with ARVN soldiers rushing back home without clearing out another supposed headquarters of the insurgency. What had been planned in Washington as a means of demonstrating how well the South Vietnamese could fight became instead proof that they could not hold their own.

At the same time, the American economy seemed ill, with inflation running at an unacceptable rate of 5 percent per year, and Europeans were angry that the United States had exported the cost of the war to them. German and French central bankers made their distress known by demanding payment in gold for the dollars they held. On August 15, 1971, Nixon made a dramatic about face in economic policy, announcing the imposition of wage and price controls, something he had previously said he would never do. He also cut the remaining link between the dollar and gold; no longer would the United States Treasury repay foreign dollar holders with the precious metal. Nixon had little choice, for foreigners held four times as many dollars as the United States possessed gold. He devalued the dollar by 10 percent in terms of other currencies. Nixon hoped for a decline in the value of the American currency which would accordingly decrease the flood of exports from Japan and Europe. The Japanese economy had, in fact, boomed during the Vietnam War as the United States used that nation's facilities to repair equipment.

AN OPENING TO CHINA

Nixon also moved in 1971 and 1972 to isolate Vietnam from China and the Soviet Union, reasoning that if the North Vietnamese lost their major backers they would make peace on America's terms. Accordingly, Nixon and Kissinger recognized the Soviet-Chinese split while at the same time attempting to become friendlier with both Communist powers. The negotiations with the two nations went along at the same time although the opening to China was the more dramatic. Secret talks began in Warsaw, Poland, between the American and Chinese ambassadors in 1970. During that year, Kissinger took over the negotiations, letting Secretary of State Rogers know what he was doing only when he found it convenient. In March 1971, the Chinese sent friendly signals to the United States by inviting a traveling American Ping-Pong team to visit China. Americans were as bad at Ping-Pong as the Chinese excelled, so acceptance of the invitation implied that the Americans would gladly lose to their hosts to improve relations. The following July, Kissinger himself went to Beijing after first disappearing from sight on a visit to Pakistan. The press reported that the national security adviser had a stomachache, and the next day he showed up in the Chinese capital to announce that the president of the United States would be coming to China to open "normal" relations between the two countries. Other White House aides foresaw Kissinger's emergence as "the mystery man of the age" upon his return from Beijing. He instantly became a celebrity in the press. *U.S. News and World Report* thought that "Kissinger's secret mission to Red China [had] few parallels in the annals of U.S. diplomacy." One of the security adviser's admirers proclaimed that his secret trip confirmed his standing as "the smartest guy around."

Kissinger's gastric distress may have been invented, but other diplomats and politicians experienced genuine pain at the handshake between him and Chinese premier Zhou Enlai. The Japanese, who had followed American suggestions and improved relations with the Nationalists on Taiwan, were caught unaware. They read of the American reversal in the newspapers. Secretary of State Rogers played no part in the planning for the trip to China, and he had to watch the most important departure in recent American diplomatic history from the sidelines. H. R. Haldeman heard the national security adviser complain that "Rogers is trying to stop Kissinger as the negotiator with the Chinese." The prospect of the old anti-Communist warrior, Richard Nixon, breaking with the government of Jiang Jieshi (Chiang Kaishek) also astonished the right wing of the Republican party. Ohio representative John Ashbrook vowed to fight Nixon for the party's presidential nomination in the 1972 primaries. In Taiwan, Jiang reacted with sputtering rage. That the American president who had hailed him earlier would now open relations with Mao Zedong flabbergasted Jiang. In Pakistan, where Gen. Ayub Khan had been the intermediary between Kissinger and the Chinese, the news won applause; for it seemed as if Pakistan were now an indispensable ally of the United States. Six months later, in December 1971, General Khan called on Kissinger for something in return when the east province of Pakistan broke away and declared itself the independent nation of Bangladesh. Khan's army fought a war with India in which the United States "tilted" toward Pakistan. India triumphed while the United States, unlike its Western European allies, supported the defeated Pakistanis. Kissinger kept control of American policy toward the India-Pakistan war. He told the president, "I can't turn it over to Rogers. We can't be frivolous about this," because it is "the one area that will screw up the trip" to China.

In February 1972, Nixon flew to Beijing. As he stepped off the plane, he shook hands with Premier Zhou. The photograph of the two leaders reversed an old snub; Secretary of State John Foster Dulles had refused Zhou's hand at the Geneva Conference of 1954. Nixon's trip to China proved a huge success. He met with the aging Mao and accepted the Chinese leader's complaints about the "hegemonism" of the Soviet Union. The two pledged to

President Richard Nixon with Chinese premier Zhou Enlai (l.) and Communist
party chairman Mao Zedong in Beijing, February 1972. *(Wide World Photos)*

end their thirty years of hostility and move toward "normal" relations. Before the decade was out, America and China had full diplomatic exchanges.
On the touchy question of Taiwan, the United States went a long way toward
acknowledging the Chinese claims to the island. The Shanghai communiqué,
announced at the end of the meeting, indicated that the United States recognized that both Chinese governments claimed that Taiwan was part of
China, and that the Untied States acknowledged the Beijing government as
the sovereign power in China. Both sides pledged to work for a "peaceful
resolution" of the dispute over Taiwan. No one knew precisely what that
meant, and the phrasing was purposely ambiguous. Kissinger outshone
Rogers in Beijing. The national security adviser helped fashion the final communiqué. His preeminence even threatened to overshadow the president.
One of Nixon's other staff members worried that reporters had "built HAK
to the point where people wonder whether he makes foreign policy or the
president." Nixon minded less, however, as Kissinger helped the administration's reputation. The president used the national security adviser to generate support among the press for the Shanghai communiqué. "Deep six
Rogers," the president commanded as he ordered Kissinger to explain the
implications of the agreements with the People's Republic.

WHITE HOUSE ABUSES

While Kissinger decried leaks from NSC staff, other Nixon aides were appalled by certain stories in the press. In June 1971, Daniel Ellsberg, a former Pentagon analyst who had cast off his hawkish ideas on the war, turned
over copies of the special Pentagon history of the Vietnam War to Neil Sheehan of the *New York Times*. Despite orders from Attorney General John N.

Mitchell not to publish the documents, the *Times* did so on June 21. Immediately thereafter, the special assistant to the president for domestic affairs, John D. Ehrlichman, created a White House "plumbers" unit to plug leaks of embarrassing information. Their first stop was a break-in at the office of Ellsberg's psychiatrist to find discrediting information. Soon the plumbers cast a wider net. By the fall, they were following one Dita Beard, a lobbyist for the International Telephone and Telegraph Company, who had slipped documents to Jack Anderson suggesting that her company had paid $500,000 to the president's reelection campaign in return for help around the world, especially in Chile. While Beard recovered from a nervous breakdown at a Denver osteopathic hospital, E. Howard Hunt, one of the planners of the Guatemalan invasion in 1954, the Bay of Pigs operation of 1961, and the commando attacks on Cuba, dressed in a red fright wig and entered her hospital room to persuade her to recant her damaging allegation.

The Democratic National Committee's headquarters at the Watergate office complex in Washington appeared next on Hunt's ridiculous agenda. He recruited five anti-Castro Cubans to obtain Democratic party secrets. While attempting to do so, they were apprehended at the building complex on the night of June 18, 1972.

DETENTE WITH THE SOVIET UNION

That "third-rate burglary," as Nixon's press secretary, Ronald Ziegler, dismissed it, created barely a stir in the summer of 1972 as Nixon successfully relaxed tensions with the Soviet Union. In late May, he became the first American president to visit Russia since FDR conferenced in Yalta in 1945. Nixon's trip to Moscow was all the more surprising as it came on the heels of another major escalation of the war in Vietnam by the United States. A North Vietnamese offensive in the spring of 1972 had once again exposed the weakness of the ARVN troops. Nixon, politically unable to rush more American soldiers into battle, responded instead by spending an evening watching the movie *Patton* and then ordering American bombers to attack the ports of Haiphong and Hanoi in the Operation LINEBACKER. Nixon expected that Soviet ships would be hit in these raids, which dumped one hundred twelve thousand tons of bombs on the North. But if the Kremlin leaders offered no formal protest and did not cancel his proposed visit to Moscow, he would conclude that they wanted an accommodation with the United States despite their friendship with North Vietnam.

Soviet president Leonid Brezhnev went ahead with the invitation to Nixon for reasons of his own. With the scheduled opening of the Twenty-Fourth Congress of the Soviet Communist party at the end of June, the Soviet premier desired some international success to show his docile delegates. The Soviet economy was in far worse shape than the American, with the consumer goods promised under Khrushchev still in short supply and chronic food shortages threatening stability. The Soviet invasion of Czechoslovakia in August 1968 had temporarily stopped the Eastern Europeans from showing their independence, but the Soviets had constantly to worry about the loyalty of their allies. The conditions on the Chinese border were even worse, with Mao Zedong officially calling the Soviet Union a "revisionist" power which had betrayed the revolutionary heritage of Leninism. (Mao had shown how much of a revolutionary he was by embracing President Nixon!) Economically, the Soviet Union could gain immensely by opening trade relations with the United States. New technology would help the struggling consumer industry, and imports of Americn grain could raise meat production. If the United States and the Soviet Union worked out a limit to the arms race, the Soviet Union, already spending twice as much of its gross national product as the Americans on arms, could divert resources to consumer goods. Finally, an agreement with the United States in the face of the opening to China would mean that the Soviet Union had effectively countered the pull of Beijing.

Accordingly, both sides had much to gain from an agreement in Moscow. The two leaders culminated years of disarmament conversations in Vienna when they signed a Strategic Arms Limitations Agreement (SALT I). In return for a mutual pledge to drop production of an antiballistic missle (ABM) system, Nixon and Brezhnev set upper limits on the number of offensive missiles each side could husband. The Soviet Union would have 1,600, and the United States would be allowed 1,054. Despite these lopsided numbers, the United States actually gained in the exchange. The antiballistic missile system, a project with a price tag in excess of $50 billion, was given little chance by experts of accomplishing its difficult mission of shooting Soviet missiles out of the sky. The idea had been floated in the Johnson administration and dropped since weapons specialists did not believe it would work and a financially strapped government could not afford it. The ABM was resurrected by Nixon's secretary of defense, Melvin Laird, in 1969 as a way of showing that the new administration would be tougher with the Russians than its predecessor had been. Henry Kissinger, whose academic work had included a discussion of the role of nuclear weapons, had backed the system for diplomatic, not strategic, reasons. The United States could threaten to complete the ABM as a bargaining chip which it would return to the Soviets for an agreement limiting the number of missiles.

In the case of intercontinental ballistic missiles (ICBMs), the United States actually came out ahead. While SALT I froze the number of missiles, it said nothing at all about the new technology of multiple warheads in which the United States had a huge lead over the Soviet Union. With the introduction of MIRVs (multiple independently targeted reentry vehicles), the United States possessed a new weapon that had several warheads, each capable of hitting targets miles apart. The MIRVs gave the United States a two-to-one lead in deliverable warheads.

The arms race continued in the seventies, with each side trying to outdo the other in new technology. The United States developed a new strategy for avoiding a nuclear holocaust with the Soviet Union. Instead of protection, the United States and the Soviet Union would follow a MAD (mutual assured destruction) plan. The strategy was as frightening as the acronym which described it. Each side supposedly held the weapons of its adversary hostage, and each knew that an attack would be met with the assured destruction of its capacity to wage war. The Soviets never accepted the American definition of how the next war would be fought, but American planners dismissed Russian complaints about "inhumanity" of the strategy as hypocrisy and proclaimed that the job of American defense intellectuals was to "raise the Soviets' learning curve" about modern strategic thinking.

In fact, the SALT agreements did not arrest the slide toward destabilizing weapons. Barred from some fields by the treaties, weapons planners on both sides turned their inventive energies to areas left uncovered by the agreements and speeded production of new generations of missiles not covered by SALT. The Soviets went to work on highly accurate land-based missiles—the SS16s. The United States worked on an invulnerable, accurate land-based missile of its own, the MX.

THE ELECTION OF 1972 AND THE VIETNAM NEGOTIATIONS

Nixon returned from Moscow to a coronation ceremony at the Republican National Convention, which had been hastily moved from San Diego to Miami after the whiff of scandal came from Dita Beard. Thugs from the Committee to Reelect the President (CREEP) had planned to kidnap radical leaders of demonstrations scheduled to disrupt the proceedings. The assembled Republicans cheered a man they expected easily to defeat the Democrats' Sen. George McGovern, a left-liberal who had been one of the first to oppose the war. CREEP had done what it could to disrupt the campaigns of the other Democratic candidates in the hopes that McGovern's liberal views went beyond those of most voters.

The election proved no contest. McGovern's campaign self-destructed early with the selection for vice-president of Missouri senator Thomas Eagleton, who admitted having received shock treatments for depression. McGovern pledged "1,000 percent support" for Eagleton and then dumped him uncerimoniously from the ticket. The public distrusted McGovern's economic proposals to guarantee $1,000 annually to every American, and they ignored his warnings that the Nixon administration had not moved to end the war in Vietnam. Instead, voters were heartened by Henry Kissinger's announcement in the last week of October that he had arranged a settlement with the new negotiator for North Vietnam, Le Duc Tho. "Peace is at hand," Kissinger assured a press conference, and a week later Nixon rode the euphoria of the war's end to a crushing defeat of McGovern. He carried every state but Massachusetts and captured nearly 61 percent of the vote.

Peace was not at hand in late October, and Kissinger received a severe dressing down from H. R. "Bob" Haldeman, the grim-faced, crew-cut chief of staff at the White House, for his indiscreet revelation on November 2 of why the public admired him. "Americans like the cowboy who leads the wagon train by riding ahead alone on his horse," the national security adviser informed an Italian journalist. Haldeman, wondering what role Kissinger saw for the president if his principal diplomat "rides into town and does everything by himself," temporarily banished him from the White House and forbade him to meet the press until an agreement was signed.

The snag in the negotiations arose from objections by South Vietnamese president Thieu to a peace settlement which would have the United States remove the last of its troops while the North Vietnamese agreed only not to introduce any new forces in the South. The United States had separated the military from the political aspects of the war by permitting the North Vietnamese and the Provisional Revolutionary Government (the new name for the National Liberation Front) to work out the best deal they could with the Thieu government. The United States had resisted the calls to depose Thieu, but still the South Vietnamese president did not want to face the armies of his enemies alone. He had a sinking suspicion that the United States had fled Vietnam and let the North know that it awaited only a "decent interval" before the Communists could take over the country. Thieu therefore rejected the importunities of Kissinger's deputy, Gen. Alexander M. Haig, who scurried to Saigon to secure South Vietnamese assent to the peace treaty before election day. Thieu was rude to Haig and refused to sign.

The Paris talks were at a standstill in November and December when the president decided that a dramatic demonstration could loosen the South Vietnamese and frighten the North. Two days before Christmas, Nixon ordered the B-52s, which previously had seen service only in the South and over Cambodia, to attack North Vietnam. Every city in the North came under fire, hospitals were exploded in Hanoi, and hundreds of civilians were killed. Denunciations came in from the usual peace groups, but Nixon treated their complaints with disdain. He justified the bombing by saying that it would secure the release of the American prisoners of war held in the North despite the fact that thirteen of the B-52s were shot down over the North and forty-five of their crew members held captive. While Nixon sought support from the silent majority, diplomats were at work on both North and South Vietnamese. Kissinger continued his talks with Le Duc Tho and indicated that his boss might be mentally unhinged. Nixon himself carefully cultivated the fears that he might go to irrational lengths to get his way. Chief of Staff Haldeman later dubbed this procedure the "madman strategy": if the North Vietnamese doubted that Nixon felt bound by conventional restraints, they would sign before risking destruction. While Kissinger played upon these fears, Haig returned to Thieu in Saigon with some brutally frank messages. The United States was determined to have a settlement, withdraw all of its troops, and get its prisoners back. If Thieu refused, the United States would make peace anyway, leaving the South in the lurch. If, however, Thieu swallowed his misgivings, the bombing of the North offered only a taste of what the United States might do later to back its friend in the South. In a secret memorandum, which he later denied writing, Kissinger pledged the reintroduction of United States troops should the South need them. The United States also assured North Vietnam of future reconstruction aid if it would sign.

Thieu agreed to peace the second week of January 1973, and a smiling Henry Kissinger and a grinning Le Duc Tho put their initials on a treaty on January 23, three days after Nixon was inaugurated for a second term. The news that Nixon had actually withdrawn American troops may have been the final blow to an ailing Lyndon Johnson, who died at his ranch on the Pedernales on January 22. Kissinger was luckier, winning the Nobel peace prize in December 1973 along with Le Duc Tho.

The North Vietnamese diplomat refused to share the prize with Kissinger, whom he blamed for prolonging the war. Benjamin A. Schwartz, an expert on China and a former Harvard colleague, observed, "I'm no fanatical enemy of Kissinger, but this is a bit much. I think he's done some good things, but the Peace Prize? There's no peace, and we stayed too long." The *Los Angeles Times* expressed "some surprise," since "Southeast Asia is still not associated in most people's minds with peace." But, the paper went on, the prize was earned by "a professional and brilliant feat of diplomacy by two remarkable men."

In September, Kissinger received the prize he really wanted when Nixon dropped William Rogers as secretary of state and appointed his national security adviser in his place. Since becoming a public figure with his trip to Beijing, Kissinger had delighted reporters, who loved his leaks, his wit, and his ability to mock his own German accent. Upon his appointment, the liberal *New Yorker* praised him as "prodigiously intelligent, articulate, talented." One foreign service officer predicted, "we'll consider ourselves God's chosen children for a couple of months." The *Christian Science Monitor* reported that Watergate "may have been a catalyst in President Nixon's decision to make the change. It has already enabled him to say that he is 'getting the work out' in the departments where it belongs."

CHILE'S AGONY

Immediately upon appointment, Kissinger became involved in the overthrow of the socialist government of Chile. Salvador Allende Gossens, the candidate of an alliance of Socialists, Communists, and radicals, had been elected president of one of the most thriving democracies of Latin America in 1970 with about 36 percent of the vote in a three-candidate race. The CIA followed its usual practice and funneled money to the Christian Democratic candidate, who came in third. When it became clear that Chile's Congress would fulfill its traditional role of confirming as president the candidate with the most votes (Allende), the CIA station chief in Santiago panicked. He sent frantic messages to the Forty Committee, the Washington interagency body which supervised the CIA, asking for authorization to "destabilize" the government. Despite a secret CIA assessment that "no vital U.S. economic interests" would be threatened by Allende's accession to the presidency, the Forty Committee believed that his victory "created considerable political and psychological costs." The agency's deputy director for plans recalled that Secretary of State Kissinger "placed the heaviest of pressures" on him to block Allende's elevation. Accordingly, the agency developed a proposal to bribe Chilean congressmen to vote against Allende and, should that fail, encourage the military to mount a coup. The Congress in Santiago confirmed Allende, and the military plot resulted only in the murder of Chile's chief of staff.

No coup followed, and for the next three years Allende embarked on a course of equalizing the gross inequalities in wealth plaguing his country. He nationalized the American-owned copper mines and expropriated the telephone system owned by the International Telegraph and Telephone Company (ITT). In Washington, the American government responded by cutting off economic aid and using its influence with the World Bank and Inter-American Bank to refuse further credits to Allende's government. The aim, Kissinger explained, was "to make the economy scream." Despite the hostility of international business, Allende's government actually increased its share of the popular vote in the 1972 congressional elections, where leftist candidates gained 42 percent of the vote. By the beginning of 1973, however, the Chilean middle class had joined with the elite and the foreign businesses in wanting the socialists out. CIA operatives were generous with their money, supporting demonstrations by angry middle-class housewives and a strike by truckers and taxi drivers, the best-paid members of the Chilean working class.

The military, proud of its long history of political neutrality, began plotting Allende's overthrow in the summer of 1973. The Chilean left insisted that Allende provide arms for the population, but the president, fearing a civil war and trusting the assurances of his military advisers that they would stand by him, refused to open the armories. On September 17, the generals who had given their pledge led the attack against Allende, and the president is supposed to have committed suicide. The United States helped the insurgents and immediately recognized the new regime. When asked about the morality of the overthrow of a duly elected democratic government, Kissinger replied that he saw no "right for people to vote in Communists" since presumably once they were in power they never left.

THE MIDDLE EAST WAR

Maintaining American domination over the Western Hemisphere came easier than asserting influence in the Middle East. A new war broke out between Israel and its neighbors when Syria and Egypt attacked on October 6, 1973, on the holiest day of the Jewish year, Yom Kippur. The Nixon administration had done little to defuse tensions since 1969. It had become the major arms supplier to Israel while at the same time floating a scheme in the summer of 1970 to have the Israelis withdraw to their 1967 borders. So little interested in the problem were Nixon and Kissinger that the American proposal for an Israeli retreat bore William Rogers's name, a sure sign that the men at the top had better things to do. Kissinger himself may have been reluctant to inject himself into the Arab-Israeli dispute because he was Jewish, but the Yom Kippur War jolted him into action. The Middle East became a region where the United States could block the Soviet Union.

In the first three days of the war, Egyptian troops crossed the Suez Canal, forcing the surrender of hundreds of surprised Israeli soldiers. In the north Syria's army posed an even greaver threat to the Jewish state. It nearly broke through Israeli defenses on the Golan Heights to cut the country in two. Israeli prime minister Golda Meir telephoned urgent requests for American military aid and considered using the Israeli atomic bomb against the Arabs. American military officers were split over the kind of aid which should be offered to the Israelis. Some agreed with the European assessment that the Israelis should be brought down a few notches since they had not reached an accommodation with the Arabs after the 1967 Six Day War. If the United States were seen to be too enthusiastic in its support for Israel, whatever leverage America had with the Arab states would disappear. Still, Israel retained considerable support among the American public, and American Jewish leaders worried that the war seemed to be going so badly for the Jewish state.

Accordingly, Nixon and Kissinger devised a strategy of helping Israel repel the attack while simultaneously pressuring the Meir government to acknowledge its dependence upon the United States. A war which resulted in a stalemate between Arabs and Israelis might make both sides ask America to act as an honest broker. Nixon authorized an airlift of replacement arms and ammunition to Israel on October 21. Sure that they could receive additional supplies from the Americans, the Israelis committed the remainder of their equipment and turned the tide. They threw the Syrians back beyond the original line of the Golan Heights, and they crossed the Suez Canal and surrounded the Egyptian Third Army. At this point, the Soviet Union threatened to intervene on the Egyptian side while Nixon countered with an alert for American troops around the world. In October, both the Untied States and the Soviet Union stood down, and they joined in a United Nations Security Council resolution demanding a cease-fire. The Israelis reluctantly agreed despite their hopes of delivering a telling blow to the Egyptians. As Israeli defense minister Moshe Dayan explained to his country's parliament, "I tell you gentlemen, the tanks and ammunition our forces are firing in Egypt three weeks ago were in the United States."

With a cease-fire in effect between the Arabs and Israelis, Secretary of State Kissinger moved to have the United States become the major go-between in the dispute, and to evict the Soviet Union from the Middle East. Egyptian president Anwar Sadat had begun the process a year before when he had thrown out ten thousand Soviet advisers. In mid-December, a United Nations peace conference opened in Geneva with the United States and the Soviet Union as co-chairmen. For the first time in the history of the Arab-Israeli dispute, both sides sat down at the same table, but this icily correct meeting had only one session. Neither Israelis nor Egyptians wanted the Soviet Union involved. Instead, Kissinger began a process of "shuttle diplomacy" in the spring of 1974, flying from Cairo to Jerusalem and back to obtain a disengagement between the two armies. Since the Israelis stood on the west bank of the canal while the Egyptians held positions on the east, both had reason to withdraw. After months of subtly shading what each had to say, Kissinger prodded them to an agreement in May. Negotiations between Israel and Syria were harder to carry off as the Syrians were closer to the Soviets and hated the Israelis more than the Egyptians did.

WATERGATE'S IMPACT AND THE FALL OF RICHARD NIXON

The Yom Kippur War occurred as the Watergate scandal reached new heights. In his announcement of the international alert, Nixon tried but failed to divert attention from the resignation of Attorney General Eliot

Richardson, the firing of the deputy attorney general, the dismissal of the special prosecutor, Archibald Cox, and the closing of his office in the "Saturday night massacre" of October 20, 1973. Immediately calls went up for the impeachment or resignation of the president. Kissinger had the sickening sense that Nixon no longer could control a docile Congress. These premonitions were confirmed on November 7 when the House and Senate passed the War Powers Act over the president's veto. The new law represented a pendulum swing of congressional resentment over the "imperial presidency" which had stripped Congress of its right to make war. Under the terms of the War Powers Act, the president had to inform Congress whenever he committed American troops overseas. After sixty days, the use of military power had to win specific congressional approval. The law had been introduced by Sen. Jacob Javits (R., New York) as a means of preventing any open-ended commitment, such as the Gulf of Tonkin Resolution, from besmirching the reputation of the Congress, but critics charged that the act actually enhanced the president's power. Now, as never before, the president had a legal authorization of sixty days in which to do what he wanted in foreign affairs.

While the shuttle between Damascus and Jerusalem slowed, the Watergate scandal threatened finally to topple the president. Nixon's popularity fell steadily in 1973 and the spring of 1974 as the House Committee on the Judiciary prepared an impeachment bill against him. By June, 55 percent of the public thought that Nixon should resign or be impeached. His approval rating stood at a minuscule 23 percent. Believing that his success at arranging detente with the Soviet Union retained some support among a public that believed the new vice-president, Gerald Ford, lacked the stature to continue diplomacy, Nixon traveled to the Middle East and Moscow in June. The cosmetic character of these trips seemed obvious, and the histrionic effect of Nixon's suffering from a potentially fatal blood clot in his leg did not arouse the public sympathy he wanted. Millions of Egyptians turned out for a campaign-style swing from Cairo to Alexandria, but the Israelis who watched his motorcade from Tel Aviv to Jerusalem were more subdued. Some bore signs reminding the president of the hot breath of the impeachment process: "MR. PRESIDENT, YOU CAN RUN, BUT YOU CAN'T HIDE." Others expressed more basic fears: "DON'T SELL US OUT." En route to another summit with Premier Brezhnev, who thought that the Watergate impeachment process had been created by "right-wing enemies of detente," Kissinger erupted into an angry denunciation of the press. Documents leaked from the House Judiciary Committee's investigations indicated that the national security adviser had directed his deputy, Colonel Haig, to install taps on his subordinates' phones. Accusing the newsmen traveling with his party of wanting to undermine his ability to direct foreign policy, he refused to answer any questions about this

Secretary of State Henry Kissinger briefs the new president, Gerald Ford.
(Gerald R. Ford Presidential Library)

electronic eavesdropping. He promised to resign if they kept insisting, a prospect all reporters present agreed would leave the country without its most respected diplomat.

The House Judiciary Committee opened public debate on Nixon's impeachment in late July, and the Supreme Court ruled that the president had to hand over possibly incriminating tape recordings. The next week the committee voted three counts of the impeachment indictment—abuse of power, obstruction of justice, and contempt of Congress. Significantly, the charges of violating Congress's power to make war by the secret bombing of Cambodia failed to carry. On August 4, the White House released the transcripts called for by the Supreme Court order. One of them contained a "smoking gun," Nixon's directive for H. R. Haldeman to make the CIA stop the FBI's inquiry into the Watergate break-in. Kissinger, Haig, and Republican Senate leaders convinced Nixon that his position looked hopeless. The House surely would go along with the Judiciary Committee, and the Senate would convict the president. The secretary of state reportedly fell to his knees and joined the president in prayer on the floor of the White House's master bedroom on August 7, the night before Nixon announced his resignation.

The new chief executive, Gerald Ford, did not pretend to challenge the preeminence of Secretary of State Kissinger, who retained his title as national security adviser. While Ford's own popularity sank after he issued a blanket pardon of Richard Nixon in early September 1974, Kissinger continued to work his magic with reporters. That fall he revived his shuttle between Syria and Jerusalem.

THE OIL EMBARGO AND IRAN

Part of the urgency of the shuttle resulted from a Middle Eastern embargo on petroleum to the United States as punishment for its support of Israel. All Arab oil producers joined in cutting shipments to the United States, causing the lights on the national Christmas tree to be banked and drawing a pledge from President Nixon "to make the United States energy-independent by 1980." Iran continued to provide petroleum to the United States, but the shah realized that here was an excellent opportunity to raise the price. By the spring of 1974, Iran had led the Organization of Petroleum Exporting Countries (OPEC) into a 300-percent rise in the price of crude oil from $2 to $8 a barrel. To offset the bill for Iranian petroleum, the Nixon administration augmented the already huge arms shipments to Iran. "In the future," Nixon ordered, "arms requests from Iran should not be second guessed." The United States had forwarded $1.2 billion worth of war materials to Iran from 1950 to 1971. In the next seven years, sales hit $21 billion. The shah's government spent 25 percent of its budget on the longest weapons shopping list in the world. The most advanced airplanes in America's arsenal—225 F-4s, 41 F-5s, 80 F-14s, 160 F-16s, and over 900 helicopters—went to Iran accompanied by five thousand military instructors for their use. Another forty thousand civilians went to the oil-drenched country to build the telephone system, construct modern airports and seaports, and operate the petroleum fields and refineries. They lived in ranch-style houses in isolated American colonies, bought imported food at familiar-looking supermarkets, refused to learn Farsi, the local language, and sowed seeds of nationalist resentment. At the same time nearly one hundred thousand Iranian students, supported by their nation's oil profits, enrolled in technical courses at universities in the United States. While in America, they discovered that they could not get jobs at home. They blamed the shah's government for corruption, arrogance, and surveillance of their personal activities and enlisted in the opposition to the monarch's rule.

THE END IN VIETNAM

Lost in the excitement of presidential and secretarial travel and the fall of Richard Nixon was the continuing war in Southeast Asia, which reached a climax in the spring of 1975. President Thieu had broken the cease-fire in March 1973, and the North Vietnamese responded by sending thousands more troops south. The ARVN had fought as badly in 1973 and 1974 as it had while the Americans were there to assist it. In early 1975, Ford asked Congress for an additional billion in aid in South Vietnam, Laos, and Cam-

A Roman Catholic priest looks up as one of the last helicopters departs the roof of the United States embassy in Saigon, April 29, 1975. *(Wide World Photos)*

bodia. The Pentagon flew a delegation of congressional doves to Vietnam to show them how badly the situation had deteriorated. But old opponents like New York congresswoman Bella Abzug were not persuaded that they should throw good money after bad. In February, Congress voted to cut off all further aid to South Vietnam, Cambodia, and Laos. An angry Henry Kissinger asked newsmen, "What kind of people are we?" when he heard the news of Congress's cutoff.

Even congressional doves seemed astonished at the swiftness of the South Vietnamese collapse. In March, North Vietnamese troops captured Danang in the North, and ARVN troops clamored aboard United States charter aircraft for the flight south to Saigon, throwing women, children, and sick men off the plane. Even worse chaos awaited the fall of Saigon in late April. American "relief" operations spirited hundreds of supposed "orphans" out of the country. One giant C-5A transport crashed killing over two hundred children, and Vietnamese critics claimed that well-meaning but misguided Americans were stealing babies from Vietnam. When it became obvious that Saigon would fall, thousands of employees of the Americans feared for their lives at the hands of vindictive Communists. They crashed the gates at the American embassy in Saigon, demanding visas to enter the United States. Marine guards threw them back, but some managed to secure places on helicopters bound for the American aircraft carriers off the coast. To make way for refugees, the navy pushed millions of dollars' worth of planes into the ocean. Finally the last helicopter, bearing Ambassador Graham Martin, left the roof of the American embassy in April. About the same time, Communist forces triumphed in Laos and Cambodia, writing another tragic chapter in the history of the latter country. Immediately upon seizing control of Phnom Penh the Khmer Rouge began a mass evacuation of the capital, forcing city dwellers onto the land. As noted earlier, perhaps three million Cambodians died in the next three years.

In Washington, the fall of Southeast Asia was greeted with recriminations from Ford and Kissinger, who blamed Congress for not providing more aid. They also made use of the Cambodian seizure of the American cargo vessel *Mayaguez* on May 12 to demonstrate their continued toughness. As soon as word reached Washington that the Cambodians had captured the ship, Ford ordered an American assault to free the crew. Thirty-eight American marines lost their lives in a needless rescue launched after the Cambodians had already set the crew free. Ignoring the War Powers resolution, Ford had authorized the rescue without notifying Congress. No one complained, however, as lawmakers joined the applause for the show of resolve. Kissinger himself announced, "We did not do this to show our macho," but careful observers noted an element of guilty conscience: no one had publicly raised the suggestion. A week after the *Mayaguez* rescue, President Ford received a standing ovation from students at the University of Pennsylvania, formerly a center of antiwar demonstrations.

COMING TO TERMS WITH VIETNAM

As the first war the United States clearly lost, the Vietnam debacle produced an anguished emotional response among politicians, diplomats, and observers looking for ways to avoid future entanglements. Congress, shaken by the sordid revelations of Watergate, spent 1975 and 1976 investigating the CIA. Subcommittees led by Congressman Otis Pike (D., New York) and Senator Frank Church (D., Idaho) poked through the evidence of twenty-five years of covert CIA operations in Asia, the Middle East, Europe, Latin America, and the United States. President Ford appointed his own task force, chaired by newly named Vice-President Nelson Rockefeller, to look into intelligence activities and quiet Congress. While none of these investigations aroused the intense public attention the earlier Watergate or impeachment hearings had created, they did build a case that foreign policy since the Second World War had often gone down a second, secret track, outside the scrutiny of public, Congress, or the State Department.

Writers have puzzled over the proper lessons of the Vietnam experience. All agree that the war ended badly, but that is the limit of consensus. Earl Ravenal speaks for many disillusioned diplomats in *Never Again* (1976), a manual for noninterventionism. Anthony Lake, one of the National Security Council staff members who resigned in protest over the 1970 Cambodian invasion, edited the Council on Foreign Relations' collection of essays, *The Vietnam Legacy* (1976). Few of the diplomats, foreign affairs academics, or politicians who contributed go so far as pledging strict noninterference in other nations' civil wars. Yet this representative sample of centrist opinion seems united in the conviction that the United States had gone too far in the use of force. The writers suggest that future American overseas involvement should concentrate on economic, social, and political questions. By 1978, an abrupt reversal occurred in writing on America's Vietnam experience. Guenter Lewy, a political scientist at the University of Massachusetts, received Defense Department permission to look at files barred to other scholars. From these documents he wrote *America in Vietnam* (1978), a pugnacious revisionist history suggesting that the United States forces had used the utmost restraint, that American initial involvement had been justified, and that the Communist foe had been far more brutal in the way it waged war. The next year, Henry Kissinger published the first volume of his memoirs, *White House Years,* which tries to rebut the charges of international lawlessness contained in British journalist William Shawcross's *Sideshow: Nixon, Kissinger, and the De-*

struction of Cambodia (1979). Leslie Gelb, once the editor of *The Pentagon Papers,* published *The Irony of Vietnam* the same year. He acknowledges that the war itself was a colossal failure but writes that the foreign policy decision-making system "worked" as it had been designed to during four presidential administrations from 1945 to 1968. In 1982, Norman Podhoretz, the editor of *Commentary* magazine and once a doubter of the wisdom of American intervention, published a spirited defense of the war, *Why We Were in Vietnam.* While admitting that the United States never could have prevailed, he stresses the nobility of American intentions and challenges the morality of antiwar activisits. Walter LeFeber, a reviewer of several of these revisionist accounts, notes sadly that authors were "rewriting the record of failed military interventionism in the 1950 to 1975 era in order to build support for interventionism in the 1980s."

ASSERTIVE OUTBURSTS AFTER VIETNAM

The search for a place to show American resolve continued in 1975, and the site selected was one of the most remote in the world, the southwest African country of Angola, formerly a colony of Portugal. The right-wing government of Portugal fell in a coup led by army officers fed up with the grueling, unwinnable guerrilla combat in Africa in 1974. Despite Kissinger's fears that the triumphant generals actually were disguised Communists, Portugal emerged as a democratic government after liquidating its African colonies of Mozambique, Guinea-Bissau, and Angola. In the last, a struggle erupted for control of the new government between three factions. The alignment of outside forces defied conventional expectations, with the United States, South Africa, and China on one side opposing the Soviet Union, which backed the strongest of the three rebel groups, the MPLA (Popular Movement for the Liberation of Angola). Kissinger ordered the Central Intelligence Agency to give covert support to pro-Western factions, but the memory of Vietnam remained strong. A cartoonist had a sergeant remark, "If you liked Vietnam, you'll love . . . Angola." A balky Congress feared any aid might become the beginning of another wholesale commitment, and in December it passed an amendment to an appropriations bill by Sen. Dick Clark of Iowa prohibiting the use of CIA funds for the war in southern Africa.

The Angola crisis indicated that the detente with the Soviet Union was limited to Europe. There at least the East-West tensions seemed to ease in August 1975 when the two nations met with thirty-three others at the European Security Conference in Helsinki. They produced a treaty which finally ended the border disputes festering since 1945. In effect, the Helsinki accords became the peace treaty which had eluded diplomats since the Second World War. East and West agreed to respect the divisions which now existed. The United States exchanged ambassadors with East Germany. The Western powers also extracted from Moscow guarantees about the protection of human rights within the Soviet sphere, including the rights of citizens to emigrate. The last guarantee proved especially gratifying to congressmen who wanted the United States to aid Jews wishing to leave the Soviet Union for Israel, Europe, and the United States.

THE DECLINE OF DETENTE AND THE ELECTION OF 1976

The Helsinki accords could not arrest the decline in Kissinger's prestige among conservative members of the Republican party. They criticized the extension of the SALT agreement worked out at a summit between Ford and Brezhnev in Vladivostok in November 1974. Ronald Reagan, the former governor of California who was challenging Ford for the presidential nomination, kept up a stream of denunciations of Kissinger's detente with the Soviet Union and the treaty being negotiated to turn the Panama Canal over to Panamanian control. Partially to satisfy conservative criticism and to make Kissinger a less visible figure, Ford stripped him of his title of national security adviser, which he had retained since being named secretary of state. An air force general, Brent Scowcroft, replaced Kissinger in his national security job in December 1975. Newspapers were filled with rumors that Kissinger himself would step down as secretary of state if Ford won reelection. Early in the campaign of 1976, Ford acknowledged that *detente* had become a term of abuse, and he banned it from his vocabulary. For a conventionally conservative Republican, Ford found the attack from his right distressing and unfair. He manfully defended Kissinger's detente without using the word, and he repeated that the Panama Canal Treaty was the only way the United States could maintain its standing among nationalist states of the Western Hemisphere. Using all the powers of incumbency, he barely beat back the challenge of Ronald Reagan at the Kansas City convention.

In the election itself, Ford faced a formerly unknown ex-governor of Georgia. Jimmy Carter's anonymity proved his principal advantage in campaigning against the "Washington establishment," which he accused of having been responsible for the Watergate scandal. After leaving the governorship of Georgia in 1974, Carter had received some brief exposure to international affairs when David Rockefeller, the chairman of the Chase Manhattan Bank, had invited him to join the Trilateral Commission, a private group of business leaders, academics, and politicians from North America, Europe, and Japan. The executive director of the group was a Columbia University political scientist, Zbigniew Brzezinski, who had complained about the

"Lone Ranger" style of Kissinger's diplomacy. In the campaign of 1976, Carter used symbolic language carefully constructed to appeal to the sensitivities of whatever group he addressed. In a masterpiece of unintended irony, he promised to "give America a government as good as its people." He chided the style of Kissinger's diplomacy for its flamboyance and sudden shifts, suggesting that he would be more attuned to the needs of America's allies. He supported the arms treaties negotiated with the Soviets but intimated that the Republicans had taken insufficient interest in human rights violations in the Soviet bloc. He denounced the "almost completely unrestrained" arms transfer policy for being "as cynical as it is dangerous." During the televised debates with Ford, Carter flashed a self-satisfied grin as the president blundered into suggesting that Poland no longer felt the sting of control by the Soviet Union. Carter's apparent sincerity, his promise "I'll never lie to you," and his ostentatious Christianity won many supporters early in the campaign; late August polls showed him ahead of Ford by more than thirty percentage points. Then disillusionment with both candidates set in as voters had to decide whether, in Arthur Schlesinger's words, to choose a candidate afflicted with the "dumbness factor" (Ford) or the "weirdness factor" (Carter). They chose a change, with Carter's fellow Southerners carrying the day. Shortly after the election, Carter's aide Hamilton Jordan explained that the new administration's diplomacy would mark a clean break with the discredited policies and tired individuals who had led American diplomacy since the Second World War. "If after the inauguration you find a Cy Vance as secretary of state and Zbigniew Brzezinski as head of national security, then I would say we failed. And I'd quit. . . . You're going to see new faces, new ideas." In December, Carter selected Vance for secretary of state and Brzezinski as national security adviser. Jordan did not quit. A new administration came to town vowing to put Vietnam behind the United States, open a dialogue between the rich and the poor nations, recapture the American commitment to human rights, place the Soviet Union on the defensive, and reduce the American role as the major arms supplier to the world.

CHAPTER FOURTEEN

The Resurrection and Death of the Cold War, 1977–1988

By the middle 1970s, the world had changed. Twenty years of rapid economic growth in Western Europe and Japan allowed those industrial nations to produce twice as much as the United States. Robust expansion stopped, however, in the wake of a tripling of energy costs. Poorer nations, concentrated mostly in the Southern Hemisphere, demanded greater shares of the world's prosperity. They pressed for a "new international economic order" to replace sterile Cold War competition between East and West as the centerpiece of world politics. Some Americans, stung by the bad memory of Vietnam, also hoped to focus attention on social and economic issues rather than military confrontation. Cyrus Vance, the new secretary of state, had grown dismayed by the waste of resources in Vietnam when he served as delegate to the peace talks in 1968. Harold Brown, Jimmy Carter's choice as secretary of defense, a physicist who once served as secretary of the air force, also doubted the relevance of the application of military force to social questions. Zbigniew Brzezinski, Carter's national security adviser, sought to combine a commitment to advancing the interests of postindustrial Western societies with competition with Soviet-style communism. The new ambassador to the United Nations, Andrew Young, a black former congressman from Carter's home state of Georgia, looked forward to improved relations with the southern, nonwhite regions of the world.

At the outset, the Carter administration seemed to press a new agenda, "the management of interdependence." Campaigning for the presidency in 1976, Jimmy Carter demanded that "we replace balance of power politics with world order politics." He predicted that "in the near future issues of war and peace will be more a function of economic and social problems than of the military security problems which have dominated international relations since World War II." In May 1977, he told a commencement day crowd at Notre Dame University that "an inordinate fear of communism has led us to embrace any dictator who joined in our fear." He suggested that his administration would pay more attention to human rights wherever they were threatened.

The commitment to "world order politics" lasted about two years. From 1977 to 1979, the United States pressed human rights, sought a "North-South dialogue" on economic issues, and moved to limit the global arms race. None of these initiatives reached its goals. And two of Carter's successes—concluding agreements with Panama over the canal and mediation of formal peace between Israel and Egypt—followed traditional, not novel, diplomatic practice.

Within the administration, National Security Adviser Brzezinski raised alarms over a Soviet threat. In 1979, the president returned to assertive themes of the early Cold War. The seizure of the American embassy by Iranian revolutionaries in November and a Soviet invasion of Afghanistan in December 1979 completed Carter's conversion into a Cold Warrior. Yet his new course did not save him at the polls in 1980. Voters selected Republican Ronald Reagan to be the most conservative president since Calvin Coolidge. He provided an assertive foreign policy that confronted the Soviet Union, communism, and revolution. In the first few years of the Reagan administration, American combativeness raised fears of war at home and abroad. After 1985, however, Reagan shrewdly adapted to changes in the Soviet Union fostered by Mikhail Gorbachev. By 1988, Reagan, the most ardently anticommunist president of the post–World War II era, formed a close personal friendship with the leader of the Soviet Union. The Cold War was about to expire.

HUMAN RIGHTS, IMMIGRATION, AND THE LAW OF THE SEA

The Carter administration's advocacy of human rights in other countries recorded some achievements but was ridden with inconsistencies. Congress created a Bureau of Human Rights within the State Department. Headed by Patricia Derian, a former professor and political activist, the bureau published a yearly account of the state of civil and political liberties abroad. It denounced nations previous Republican administrations had wanted to use as surrogates against the Soviet Union under the terms of the Nixon Doctrine. The Philippines, South Korea, Chile, Brazil, and Argentina all came under the lash. The administration cut economic aid, pressured the World Bank, the International Monetary Fund, or the Inter-American Development Bank to curtail assistance, and publicly called for the release of political prisoners.

The administration did not, however, follow a consistent human rights policy. Old ideas of national security, presumably outmoded in the new era, led Carter to support several unsavory rulers. The need for oil prompted an embrace of the shah of Iran. Carter praised the shah for having created an "island of stability" in the turbulent Middle East. The administration muted criticism of human rights violations despite reports from Amnesty International, a respected London-based human rights group, that SAVAK, Iran's secret police, held as many as fifty thousand political prisoners. In 1977, the United States sold the shah $5.7 billion worth of weapons, two-thirds of his country's arms imports.

Joseph Mobutu, ruler of Zaire in central Africa, also received help from the new administration despite an appalling record on human rights. Gen. Mobutu had consolidated his hold on the former Belgian Congo in 1967. He created a single-party state, jailed opponents, and encouraged friends and relatives to loot the wealth of the country. On the verge of bankruptcy, kept afloat only by the willingness of foreign bankers to "roll over" loans to avoid a default, Zaire also faced the secession of Shaba province in the spring of 1978. Rebels based in neighboring Angola mounted an invasion in June. Immediately, the Carter administration ordered the air force to ferry French Foreign Legion and Moroccan troops to the town of Kolwesi, headquarters of a huge copper mine, to rescue two hundred white missionaries and mining engineers.

The Carter administration also ran into difficulties applying consistent human rights standards at home, where the issue was immigration, always a complicated mixture of diplomacy and domestic politics. Immigration policy became a way of punishing unfriendly, usually Communist governments, rather than of assisting individual refugees. The United States opened its doors to two hundred thousand "boat people" fleeing the Communist governments of Vietnam, Laos, and Cambodia. State Department officials pressured European and South Asian nations to accept their share of refugees. American officials took the floor at international refugee meetings to assail the Vietnamese practice of demanding gold bribes before frightened citizens could disembark on a fleet of leaky, rotting, unsanitary small boats.

Carter also used the plight of refugees to score points from an old American nemesis, Cuba's Fidel Castro. In April 1980, ten thousand disgruntled Cubans flooded the Peruvian embassy in Havana asking for asylum. From the middle of April until the middle of June, a flotilla of boats ferried over one hundred thousand Cubans from the island to Florida, and by the time it was over, the administration wished it had never raised the issue. The government sent the Cubans to sports stadia and army bases, where they set up tent cities, became hot and bored, and demanded to leave. Some Americans wanted them to stay incarcerated.

While the Carter administration made a show of welcoming the Cubans, it tried to deport thousands of Haitians who fled a government which maintained the traditional standards of tyranny for that unhappy island. Yet the State Department was reluctant to offer refugee status, fearing that it would offend the friendly government of Jean-Claude "Baby Doc" Duvalier. Civil rights groups in the United States charged that the State Department did not want Haitians because they were blacker than Cubans.

A failed attempt to reach international agreement regulating the use of the world's oceans also dashed hopes that the Carter administration could focus attention on nonsecurity issues. In 1972, a UN-sponsored Law of the Sea Conference opened to resolve differences among one hundred thirty nations over warship rights, fishing, and deep seabed mining. Talks stalled under Nixon and Ford, but Carter appointed Elliot Richardson as his special representative to breathe life into the law of the sea. Despite these high sentiments and his acceptance of the fact that the oceans represented the "common heritage of mankind," Richardson was unable to reach agreement before the election of 1980.

THE PANAMA CANAL TREATIES AND CENTRAL AMERICA

Carter found more success following a traditional path of negotiation to heal the seventy-year wound left by Theodore Roosevelt's high-handed actions during the Panamanian revolution of 1903. Each American president since 1965 had conducted desultory talks with Panama over the future of the canal. In that year, street demonstrations broke out in Panama City and Colón protesting the haughtiness of the United States residents of the Canal Zone— the five-mile-wide strip of territory bisecting the isthmus in which the United States acted "as if it were sovereign." Panamanians could be jailed under United States laws by American courts using English, a language they did not understand. While Panamanians took low-paying, unskilled jobs in the zone, none was found operating the locks or piloting ships through the canal. The government of Panama argued that the behavior of the Zonians represented the worst sort of "Yankee colonialism."

After ten years, a deal was nearly struck in 1975. The United States was willing in principle to yield its perpetual lease. Panama insisted that the United States leave in twenty or thirty years while the Pentagon held out for longer, perhaps another fifty. An ominous note was sounded, however, when conservative South Carolina Republican senator Strom Thurmond got the signatures of thirty-eight senators (five more than needed to block ratification) on a letter opposing any release of sovereignty. During the 1976 Republican primary season, Ronald Reagan charged Gerald Ford and Henry

Kissinger with "giving away our canal." Ford quietly shelved negotiations during the heat of the campaign, leaving the nearly completed treaty for his successor. During the lull in the talks, Panama's leader, Omar Torrijos, engaged in a "banana war" with the United Fruit Company and new riots broke out in September 1976.

Carter appointed Sol Linowitz as head of the American negotiating team. Within seven months, he produced two treaties. The first returned legal jurisdiction over the zone to Panama. The United States would continue to operate and defend the canal until December 31, 1999, after which Panama would take over. The first treaty also protected the jobs of the Americans operating the canal. The second agreement gave the United States the permanent right to defend the "neutrality of the waterway."

When Carter presented the treaty to the Senate in August, it provoked a storm. Public opinion polls revealed that 78 percent of those who took a stand opposed yielding the canal. The administration spent the next six months changing attitudes in the hopes of gaining Senate ratification. Carter enlisted major establishment figures like Averell Harriman, John J. McCloy, and former Republican Senate leader Hugh Scott to form a Committee for the Ratification of the Panama Canal Treaties. The president took questions about the canal on a radio call-in hookup. Noting that the United States had never had sovereignty, he predicted the "assured capacity of our country in guaranteeing that the Panama Canal would be open." Over the winter, public opinion seemed to change.

The battle shifted to the Senate in February and March while Democratic leader Robert Byrd (W. Va.) and Republican Howard Baker (Tenn.) carried the brunt of the argument. Carter had more trouble with Democrats Richard Stone (Fla.) and Dennis DeConcini (Ariz.). Stone, who described Torrijos as a "Left-leaning, rickety, tin-horn dictator," agreed to vote yes out of the close ties to his home state had with Central America. DeConcini offered his support only after Carter accepted a "condition" allowing the use of American forces *in Panama* to keep the canal open after 1999. Torrijos held his tongue about this violation of his country's sovereignty. On March 16, sixty-eight senators, one more than required for ratification, voted for the treaty. Ratification did not ensure good relations with Central American republics, but it did offer the hope of reduced tensions.

After some hesitation, the Carter administration also accommodated a revolution in another Central American state, Nicaragua. Andrew Young's mission to the UN, which tried to steer American diplomacy toward the interest of the poor southern states, pressured Secretary of State Vance and National Security adviser Brzezinski gracefully to accept the end of the Somoza dictatorship. The Somoza family had virtually owned Nicaragua ever since the departure of United States Marines in 1934. Anastasio Somoza took power in 1965. By the mid-seventies, he had alienated the Church and the small middle class as well as the traditionally exploited peasantry with his thievery and the brutality of the National Guard. Rebels, calling themselves the Sandino Liberation Front after Augusto Sandino, the insurgent murdered by the first Somoza in 1934, took up arms in 1976. In August 1978, a band of Sandinista soldiers, led by a dashing Eden Pastora, "Commander Zero," took over the National Assembly building and held Somoza's handpicked legislators for a ransom of $25 million. Commander Zero became a hero as he waved to a crowd of well-wishing Nicaraguans before boarding a plane for asylum in Venezuela. Shortly afterward national guardsmen murdered the editor of *La Prensa,* a moderate opposition paper.

On June 23 the OAS called for the "immediate and definitive replacement of the Somoza regime" by "a democratic government [and] the holding of free elections as soon as possible." The United States reluctantly endorsed this resolution, and Lawrence Pezullo, American ambassador to Nicaragua, spent the next several days trying to arrange Somoza's exile. Somoza temporized for three more weeks, as Washington scrambled to sponsor a new government in Nicaragua that would keep the Sandinistas from power. The revolutionaries would hear nothing of that. On July 18 Somoza fled Nicaragua for exile, first in the Bahamas, then in Miami, and finally in Paraguay, where he was murdered in 1980. On July 20 the Sandinistas in Managua triumphantly proclaimed a new revolutionary government. The new regime was a coalition of opponents of Somoza, but within months it became clear that a nine-member Directorate of Sandinistas had real power.

Over the remainder of the Carter administration relations between the United States and Nicaragua deteriorated. According to Robert Pastor, the administration's specialist on Central America on the National Security Council, "at the beginning the United States government deliberately suspended its suspicions about the Sandinistas." By the end of 1980, however, "the Carter administration was on the verge of terminating its aid program." In September Carter greeted Daniel Ortega of the junta at the White House and told him, "If you don't hold me responsible for everything that occurred under my predecessors, I will not hold you responsible for everything that happened under your predecessors." Everyone smiled. The United States promised to maintain a program of $80 million of economic assistance. Four days later, Carter's expression soured when Ortega told the United Nations that "the most aggressive circles of the United States and of Central America dream of restoring Somozaism to our country."

In Nicaragua itself, the revolution began to split, as more conservative members of the junta distrusted the Sandinistas. By the summer of 1980 several moderates resigned, threatening to take up arms if the revolution did not mellow. In Washington, though, Carter still sought an accommodation.

The CIA found no conclusive evidence before November that the Sandinistas were arming revolutionaries in El Salvador. He continued economic aid to Nicaragua in the midst of the 1980 election campaign, despite Republican charges that he was permitting the development of another Cuba in Central America. After Ronald Reagan won, Washington shifted course in the winter of 1980–1981. The Sandistas began shipping weapons to leftist forces in El Salvador for a "final offensive" before Reagan took office. In response, the Carter administration laid the groundwork for a more assertive course against Nicaragua as it planned to stop economic assistance.

MEDIATING BETWEEN ISRAEL AND EGYPT

Carter's most surprising accomplishment occurred at Camp David, the presidential retreat in the Maryland mountains, in September 1978, where he brokered a settlement between two old adversaries, Egypt and Israel. The summit meeting between Egyptian president Anwar Sadat and Israeli prime minister Menachem Begin climaxed a remarkable reversal of alignments begun the year before. The United States assisted the process, but not necessarily because of the shrewdness in its diplomacy. In fact, fear that American efforts to arrange a "comprehensive settlement of the Palestinian problem" might backfire encouraged Sadat to take an unprecedented trip to Jerusalem to address the Knesset, or Parliament, on November 19, 1977.

Both Israelis and Egyptians had squirmed when Carter publicly called for a "homeland" for the displaced Palestinians in the summer of 1977. Despite Carter's denial that a homeland implied the creation of a Palestinian state, Israel's newly elected conservative government headed by Begin feared that the United States might deal directly with the Palestine Liberation Organization (PLO). Neither did Sadat care for the PLO, considering it a radical organization committed to the overthrow of conservative Arab governments. Accordingly, he sent feelers to the Israelis through King Hassan of Morocco and President Nicolai Ceauçescu of Rumania. Israel's one-eyed foreign minister, Moshe Dayan, one of the most recognizable men in the world, grabbed a wig and false moustache and slipped into Fez Morocco to prepare the ground. Then, in response to a November 14 question by CBS news correspondent Walter Cronkite, Sadat stunned the world by expressing willingness to go to Israel.

Sadat did not receive the kind of reception he hoped for in Jerusalem. His hosts liked to call for "no more war," but they refused to make a grand gesture of their own by relinquishing all territory seized in the 1967 war. Instead, Begin and Dayan proposed a series of ministerial talks with the Egyptians leading to a bilateral peace treaty.

At this point, the United States entered as mediator. Sadat got his hero's welcome from Congress, press, and president when he came to Washington in February 1978. Cronkite called him the "man of the century," and Carter described him as a "great statesman." For the remainder of the spring and summer, Secretary of State Vance arranged a series of encounters between Dayan and Egyptian foreign minister Ibrahim Khalil. Eventually, the diplomats agreed to a meeting of their heads of government hosted by Carter at Camp David.

For two weeks, Sadat, Begin, Carter, and a small army of aides argued over a "framework" for a peace treaty. The suspicious Israelis tried to separate the Egyptian and Palestinian questions. They insisted that any agreement with Egypt void commitments Cairo had with Arab states to join a war against Israel. Sadat became impatient with the Israelis' legalistic quibbles. Carter and his advisers, eager for any sort of agreement to bolster their prestige, sided with the Egyptians. The president, who mastered every detail of the geography of the Sinai Desert, had been fed up with Begin's hectoring before the conference began. Nothing happened over the next two weeks to soften his opinion. The three leaders met together only once, and that encounter proved so tense that Carter decided to shuttle between the Egyptians and the Israelis. His chats with Sadat were music to his ears while meetings with Begin were filled with charges of bad faith. Finally, on Friday, September 15, Carter announced that he would dissolve the summit on Sunday night whether there was a framework or not. Fearful of being labeled an obstacle to peace, Begin put forward ambiguous language suspending for a time new Jewish settlements on the west bank of the Jordan River. He explicitly agreed to total Israeli withdrawal from the Sinai Peninsula and the dismantlement of Jewish settlements there. Sadat, for his part, accepted the separate peace. The treaty between Israel and Egypt would only be linked to continued negotiations over the future of the West Bank.

When Carter, Begin, and Sadat smiled for the camera at the White House on that Sunday evening, they thought that a peace treaty was within easy reach. In fact, it took another six months of presidential Mideast travel, cajolery, and badgering to bring the two men to the White House lawn for a signing ceremony on March 26, 1979. The president guaranteed a pact committing Israel to withdraw from the Sinai in return for peace and diplomatic recognition from Egypt. The United States promised $2 billion to underwrite the cost of moving Israel's advanced airfield from the Sinai to Israel proper. America would organize an international peacekeeping force after the Israelis completed their departure in 1982. In an additional document, Egypt and Israel left open the issue of sovereignty on the West Bank, promising continued talks leading to "full autonomy" for the Palestinian Arabs living there. The final status of the West Bank and East Jerusalem would be decided after a five-year interim period of autonomy.

Egypt's Anwar Sadat, President Jimmy Carter, and Israel's Menachem Begin at
the White House signing ceremony for the Egyptian-Israeli peace treaty,
March 26, 1979. *(Wide World Photos)*

Much to the surprise of the United States, Egypt, and Israel, no other
Arab state joined the peace process. The PLO denounced it as a betrayal of
the Palestinians and threatened any West Bank Arabs who might want to join
the autonomy talks. Egypt found itself ostracized by other Arab states. Neither Jordan nor Saudi Arabia, two states with which Washington had good
relations, joined the Camp David peace process. By May 1980, the date set
for an agreement on West Bank autonomy, Sol Linowitz, the American delegate to the talks, glumly announced that a final arrangement eluded his
grasp.

PLAYING THE CHINA CARD

The Carter administration completed the opening to China begun by President Nixon when it exchanged ambassadors with the People's Republic in
January 1979. Recognition of Beijing served to heighten tensions with the
Soviet Union while consolidating the power of National Security Adviser
Brzezinski. He went to Beijing in May 1977. On an outing to the Great Wall
of China, he challenged his hosts to race up the stairs with the words "Last
one to the top gets to fight the Russians."

By December 1978, Carter was ready to play the "China card" against the Soviet Union by restoring full diplomatic relations with Beijing. On January 1, 1979, the American embassy in Taiwan changed into a "foundation" while the United States upgraded its Beijing office to a regular embassy. In late January and early February, Deng Xiaoping, vice-chairman of the Chinese Communist party and the guiding force behind the movement away from Maoist revolutionary orthodoxy, visited the United States. Not since Nikita Khrushchev peeled an ear of corn in an Iowa cornfield in 1959 had Americans taken such notice of a foreign leader. At stops in Washington, Houston, and Seattle, Deng pointed fingers at the "hegemonists" of the Kremlin and warned of a new war unless the West woke up. He donned a ten-gallon hat, accepted "honorary membership" in NATO, and was roundly cheered by workers in a defense plant. Two weeks after his return to China, Deng put his anti-Soviet rhetoric into practice by ordering the People's Liberation Army to attack Vietnam. That friend of the Soviet Union had recently invaded Cambodia, an ally of China.

THE FAILURE OF ARMS CONTROL

The opening to China helped poison relations with the Soviet Union, and the signing of a new Strategic Arms Limitation Treaty (SALT II) in June 1979 could not stop further deteriorations. The new administration came to Washington with high hopes of actually reducing the nuclear arsenals of both superpowers. In March 1977, Secretary of State Vance went to Moscow to present a plan for across-the-board reductions to Soviet president Leonid Brezhnev. The Soviet leadership reacted coolly to suggestions which ignored the careful provisions for future arms control laid down in the SALT I agreement (1972) and the Vladivostok agreement of 1975. Rebuffed in Moscow, Vance returned to Washington and instructed the Arms Control and Disarmament Agency to continue along the path blazed by Henry Kissinger.

Vance and Paul Warnke, the delegate to the SALT talks, considered any agreement setting upper limits on armaments superior to an untrammeled arms race. In two years of bargaining, Soviet and American negotiators in Vienna, Washington, and Moscow hammered out a treaty acknowledging essential "parity" in the nuclear forces of both sides. They produced a design to lessen the dangers posed by "destabilizing" weapons systems, that is, those which raised fears that the other side planned a first strike. Each agreed to stop construction of new fixed ICBMs and pledged not to relocate fixed ICBMs, not to convert light ICBMs into heavy ones, and not to increase the "throw weight," or warhead destructive power, of their missiles. Each would limit the number of its MIRVs and cruise missiles (small, virtually undetectable flying bombs) to 1,320. Under this provision, the Soviet Union would dismantle 200 MIRV'd ICBMs while the United States foreswore testing of cruise missiles with a range greater than six hundred kilometers. The treaty would expire in 1985. Negotiators also arrived at a Joint Statement of Principles for SALT III, maintaining parity while reducing overall levels of armaments.

Jimmy Carter immersed himself in the welter of numbers in the weeks before the signing ceremony scheduled for Vienna the third week of June. He knew that the arms control process had aroused suspicious Cold Warriors who considered the Soviet Union ahead in the arms race and doubted if it would keep its end of the bargain. On the eve of his departure, he learned that Sen. Henry Jackson (D., Wash.), a longtime hawk, had decided that the treaty "favors the Soviets" and to sign it would be "appeasement in its purest form." Stung by Jackson's allusion to Neville Chamberlain's toting an umbrella home from his capitulation to Adolf Hitler at Munich, Carter stood bareheaded in a rainstorm when he disembarked from the plane at Vienna. "I'd rather drown than carry an umbrella," he growled.

Carter kissed Brezhnev on both cheeks before each put his name to the treaty on June 24. The document encountered a buzzsaw when it reached the Senate. The Joint Chiefs of Staff endorsed the treaty as reducing the likelihood of a first strike, but their representative on the negotiating team, air force general Edward Rowny, resigned and testified against the treaty. Outside Congress, a louder chorus rose against SALT and accommodation with the Soviet Union. The Committee on the Present Danger, a pressure group formed in 1975 to lobby against detente, opposed "world order rhetoric" with the observation that "the principal threat to our nation, to world peace, and to the cause of human freedom is the Soviet drive for dominance based on unprecedented military buildup." Norman Podhoretz, editor of *Commentary* magazine and a leading "neoconservative" (former liberals who focused on the dangers of communism) blamed "isolationism" and "the culture of appeasement" for producing SALT II. Faced with such charges, the Carter administration hesitated about asking for a vote on SALT II in the fall of 1979 and then withdrew the treaty in January 1980.

ECONOMIC TRIALS AND A GOVERNMENT SHAKE-UP

The world and American economies never really recovered from the fourfold rise in energy costs following the Arab oil embargo of 1973. Carter addressed the energy crisis in March 1977, soon after taking office, when he called for the "moral equivalent of war" to reduce dependence on foreign petroleum. He wore a sweater before a roaring fireplace when he delivered a folksy homily to the public on the virtues of energy conservation and substitution. Congress dallied for two years before passing a modified energy program taxing "windfall" oil company profits, allowing the eventual decontrol of oil and gas prices, and establishing a new Department of Energy. James Schlesinger, a brilliant economist who had served earlier Republican administrations as head of the CIA and the Defense Department, took over at Energy and warned that unless the United States imported less foreign oil "this society may not make it." By 1979, American consumers paid over $50 billion yearly for the eight million barrels of oil they imported each day. Things got worse in June as gasoline seemed unavailable at any price. (The official cost doubled, from $18 to $36 a barrel.) The Iranian revolution which erupted early in the year cut that country's oil production by 90 percent. Four-hour-long gasoline lines formed at filling stations as angry motorists punched each other, pulled guns on line jumpers, and cursed President Carter.

This second oil shock helped produce worldwide recession even sharper than the 1974–1975 downturn. Many nations turned in desperation to Western banks, awash in petrodollars. In late June 1979, Carter went to Tokyo for the annual meeting of the heads of the seven largest economies in the nonCommunist world (the United States, Great Britain, France, West Germany, Italy, and Japan). He heard complaints from each of his fellow summiteers, who hated the sinking dollar, wondered when the United States would reduce its inflation rate of 13 percent, and pressed Carter to halve American oil imports. Upon returning, Carter's advisers gave him the grim word that the country blamed him for gas lines and economic stagnation. Carter then went to Camp David where he brooded for ten days. Returning to Washington on July 19, he delivered a public excoriation and apology to his countrymen. He noted a "spiritual malaise" in the land, confessed that he had been "managing not leading this country," and revealed that no cabinet member's job was safe. Four days later, he dropped four secretaries, including Schlesinger and Blumenthal, and requested loyalty oaths from those who remained.

One cabinet-level appointee who survived temporarily was UN ambassador Andrew Young. His days were numbered, though, in July 1979. He had been prone from the start to offhand comments about foreign affairs—calling the British "the most racist society in history," welcoming a Cuban brigade in Ethiopia as a "stabilizing force," and describing Ayatollah Ruhallah Khomeini, leader of Iran's religious fundamentalists, as "something of a saint." When Carter called his principal advisers to Camp David in July, he dressed Young down as an "embarrassment to this administration." Nevertheless, he decided to keep him because of his appeal to black Americans. Not only did Young occupy a highly visible position in the administration, but he had helped change American policy toward Africa. At his urging, the

United States joined Great Britain in arranging majority rule in Rhodesia, renamed Zimbabwe after 1979. He made friends for the United States in Nigeria, a major oil supplier, by his criticism of the system of racial segregation, *apartheid,* practiced in South Africa. At the UN, he speeded negotiations for an end to South African occupation of Southwest Africa (Namibia) and the creation of a black majority government there. In August, however, Young resigned under pressure when reports appeared that he had secretly conferred with Zehdi Terzi, the Palestine Liberation Organization's permanent observer to the UN. Israel's supporters expressed outrage at this apparent violation of a five-year-old United States pledge to have nothing to do with the PLO. Angry black leaders for their part accused American Jews and Israeli diplomats of forcing Young's exit. Carter said nothing to reduce inflamed passions over the Young affair.

AMERICA'S IRANIAN BONDAGE

Journalists wrote of a "failed presidency" in the summer of 1979. None of Carter's problems matched those created by the encounter with revolutionary nationalism in Iran. Opposition to the rule of Shah Mohammed Reza Pahlevi built in early 1978, soon after Carter raised his glass to the "respect, admiration and love" in which the Iranian people held their monarch. Widespread street demonstrations broke out in January and February. The mullahs and ayatollahs (religious leaders of the Shi'ite Muslims, who made up 90 percent of the population) joined bazaar merchants, students, and opposition politicians in objecting to the quality of the shah's rule. They could not agree on what they disliked most, but none had good words for the presence of fifty thousand Americans training the military, building industrial plants, and operating the oil fields which provided some $20 billion in annual revenue. Opposition coalesced behind Ruhallah Khomeini, an eighty-year-old ayatollah who had lived in exile, first in Iraq and then in France, for the previous fourteen years. Cassette tapes circulated of Khomeini's calls to rid the country of the shah, his family, SAVAK (the secret police), and the Americans and create an Islamic republic committed to traditional Muslim virtues.

Throughout the upheavals the shah dismissed his opponents as "people who are easily instigated. They hear a few words and immediately they are electrified and stop thinking." Yet he responded slowly to the challenges to his rule. In February, French doctors diagnosed a fatal cancer which affected his judgment, so he relied on guidance from confused officials in faraway Washington. While National Security Adviser Brzezinski urged firmness, Secretary of State Vance decided that the monarch had to step aside for a civilian government. In late August, a theater fire killed 377 Iranians, and the opposition blamed SAVAK agents for setting the blaze and blocking the exits. Hundreds of thousands took to the streets. On September 6, the shah, acting on advice from Brzezinski in Washington, proclaimed martial law. The next day troops fired on a demonstration killing between 700 and 2,000 protestors.

Carter sided with Vance over Christmas, and on December 30 the shah named Shapour Bahktiar as prime minister. In mid-January, the monarch left the country for Egypt. Bahktiar lasted two more weeks before Khomeini returned in triumph from Paris and ordered his arrest. The prime minister fled in fear for his life, and the ayatollah appointed as premier Mehdi Bazargan, a veteran of the nationalist party of Mohammed Mossadeq, overthrown by the CIA in 1953.

From February to October 1979, Ambassador William Sullivan in Iran and officials in Washington urged an accommodation to the new Islamic Republic. American civilians quietly left the country, but the embassy continued to operate. The staff received a temporary fright in late February when demonstrators entered the forty-acre compound, but the Iranian police evicted them. Marches on the compound took place weekly as hundreds of thousands chanted, "Death to the United States, death to Carter!"

The United States had not offered asylum to the deposed shah, who spent the first ten months of 1979 wandering from Egypt to Morocco to the Bahamas to Mexico. His friends Henry Kissinger and David Rockefeller pressed the Carter administration to permit him to come to New York for an operation on his cancerous spleen. Convinced that relations with Iran had stabilized, Carter authorized the admission of the deposed ruler on humanitarian grounds on October 22.

In Tehran, Khomeini greeted the news with "America expects to take the shah there, engage in plots, and our young people are expected to simply remain idle." He encouraged his followers to take to the streets once more. The largest demonstrations in history convulsed the capital as three million people marched on the embassy on November 1. On November 4, hundreds of the most militant revolutionaries stormed the fence, but this time the police did not evict them. Instead Khomeini called the compound a "nest of spies." Praising the militants as "ten thousand martyrs," he called on the "Great Satan Carter" to return the shah for trial and hand back his fortune, estimated at a preposterous $40 billion, to pay for his crimes. Unless these conditions were met, the militants at the embassy would keep sixty-nine diplomats, marine guards, and private American citizens imprisoned. Parading their blindfolded hostages, they threatened to try and execute them as spies.

The seizure of the hostages became the news story of the year in the United States. The number fell to fifty-three after the militants released some of the black and female captives in December, but those who remained became the focal point of national shame. CBS began introducing its evening news listing as "Day #4 . . . 5 . . . 6 . . ." for the prisoners. ABC started a special evening edition at 11:30 P.M. called simply "America Held Hostage."

Carter announced that he would not leave the White House until he secured the hostages' release. In December, Carter froze $8 billion in Iranian assets, doused the lights on the national Christmas tree, and told a visiting group of congressmen that American "national honor" would not be assuaged even after the return of the hostages. Later in the month, Brzezinski and Jordan encouraged the shah to leave for Panama.

Tough talk and symbolic action did not bring the fifty-three home, but it did offer a temporary boost to Carter's popularity. In December, 66 percent of those polled favored his handling of the crisis versus 32 percent who opposed it. Carter also overtook the challenge from Massachusetts senator Edward M. Kennedy, who decided in November to make a try for the Democratic presidential nomination. At one time, Kennedy led Carter by two to one in the polls, but the incumbent's "Rose Garden strategy" of looking presidential to resolve the hostage problem wounded the challenger's chances in early 1980. By March, however, Kennedy seemed to have recovered with a victory in the New York primary. New polls showed that only 31 percent of the public thought Carter's strategy was successful in dealing with Iran while 47 percent perceived that it had failed.

Having successfully avoided the stump as he bargained for the hostages, Carter now felt a prisoner himself in the White House. If the militants held the Americans through November, he might never campaign against the Republican nominee, and the continued humiliation would remind voters of presidential failure. He therefore approved a military rescue mission despite Secretary of State Vance's assurances to Europeans that the United States would not use force. On April 24, eight air force helicopters took off in a dust storm from the carrier *Nimitz* for a rendezvous at Tabriz in the Iranian desert, a staging area for an assault on the embassy. The rescue mission got no farther. Two of the machines choked on the dust and started to turn back when they collided with one another and a transport plane which crashed, killing eight servicemen. Carter canceled the project. The militants dispersed the fifty-three hostages, thereby making future rescues impossible.

The mission prompted Vance's resignation, as he had opposed the use of force and seen his world order viewpoint gradually lose ground to Brzezinski's proposals over the previous year. Carter appointed Maine senator Edmund Muskie as the new secretary of state. The rescue attempt did liberate the chief executive from the White House. Saying he "had never dreamed" the crisis would last so long and that it now was "manageable," he departed the Rose Garden for the campaign trail. Public interest in the hostages diminished too, as any mention of the captives was painful. As the summer

A blindfolded American hostage being paraded before Iranian revolutionaries at
the United States embassy in Tehran, November 1979. *(Wide World Photos)*

wore on, a new government took power in Iran headed by Abdul Hassan
Bani-Sadr. Since the shah died in Egypt in late July, the United States no
longer could return him even if it wanted to. Negotiations opened in August on exchanging the remaining hostages for Iran's frozen assets. The talks
made headway through the fall but stalled the week before the American
presidential election. After Ronald Reagan won, Carter worked incessantly
in the last months of his term to arrange the hostages' release. His patience
paid off in the final hours of his administration, when Algeria helped broker the return of the captives in exchange for the unfreezing of Iran's assets. Tehran let the Americans fly out of Iran as soon as Carter left office
and Reagan was sworn in as president.

THE RETURN OF THE COLD WAR AND THE ELECTION OF 1980

Another, more important, foreign policy issue, renewed conflict with
Moscow, appeared in early 1980. On December 27, 1979, some eighty thousand Soviet troops poured into the neighboring country of Afghanistan to
prop up the shaky government of leftist Babrak Karmal. Carter responded
with typical hyperbole. He regretted that the Soviets had "lied" to him and

called their move "the gravest threat to peace since the Second World War." In early January, he withdrew the SALT II Treaty from the Senate where it was doomed anyway. He forbade Americans to participate in the Moscow Olympic Games the following July, slapped an embargo on American grain and sophisticated electronic equipment bound for the Soviet Union, promised to raise defense spending by 5 percent in real terms for each of the next five years, ordered young men to register for a potential draft and proclaimed a Carter Doctrine under which the United States would fight for its "national interests" should the Soviet Union threaten the oil of the Persian Gulf.

Yet Carter's new anti-Soviet line did not stop the erosion of public support. The Committee on the Present Danger endorsed the candidacy of Republican Ronald Reagan with the charge that the president's change of heart had come too late. Reagan on the right, Kennedy on the left, and John Anderson, an Illinois Republican congressman running an independent presidential campaign from the center of the political spectrum, all questioned the incumbent's "competence."

Once nominated by the Republicans, former California governor Reagan promised a "strong America." Telling the Veterans of Foreign Wars that the war in Vietnam had been a "noble cause," he implied that a "Vietnam syndrome"—fear of intervention—had paralyzed Carter. He denigrated the emphasis on human rights for having undermined the shah and led to the hostage crisis. He did not indicate what he would do to secure the captives' release but hinted that had he been president they would not have been imprisoned in the first place. The Republican promised to rearm America at a faster rate, kill SALT II, and most of all, "speak with a single voice" in foreign affairs.

Carter's pollsters told him that the voters finally turned against him the last weekend of the campaign when it appeared that no deal would be reached with Iran to free the captives. On November 4, exactly one year after the seizure of the Tehran embassy, Reagan won the election with 51 percent of the vote. Carter received 42 percent, and Anderson captured 6 percent. As significant as Reagan's victory was the election of a Republican Senate majority for the first time since 1952.

Jimmy Carter's efforts to shift the focus of American diplomacy away from competition with the Soviet Union to the management of interdependence failed. Bad luck plagued Carter. He was elected in 1976 at a time when Americans responded to moral appeals. Two years later, a sour world economy and domestic inflation cancelled voters' enthusiasm for helping poorer nations in the Southern Hemisphere. Soviet behavior also contributed to Carter's downfall. Moscow's assertiveness in the Third World made it harder for Carter to declare the end of the Cold War. The Iranian revolution and the seizure of hostages at the American embassy in Tehran virtually ensured Carter's defeat at the polls.

Even if fortune had been kinder, though, the Carter administration's foreign policy would have experienced troubles. Cyrus Vance and Zbigniew Brzezinski, his two principal international lieutenants, clashed repeatedly. As historian Gaddis Smith writes, "only a President with deep experience in foreign affairs and a grasp of the issues equal or superior to that of such contending advisers could have prevented crippling contradictions. Carter lacked such experience and grasp." He appeared to vacillate before finally siding with the anti-Soviet positions of Brzezinski. At that point, his rhetoric sounded harsh and unsophisticated. An outsider who distrusted Washington, Carter warred with Congress. When he needed lawmakers' help in 1980, they rejected him. The public did too in 1980, replacing him with an administration that tried to restore American preeminence.

THE REAGAN FOREIGN POLICY APPROACH

Ronald Reagan and his principal foreign policy advisers came to power in 1981 with a clear idea of reversing the course of the last fifteen years of United States foreign policy. They looked back to the decades immediately after the Second World War when the United States was the unquestioned leader of an anti-Soviet alignment. The new administration expected to confront the Soviets assertively. It looked forward to battling Third World Communists from Nicaragua to Afghanistan. It pledged to elevate the fight against terrorism over the Carter administration's concentration on human rights. It promised to erase the dishonorable stain of Iran's seizure of the United States embassy and its captivity of fifty three American hostages for 444 days.

By the end of the Reagan administration, however, many of these promises had been altered, abandoned, or overtaken by events. The world of 1988 was far different from that of just eight years earlier. The United States did not cause the dramatic changes in the Soviet Union, but the Reagan administration did nimbly respond to calls from Mikhail Gorbachev for "new thinking" in world affairs. Reagan, who had won the presidency deriding arms control and detente, signed in 1987 one of the most far-reaching arms reduction agreements of the Cold War era. In 1987 and 1988 he also formed a close personal bond with Gorbachev, leading the way to the end of the Cold War.

Although the Reagan administration reacted intelligently to Soviet overtures after 1985, U.S. foreign policy in the Reagan years never provided the coherence and consistency promised in the 1980 presidential campaign. Much of the difficulty was of the Reagan administration's own making. From the beginning it was bedeviled with internal dissension. The White House staff warred with the heads of the departments of State and Defense, who often were at each other's throats as well. Six different men held the post of national security adviser, two of whom, Richard Allen (1981) and John Poindexter (1985–1986), left in scandal. There were two secretaries of state, the first of whom, Alexander Haig (1981–1982), also quit under a cloud. The second, George P. Shultz (1982–1989), compiled a more successful record. There were also two secretaries of defense, Caspar Weinberger (1981–1987) and Frank Carlucci (1987–1989), a normal turnover for a long administration.

Congress was at best skeptical and often hostile to the administration's foreign policy. For the first six years of the administration, Republicans held the Senate while Democrats controlled the House of Representatives. With the congressional elections of 1986, Democrats organized both houses. Immediately thereafter the gravest scandal of a presidency since Watergate erupted when it was revealed that the United States had secretly sold weapons to Iran in return for the promise of the release of American hostages taken in Lebanon after 1983. Soon the public learned that profits from the sale of the weapons had gone to support the rightist counterrevolutionaries (contras) fighting the government of Nicaragua. For a while it appeared that public support for the Reagan administration's foreign policy had collapsed. The decline was temporary, though. As relations between the United States and the Soviet Union improved in 1987 and 1988 over two-thirds of the public approved of Reagan's handling of foreign affairs at the end of his term.

FROM CONFRONTATION TO DETENTE WITH THE SOVIETS

United States–Soviet relations underwent a remarkable transformation in the eight years of the Reagan administration. The most anti-Soviet administration in decades eventually presided over a new era of detente. At his first news conference the president denounced the Soviet leaders as scoundrels who reserved the right to "lie, cheat, and steal" to advance the Communist cause. In June 1982 he told the British Parliament that Soviet-style communism would one day be consigned to the "ash heap of history." He identified the Soviet Union as "the focus of evil" in the modern world, as he told a convention of religious broadcasters that the Kremlin had amassed an "evil empire."

Throughout his first term, he and Secretary of Defense Caspar Weinberger pushed forward with the largest peacetime military buildup since 1940. "We do not know how much time we have left," the secretary warned the Senate in 1982. Fear of a superpower war rose further when, in March 1983, the president promised a defensive shield against incoming ballistic missiles. Called the Strategic Defense Initiative (SDI) by its supporters and derided by critics as "Star Wars," a science-fiction fantasy, this twenty-year re-search and development project carried a price tag that could not be esti-mated. Guesses ranged from $100 billion to $1 trillion. More concretely, the Reagan administration and the NATO allies went forward with plans, cre-ated at the end of the Carter administration, to deploy medium-range bal-listic and cruise missiles in Western Europe. The Soviets responded in late 1983 by walking out of all arms control talks with the United States. At the beginning of the election year of 1984, therefore, there had been no progress on either Strategic Arms Reduction Talks (START), the Reagan adminis-tration's new name for Strategic Arms Limitation Talks (SALT), or a treaty reducing Intermediate Nuclear Forces (INF) of the sort both the Soviets and the United States had installed in Europe.

To domestic critics, the Reagan administration's harsh anti-Soviet rhetoric and military buildup raised the specter of nuclear war. A grassroots movement favoring a "nuclear freeze" spread quickly in 1982 and 1983. One of its proponents, Sen. Edward M. Kennedy (D., Mass.), brought cheers from the delegates to the Democratic National Convention in 1984 when he as-sailed the refusal of the president to meet with the leaders of the Soviet Com-munist party. Every president since Herbert Hoover had done so, Kennedy thundered, "but not Ronald Reagan." Democratic presidential candidate Walter Mondale recommended that the leaders of the Soviet Union and the United States agree to meet yearly, at the summit. The president and his campaign managers scoffed in turn that this represented the sort of woolly minded idealism their assertive foreign policy was designed to combat.

Maybe not surprisingly, Reagan put Mondale's suggestion into practice over the course of his next term. In the next four years, Reagan had more meetings with the leader of the Soviet Union than any of his predecessors. He and Mikhail Gorbachev had summits lasting from two and a half hours to four days in Geneva in November 1985; in Reykjavik, Iceland, in October 1986; in Washington in December 1987; in Moscow in June 1988; and in New York in December 1988.

Gorbachev became party chairman in early 1985 after two dizzying years of changes at the top. Leonid Brezhnev died in November 1982, replaced by Yuri Andropov, former head of the KGB, who became ill within the year. The problem remained throughout 1984 when Konstantine Chernenko, also ill, took over. He died in March 1985, succeeded by Mikhail Gorbachev.

The new chairman was far different from his predecessors. Fifty-four years old, young by the standards of recent Soviet leaders, well educated, Gor-bachev plunged into a major reform of the Soviet system. Denouncing the eighteen-year Brezhnev era as "the period of stagnation," he promised *pere-stroika,* liberalization of the stagnant economy, and *glasnost,* greater open-ness in politics. He worried that his country might not be able to bear the weight of the military buildup created since the Cuban missile crisis of 1962.

He vowed to reach an agreement with the United States to free resources for his economic program.

Over the next four years Gorbachev was everywhere: at home, in Europe, in Latin America and the United States. Old anti-Communists like Conservative prime minister Margaret Thatcher of Britain found him charming and called him "a friend." He presented more of a challenge to the Reagan administration than the slow, unimaginative men who had led the Kremlin in recent years.

In the five meetings between Gorbachev and Reagan, the two gradually revived detente, even if Reagan resisted using the word. Their first two summits, at Geneva in November 1985 and at Reykjavik, in October 1986, were tentative, even stormy affairs. The two men's wives did not get along at first. "Who does this dame think she is?" Nancy Reagan complained about Raisa Gorbachev.

Worse followed at Reykjavik. Neither President Reagan nor Secretary of State Shultz nor Secretary of Defense Weinberger was prepared for the far-reaching proposals that Gorbachev sprang on them. The Soviet leader offered 50-percent cuts in strategic ballistic missiles, leading to their elimination. In return, he demanded that the United States stop work on Star Wars or SDI. Reagan refused, and Shultz looked miserable as he announced the collapse of the meeting to a press conference on a cold Sunday afternoon. The secretary could not even predict when, or if, there would be another meeting of the heads of government.

Events proved that the momentum of better relations between the superpowers was too strong to be derailed by the failure in Iceland. A summit did take place in Washington in December 1987, which bore concrete results in a secondary field of arms control. On December 6, Reagan and Gorbachev signed a treaty on Intermediate Nuclear Forces. The two powers agreed to withdraw and destroy all of the intermediate-range missiles they had stationed in Europe over the past decade. The treaty had been drafted over the previous several months, so there was no repetition of the frantic negotiations between Henry Kissinger, Richard Nixon, and Leonid Brezhnev which had occurred at the Moscow summit in May 1972. Unlike Nixon, Reagan was not hailed as a master geopolitician, and his deputies were not lauded as geniuses as Kissinger had been. But Reagan did win praise for a general improvement of relations with his main rival. "The atmospherics at the December summit in Washington was positive," admitted Marshall D. Shulman of Columbia University, who had earlier served as President Carter's special adviser on the Soviet Union. The INF treaty went forward despite the lack of progress on the thornier issue of strategic weapons. Only Nancy Reagan and Raisa Gorbachev continued to get in each other's way, as the American First Lady believed that her Soviet counterpart tried to upstage her on their tours of art galleries.

The last year of the Reagan administration saw further improvements in superpower relations. In April representatives of the two governments concluded an agreement in Geneva calling for the phased withdrawal of Soviet forces from Afghanistan. When President Reagan went to Moscow for another summit with Gorbachev in June, he explained that the new Soviet leader had not been responsible for sending the troops to Afghanistan in the first place. "They've changed," he added when asked whether he believed that the Soviet Union still represented the "focus of evil in the modern world." He received an enthusiastic welcome from students at Moscow State University. The presence of an old foe like Reagan in the heart of the Soviet Union was the most important symbolic result of the Moscow meeting. He seemed to get along famously with Gorbachev, whom he now referred to as a "friend."

Relations between the two superpowers continued to get better for the remainder of the Reagan administration. By the fall Prime Minister Thatcher asserted that "the cold war is over." Gorbachev and Reagan met once more, before the expiration of the American president's term, when the Soviet leader, now president as well as party chairman, addressed the United Nations General Assembly in New York on December 7, 1988. He announced that his country would unilaterally reduce its military forces by five hundred thousand men and ten thousand tanks over the next two years. This was a very different performance from that of the last Soviet leader to address the UN, Nikita Khrushchev's pounding the table with his shoe in 1960. The usually sober *New York Times* exulted, "perhaps not since Woodrow Wilson presented his Fourteen Points in 1918 or since Franklin Roosevelt and Winston Churchill promulgated the Atlantic Charter in 1941 has a world figure demonstrated the vision Mikhail Gorbachev displayed yesterday at the United Nations." President Reagan said, "I heartily approve" of the proposal to reduce Soviet conventional forces, before lunching with the Soviet president after his UN speech. The warmth between the two powers seemed genuine as the wives of the presidents dropped their earlier frostiness. The *New York Times* headlined this sort of detente "ANOTHER OBSTACLE FALLS: NANCY REAGAN AND RAISA GORBACHEV GET CHUMMY." By the end of the Reagan administration, the detente promised in the early 1970s had revived, and serious people contemplated the end of the Cold War.

CRISES IN CENTRAL AMERICA AND THE CARIBBEAN

The Reagan administration returned to an earlier era of attempted United States domination over the political destiny of Central America and the Caribbean. Official Washington sought to erase the memory of Vietnam and the supposed weakness of the Carter years by confronting leftists in Central

America. It helped keep the revolutionaries from power in El Salvador, militarily overthrew the Marxists on the Caribbean island of Grenada, but failed in its principal objective—making the Sandinista government in Nicaragua "cry uncle," as the president once put it. Support for the contras strained relations with friendly states in the hemisphere, provoked public protests at home, angered Congress, and led to the greatest foreign policy scandal of the Reagan administration.

"Let's win one in El Salvador," urged columnist William Safire, early in 1981. For conservatives like Safire or Secretary of State Alexander Haig, the growing tension in Central America reminded them of Vietnam. This time, they believed the outcome for the United States would be different. The administration quickly sent fifty-five American military advisers to El Salvador to assist the army in its war against a combined front of Marxist and Social Democratic guerrillas. Washington also underwrote the cost of an ambitious land reform program undertaken by the moderate Christian Democratic government of José Napoleon Duarte.

The Christian Democrats held on in El Salvador throughout the Reagan administration, but their tenure was never secure. Duarte faced challenges from the right as well as the left. Death squads associated with the Salvadoran armed forces roamed the country killing tens of thousands of civilians, including teachers, physicians, common farmers, and church workers. Haig alienated many Catholics when he speculated that four American churchwomen—three nuns and a lay worker—who had been murdered in December 1980 may have "run a blockade" or been "caught in a crossfire." Campuses erupted as demonstrators carried signs demanding "NO MORE VIETNAMS. U.S. OUT OF EL SALVADOR." Congress passed legislation requiring presidential certification of "improvement" in human rights before additional aid could be granted. Duarte tried to comply, but rightists in the army and legislature dogged his tracks. In 1982 and 1988 the extreme right won control of the National Assembly, severely restricting Duarte and the Christian Democrats.

As in Vietnam, American military advisers were frustrated as they helped the Salvadoran army fight a "nine-to-five war" against well-motivated guerrillas. This time, however, the war was closer to the United States, and the guerrillas lacked the material support the Vietnamese had enjoyed from China and the Soviet Union. Reagan went on a public relations offensive in 1983 to shore up public and congressional support for military aid to El Salvador. He urged critics to set aside "passivity, resignation and defeatism" in the face of a "challenge to freedom and security in our hemisphere." Doubters would not be stilled. Senator Christopher Dodd offered the official Democratic party response immediately after Reagan spoke. Labeling the search for military solutions a "formula for failure," he recollected the disillusionment of Vietnam.

The public seemed bewildered and frustrated. A *New York Times*–CBS News poll revealed that only 25 percent knew that the United States supported the government of El Salvador, 12 percent knew that it backed the contras in Nicaragua, and a meager 8 percent understood both alignments. Fifty-seven percent opposed sending troops to El Salvador, while 32 percent would back such a move if it would avert a Communist takeover. Philip Converse, a public opinion specialist at the University of Michigan, noticed a "sort of Vietnam pall across these numbers. People have less of a support reflex than they would have, pre-Vietnam."

From the administration's point of view something had to be done to arrest the downward slide in public support for the assertive policy in Central America. In June 1983 Reagan reached out to Henry Kissinger, an old target of scorn, to head a Bipartisan Presidential Commission on Central America. The Kissinger Commission spent six months studying the complex issues and published their findings in early 1984. It tried to satisfy everyone, explaining that the roots of the problems in Central America were social, not the result of Communist plots. It noted that Soviet policy in the region had been "gradualist and ambiguous," not reckless. It urged a major increase in U.S. involvement in all aspects of Central America's problem. It called for an additional $8 billion in American economic assistance to the region over the next five years. Congress provided less than half that amount. It also recommended that Washington continue to support the military in El Salvador and the contras in Nicaragua. The effort at balance only sounded weak.

As the Kissinger Commission went about its work, the focus of attention shifted to the Caribbean, where the United States sent troops to overthrow the revolutionary government of Grenada. The Reagan administration had objected to the Marxist government of Prime Minister Maurice Bishop which had ruled since 1979. The United States had suspended all foreign aid and sought to isolate Grenada. By 1983 the only United States presence on the island was at the St. George's University School of Medicine where five hundred aspiring young American doctors were studying. Bishop had good relations with Fidel Castro, and his New Jewel movement galvanized anti-American nationalism in other Caribbean states. In the summer of 1983, however, Bishop seemed to draw away from Cuba, softened his anti-Yankee rhetoric, and signaled a readiness for a rapprochement with Washington. On October 12, a more militant faction of the New Jewel movement, led by Gen. Hudson Austin, staged a coup, murdered Bishop, declared martial law, and imposed a strict curfew on the island.

The Reagan administration perceived a challenge. If the new government flourished, Washington's brave talk about turning back revolution in the hemisphere would ring hollow. Direct military intervention, on the other hand, promised value for the billions invested in the military since 1981. On

An American medical student returns from Grenada to Charleston, S.C., and thanks his rescuers. Pictures like this generated intense public support for the intervention in Grenada. *(Wide World Photos)*

Sunday, October 23, the American public was stunned when commandos bombed a marine barracks in Beirut, Lebanon. The shock of this raid could further erode public support for the use of force. Before dawn, on Tuesday morning, October 25, a force of nineteen hundred United States marines and army airborne forces landed on the island. After three days of fighting with the Grenada army and six hundred Cuban construction workers, the Americans arrested the new government and proclaimed the island liberated. Reagan announced that he had acted against "a brutal gang of leftist thugs" to save the lives of the American medical students and at the request of a little-known five-member Organization of Eastern Caribbean States.

Initially some members of Congress were outraged. "We do not have the right" to invade a sovereign state, said New York Democratic senator Daniel Patrick Moynihan. Speaker of the House Thomas P. O'Neill (D., Mass.), upset that he had not been consulted as provided by the 1973 War Powers Act, called it "gunboat diplomacy" and grumbled that the president "is going down the wrong road." Seven members of the House drafted a resolution of impeachment against the president.

Yet public support for the military action soared. Recruitment offices were briefly swamped. Nothing did more to generate public enthusiasm than pictures of medical students falling to their knees and kissing American soil upon their return home. Such scenes and remarks like "I don't think there's any more beautiful sight than the United States and the rangers who arrived to save us" erased earlier declarations by the director of the school that the students had never been in danger. Within two weeks, Speaker O'Neill exercised a strategic retreat, led a fourteen-member congressional delegation to the island, and announced that the invasion had been "justified." During the presidential election campaign of 1984, Republican ads featured footage of the grateful medical students with devastating effect against former vice-president Walter Mondale, the Democratic nominee, who had initially condemned the military action.

Memories of Grenada faded, though. Of greater significance were the unsuccessful attempts by the Reagan administration to evict the Sandinista government of Nicaragua led by President Daniel Ortega. In March 1981, Reagan signed a "Presidential Finding" authorizing the CIA to pay, train, and arm disaffected Nicaraguans to overthrow the Sandinistas. The CIA recruited between five and ten thousand of these contras in the first two years, rising to nearly twenty thousand in 1985. Many of the fighters and commanders were former Somoza national guardsmen; a few of the top political leaders had originally been part of an alliance against the Somoza dictatorship.

Within a year this "secret war" became common knowledge. Congress passed a resolution sponsored by Rep. Edward Boland (D., Mass.), chairman of the House Committee on Intelligence, expressly forbidding the use of American funds to overthrow the government of Nicaragua. Other Latin American states warned Washington that it was pursuing a dangerous course. In January 1983 the foreign ministers of Colombia, Mexico, Panama, and Venezuela met on Contadora, an island off the Panama coast, to forge a diplomatic solution to the impasse between Washington and Managua. Over the next two years "the Contadora process" became a shorthand code for a negotiated settlement of the U.S.-sponsored contra war against Nicaragua.

Washington displayed little interest in negotiations, however. In September 1983 President Reagan signed another finding authorizing support to the contras for the vague purpose of "putting pressure on the Sandinistas" to stop sending arms to the leftist guerrillas in El Salvador. Since this finding did not promise the overthrow of the government, it circumvented the first Boland amendment. In a nationally televised speech, Reagan urged the public to pressure Congress to provide $24 million for the contras. "Communist subversion is not an irreversible tide," he said. "We have seen it rolled back in Grenada."

Congress could not be moved, though, after the news broke in April 1983 that the CIA had mined Nicaragua's harbors and bombed the oil storage facilities at Corinto. Aid for the contras, appropriated by Congress, expired on October 1, 1984. Lawmakers thereupon passed another version of the Boland resolution, banning government funds for the contras. This prohibition remained in effect until mid-1986, when Congress once more provided money for the contras.

In 1987 and 1988 the contras did poorly in their war against the Sandinistas, as the United States backed away from its earlier support. The growing scandal of the diversion of funds from Iran arms sales to the contras undermined always tenuous congressional support. The Nicaraguan forces fought better than the contras. The long-dormant Contadora process revived, after President Oscar Arias of Costa Rica urged a cease-fire and an amnesty in 1987. He won a Nobel Peace Prize for his efforts. In March 1988, the contras signed a cease-fire with the Sandinistas, agreeing to lay down their arms in return for negotiations leading to an opening of the political system.

MUDDLING IN THE MIDDLE EAST

The Reagan administration wrestled with the problems of the Middle East for eight years but had little success in resolving them. A public opinion poll taken in April 1985 revealed that Americans regarded the Camp David accords, brokered by Jimmy Carter in 1978 and 1979, the greatest achievement of recent foreign policy, while they considered the Reagan administration's involvement in Lebanon in 1982–1984 its greatest failure.

In September 1982 the United States landed troops in the eastern Mediterranean for the first time since 1958. This unplanned and poorly executed effort to mediate a war between Israel and the Palestine Liberation Organization quickly bogged down in the complicated civil war of scores of religious and political factions in Lebanon. Originally the Reagan administration had hoped to change the subject of Mideast disputes from the Arab-Israeli conflict to the new Cold War between East and West. Secretary of State Alexander Haig sought to forge what he called a "strategic consensus" between Jerusalem and anti-Communist Arab states. Neither side was interested, and Washington pulled away from the effort to further the mediation between Israel and the Arabs as envisioned in the Camp David formula.

In June 1982 Israel, perceiving a "green light" from Haig, attacked the PLO in Lebanon. Instead of a brief, successful campaign, the war dragged on. Haig resigned on June 25, angry that National Security Adviser William P. Clark had opened his own channels of communications with the PLO. Haig left with the admonition that Reagan had shunned the path of "consistency, clarity and steadiness" he had promised. The president immediately named George P. Shultz as his new secretary of state.

Shultz's first test came later that summer as the Israelis had blasted their way to the outskirts of Beirut. The PLO remained intact. Shultz and special envoy Philip Habib worked out a plan for the PLO to evacuate Beirut under the protection of a multinational force made up of American, French, and Italian marines. A smiling PLO leader Yassir Arafat led his fighters from the bombed-out city in late August, and the multinational force withdrew. The new secretary of state thereupon persuaded President Reagan to announce a "fresh start" in Mideast peace negotiations. On September 1, he proposed a formula of "peace in exchange for territory." Israel would yield the West Bank to a Palestinian "homeland in confederation with Jordan" in return for security and normal relations with its neighbors. Neither Israel nor the Arab states accepted the plan.

All hell broke loose less than three weeks later, following the September 14 assassination of Bashir Gemayal, leader of the Christian Phalange party who had just been elected president of Lebanon. Israel's army occupied Muslim West Beirut on the 15th; two days later Gemayal's Christian militia entered two Palestinian refugee camps and went on a bloody rampage. They slaughtered anywhere between two hundred and eight hundred Palestinian men, women, and children. Immediately afterward, the multinational force of American, French, and Italian marines returned for an indefinite stay.

Originally the marines were welcomed by most factions in Lebanon as peacekeepers, but soon they provoked resentment from Shi'ite Muslims and Syrians, who also had troops in Lebanon. Washington never made clear the precise purpose of the force or how long it would remain in the midst of an ever more dangerous civil war. On April 18, 1983, a suicide squad bombed the American embassy in Beirut, killing sixty three, including seventeen Americans. By the fall, the marines were siding openly with some Christian factions, shelling Muslim and radical positions. Early on Sunday morning, October 23, suicide terrorists driving trucks loaded with TNT blew up the American marine headquarters near the Beirut airport, killing 241 marines and navy personnel as they slept.

American policy lay in ruins along with the barracks. For a while Reagan put on a brave face, insisting that the United States force would remain in Beirut. "If others feel confident they can intimidate us and our allies in Lebanon, they will become more bold elsewhere." In his January 25, 1984, State of the Union message, Reagan reiterated that the marines would stay in Beirut. This was just talk. Two weeks later, Lebanon's fragile government collapsed, and chaos reigned in the capital. Restless House Democrats prepared a resolution demanding the marines' withdrawal. The president removed them to ships offshore, but still said he had not "bugged out" under fire.

The United States lowered its public profile in the Arab-Israeli dispute over the next five years. A new coalition between the more moderate Labor party and the nationalist Likud bloc took power in Israel in September 1984 and began the process of removing Israel's army from southern Lebanon. Washington watched and hoped that the issue would recede from public view. It did, but in the meantime peace between Israel and the Arabs remained only a dream.

The unreal calm was shattered on December 9, 1987, when Palestinians in the West Bank and Gaza Strip, dominated by Israel and ignored by other Arabs, began an uprising, or *intifada,* against the twenty-year-old occupation. Over the next year Palestinians demonstrated, scrawled slogans on walls, struck, threw rocks, hurled gasoline bombs, and stabbed Israelis. The Israelis responded with tear gas, rubber bullets, clubs, and live ammunition. In the first year of the *intifada* Israeli soldiers and settlers killed over 330 Arabs, while 13 Israelis lost their lives to the insurgents. Caught by surprise, the United States tried once more to breathe life into the moribund peace process. In March, Secretary Shultz called for the revival of the land-for-peace formula and the interim autonomy arrangement of the Camp David agreement. Israel, however, rejected Shultz's proposal of an international conference to formulate a framework for resolving the Palestinian issue. Shultz's initiative died.

Nine months later, after the presidential elections, the United States abruptly reversed a thirteen-year ban on official contact with the PLO when Shultz announced on December 14 that Washington was willing to open a "dialogue" with Yassir Arafat. The PLO chairman recognized Israel's right to exist, observed that two UN Security Council resolutions adopted after the 1967 and 1973 Arab-Israeli war provided a framework for negotiations, and "renounced" terrorism. Shultz made it easier for his successors in the Bush administration to act as a broker between Israel and the Palestinians.

Farther west in the Mediterranean the United States engaged in smallscale warfare with Libya. This radical Islamic state, ruled since 1969 by a charismatic and demogogic strongman, Col. Muammar Khaddafy, used its oil wealth to bankroll some of the more violent terrorists operating in Europe and the Middle East. Hoping to put Khaddafy "back in his box," as Secretary of State Shultz once observed, American ships and planes patrolled the Gulf of Sidra, North of Libya's coast, throughout the Reagan administration. The Libyans rose to the bait twice. In August 1981 and December 1988, American navy jets downed Libyan warplanes approaching for an attack. A far more serious episode took place on the night of April 14–15, 1986, when American jets from carriers in the Mediterranean and bases in Britain bombed five targets in Libya. The raid was ordered in retaliation for a series of terrorist episodes in Europe linked to Libya, the most recent of which was the bombing of a Berlin nightclub frequented by GIs. One of the aims of the raid was the death of Khaddafy. He escaped, but his daughter was killed and two of his sons were injured. Seventy-seven percent of the American public polled immediately after the bombing approved of it.

The United States also reacted to events, rather than planned carefully, as the war between Iran and Iraq dragged on for nearly nine years, from 1980 to 1988. With bad relations with both Baghdad and Tehran, the United States watched from the sidelines, supporting neither for six years. As many as two million soldiers and civilians lost their lives in the bloodiest fighting since the Second World War. In 1985–1986 the White House became more directly involved, secretly arming Iran. When news of the clandestine shipments fanned an outraged backlash at home, the administration reversed course and sided with Iraq. In May 1987 the U.S. navy began escorting Kuwaiti oil tankers, reflagged as American vessels, through the Persian Gulf. In May 1987, an Iraqi fighter mistook the destroyer *Stark* for an Iranian vessel, fired a French Exocet missile at it, and killed thirty seven sailors. The navy continued its patrols, still siding with Iraq against Iran. In August, one of the reflagged tankers, sailing in front of warships supposed to protect it, hit an Iranian mine. The following July 3 the crew of the U.S.S. *Vincennes* became as confused as the Iraqi pilots, mistook an Iranian civilian airliner for a hostile jet, and blasted it out of the sky, killing 290. Washington compensated the victims, an act of generosity hardly welcomed by an American public which still detested all things Iranian. A month later, in August, Iran and Iraq, exhausted by their losses, signed a cease-fire.

THE IRAN-CONTRA CONNECTION

On November 3, 1986, an obscure Lebanese weekly, *Al Shiraa,* with close ties to the revolutionary government of Iran, reported that former United States National Security Adviser Robert McFarlane had secretly visited Tehran in May. He carried a Bible and a cake in the shape of a key with a mission to negotiate the release of American hostages in Lebanon in return for a supply of spare parts for Iran's military. This article opened a window on a hitherto secret American foreign policy, staffed by White House operatives, former CIA agents, and shadowy arms dealers, beyond the control of the State or Defense departments or the knowledge of Congress.

As the story unfolded over the next eight months it engulfed the White House and seriously undermined public support for Reagan's foreign policy. On November 25, Attorney General Edwin Meese revealed that Lt. Col. Oliver North of the National Security Council staff had arranged for the transfer of $10 million to $30 million in payments Iran had made for arms in 1985 and 1986 to rebels fighting the Nicaraguan government. During that time the Boland amendment had prohibited any U.S. government funds for the contras. David Durenberger (R., Minn.), chairman of the Senate Intelligence Committee, threatened, "It will be a cold day in Washington before any more money goes into Nicaragua." At the same time Reagan fired North and his superior Admiral John Poindexter, who had succeeded McFarlane as national security adviser in December 1985. Even as the president dropped North, he described him as a "national hero" and telephoned to say that "your work will make a great movie some day."

Before the filmmakers went to work, though, a presidential commission and Congress exposed North's network. Reagan appointed a special review board chaired by former senator John Tower (R., Tex.) working with former national security adviser Brent Scowcroft and former secretary of state Edmund Muskie. They investigated from December 1986 to February 1987 and found that the initiative to Iran was the brainchild of McFarlane, CIA director William Casey, North, several Israelis, and an Iranian go-between. Throughout 1985 and 1986 the United States had helped Israel and private arms merchants ship hundreds of tons of missiles and spare aircraft parts to Iran. The objective had always been to encourage Iran to release American hostages held in Lebanon. The Tower Commission concluded that the scheme "was handled almost casually . . . with an expectation that the process would end with the next arms-for-hostage exchange." They portrayed Reagan as remote, unaware of what subordinates did in his name, and ignorant of the implications of their actions. They decided that the president had "a concept of the initiative that was not accurately reflected in the reality of the operation." They faulted Chief of Staff Donald Regan, Secretary of Defense Weinberger, and Secretary of State Shultz for not forcefully stopping dealing arms for hostages, even though they thought it a terrible idea. "That policy was a wrong policy," said Muskie, "and it was the President's policy." The Tower board recognized that news of the Reagan White House negotiating with agents of the Ayatollah Khomeini was a public relations catastrophe. The connection "ran directly counter to the administration's own policy on terrorism," they wrote. "The result," they observed, "was a U.S. policy that worked against itself . . . an unprofessional, and, in substantial part, unsatisfactory operation."

While the Tower board damned the president for managerial negligence, it did not directly connect him with the illegal decision to divert profits from the arms sales to the contras. A congressional investigation followed the money trail to discover who knew of the diversion. The committees, chaired by Daniel Inouye (D., Hawaii) in the Senate and Lee Hamilton (D., Ind.) in the House, held joint hearings to determine, as Sen. David Boren (D., Okla.) asked, "Did the president faithfully carry out the spirit of the law, or was he ignoring it? Did he subvert the process himself by trying to raise funds to get money to the contras?"

Lt. Col. Oliver North testifies before the joint House-Senate Committees
investigating the Iran-Contra affair in July 1987. *(Wide World Photos)*

From May until July the committees heard secondary figures explain how
North had solicited money for the contras from wealthy Texas widows,
rightwing brewers, the Sultan of Brunei, and the governments of Taiwan and
Saudi Arabia. By July a picture of North had emerged as a driven, ambitious
young man who, one colleague described, "came into the NSC as an easel
carrier and ended up the world's most powerful lieutenant colonel."

Media excitement boiled over as North himself began four days of televised testimony on July 7. North revealed that he held a "shredding party,"
destroying the written record of his activities as Justice Department officials
entered his office in November. He explained, "I thought I had received authority from the president," even though he never heard from Reagan directly. He explained that CIA Director Casey and he arranged for him to be
the "fall guy" should the scheme be revealed. "I was supposed to be dropped
like a hot rock," he said, but "I wasn't willing to become the victim of a criminal prosecution." That was why, he explained, he was now implicating his
superiors in the plan to divert money from the arms sales to the contras.
Two weeks later, John Poindexter told the committee, "the buck stops with
me," when lawmakers pressed him to explain if Reagan had been involved
in the diversion. Poindexter also revealed that he "tore up" a presidential

finding on the arms sales. Frustrated committee members knew that with the record destroyed they never would learn for certain about Reagan's role.

North's testimony temporarily altered public opinion about the diversion to the contras and the colonel himself. He offered a more spirited defense of the Nicaragua rebels than Reagan had, and opinion polls briefly showed that a majority of the public now backed aiding them. That majority melted within a month.

Just as short-lived was the "Ollie mania" which swept the country after he testified. *U.S. News and World Report* explained that his blue eyes and boyish grin "erased the impression that he was a man with Walter Mitty's grip on reality." One Minnesota woman remarked, "He turned my whole mind around. He's fabulous." Bumper stickers reading "THANK YOU, OLLIE" popped up. Congress was deluged with letters and telegrams running twenty to one in favor of North. Friends raised hundreds of thousands of dollars which they promised to his legal defense fund.

Passions quickly faded. Much about North encouraged manipulators and confidence operators. The telegram wave had been orchestrated by local Republican parties and abetted by Western Union, which profited from the business. Over 75 percent of the money raised for his defense remained with the fund-raisers and never reached his legal team. In March 1988 a special prosecutor indicted North, Poindexter, and two of the arms dealers for violating the ban on aiding the contras, defrauding the government, and obstruction of justice. Now needing millions, North resigned from the Marine Corps and toured the country, speaking on behalf of conservative politicians and raising money for his own defense. His supporters urged President Reagan to issue a preemptive pardon before North went to trial.

While the public sobered up about North, his testimony deflated the congressional effort to attach responsibility for Iran-contra to the president. Reagan declined to damage his own standing with the public by pardoning his subordinates for their role in the Iran-contra affair. North, Poindexter, and several lesser arms dealers and go-betweens were tried and convicted of perjury and the misuse of government funds. A federal appeals court later overturned the convictions of North and Poindexter on the ground that they had been promised immunity from prosecution in return for their testimony before the congressional committee investigating Iran-contra. In 1992 the special prosecutor handling the case brought charges of perjury against former Secretary of Defense Caspar Weinberger. Although Weinberger had opposed the sale of weapons to Iran, he had denied to Congress that he had kept notes of his activities during crucial meetings in early 1985. Discovery of Weinberger's handwritten diary led the prosecutor to bring the indictment.

FOREIGN POLICY IN THE ELECTION OF 1988

When candidates addressed foreign affairs during the election campaign of 1988, they concentrated on the past. Like nearly all of their fellow citizens, the men seeking the Democratic and Republican presidential nominations could not anticipate the earthquake about to topple the Communist world. Instead of preparing for the end of the Cold War, both the winner of the November election, Republic vice-president George Bush, and the loser, Massachusetts' Democratic governor Michael Dukakis, remained frozen in a traditional debate over how to confront the Soviets and project American military power around the world. The credentials and experience each man might bringing to the job counted for more than specific proposals each made for the future direction of American foreign relations. The vice-president presented an impressive résumé in foreign affairs—ambassador to the United Nations, representative to the Peoples' Republic of China, and director of Central Intelligence in the Nixon and Ford administrations. Dukakis, on the other hand, had little overseas experience, having devoted himself to public service and politics in Massachusetts after returning from two years of duty as an army private in 1954.

The discussion of foreign affairs in the 1988 election became a referendum on the Reagan administration's accomplishments and failures. Dukakis tried to use Bush's service in the Reagan administration against him by tying the vice-president to the Iran-Contra scandal. The governor noted that the vice-president claimed to regard Oliver North as a "national hero" and had invited him to his 1987 Christmas party. But the issue faded as Reagan refused to offer preemptive pardons to North and Poindexter. Furthermore, Bush refused to answer specific questions about his participation in the arms-for-hostage swap, other than to affirm that he had been "out of the loop" when top Reagan officials contemplated supplying weapons to Iran.

Bush had more success than Dukakis in deriding his opponent's foreign affairs positions. Bush pointed to the genuine warmth developed between Reagan and Gorbachev to demonstrate that the military buildup of the Reagan administration had not let to war, as some critics had predicted. Bush assailed Dukakis for advocating deep cuts in overall defense spending and a halt to the development of the Strategic Defense Initiative.

Dukakis had little success raising other foreign policy disappointments of the Reagan years. Dukakis concentrated his criticism on the failed effort by the Reagan administration to evict General Manuel Noriega from power in Panama. A federal grand jury in South Florida indicted Noriega in February 1988 for running cocaine into the United States. Soon after his indictment, news leaked that the Panamanian strongman had been on the

CIA's payroll for over a decade. Dukakis raised the specter that Bush, director of Central Intelligence in 1976, had overlooked Noriega's unsavory behavior. Noriega's ability to stay in power despite Washington's economic pressure allowed Dukakis to cast doubt on the foreign affairs competence of the Reagan-Bush administration. Dukakis promised that his administration would not "do business with a drug running Central American dictator." Dukakis's charges did not strike a deep chord with the general public, but they did irritate Bush. What to do about Noriega became an immediate problem for the new Bush administration.

Dukakis's intermittent discussion of foreign affairs had little effect on the outcome of the election, which Bush won comfortably. In the end, voters appreciated Reagan's accomplishments with the Soviets and felt comfortable with the continuity promised by Bush.

THE REAGAN RECORD

The foreign policy record of the Reagan administration was one of the most surprising of the twentieth century. The president and his principal advisers came to office with a narrowly ideological view of the world. Harshly antagonistic toward Soviet-style communism, they appeared to consider compromise with Moscow as a sign of weakness or folly in their predecessors. Yet the Reagan administration proved to be exceptionally skillful in its negotiations with the Soviets after the advent of Mikhail Gorbachev. Throughout his presidency Reagan held a series of simple ideas about foreign policy. He believed in strength—especially of the military sort—the moral virtues of the United States, and the evils of communism. His critics derided him for the lack of sophistication of these opinions. Indeed, in Reagan's first term, such ideas threatened to bring the nuclear superpowers to the brink of war. By 1987, however, Reagan had adapted to the new face of the Soviet Union. Despite his intellectual limitations, Reagan exercised real political leadership in his dealings with the Russians.

It was to Reagan's credit that he understood the changes in Soviet policy undertaken by Mikhail Gorbachev, and he thereupon dropped his hostile anti-Soviet rhetoric, allowing the Cold War to end. Yet more of the credit for ending the Cold War probably goes to Gorbachev than to any other single individual. Gorbachev acknowledged the deep structural flaws in the Soviet system, and he believed that only an end to the Cold War would allow his country to survive into the twenty-first century. He was only half right, as events were to prove that the Soviet Union was doomed. Reagan and supporters of his hostile policies argue that the American toughness eventually convinced Gorbachev to change. The reality is somewhat different. As Raymond Garthoff, the foremost analyst of the end of the Cold War, writes, "the crusading spirit evidenced by American leaders and their indictment of the Soviet system were largely irrelevant to the outcome." Indeed, the adversarial attacks coming from Washington before 1988 probably "made it harder for Gorbachev to liberalize Soviet internal and international behavior because the powerful domestic conservative forces with which he was in constant struggle objected that he was giving in to American pressures, sacrificing Soviet interests and kowtowing to the West."

American diplomacy descended into illegality during the Iran-contra scandal; the disregard for congressional constraints on the executive intensified the already high level of public distrust of government officials. By reversing the Carter administration's emphasis on the protection of human rights, already weakened in 1980, the Reagan administration diminished affection for the United States abroad. The United States was often too quick to use force in the 1980s, and the military buildup of the Reagan years contributed to a crushing burden of debt. Nevertheless, the ability of Ronald Reagan to seize the moment contributed to lifting the fear of nuclear annihilation that had made the Cold War a nightmare.

CHAPTER FIFTEEN

Toward the Twenty-First Century, 1989–1996

Soviet-style communism collapsed with breathtaking speed from 1989 to 1991. On November 9, 1989, the Berlin Wall tumbled down. Less than a year later, Germany was reunited as a capitalist, democratic country. Revolutions swept away Communist governments across Eastern Europe in 1989 and 1990. Most spectacularly of all, the Soviet Union ceased to exist by the end of 1991. On December 25, Mikhail Gorbachev, who three months earlier had stepped down as the final general secretary of the Communist party, resigned as president of the Soviet Union. Seven days later, the red banner of the Bolshevik revolution of 1917, bearing the hammer and sickle of the international workers' movement, came down for the last time from a flagpole over the Kremlin, to be replaced by the old red, white, and blue flag of the Czars, adopted as the emblem of the new Russian Republic. President George Bush characterized the end of the Soviet system as "one of the most important developments of this century—the revolutionary transformation of a totalitarian dictatorship and the liberation of its people from its smothering embrace."

For a brief period from 1989 to 1991, Bush, high officials in his administration, and numerous articulate observers of international affairs spoke with confidence about how the death of communism in Europe portended a "new world order." While the contours of that order never came sharply into focus, its advocates anticipated an arrangement of world politics similar to the one envisaged by Franklin D. Roosevelt near the end of the Second World War. The United States, enjoying unquestioned military superiority, would work with partners directly and within the United Nations to diminish international conflict and eliminate aggression.

Reality confounded the image of international cooperation and harmony promised by American advocates of a new world order. In 1990 and 1991, the Bush administration successfully organized a vast and unprecedented multinational military coalition under United Nations auspices to compel Iraq's armed forces to evacuate the oil-rich emirate of Kuwait. But in the aftermath of the six-week Persian Gulf War in the beginning of 1991, the Bush administration could not deliver the international stability many people hoped would follow the Cold War. In 1992, Bush dropped references to American sponsorship of a new world order. He expected that the respect he had earned for his stewardship of foreign policy would result in an easy victory in his 1992 reelection bid. Instead, many Americans turned inward, believing that the need to overcome a sharp economic slump required their attention. Now that the threat of nuclear war no longer hung over their heads, Americans focused on unmet domestic needs. Bush's emphasis on foreign affairs became a disadvantage with a public that perceived him as out of touch with the daily concerns of ordinary people. Bill Clinton, the successful Democratic candidate in 1992, won the White House by empathizing with the problems of the middle class. As soon as he was elected, he promised to "focus on the economy like a laser. Foreign policy in large measure will come into play as it affects the economy."

Like many of his predecessors, however, Clinton found that foreign affairs took on increasing prominence during his first term. The Democratic administration pressed trade expansion to sharpen the country's competitive edge in a global economy. In 1993, the Senate, at Clinton's urging, ratified the North American Free Trade Agreement (NAFTA) negotiated during the Bush administration, promising to end trade barriers between Canada, the United States and Mexico over a twenty-year period. The Clinton administration aggressively promoted better commercial ties with the booming economies of East and Southeast Asia. From 1993 to 1996, the United States continued work on numerous problems left unresolved at the end of the Cold War—mediating between Israelis, Palestinians, and other Arabs; promoting democracy in the states of the former Soviet Union and Eastern Europe; trying to dampen ethnic tensions in the Balkans; restoring democracy to Haiti; and providing humanitarian assistance to Africa. Some of these initiatives succeeded, some failed, and others achieved mixed results. At century's end, American foreign policy no longer displayed the clarity of purpose it had shown at the height of the Cold War. Yet the very ambiguities of America's attempts in the 1990s to come to grips with the emerging post–Cold War world reflected the reality of that world.

THE BUSH FOREIGN AFFAIRS TEAM

Bush dropped subtle hints during the 1988 presidential election campaign that he would approach his duties more energetically than had Ronald Reagan, his often disengaged predecessor. In international affairs, Bush indicated that his foreign policy experience in the Nixon and Ford administrations—as well as the numerous diplomatic assignments he had undertaken for the Reagan administration—had prepared him perfectly to take personal charge of the nation's foreign policy. Bush had acquired a wide circle of political friends around the world before assuming the presidency; as president, he boasted of the numerous daily overseas telephone conversations he had with world leaders in times of international crisis.

Bush signaled his personal control over foreign affairs with his first appointment. He nominated his closest political friend and adviser, James A. Baker III, as secretary of state. Baker had served as Reagan's first chief of staff from 1981 to 1985 and then became secretary of the treasury at the beginning of the second Reagan term in 1985. At the Treasury Department, Baker's greatest international experience came when he supervised U.S. participation in the annual meetings of the leaders of the Group of Seven non-Communist industrial powers. The new president went back to his associates in the Ford administration with his choice for national security adviser. He returned retired air force general Brent Scowcroft to the position he had held from 1975 to 1977, the period during which Bush had been director of Central Intelligence.

After the Senate rejected Bush's first nominee to be secretary of defense, the president turned to another old friend from the Ford administration, Wyoming congressman Richard Cheney, Ford's chief of staff from 1975 to 1977. To round out his set of senior foreign policy advisers, Bush elevated General Colin Powell, Reagan's last national security adviser, to become the first African-American chairman of the Joint Chiefs of Staff.

Baker, Scowcroft, Cheney, and to a lesser extent Powell formed an unusually tight team, and they worked well with the president. Their partnership ended the frustrating bickering among the president's top foreign policy aides that had bedeviled the Reagan administration. While united and mostly comfortable with one another, Bush's foreign policy team held a narrow vision of U.S. interests. Scowcroft saw his role as a manager of options for the president rather than an initiator of grand strategy. This approach perfectly suited Bush, who continuously stressed his "obligation to temper optimism with prudence" in foreign affairs in his first year in office. All veterans of the Cold War, the Bush foreign policy team focused on state-to-state relations, felt uncomfortable stressing the advancement of human rights, and slowly realized that confrontation with the Soviet Union had ended. Bush's own experience as representative to the Peoples' Republic of China, combined with his subordinates' recollection of the partnership between Washington and Beijing forged in the 1970s, led the administration to express constant sympathy for China and its aging leaders.

By the end of 1989, Bush and his principal foreign policy advisers acknowledged the extraordinary changes in the Communist world and tried to fashion the future. By 1990, the president became more expansive as he projected hopes for a new world order. Under this vague system, the states of Western Europe, Japan, and the former Communist nations of Eastern Europe and the collapsing Soviet Union would work with the United States, directly and through the United Nations, to harmonize international relations. For a while this hope seemed justified as Bush achieved his greatest triumph—leading a United Nations–sponsored coalition against Iraq. In the eighteen months after the Iraq war, however, hopes for the new world order faded quickly. Bush retired the phrase, which then was used only derisively by his critics.

THE END OF COMMUNISM

The Bush administration moved with painstaking caution in its first year toward a new relationship with the Communist states, and Bush's initial moves scarcely foretold the earthquake in the Communist world in the summer of 1989. The Soviet Union's economy had stagnated for four years despite, and partially because of, Gorbachev's economic reforms. The Soviet leader recognized the enormous burden imposed by maintaining armed forces outside the borders of the Soviet Union. In July, Gorbachev informed the annual meeting of the leaders of the Warsaw pact that Moscow no longer wanted to control their political or social systems. Within eighteen months, all of the Communist states of Eastern Europe had adopted capitalism, free markets, multi-party electoral systems, and anticommunism.

Popular revolutions overturned all the Communist governments of Eastern Europe. The Communist regime of East Germany collapsed, and quickly thereafter the German Democratic Republic disappeared as a separate nation. The fall of the Berlin Wall seemed to recapitulate the emigration crisis from East Germany that had preceded the Wall's construction in the summer of 1961. Hundreds of thousands of East Germans fled their country to the West in the summer of 1989. Thousands of Germans who remained behind in the East went to the streets in massive demonstrations against their own government in the autumn. The East German Communist authorities considered using police or troops against their own people, but Gorbachev discouraged them. Instead of resisting, the Communists ordered the Wall opened on November 9, allowing anyone who wanted to leave to do so. Wrecking balls began dismantling the remainder of the Wall during the winter. On October 2, 1990, the German Democratic Republic ceased to exist and its constituent states became part of the German Federal Republic. Hel-

mut Kohl, chancellor of West Germany, became leader of the unified country.

Similar revolutions—mostly peaceful, but occasionally bloody—occurred in all the Communist nations of Eastern Europe. Everywhere governments came to power promising the end of communism, the creation of free market economies, and, eventually, the prosperity that existed in the West. The new regimes retained popular support for about a year, but their citizens became restless. Prosperity did not come quickly, but social and ethnic tensions did. Unemployment and high prices dampened enthusiasm for market reforms in many places, especially in Albania, Bulgaria, Poland, and Rumania. The Slovaks resented the Czechs, and they forced the dissolution of Czechoslovakia into separate Slovak and Czech republics.

The worst repercussions of the fall of communism occurred in Yugoslavia. The Yugoslav federation disintegrated into at least four separate republics. In the aftermath, a brutal civil war erupted in which the most gruesome atrocities against civilians to have occurred in Europe since 1945 took place. Anywhere from 3,000 to 20,000 mostly Moslem residents of Bosnia and Herzegovina lost their lives to Serbian militiamen after May 1992. The United States offered a low profile toward the conflict, preferring that the European powers take the lead in offering a solution.

The 1989–1990 ferment in Eastern Europe spread eastward into the Soviet Union. The Baltic states of Lithuania, Latvia, and Estonia, annexed by Stalin in 1940, declared independence in 1990. Moscow refused to recognize their independence. In January, Soviet troops fired on peaceful demonstrators in Vilnius, the capital of Lithuania, killing fourteen. The Bush administration issued only mild protests, not wishing to discourage Gorbachev from supporting the UN-led military coalition against Iraq. Reformers in the Soviet Union lost faith in Gorbachev, as he proved powerless to stop the drift toward repression. His economic reform programs also seemed incapable of reversing the collapse of industrial production within the Soviet Union. Russia elected a parliament with a non-Communist majority in 1990. In 1991, Boris Yeltsin won election as the president of the Russian Federation, an office of undefined powers which he quickly expanded into the principal center of opposition to Gorbachev.

The U.S. government seemed disinclined to become directly involved in the drama unfolding behind what used to be called the Iron Curtain. Bush considered it only prudent not to appear openly to gloat over the collapse of communism. Bush and Gorbachev held their first summit in Malta in December 1989. Meetings between them then became routine, and over they next nineteen months Bush and Gorbachev held six high-level summits. One of their most significant meetings took place in Paris in November 1990. There, the two leaders joined representatives of thirty-two other European and North American states at the Conference on Security and Cooperation in Europe and officially proclaimed the end of the Cold War.

In the summer of 1991, Gorbachev undertook to erase the vestiges of his country's domination of Eastern Europe. He did so in the plaintive hopes of garnering Western economic assistance for his nation's collapsing economy. In June, the Soviet Union and its former allies in Eastern Europe disbanded the Warsaw Pact, the anti-NATO alliance of Eastern bloc countries, and COMECON, the Eastern bloc's response to the European Economic Community. The next month, Bush traveled to Moscow to sign a Strategic Arms Reduction Treaty, a far-reaching arms control pact that promised to reduce each side's nuclear missiles by one third. Gorbachev's preoccupation had shifted from the dangers posed by East-West military confrontation to the dire straits of the Soviet economy.

Probably there was nothing the West could have done to keep Gorbachev in power, because he remained a committed Communist when communism had long since died among most citizens of the Soviet republics. His tenuous grip on power loosened further when opponents in the military, the Communist party, and the secret police tried to depose him in a coup d'e-tat on August 19. The plot failed within three days, after Yeltsin led scores of thousands of Moscovites into the streets in protest.

The coup hastened the death of the Soviet empire and transformed East-West relations. During the height of the coup crisis, Bush telephoned Yeltsin to offer his unqualified support for the democratic forces. On August 21, the plotters surrendered. Gorbachev returned to Moscow, but he seemed confused and unaware that the Communist party he had headed since 1985 had been thoroughly discredited. A Moscow newspaper asked "Does Gorbachev understand that he has returned to a different country?" Shortly after the coup, Gorbachev and Yeltsin appeared together on the ABC television program *Nightline*. The former defended some aspects of seventy years of Communist rule, but Yeltsin rejected it all, saying "I wish this experiment had been tried in some other country." A triumphant Yeltsin now held unchallenged power, and he moved quickly to shred the remnants of communism. He outlawed the Communist party, closed its newspapers, and seized its property. Throughout the country, crowds tore down statues of Communist heroes and restored the pre-revolutionary names to street, squares, and cities. In the fall, Leningrad became St. Petersburg once more. On December 25, Gorbachev resigned as the last president of the Soviet Union, and a week later that country ceased to exist. Yeltsin remained president of Russia, the most powerful of the successor nations.

The collapse of communism in Europe and the Soviet Union did not extend eastward to China, the largest Communist country. In the spring of 1989, Chinese university students, influenced by Western ideas, staged a series of demonstrations calling for democracy, economic reform, and the resignation of China's aging leaders. In Beijing, thousands of students occupied Tiananmen Square in front of the Forbidden City and the tomb of revolutionary leader Mao Zedong for six weeks. They constructed a giant statue, the "Goddess of Democracy," modeled roughly after New York's Statue of Liberty. They demanded freedom of expression, the opening up of the Communist system to competing political parties, and better positions for graduates of China's universities and technical academies. Many students went on hunger strikes to force the government's hand, and the prime minister held a dramatic meeting with a few of the strikers. Hundreds of U.S. television reporters followed every move in Tiananmen Square, and the Cable News Network (CNN) broadcast continuously from China. Naturally, most Americans felt flattered that their cherished national symbols had been

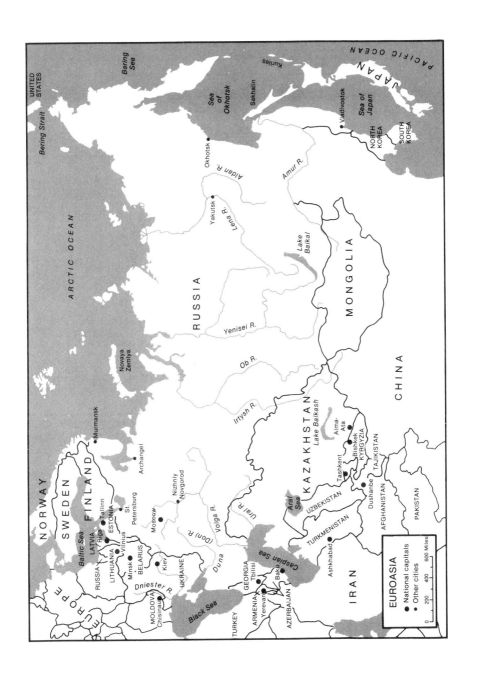

adopted by such attractive, earnest young students. Yet China's government considered the international attention given to the demands for greater freedom a serious threat. Deng Xiaoping, China's leader since the late 1970s, ordered the army to crush the demonstrations on June 3. Television pictures of tanks bearing down on unarmed demonstrators shocked viewers throughout the world.

Yet the Bush administration expressed only the mildest objections toward the suppression of the pro-democracy movement. Bush himself believed that his experience as representative to Beijing in 1974–1975 provided him with great insight into the mentality of Deng Xiaoping and his associates. "The Chinese army loves the Chinese people," Bush said the week before the tanks rolled against the students. The administration resisted congressional efforts to punish China after the suppression of the democracy movement. For the remainder of his term, Bush steadfastly refused to drop China from the list of countries entitled to receive most-favored-nation status for their exports to the United States.

THE UNITED STATES AND DISORDER IN THE THIRD WORLD

The end of the Cold War highlighted the disorders of non-industrial nations. At the beginning of its term, the Bush administration attempted to reformulate policy toward the Western Hemisphere to follow a pragmatic rather than ideological course. It minimized the zealous anticommunism characteristic of the Reagan administration's approach to the conflicts in Central America. The nations of that region themselves moved toward reducing their civil and international wars. The presidents of the Central American republics agreed in February 1989 to a framework ending the civil war in Nicaragua. The leftist Sandinista government agreed to hold free elections no later than February 25, 1990. The guerrilla war in El Salvador also wound down in 1989.

Nicaragua slipped from North American consciousness until the beginning of 1990, when the election campaign in that country attracted attention. An anti-Sandinista coalition rallied behind Violeta Barrios de Chamorro's candidacy for the presidency. On February 25, 1990, Chamorro, the widow of a political martyr of the hated Somoza era, defeated Daniel Ortega by a margin of 13 percent of the vote. Official Washington expressed jubilation at the end of Sandinista rule, but the new Chamorro government soon dashed the hopes of both the U.S. administration and many Nicaraguans who had elected it. Chamorro offended the United States by not purging the country's armed forces of Sandinistas. At the same time, the Nicaraguan economy did not revive. Chamorro completed her term in 1996.

In October of that year, Nicaraguans went to the polls again, and once more they rejected Daniel Ortega. Instead, they chose Arnoldo Aleman, leader of the rightist Liberal Alliance, who had supported the contras during the civil war, as their new president.

In 1989, one academic expert concluded that Latin America "has become synonymous with drugs, illegal immigration, death squads, guerrillas, capital flight and that nefarious term "U.S. intervention.' " U.S. relations with Panama confirmed this bleak assessment. The question of Panama had bedeviled Republicans during the election campaign of 1988, and the new president intervened in that country to end the embarrassment. U.S. relations with Panama had remained unsettled since the 1978 ratification of treaties in which the United States had agreed to return control of the canal and canal zone to Panama. Panamanian strongman Omar Torrijos had died in a plane crash in 1981. The Reagan administration quickly established friendly relations with his successor, General Manuel Noriega. Noriega had a long-standing relationship as an informant for the Central Intelligence Agency. After consolidating his power in 1983, he continued to make himself available to the CIA while simultaneously making himself useful to a bewildering array of completing movements and individuals—a Colombian drug cartel, Fidel Castro, and Nicaragua's contra rebels. His involvement in the drug trade became an open secret by 1988, and a federal grand jury in Florida indicted him for the transport of cocaine into the United States.

Regardless of what Bush may have done to encourage Noriega during his time as director of Central Intelligence, as president Bush considered the Panamanian dictator an adversary. Noriega's rule became more authoritarian and abusive in 1989, and the United States threatened economic sanctions. Noriega responded with a call for national elections in May, expecting that his loyal national guardsmen would stuff ballot boxes with fraudulent votes for Noriega's handpicked presidential candidate. To his astonishment, a huge majority of Panamanians cast ballots for opposition candidate Guillermo Endara. Public demonstrations erupted to force Noriega to honor the result of the vote, but he voided the election. He also encouraged mobs known as "Dignity Battalions" to beat up protesters, among them the winning presidential and vice-presidential candidates. At that point, opposition politicians called on the United States to do what it could to stop Noriega.

In December, Bush and his military advisers responded. Certain that an invasion of Panama would be cheap, easy, and widely popular among Panamanians, Bush ordered an attack on Panama to protect the lives of U.S. soldiers in the canal zone and arrest Noriega. At 1 A.M. on December 20, American paratroopers began dropping into Panama City, beginning a seventy-two-hour conquest of the country, code named Operation Just Cause. Fifty-five Panamanian National Guard troops and twenty-three United States soldiers lost their lives in the fighting. Civilian casualties were higher, with approximately 500 bystanders killed by crossfire. Noriega fled his military headquarters, but soon took refuge in the Vatican embassy. United States forces surrounded his sanctuary and blasted rock music, which Noriega was known to hate, twenty-four hours a day. Unable to sleep and terrified that capture by angry Panamanians could mean death, Noriega gave up to the U.S. Army on January 3, 1990. The new Panamanian government quickly agreed to extradite him to Miami for trial on drug charges. Noriega was convicted of conspiracy to transport cocaine into the United States in April 1992.

The Bush administration seemed most successful in improving relations between the United States and Mexico. The U.S. president formed a close personal friendship with Mexico's president, Carlos Salinas de Gortari, who, like Bush, was elected in 1988. Salinas, a youthful, Harvard-educated economist, won a narrow and tainted victory, but he quickly promised political and economic reform. He deregulated and privatized much of Mexico's state-run industry. The United States tried to help Salinas, in the hopes that a politically stable and prosperous Mexico would reduce the impulse for hundreds of thousands of desperately poor Mexicans to cross the northern border into the United States looking for work. In 1990, Bush won approval from Congress to hasten negotiations with Mexico and Canada on the North American Free Trade Agreement (NAFTA). Bush signed the treaty in October 1992, and the Clinton administration obtained senatorial ratification one year later. Most economists predicted that NAFTA would eventually encourage economic development throughout the hemisphere. The Clinton administration proposed to expand NAFTA to include the major economies of South America as well.

But before the bounty of free trade could be harvested, Mexico sank into a political crisis and a deep economic recession. On January 1, 1994, the day NAFTA went into effect, civil war erupted in the poorest area of Mexico. Guerrilla fighters calling themselves the Zapatista Liberation Front, named in honor of the revolutionary hero Emiliano Zapata, attacked government forces in the impoverished, mostly Indian southern state of Chiapas. Over the next three years, the Mexican government alternately counterattacked and negotiated with the guerrillas. By 1996, an uneasy truce held.

Moreover, the political reforms promised by President Salinas never came, and corruption and bribery remained rampant throughout the Mexican political system. Salinas' elder brother Raul became deeply involved in some of the seamiest activities of Mexico's drug lords. He amassed over $100 million in bribes and kickbacks and evidence strongly suggested that he had arranged the murder of rivals. A series of political assassinations rocked Mexico. The most dramatic murder occurred in March 1994 when Donaldo Colosio, Salinas's hand-picked successor as the presidential candidate of the Institutional Revolutionary Party (PRI), was gunned down in Tijuana. Evidence pointed to the involvement of officials of the ruling PRI in Colosio's murder.

The PRI then turned to Ernesto Zedillo, another Ivy League–educated economist, as its candidate. He won handily in August 1994. Zedillo was personally honest but shy, lacked charisma, and was afflicted with terrible luck. He had the unhappy duty to try to repair the damage left from the corruption of the Salinas years. Almost immediately after he assumed office in December 1993, just weeks after the U.S. ratification of NAFTA, Zedillo was forced to devalue the peso by 50 percent against the dollar. Mexico plunged into a depression, with unemployment doubling in the first six months of 1994. Many Mexicans blamed former president Salinas and his family for their country's misfortunes. Salinas went into self-imposed exile and his brother went to jail. Immigration across the U.S. border surged. After two years of political intrigue and economic depression, the economy began to grow once more in 1996. By then, the optimism of the early days of NAFTA seemed to have been wildly overblown. The U.S. ambassador to Mexico likened Mexico in the 1990s to the United States during the Great Depression of the 1930s. "Opportunities have got to become real" for the poorest Mexicans, he warned. "Otherwise these people are going to lose faith in free markets and democratic freedoms." The *Economist* of London, one of the staunchest advocates of free trade, privatization, and free markets, noted a backlash against all such forms of economic liberalization in Latin America. "Almost everywhere" in the Spanish- and Portuguese-speaking Western Hemisphere, the newspaper noted, "both rich and poor feel less secure, as drugs, guns and violent crime take an ever-stronger hold on the shanty towns that ring so many cities."

About a year after the invasion of Panama, a few poor residents of that country who had welcomed the arrival of the Americans as saviors now cursed them and shouted their support for Saddam Hussein, the dictator of Iraq, Washington's latest nemesis. For over half a year, from August 1990 to April 1991, Americans became obsessed with events in Iraq, Kuwait, and the Persian Gulf. On August 2, 1990, Iraq invaded and annexed its neighbor Kuwait, seizing that country's vast oil reserves and effectively cancelling payment on the billions of dollars of loans provided by Kuwait during Iraq's eight-year war with Iran. Within days of the invasion, President Bush began organizing an international coalition to roll back Iraq's conquest of Kuwait. Asserting that "this is naked aggression; it will not stand," Bush personally encouraged leaders of the members of the United Nations Security Council to resist Iraq. By November, the Council had imposed the tightest economic sanctions ever adopted against a country and passed twelve separate resolutions demanding an Iraqi withdrawal. Constantly working the telephones to foreign lead-

ers, Bush assembled a vast force of 700,000 troops from twenty-eight countries. This air, land, and sea coalition was stationed in Saudi Arabia and in
the ocean near Kuwait and Iraq.

Originally, Bush sent a contingent of 200,000 American troops to Saudi
Arabia, under the mission name "Operation Desert Shield," to defend that
country from a potential Iraqi attack. Two days after the November midterm
congressional election, Bush doubled the size of the United States expeditionary force to over 500,000, to provide what Defense Secretary Cheney
characterized as an "offensive capacity" to evict Iraq from Kuwait. The twelfth
UN Security Council resolution demanded that Iraq relinquish Kuwait by
January 15, 1991, or face the possibility of military attack.

Saddam Hussein never expected the angry reaction the annexation of
Kuwait provoked among other Arab states, the United States, the United Nations, and even the Soviet Union, Iraq's longtime military sponsor. He had
every reason to suspect that the non-Arab world would consider his quarrel
with the Emir of Kuwait to be a local dispute, to be resolved by the two countries with the assistance of the Arab League. Saddam Hussein found President Bush's fury especially difficult to understand or take seriously. Before
the invasion, the Reagan and Bush administrations had eagerly tried to improve relations with Saddam's regime. U.S. intelligence agencies had shared
information with their Iraqi counterparts during and after the Iraq–Iran war.
The Bush administration had resisted congressional efforts to restrict agricultural credits to Baghdad. It had also encouraged clandestine and illegal
bank loans to Iraq; Saddam's military used the money to purchase $2 billion
in sophisticated Western equipment for its flourishing nuclear, chemical,
and biological weapons programs. The State Department had also ordered
the U.S. ambassador to apologize personally to Saddam for Voice of America broadcasts critical of Iraq's dreadful record on human rights.

Americans became anxious as the UN's January 15, 1991, deadline for
Iraqi withdrawal approached. Opinion polls conducted in late December
and early January indicated that huge majorities of Americans opposed Iraq's
invasion of Kuwait, but only a much smaller majority supported the use of
American force. Bush, Defense Secretary Cheney, and Chairman of the Joint
Chiefs of Staff Powell decided in late December that the crisis would not be
resolved diplomatically. They believed war necessary, but Bush wanted congressional support before ordering an attack. Congress conducted a thoughtful debate over whether to authorize action immediately after January 15.
On January 12, Congress approved Bush's request and authorized the president to use force under UN auspices. Nearly all Republicans in the House
and Senate voted for the war resolution. Two thirds of House Democrats and
forty-five of fifty-six Democratic senators voted no. The Democrats voting yes,
however, provided the margin of approval in both houses.

On January 16, eighteen hours after the expiration of the UN's deadline, Operation Desert Shield became Operation Desert Storm. War began with a ferocious aerial bombardment of Iraq positions in Kuwait. U.S. planes made up the majority of attackers, but they were joined by bombers from Britain, Italy, France, and the exiled government of Kuwait. They inflicted terrible losses on Iraqi forces, military installations, and cities. Postwar estimates varied widely about the number of Iraqi casualties; they ranged from 25,000 to 250,000 deaths.

The sullen and fearful American mood lifted immediately with the beginning of the air war. The price of a barrel of oil fell from $38 to $18. Advances in satellite technology allowed Americans to see, as it happened, bombs drop on Baghdad and Patriot missiles, fired by U.S. Army crews, shoot down Iraqi Scud missiles aimed at targets in Israel and Saudi Arabia.

Bush's management of the coalition against Iraq won high praise from articulate observers and the general public. He constantly worked the telephone with dozens of foreign leaders. He kept such disparate Arab countries as Egypt, Morocco, the Gulf states, and Syria aligned against Iraq despite differences among themselves and the support for Saddam expressed by the Palestine Liberation Organization and Jordan. He discouraged Israel from retaliating militarily for the Scud attacks on its cities, since the involvement of Israel's air force would have driven most Arab states out of the coalition.

Five weeks of nonstop bombing devastated Iraq and destroyed the morale of its armed forces. In February, General H. Norman Schwarzkopf, the U.S. supreme commander of the allied forces, decided that his troops could mount a ground assault without fear of substantial resistance. On the night of February 23, hundreds of thousands of coalition ground troops attacked Kuwait and Eastern Iraq. Despite Saddam's boast that a ground war would become a fiery "mother of all battles" in which the Americans would suffer tens of thousands of deaths, Iraq's weakened forces put up virtually no fight. Scores of thousands of tired, cold, frightened, and defeated Iraqi soldiers surrendered to the advancing coalition troops. On February 27, exactly 100 hours after the ground war began, Bush announced the liberation of Kuwait and the end of the war. Iraq and Kuwait had suffered terrible death and destruction.

The United States and its president briefly appeared triumphant in victory. The 540,000-member American expeditionary force returned home quickly to huge and jubilant victory parades in the nation's major cities. The president's approval rating hit a stratospheric 89 percent in a Gallup poll conducted in March 1991. No president had been so popular since Harry Truman had reached a similarly lofty rating immediately after Japan surrendered in September 1945. Bush probably should have kept Truman's subsequent difficulties firmly in mind in the succeeding months, since the memory of victory over Iraq—and Bush's popularity—soon faded.

One enduring international conflict of interest to the United States— the dispute between Israel, its neighbors, and the Palestinians—did appear closer to resolution as a result of the Gulf War. Israel had found itself on the same side of the Iraq dispute with several of its longstanding Arab adversaries (Saudi Arabia, Kuwait, and Syria). At the same time, the Palestine Liberation Organization had angered many of its backers among the wealthy Arab states by ardently supporting Saddam Hussein during the war. Days after the war ended, Bush promised to "do all that we can to close the gap between Israel and the Arab states—and between Israelis and Palestinians." For the next four months Secretary of State Baker traveled constantly to the Middle East, Europe, and the Soviet Union to arrange an international conference on the Middle East. In the summer, Baker hammered out a delicate compromise under which the United States and the Soviet Union would jointly sponsor an international conference involving Israel, Syria, Lebanon, and a joint Jordanian–Palestinian delegation. The parties agreed to Israeli demands that the PLO not be directly represented and that the plenary sessions quickly break up into face-to-face bargaining sessions. Israel accepted Arab insistence that the talks proceed on the basis of UN resolutions 242 (passed after the 1967 war) and 338 (passed after the 1973 Mideast War), both of which envisaged a settlement on the basis of the exchange of territory for peace. The Middle East pace conference opened in Madrid on October 30, and the face-to-face negotiations commenced shortly afterward in Washington. Virtually no progress occurred until Israel's election on June 23. The frosty atmosphere improved remarkably with the return to power in July of Israel's Labor party, whose leader, Yitzhak Rabin, assumed the prime ministership he had left in 1977. Rabin's victory derived in part from American pressure. Bush's friendship with foreign leaders did not extent to Yitzhak Shamir, Rabin's intensely nationalist and hawkish predecessor as prime minister. Bush did not trust Shamir and the personality conflict between the two men became an issue in Israel's election campaign. The Bush administration also withheld U.S. government guarantees on $10 billion in private loans Israel had sought to help resettle hundreds of thousands of Jewish immigrants from what was by that time the former Soviet Union. Washington believed that Shamir's nationalist government wanted to use the money to continue to build Jewish settlements on the West Bank. Once Rabin became prime minister, he froze settlement activity on the West Bank and the Bush administration and Congress authorized the loan guarantees. The new Israeli government increased the pace of the bilateral talks with the Arab states and the Palestinians in hopes of fulfilling Rabin's campaign promise of reaching agreements within nine months of assuming office.

THE ELECTION OF 1992 AND THE FUTURE OF
AMERICAN FOREIGN POLICY

In mid-1991, most Americans, including nearly all potential Democratic presidential candidates, believed that the extraordinary popularity George Bush
had earned during the Persian Gulf War would make him an invincible candidate for reelection in 1992. One by one, prominent Democratic senators
and governors announced that they would not seek their party's presidential nomination, leaving what appeared to be a weak field of contenders.
Among them was Arkansas governor Bill Clinton, whose dogged determination and sharp focus on the nation's domestic economic woes won him
the Democratic nomination. Clinton and his advisers considered that the
end of the Cold War and Bush's apparent successes in foreign affairs would
work, surprisingly, to their advantage. The contrast between Bush's mastery
of international relations and his befuddlement over the nation's lingering
recession sapped public confidence in the president's leadership. By the fall
of 1991, half of the public who had given Bush an 89-percent approval rating in March had withdrawn their support. Anxious about their current economic prospects and fearful that the future would be worse for themselves
and their children, Americans throughout 1992 demanded that Bush deliver
the same energy and commitment to restoring domestic economic growth
that he had devoted to foreign affairs. Bush proved temperamentally and
politically incapable of becoming a successful domestic president. In the November election, voters rejected him in favor of Clinton. Bush won only 38
percent of the popular vote, the lowest proportion for a Republican candidate since 1936. Clinton, however, only received 43 percent. An exceptionally high portion of the electorate, 19 percent, cast their ballots for Ross
Perot, an extremely wealthy Texas businessman who promised a radical over-
haul of the country's government finances and an intensely nationalist foreign policy.

Despite Clinton's success during the election campaign at keeping the
focus on economic issues, foreign affairs questions arose intermittently. The
similarities and differences between Bush's performance and Clinton's
promises offered clues to U.S. foreign policy after January 20, 1993. Throughout the campaign, Bush harkened back to triumphs in the Cold War and in
the conflict with Iraq. The management of traditional diplomatic-military relations was his strength. He seemed incapable of successfully implementing
policies dealing with international trade, the global environment, or human
rights. Clinton, on the other hand, carefully crafted a foreign affairs strategy
to continue to project American military power abroad. At the same time,
he criticized Bush's record on human rights, accusing him of "coddling dictators from Baghdad to Beijing." He claimed that Bush had been slow to of-

fer aid to Russia after the fall of communism. The challenger also promised a much more forceful U.S. policy on international economic and environmental issues.

Foreign affairs faded into the background during the election campaign. Bush undermined some of the value he had put on foreign policy by insisting that his friend James Baker resign from the State Department to return to his old position as chief of staff at the White House. For the remainder of 1992, Acting Secretary of State Lawrence Eagleburger served as a caretaker. Clinton said little about international relations other than to voice approval for a strong national defense and repeat that restoration of economic growth would be his first priority. He left most of the criticism of Bush's diplomatic record to his vice-presidential candidate, Democratic senator Albert Gore of Tennessee. One of Bush's sharpest critics on the global environment, Gore assailed Bush on foreign affairs. "If they [Bush and Vice-President Dan Quayle] are such whizzes at foreign policy," Gore complained, why then did the United States support Saddam Hussein before the Gulf War and why was the Iraqi dictator still in power? Gore and other Democrats also criticized Bush for his support of the Reagan administration's decision to sell weapons to Iran in 1985. In the fall, Bush desperately sought to raise doubts about the Democrats' foreign affairs backgrounds, knowledge, and judgment. The president derided Clinton as a draft dodger during the Vietnam War. Most of the public considered Clinton's behavior twenty-three years earlier ancient history, as irrelevant to the future of American foreign policy than Bush's heroic service in World War II.

As election day neared, Bush seemed frantic. He began calling Gore "Ozone Man," and he seemed undignified when he shouted to a crowd of supporters that "my dog Millie knows more about foreign affairs than those two bozos." The public, however, thought Clinton and Gore knew enough. Bush, too, should have known that most people did not have foreign affairs uppermost in their minds. Clinton's moderate approach and his promise to maintain the broad outline of American foreign policy seemed sufficiently reassuring to mitigate doubts about his capacity to handle foreign affairs.

CLINTON'S FOREIGN POLICY AIMS AND LIEUTENANTS

Despite Bill Clinton's concentration on domestic affairs during his successful challenge to George Bush for the presidency in 1992, the Democratic candidate did offer a few clues about his plans for foreign policy. Clinton promised to work harder than Bush to expand American trade with the rest of the world. He would try to help the states of the former Soviet Union manage their transitions to capitalism and democracy in ways that minimized the danger of nuclear weapons. Like Bush, he would use the opportunities created by the end of the Persian Gulf War to find a permanent solution to the enduring Israeli–Palestinian/Arab conflict. But Clinton also criticized Reagan and Bush for ignoring violations of human rights abroad. He suggested that the United States would take a stand to alleviate suffering in Haiti and the former Yugoslavia, and would press China to relax its crackdown on advocates of democracy.

When Clinton took the oath of office on January 20, 1993, a Democrat had occupied the White House for only four of the previous twenty-four years. The ranks of prominent Democrats with foreign policy experience able to assume high positions had thinned, and Clinton had to scramble to assemble a foreign policy team. For secretary of state he selected Warren Christopher, a veteran of the Johnson and Carter administrations where he had served, respectively, as deputy attorney general and deputy secretary of state. Christopher, a respected Los Angeles lawyer, was reserved, thoughtful, and an accomplished mediator. In both his private practice and government service, he saw his role as solving problems as they arose, rather than fashioning grand designs. Christopher served as head of the committee that guided the transition from the Bush to the Clinton administration, and the new president admired his lawyerly skills. But the two men were of different generations and did not spend hours discussing public policy issues, the way Clinton did with people of his own age. One of the latter, Strobe Talbott, a writer for *Time* magazine who had become a close friend of Clinton's when the two were Rhodes scholars at Oxford University in 1969 and 1970, became deputy secretary of state. As his national security adviser, Clinton appointed Anthony Lake, a foreign service officer who had served on the National Security Council staff under Henry Kissinger before resigning in protest over the U.S. invasion of Cambodia in 1970. During the Carter administration, Lake had returned to direct the State Department's Policy Planning Staff.

The new administration faced formidable obstacles in putting its stamp on U.S. military policy after the Cold War. The end of the Cold War vastly altered the world military balance, since the U.S. now stood alone as a superpower. Before he could take full advantage of the new environment, Clinton had to overcome the suspicions of supporters of the military who resented his lack of military service during the Vietnam War. For secretary of defense, Clinton tapped Representative Les Aspin (D.-Wisc.), chairman of the House Committee on Armed Services. A man who had reflected deeply on the needs of the military in the post–Cold War era, Aspin seemed a good choice, but he his relationship with the top brass of the armed services quickly soured. Leading generals and admirals opposed his efforts to fashion a compromise on the heated issue of allowing gay servicemen and -women to serve.

Under the new policy, the armed services would stop inquiring into personnel's sexual orientation and they, in turn, would not openly state that they were gay. The compromise, characterized as "don't ask, don't tell," satisfied neither gay activists nor traditionalists opposed to gays serving in the military. The new secretary of defense undertook a detailed "bottom-up review" of the military needs of the United States in the post–Cold War world. The Defense Department concluded that in the absence of a threat from the Soviet Union, the United States should be prepared in the future to fight two regional wars simultaneously. Aspin's very ability to comprehend the complexity of world politics and military affairs, his rambling speech patterns, and his rumpled appearance also landed him in trouble with military leaders, who wanted crispness and an authoritative bearing in their civilian secretary. Aspin resigned after a year. From 1994 until 1996, William Perry, a former weapons analyst and strategic thinker from the Massachusetts Institute of Technology, served as secretary of defense. At the beginning of his second term, Clinton nominated former Republican Senator William Cohen from Maine as the new Secretary of Defense.

There was also turnover as Director of Central Intelligence. Clinton's first head of the CIA was Admiral James Woolsey, who also lasted barely a year. From 1994 until 1996 John Deutch, like Secretary of Defense Perry a former college professor who had studied the nation's weapons systems and the organization of its intelligence operations, led the CIA. Under both Woolsey and Deutch, the CIA struggled to find a role in the post–Cold War world. Despite the vast resources poured into analyzing data from the Soviet Union during the Cold War, the agency had shown a poor record at predicting the collapse of Communist regimes. The intelligence community seemed even less equipped to deal with the problems of the post–Cold War world: ethnic fighting, environmental degradation, and economic competition among the wealthy nations of the world. Many dedicated and honorable officials of the CIA were further demoralized when several agents were convicted of having sold some of the most sensitive secrets to the Soviet Union before its collapse and to Russia after 1992. Aldrich Ames, whose work for the Soviet Union was unearthed in 1994, had actually caused the death of several American agents inside the Soviet Union. Deutch strove to bolster the morale of CIA employees and comply with public demands for greater openness and accountability. He left government at the end of Clinton's first term, and the President appointed Deputy Director of Intelligence George Tenet to succeed him as Director. At the same time, the President promoted Deputy National Security Adviser Samuel Berger to replace Anthony Lake (who failed to receive Senate confirmation as director of Central Intelligence) as national security adviser.

The U.S. delegation to the United Nations and the Commerce Department assumed high profiles in Clinton's first term. Madeleine Albright, a foreign policy analyst who had worked for Senator Edmund Muskie in the 1970s and served on the Policy Planning Staff of the State Department during the Carter administration, became the U.S. representative to the United Nations. Born in 1937, she was the daughter of a Czech diplomat who had fled his homeland twice—once when the Nazis occupied Czechoslovakia in 1939 and again when the Communists seized power in 1948. Albright often spoke publicly of her family's experience with despotic regimes and believed that the United States should act as a beacon of hope to people resisting tyranny. She noted that the formative foreign policy experience for many people of her generation had been the Vietnam War, but for her it had been the 1938 Munich conference in which the major Western democracies had appeased Hitler. Yet she was no reflexive Cold Warrior; she understood how vastly the world had changed after the demise of the Soviet Union. Within the administration, she advocated the use of American military force to obtain multilateral foreign policy objectives. From the beginning, she encouraged the administration to make good on Clinton's 1992 campaign promise to intervene to stop the growing bloodshed in the former Yugoslavia. Clinton nominated her to be secretary of state at the beginning of his second term. In 1993, Clinton appointed Ronald Brown, former chairman of the Democratic National Committee and a prominent Washington lawyer, as his commerce secretary. Brown drew on his many connections in the worlds of finance, manufacturing, and commerce to travel the world promoting U.S. exports. On one of his trips to the former Yugoslavia in the spring of 1996, Brown died in a plane crash.

During its first four years, the Clinton administration sought to adjust American foreign policy to the complexities of the post–Cold War world. After a rough start, the president and his principal advisers recovered their balance by 1994. The United States pursued a foreign policy that mixed intervention to achieve humanitarian purposes, mediation of seemingly intractable disputes, management of relations with other powerful states, trade expansion, and the promotion of economic interdependence.

INTERVENTION AND MEDIATION

To the surprise of most people, the United States continued to send troops around the globe despite the end of the Cold War. The United States also used its status as the world's only remaining superpower to help mediate military disputes. With the passing of the Soviet Union and the rare election of a Democrat to the White House in 1992, the domestic constituencies supporting and opposing the deployment of U.S. forces abroad shifted. While there were exceptions to the rule, many Democrats or liberals who had resisted the use of U.S. troops since the Vietnam War now endorsed military engagement to promote humanitarian ends. On the other hand, many Republicans and conservatives who had backed the Reagan and Bush administrations when they had sent soldiers into combat opposed exposing American uniformed forces to harm abroad after the Cold War. Some of the disagreements were political, with Democrats wanting to stand by a president of their own party and Republicans looking for ways to embarrass an opposition leader, but the differences also reflected disputes over the proper role of the United States in world affairs. Long before the end of the Cold War, many liberals wanted the United States to stress humanitarian aims more and be less fixated on ending communism. The post–Cold War situation gave them the chance. Some conservatives, on the contrary, believed the military should only be used to meet what they characterized as real security threats. They continued to advocate large military budgets, but resisted using soldiers for any purposes other than fighting wars.

The Clinton administration followed the example of President Bush in his last weeks in office and deployed U.S. forces to Africa, for many years the continent of least importance for U.S. policy makers. The end of the superpower rivalry harmed many of the world's poorest countries, which found they could no longer play the United States and the Soviet Union off against one another to gain additional foreign aid. African countries were especially hard-hit. The East African country of Somalia, once a Soviet client, fell into chaos and famine in 1991. By the fall of 1992, grim pictures of hundreds of thousands of hopeless, starving refugees, forced to flee a growing civil war, were flashed to television screens around the world. International relief workers who went to Somalia to help feed the hungry quickly found themselves in danger as competing warlords stole the food international agencies hoped to distribute to the desperate victims of inter-ethnic conflict. Relief agencies predicted that nearly 500,000 would die within six months unless a way were found to get food to the starving. The heart-wrenching television reports produced an outcry and a demand for action among sympathetic ordinary people in the United States and Europe. In December 1992, four weeks after Clinton's victory over Bush but while Bush remained president, the United States dispatched a force of 28,000 marines and army troops to Somalia as part of a multinational UN-sponsored force to make certain that the food sent actually reached the mouths of the innocent people it was intended for.

The relief mission went well in early 1993, but the early successes led the U.S. to overreach. Warlords stopped stealing relief supplies, famine subsided, and some refugees returned to their villages to plant crops. By March, the U.S. began withdrawing its combat soldiers from Somalia, and more and more of the duty of preserving order on the streets of Mogadishu, Somalia's capital, was turned over to other nations whose troops were part of the UN force. Yet some 8,000 U.S. logistical soldiers remained. Meanwhile, the UN shifted its attention to a doomed effort to create an effective and responsible government for Somalia. Encouraged by the early success of providing relief, the United States urged the UN to try, in the words of Ambassador Albright, to restore "an entire country as a proud, functioning, and viable member of the community of nations." To that end, UN forces began to disarm the factions. Sadly, the various warlord factions now turned their fire on the UN peacekeepers. Fighting intensified over the summer, culminating in a disaster for the Americans in the fall. In October, seventeen American soldiers were killed in a firefight in Mogadishu, and one of the dead was stripped naked and dragged through the streets by jubilant Somali fighters. Just as Americans had been roused to actions by television pictures of the suffering Somalia in 1992, horrifying images of the desecration of the soldier's body made people demand withdrawal a year later. Chastened by the loss of American life in what had begun as a humanitarian mission, the Clinton administration ordered the withdrawal of U.S. forces by March 1994. The sad end to an effort of mercy also hastened the departure of Defense Secretary Aspin.

Somalia left a bitter aftertaste, as both the Clinton administration and the public became more cautious about using the military to promote humanitarian ends. After October 1993, the United States occasionally delayed sending help abroad, with the paradoxical result that ethnic tensions and civil strife were made worse than they would have been had the U.S. acted earlier.

Such was the case in the landlocked East African country of Rwanda in 1994. For years, two ethnic groups—the majority Hutu and the minority Tutsi, who comprised about 15 percent of Rwanda's population—had vied for control. In April 1994, an extremist Hutu government commenced a campaign of genocide against the minority Tutsi. For the next hundred days, Hutu militiamen slaughtered Tutsis and Hutus who stood in their way with machetes, clubs, rifles, and fragmentation grenades. In late April, the UN Security Council authorized a force of 5,500 peacekeepers, including a contingent of 2,000 U.S. soldiers, to go to Rwanda, but the U.S., averse to putting its soldiers in harm's way, delayed sending forces until July. By the time they reached Rwanda, 750,000 people lay dead, and rivers and lakes were choked with decaying bodies. Once more, television pictures relayed the extent of the catastrophe to the rest of the world. Tutsis had organized their own armed forces and ousted the Hutu-led government. The Tutsi victory led in turn to more widespread human suffering as approximately one million Hutus, fearing the wrath of the Tutsis, fled into neighboring Zaire. They remained there in miserable camps until the end of 1996, when hundreds of thousands returned within days to Rwanda. Again, TV showed pictures of waves of desperate people carrying their belongings on their backs, trudging home. The United States initially agreed to send soldiers to keep order during their repatriation, but once again the Clinton administration decided that Rwandans could sort out their own affairs.

Closer to home, in September 1994 the Clinton administration sent U.S. troops to restore democracy to the impoverished Caribbean island nation of Haiti, ruled by a violent and repressive dictatorship since 1991. In September of that year the armed forces, led by General Raoul Çedras, overthrew the democratically elected and reform-minded government of Jean Bertrand Aristide, who fled into exile in the United States. In the aftermath of the coup, tens of thousands of Aristide's fellow Haitians tried to join him by escaping in small wooden boats, crossing hundreds of miles of dangerous Caribbean waters, seeking asylum in the United States. The Bush administration, mindful of the hostility earlier boat people from Haiti had provoked in south Florida, characterized them as people seeking economic advantages, not refugees who realistically feared persecution if they returned home. In 1991 and 1992, Bush sent the Coast Guard and navy to intercept them and haul them back to Haiti.

During the election campaign of 1992, Clinton assailed Bush for allowing dictatorship to flourish in Haiti and abusing the rights of the Haitian boat people. The challenger suggested that were he to become president he would help Aristide regain his office and would let more Haitians into the United States. In 1993, however, Clinton continued to arrest Haitians and send them back, and the dictatorship remained in office. The United States tightened economic sanctions, but the hardship fell heaviest on the poor, who had supported Aristide. The Çedras government remained and its soldiers continued to beat and kill opponents. By 1994, many human rights advocates and African Americans complained that the Clinton administration's Haitian policy was no better than Bush's. Clinton responded by appointing a prominent African American, former Philadelphia congressman William Gray III, to oversee U.S. policy toward Haiti. In July, the U.S. sponsored a UN Security Council resolution authorizing the use of military force if necessary to evict Çedras and restore Aristide's legitimate government. Conservatives in the U.S., led by Senator Jesse Helms (R.-N.C.), opposed the use of force to replace Çedras with Aristide. Helms and other conservatives, joined by some Democratic lawmakers mindful of the bitter lessons of Somalia and protective of Congress' war-making powers, passed a Senate resolution in August declaring that the president could not use U.S. force to oust Çedras without prior congressional approval.

Nevertheless, in September the Pentagon went forward with plans to invade Haiti, oust Çedras and restore Aristide. Former president Jimmy Carter, a supporter of human rights but an opponent of U.S. military actions, asked

Clinton's permission for him to make a personal appeal to Cedras to leave office peacefully. Clinton reluctantly agreed, and a team made up of Carter, former chairman of the Joint Chiefs of Staff General Colin Powell, and Senator Sam Nunn (D.-Ga.) flew to Port-au-Prince on September 17. They spent two days negotiating with Çedras, alternately flattering him as a man of honor and praising his wife's slimness, grace, and beauty, and threatening him with the imminent arrival of an American invasion force. On the evening of September 19, as U.S. planes were in the air preparing to parachute troops into Haiti, Çedras agreed to relinquish power by October 15. The U.S. forces then landed to a tumultuous welcome. As agreed, Aristide returned to power the next month. U.S. forces remained for eighteen months to maintain order and supervise a new presidential election. In February 1996, Rene Preval, Aristide's handpicked successor, won an overwhelming victory. After a slow start, Clinton's Haitian policy had turned into a significant success. Haiti remained impoverished, but democratic rule was restored. Despite the anxieties generated by the killing in Somalia, the United States deployed troops, and no American soldiers lost their lives to hostile fire during the Haitian occupation.

In December 1995, the Clinton administration also deployed U.S. forces as part of a NATO peacekeeping force in Bosnia. Once more, the U.S. acted more slowly than might have been anticipated by someone listening to Clinton's pledges during the 1992 presidential campaign. At that time, the challenger had denounced Bush for standing idly by while genocide occurred in Bosnia-Herzegovina (often called simply Bosnia), one of the states that had emerged from the collapse of Communist Yugoslavia.

Three ethnic groups—the mostly Muslim Bosnians, the mostly Catholic Croats, and the mostly Orthodox Serbs—had contended for supremacy for nearly a thousand years. Each had significant outside backers. Muslims sympathized with their coreligionists, the Bosnians; Germany supported the Croats; and Serbs found succor among their fellow Slavs in Russia. In 1991 and 1992, Bosnians and Croats formed an uneasy coalition in a new government of Bosnia, but Serbs began fighting in order to join their part of Bosnia to Serbia, another successor to Yugoslavia. The Serbs were the better armed, having obtained most of the weapons of the former Yugoslavian army. In 1991, Serbs began a campaign of "ethnic cleansing," evicting non-Serbs— mostly Bosnians—from their homes in cities and farms in the countryside. Hundreds of thousands fled; tens of thousands died. Serbian troops surrounded Sarajevo, the capital of Bosnia, and their gunners rained down thousands of artillery shells on the once magnificent city. Such brutality based on ethnicity had not occurred in Europe since the days of the Holocaust against the Jews committed by Nazi Germany during the Second World War. In 1992, the world knew about the forced evictions, murders, and rapes from eyewitnesses and television pictures, but neither the European states nor the United States nor the UN wished to send soldiers to make peace. The Bush administration wanted to avoid offending the government of Russia, a traditional backer of the Serbs; considered the Balkans a European problem; and feared entering a Vietnam-style morass in Bosnia. Instead of calling for armed intervention, the Bush administration endorsed a UN-sponsored embargo on arms shipments to the warring factions. The embargo hurt the legitimate Muslim-led government more than it did the Serbs, since the latter had most of the tanks and artillery of the former Yugoslav army.

During the election campaign of 1992, Clinton offered an alternative policy of "lift and strike." Under this proposal, the United States would press the UN to lift the embargo, allowing the Bosnians to obtain weapons and level the military playing field, and the U.S. and its NATO allies would conduct air strikes to destroy the Serbs' heavy weapons and possibly attack neighboring Serbia to prevent it from supplying more weapons to the Serb armed forces operating in Bosnia. Once in office, however, the Clinton administration initially followed a policy very similar to that of its predecessor. Clinton, like Bush, feared that direct U.S. military involvement in Bosnia might be easier to start than to end. By late 1993, the president became more attuned to the ancient history of ethnic strife in the Balkans, and he wondered if the hatreds there ran too deep for any outside power to resolve. Moreover, no one could confidently predict what Russia's reaction might be to outside intervention.

Within the administration, only UN Ambassador Albright consistently recommended that the U.S. do more to stop the civil war in Bosnia. Outside the administration, human rights advocates urged greater involvement, as did Senator Robert Dole (R.-Kan.), the Republican leader preparing a bid for the presidency in 1996. In 1994, when he was minority leader, and in early 1995, when he led a newly elected Republican majority, Dole had advocated an end to the embargo to let the Bosnian Muslims defend themselves. The Clinton administration thought that an end to the embargo would only widen the war, but it believed that Dole's committed to the Bosnians would make it easier to obtain Republican support for deeper U.S. involvement in Bosnia.

New Serb atrocities, including the murder of several thousand men in a conquered Muslim town in mid-1995, goaded the United States and the other NATO countries to act. They finally ordered air strikes on the Serb guns that had continued to fire on Sarajevo in defiance of UN resolutions demanding a cease-fire and an end to the siege. Backed by NATO air power, the Muslims and Croats went on the offensive in late summer and fall of 1995, reconquering about one third of the territory lost to the Serbs. The Bosnian Serbs suffered the loss of backing from independent Serbia, itself reeling from the effects of an international economic embargo. Russia also decided that improved relations with the United States and Western Europe were more important to its future well-being than promoting romantic dreams of Slavic solidarity. In mid-1995, Russia endorsed international demands that the Serbs make peace with the Bosnians. By October, the Serbs felt isolated and in danger of losing the war they earlier had dominated. They reluctant accepted an American invitation to attend a conference of all the warring parties in the Bosnian conflict, to convene on November 1 at Wright-Patterson Air Force Base in Dayton, Ohio.

For three weeks, Richard Holbrooke, the U.S. diplomat Clinton had placed in charge of resolving the Bosnian conflict, mediated among Muslims, Croats, and Serbs. On November 21, the three parties reached an agreement that ended, at least temporarily, the civil war. Under the terms of the Dayton peace accord, Bosnia-Herzegovina would remain a unified state, consisting of two entities: The federation of Bosnia and Herzegovina (a Bosnian-Croat unit) would comprise 51 percent of the territory and a Serb Republic would make up 49 percent. Sarajevo would remain the single, unified capital of the country. A 60,000-member NATO peacekeeping force would come to Bosnia to take over peacekeeping duties from the United Nations. The U.S. would provide about half of the peacekeeping soldiers.

At first, the Dayton agreement produced little enthusiasm in the U.S. People who sympathized with the Bosnians as victims of Serb atrocities believed that Dayton rewarded aggression and divided the country along ethnic lines. Defenders countered that formal partition would have been even worse. In Congress, many Republicans criticized the Clinton administration for sending U.S. troops into danger without a clear strategy for taking them out. The president responded by saying that soldiers who went to Bosnia on December 20, 1995, would come home within a year. Moreover, Senate Majority Leader Dole endorsed the deployment. (Dole became the Republican presidential candidate in 1996, and his support of Dayton took the issue off the table during the 1996 election campaign.) Immediately after Clinton won another term in the White House, he announced that approximately 8,000 of the 30,000 U.S. troops would remain in Bosnia after the withdrawal deadline to continue to supervise the cease-fire.

The Clinton administration also harvested the fruit of years of U.S. mediation of the Israel–Palestinian/Arab dispute. In the summer of 1993 the Israeli government led by Labor Party prime minister Yitzhak Rabin opened secret talks with the Palestine Liberation Organization in a villa in Oslo, Norway. By late August, the two sides reached an agreement calling for a phased withdrawal of Israeli troops from the Gaza Strip and much of the West Bank over the next five years. Yasser Arafat of the PLO would rule over a Palestine National Authority in the areas to be evacuated by Israel. The two sides

On September 13, 1993, President Bill Clinton encouraged Israel's prime minister Yitzhak Rabin and Palestine Liberation Organization president Yasser Arafat to shake hands on the White House lawn. *(White House photograph)*

promised negotiations to reach an agreement on the final status of Jerusalem and the political standing of the Palestine Authority within five years. Although Israel and the PLO fashioned their peace without direct American involvement, they wanted the U.S. endorsement of their efforts. On September 13, 1993, Arafat and Rabin, two former bitter enemies, met on the White House lawn to sign their agreement. A moment later, Clinton took Arafat in one arm and Rabin in another and gently pulled them together. Arafat reached out his hand and, after a split second of hesitation, Rabin smiled wanly and shook it. The crowd of dignitaries, including most of the living veterans of twenty years of Arab-Israeli peace talks, gave a loud cheer.

Anything seemed possible in the heady atmosphere of the Arafat-Rabin handshake. Israel opened diplomatic relations with Arab states in North Africa and the Persian Gulf. Israel and Syria conducted peace negotiations designed to open relations between the two enemies in return for Israel's withdrawal from the Golan Heights it had occupied since 1967. These talks did not succeed, but in October 1994 Clinton flew to the Middle East to witness another historic treaty establishing full peace between Israel and Jordan.

Yet a significant minority of Israelis and Arabs resisted the growing amity. Militant Israeli nationalists feared that full peace would force them to abandon their dream of creating a Greater Israel in all of the territory captured during the 1967 war. Some Arabs perceived Arafat's compromise with the Israelis as a violation of the principle that Israel was an illegitimate outpost of Western imperialism that needed to be eradicated. In the two years after the signing on the White House lawn, opponents of peace killed Israeli and Palestinian civilians by the scores. Then, on November 4, 1995, minutes after he addressed a crowd of over 100,000 Israelis gathered to show their support for his peace policies, Yitzhak Rabin was assassinated by a right-wing 23-year-old religious Jew opposed to Israel yielding any territory for peace. Israelis were shocked, and many observers believed that Rabin's murder would unify Israel the way John Kennedy's death had brought Americans together in 1964. Foreign Minister Shimon Peres, the principal architect of the Oslo arrangement, took over as prime minister. For a while it seemed as if he would sail serenely to victory in elections called for May 1996, but in February a series of suicide bombings in Tel Aviv and Jerusalem, conducted by militant Islamic groups opposed to peace, killed sixty Israelis. Israeli opinion turned against Peres and his vision of peace. During the election campaign, the Clinton administration strongly backed Peres over his challenger, Likud party leader Benjamin Netanyahu, who opposed the concessions made by Rabin and Peres. But American support could not save Peres, who narrowly lost to Netanyahu. The new Israeli government sharply slowed but did not entirely stop the peace process. Netanyahu delayed implementing agreements signed by Peres, and he expanded Jewish settlements in the parts of the West Bank Israel had not yet returned to the Palestine National Authority. U.S.–Israeli relations, which had been closer than ever under the Labor government of Rabin and Peres, became much cooler.

POST–COLD WAR RELATIONS WITH THE INDUSTRIAL POWERS

The Clinton administration also sought effective approaches to manage relations with other states with large or growing economies. For those countries that did not pose a real or potential military threat, the Clinton administration's policies consisted almost exclusively of trade expansion. In 1995, the United States joined the newly created World Trade Organization (WTO), designed to eliminate most trade barriers by 2020. The U.S. and the other 128 members of the WTO each agreed to avoid practices that discriminated in favor of their own nation's exports and against the goods or services of other countries. The U.S. wanted other nations to relax restrictions on the import of U.S. computer software and have the WTO impose sanctions on countries that allowed their private firms to copy American-produced software without paying licensing fees. Other nations had their own criticism of U.S. trade practices. The Helms-Burton law (passed in 1996, under which the U.S. would punish foreign firms and their executives for trading with Cuba), seemed to be a particularly flagrant violation of the WTO pact. Under the WTO, nations could bring complaints against others they accused of unfair trade policies. The Clinton administration also pursued regional trade organizations to supplement the WTO. The U.S. promised to expand NAFTA to include all the states of the hemisphere by 2020, and Clinton attended yearly meetings of the newly formed Asia-Pacific Economic Conference (APEC), hoping to create a common market for the states of the Pacific Rim, a region that included most of the world's fastest growing economies.

Gaining American access to Vietnam, a currently poor country but one with great potential, played a major role in the Clinton administration's decision to lift the decades-old embargo and open full diplomatic relations with America's old enemy. In February 1994, the U.S. lifted all restrictions on Americans doing business with Vietnam, and in July 1995 the United States and Vietnam announced opened full diplomatic relations. "This moment offers us the opportunity to bind up our wounds," Clinton said as he announced that the two states would exchange ambassadors.

Clinton moved deliberately toward a rapprochement with Hanoi, since he wished to avoid giving his domestic political opponents an excuse to revive their accusations that he had dodged the draft in 1969. By 1994, however, American businesses were desperate not to be left behind by their European and Japanese competitors in the race to sell goods to Vietnam and set up factories there that could make use of Vietnam's large supply of cheap but educated labor. Arizona Republican senator John McCain, who had survived six years as a prisoner of war in Vietnam, forcefully advocated normalizing relations. McCain's support helped inoculate Clinton against right-wing charges that a former antiwar demonstrator had somehow besmirched the honor of the American soldiers who had fought in Vietnam by closing the book on the war.

The restoration of diplomatic relations with Vietnam went more smoothly than the U.S. relationship with the Peoples' Republic of China, a major economic power and a potential military rival of the U.S. During the 1992 presidential election campaign, Clinton had criticized the Bush administration for overlooking China's dismal record of human rights abuses. He'd suggested that Bush's personal experience as U.S. envoy to the PRC during the Nixon administration had made him willing to forgive any transgressions made by his friends among China's aging Communist party leadership. Clinton had promised to link enhanced trade with China to that country's respect for the rights of its own citizens to demand democracy.

As president, however, Clinton pursued a much more complicated China policy. He quickly dropped efforts to link China's access to U.S. markets to its human rights record. China boomed in the 1990s, with its rate of economic growth surpassing 12 percent per year.The China market, promised by dreamers for over a century, had become a reality. By the mid-1990s, China had become one of the United States' largest trading partners, and its yearly trade surplus with the U.S. of approximately $35 billion surpassed that of Japan. China had become the principal exporter of shirts, shoes, and toys to the U.S. In return, U.S. firms invested billions in China's growing infrastructure. American telephone companies, hotel chains, and computer companies were everywhere in China's rapidly developing cities.

The Clinton administration's policy of separating concerns over China's authoritarian repression of its people with American desire to expand trade disappointed advocates of human rights, who had expected Clinton to press China harder. But political relations between Beijing and China were still rocky. Chinese president Jiang Zemin and Prime Minister Li Peng rejected U.S. protests of Chinese sales of weapons or materials that could be turned into weapons to Pakistan, North Korean, and Iran. China pressed its own grievances against the United States. It complained that Washington had violated its pledge to break formal diplomatic relations to Taiwan when it permitted Lee Teng-hui, Taiwan's president, to visit the U.S. in May 1995 and receive an honorary degree from Cornell University, his alma mater. China, aware that the White House had overruled the advice of State Department experts and granted Lee a visa, derided Washington's claim that this was a purely private engagement over which it had no control.

Relations between the PRC, Taiwan, and the U.S. reached a low point in March 1996. The PRC worried that if he were reelected with a large majority in March 1996, President Lee might move Taiwan away from unification with the mainland and toward independence. The PRC sought to influence Taiwan's voters by conducting naval maneuvers off Taiwan's coast. The U.S. responded by sending its own warships into waters between Taiwan and the mainland, as a warning to Beijing. If anything, the PRC's threats strengthened Lee's position with Taiwan's voters, and he easily won reelection. Both the U.S. and the PRC then withdrew their fleets from the Taiwan Straits and looked for ways to cool their heated rhetoric. After Clinton won reelection, he met Chinese president Jiang at the Asia-Pacific Economic Conference in Manila and the two men promised to exchange visits to each other's countries over the following two years.

The Clinton administration tried to help the states of the former Soviet Union peacefully complete their transition toward democracy and market economies. Following the advice of his friend Deputy Secretary of State Strobe Talbott, a Russia expert, Clinton maintained U.S. support for Russian president Boris Yeltsin. Russia's economy had continued to sink in the

President Bill Clinton formed a partnership with Russian president Boris Yeltsin, a frequent visitor to the White House. *(White House photograph)*

years 1993 to 1995, and Yeltsin's fortunes seemed to plunge with the falling ruble. The U.S. sympathized with the Russian leader's difficulties when a deranged ultranationalist won the most votes in parliamentary elections in 1993. Washington offered only the mildest reproaches when Russian troops fought a brutal war to suppress the secession of the Republic of Chechnya in the Caucasus. The U.S. also backed Yeltsin when he ran for reelection in 1996, an election most early observers predicted he would lose to the candidate of the newly revived Communist party. Yeltsin proved more resilient than his critics imagined. Russia's economy began to emerge from its slump in 1996, and most Russians did not want to return to the bad old days of a Communist police state. Yeltsin easily won reelection.

The United States promised to continue to support International Monetary Fund aid to Russia. The Clinton administration also went forward with plans to help Russia and the other former Soviet states that possessed nuclear weapons to either destroy them or make certain they were under strict control. At U.S. urging, all the nuclear powers of the former Soviet Union signed the Nuclear Non-Proliferation Treaty and agreed to return the weapons on their territory to Russian control.

The issue of expanding NATO eastward became a potential problem late in Clinton's first term. During his campaign for reelection, Clinton promised that NATO would be enlarged to include some undetermined number of Eastern European states by 1999. Some of the likeliest candidates for NATO admission were Poland, the Czech Republic, and Hungary. Their admission would disturb no one, but the Baltic states of Lithuania, Latvia and Estonia, Ukraine, Moldova, and Belarus—all of which border Russia—also expressed an interest in joining the rich states of Western Europe and North America. If NATO remained a military alliance, against what threat was it to direct its military forces? Russian military officials naturally feared that they might still be NATO's target if the alliance included Russia's neighbors. But Russia also resisted submitting its own application to become part of a U.S.-led alliance. To do so would be too formal an acknowledgment of American preeminence at the beginning of the twenty-first century.

As the Clinton administration prepared for its second term and the world faced the next millennium, these traditional military issues vied with newer concerns over what constituted security in global affairs. Important economic forces were bringing people closer together and promising abundance for millions who previously had suffered from want. The very development promised by the global market had been accompanied by unprecedented environmental challenges. The world was literally falling apart in many places. Ethnic and religious tensions had replaced the Cold War as the central arena of conflict. Despite the spread of democracy, human rights were imperiled in many areas of the world. The United States had to deal with all of these issues in the post–Cold War world. No one inside or outside government had developed a comprehensive vision explaining these many complexities, but the very awareness of the world's complications shown by U.S. policy-makers after the Cold War provided hope for the future.

CHAPTER SIXTEEN

Selected Bibliography

The field of diplomatic history has undergone a transformation in the last decade, drawing heavily on the insights and theoretical rigor of other social science disciplines. The best introduction to this new work is Michael Hogan and Thomas Paterson, eds., *Explaining the History of American Foreign Policy* (1991). There are several recent bibliographies of twentieth-century American diplomatic history. The comprehensive work is Richard Dean Burns, ed., *Guide to American Foreign Relations Since 1700* (1982). A good account of the historiographical debates among diplomatic historians is Jerald A. Combs, *American Diplomatic History: Two Centuries of Changing Interpretations* (1983). Michael J. Hogan, ed., *America in the World: The Historiography of American Foreign Relations since 1941* (1995), covers the period since the Second World War.

Detailed factual summaries of the course of American foreign relations appear in the series *The American Secretaries of State and Their Diplomacy*. The three concluding volumes of the Cambridge History of American Foreign Relations provide a good overview of the twentieth century: Walter LaFeber, *The American Search for Opportunity, 1865–1913* (1993); Akira Iriye, *The Globalization of America, 1913–1945* (1993); and Warren I. Cohen, *America in the Age of Soviet Power, 1945–1991* (1993).

Four academic or quasi-scholarly journals which commenced publication at various times after the First World War include current information and historical research on America's international relations. They are *Foreign Affairs* (1922–), *World Politics* (1947–), *Foreign Policy* (1971–), and *Diplomatic History* (1977–). *Diplomatic History,* the journal of the Society for Historians of American Foreign Relations, regularly publishes excellent historiographical essays on chronological and topical subjects of interest to students of American diplomacy. It also carries important articles on the new theoretical approaches to the field. See also *American Historical Review, Journal of American History, International History Review,* and *American Political Science Review.*

GENERAL INTERPRETATIONS

General interpretations of American diplomatic history and foreign policy fall into three broad categories: nationalist, realist and radical or revisionist. The first "dean" of American diplomatic historians, Samuel Flagg Bemis, set forth the nationalist interpretation in the 1920s and expressed it most forcefully in *American Foreign Policy and the Blessings of Liberty* (1962). The major expressions of the realist critique of American foreign policy are George F. Kennan, *American Diplomacy* (1951) and *Realities of American Foreign Policy* (1954); Robert E. Osgood, *Ideals and Self-Interest in America's Foreign Relations* (1953); Hans J. Morgenthau, *In Defense of the National Interest: A Critical Examination of American Foreign Policy* (1951); and Reinhold Niebuhr, *The Children of Light and the Children of Darkness* (1948). Recent restatements of realism are Robert Dallek, *The American Style of Foreign Policy* (1983) and Norman A. Graebner, *America as a World Power* (1984). Revisionist writing owes much to two works by Charles Beard: *The Idea of National Interest* (1934) and *The Open Door at Home* (1935). Modern revisionist, radical, or "left-liberal" writing on foreign policy follows the path set by William Appleman Williams in *The Tragedy of American Diplomacy* (1959, 1962), *The Contours of American History* (1961), *America Confronts a Revolutionary World* (1978), and *Empire as a Way of Life* (1980). Other radicals—Richard Barnet, *Roots of War* (1972); Gabriel Kolko, *Roots of American Foreign Policy* (1969); and C. Wright Mills, *The Power Elite* (1959)—suggest that American foreign policy represents the interest of the rich, the well-born, and the powerful. The readings of Jerald A. Combs, ed., *Nationalist, Realist and Radical: Three Views of American Diplomacy* (1972), offer a good debate. Two sophisticated recent interpretations are Lloyd C. Gardner, *A Covenant with Power* (1984), and Michael H. Hunt, *Ideology and United States Foreign Policy* (1987).

Beyond the general accounts listed above, several detailed accounts reveal the competitive world in which the United States has operated. The best history of the imperial rivalries at the end of the nineteenth century remains William Langer, *The Diplomacy of Imperialism,* 2 vols. (1935). The radical economist Harry Magdoff suggests that the contemporary world continues the practices of late-nineteenth-century imperialism in *The Age of Imperialism* (1969). Richard Drinnon's *Facing West: The Politics of Indian Hating in American History* (1979) interprets all of American history as an attempt to expand at the expense of nonwhite peoples. Reuben F. Weston's *Racism in United States Imperialism* (1972) stresses racial motives. Victor G. Kiernan's *The Lords of Humankind* (1968) explains European attitudes, often shared by Americans, toward the nonwhite world.

Two British liberals, John Hobson, *Imperialism* (1902), and Norman Angel, *The Great Illusion* (1911), note the growing interdependence of the world's economies and the effects this had upon international relations. Discussions of modern interest in themes of interdependence appear in Thomas Etzold, "Interdependence, 1976" in *Diplomatic History* (1977); and Richard Barnet, *Real Security* (1981).

Among general works dealing with the process of creating foreign policy, the best are Barry Rubin, *Secrets of State* (1984); Burton M. Sapin, *The Making of United States Foreign Policy* (1966), Alexander De Conde, *The American Secretary of State* (1962); I. M. Destler, *Presidents, Bureaucrats and Foreign Policy* (1972); Francis O. Wilcox, *Congress, the Executive and Foreign Policy* (1971); and Thomas Franck and Edward Weisband, *Foreign Policy by Congress* (1979) (indispensable); Richard Neustadt and Ernest May, *Thinking in Time: The Uses of History for Decisionmakers* (1986), explains the uses and abuses of historical thought by officials.

The effects on foreign policy of nongovernmental actors appear in Barry Hughes, *The Domestic Context of Foreign Policy* (1978); Edward Crapol, ed., *Women and American Foreign Policy*, 2d ed. (1992); Robert D. Schulzinger, *The Wise Men of Foreign Affairs: The History of the Council on Foreign Relations* (1984); Charles Chatfield, *For Peace and Justice: Pacifism in America, 1914–1941* and *Peace Movements in America* (1973); Charles De Benedetti, *The Peace Reform in American History* (1980); De Benedetti's edited work *Peace Heroes in Twentieth Century America* (1986); and John W. Chambers II, *The Eagle and the Dove: The American Peace Movement and United States Foreign Policy, 1900–1922* (1992).

FROM THE SPANISH AMERICAN WAR TO WORLD WAR I, 1898–1914

Good general surveys of the causes, conduct, effects, and historiography of the Spanish-American war appear in John Offner's up-to-date *An Unwanted War: The Diplomacy of the United States and Spain over Cuba, 1895–1898* (1992); Walter LaFeber's intelligent *The New Empire* (1963); Ernest May's well-documented *Imperial Democracy* (1961); and David Trask's massive military history, *The War with Spain* (1981). Samuel Flagg Bemis claims that the seizure of colonial territory after the war represented a "great aberration" in *The Latin American Policy of the United States* (1943). The strategic importance of the war with Spain receives full treatment in John A. S. Grenville and George Berkeley Young, *Politics, Strategy and American Diplomacy, 1873–1917* (1966). Walter

Millis mocks American participation in the war with *The Martial Spirit* (1931). Julius W. Pratt explores its motives in *Expansionists of 1898* (1936). Philip Foner's *The Spanish-Cuban-American War and the Birth of American Imperialism* (1972) contains a biting indictment.

The movement against taking colonial territory is treated in Robert Beisner, *Twelve Against Empire* (1968); Thomas G. Paterson, *American Imperialism and Anti-imperialism* (1973); and Paolo Coletta, *William Jennings Bryan*, 3 vols. (1964–1969).

A good interpretive overview of the period after 1900 appears in Lloyd C. Gardner's "American Foreign Policy, 1900–1921: A Second Look at the Realist Critique of American Diplomacy," in Barton Bernstein, ed., *Towards a New Past* (1968).

The realist critique of the Open Door policy appears in A. Whitney Griswold's *The Far Eastern Policy of the United States* (1938), which argues that John Hay was naive and moralistic in proposing the Open Door policy. George F. Kennan concurs in *American Diplomacy* (1951). William Appleman Williams suggests that the Open Door policy stood at the center of American foreign policy in his *Tragedy of American Diplomacy*, rev. ed. (1962). Thomas McCormick's *China Market: America's Quest for Informal Empire* (1967), an expert revisionist account, explains that Hay played a weak hand as well as he could. Michael Hunt's subtle *Frontier Defense and the Open Door* (1973) argues that the Chinese had as much to do with writing the notes as the Americans. More general accounts of United States–Chinese relations are Warren Cohen, *America's Response to China* (1971); Michael Schaller, *The United States and China in the Twentieth Century* (1980); and Michael H. Hunt, *The Making of a Special Relationship: The United States and China to 1914* (1983).

The American war in the Philippines is covered in Stanely Karnow, *In Our Image: America's Empire in the Philippines* (1989); Peter Stanley, *A Nation in the Making: The Philippines, 1898–1935* (1977); and Richard E. Welch, *Response to Imperialism: The United States and the Philippine-American War* (1979).

The growth of the Anglo-American rapprochement after the SpanishAmerican War receives full discussion in Charles S. Campbell, *Anglo-American Understanding, 1898–1903* (1957); Lionel Gelber, *The Rise of AngloAmerican Friendship: A Study in World Politics, 1898–1906* (1938); and Bradford Perkins, *The Great Rapprochement: England and the United States* (1968).

The best study of TR's diplomacy remains Howard K. Beale, *Theodore Roosevelt and the Rise of America to World Power* (1956). Frederick Marks III, *Velvet on Iron: The Foreign Policy of Theodore Roosevelt* (1979), presents a nationalist perspective. Broader studies which put Roosevelt in the context of Progressive thought are John Morton Blum, *The Republican Roosevelt* (1958); David Noble, *The Progressive Mind* (1980); and Charles Forcey, *The Crossroads of Liberalism: Croly, Weyl, Lippmann and the Progressive Era* (1961).

Specialized studies of Roosevelt's actions during the Panama crisis are Walter LaFeber's masterly *The Panama Canal: The Issue in Historical Perspective* (1979) and David McCullough's *The Path Between the Seas: The Building of the Panama Canal* (1976). The standard account of the Monroe Doctrine and the Roosevelt Corollary is Dexter Perkins, *A History of the Monroe Doctrine* (1955). Dana Munro's *Intervention and Dollar Diplomacy in the Caribbean, 1900–1921* (1964) is comprehensive.

Discussions of Roosevelt's relations with Russia and Japan appear in Arthur Thompson and Robert Hart, *The Uncertain Crusade: America and the Russian Revolution of 1905* (1970); Raymond Esthus, *Theodore Roosevelt and Japan* (1966); Charles Neu, *An Uncertain Friendship: Theodore Roosevelt and Japan* (1967); and Akira Iriye, *Pacific Estrangement: Japanese and American Expansion, 1897–1911* (1972).

The movement for international law and international organization is covered well by Warren Kuehl, *Seeking World Order: The United States and International Organization to 1920* (1969); Calvin D. Davis, *The United States and the Second Hague Peace Conference* (1976); Philip Jessup, *Elihu Root* (1938); and Richard Leopold, *Elihu Root and the Conservative Tradition* (1954). William A. Williams's *Tragedy of American Diplomacy* (1962) places dollar diplomacy in the context of the Open Door policy. The standard account of Taft's foreign policy is Walter Scholes and Marie Scholes, *Foreign Policies of the Taft Administration* (1970).

Arthur Link is the foremost biographer of Woodrow Wilson. See his *Wilson*, 5 vols. (1947–1986), *Wilson the Diplomatist* (1956), *Woodrow Wilson and the Progressive Era, 1910–1917* (1959), and *War, Revolution and Peace* (1980). N. Gordon Levin's *Woodrow Wilson and World Politics* (1968) places Wilson's diplomacy in the context of Progressive thought, but it concentrates on World War I. Paolo Coletta's *William Jennings Bryan* (1964–1969) is a sympathetic three-volume work. William C. Widenor's *Henry Cabot Lodge and the Search for American Foreign Policy* (1980) has something on this period.

Far Eastern developments in the Taft-Wilson years receive treatment in Michael Hunt, *Frontier Defense and the Open Door* (1973); Jerry Israel, *Progressivism and the Open Door: America and China, 1905–1921* (1971); Charles Vevier, *The United States and China* (1955); and Edward H. Zabriskie, *American-Russian Rivalry in the Far East, 1895–1914* (1946).

Intervention in Central America and the Caribbean receives up-to-date coverage in Thomas Schoonover, *The United States in Central America, 1860–1911* (1991); and Lester Langley, *The Banana Wars: An Inner History of the American Empire, 1900–1934* (1983). Robert Rotberg's *Haiti: The Politics of Squalor* (1971) contains a chapter on the American occupation, a subject treated in greater detail by Hans Schmidt, *The United States Occupation of Haiti* (1971). Jules Benjamin's *Hegemony and Development: The United States and Cuba, 1890–1934* (1977) is an important book.

Good studies exist on American meddling in Mexico. P. Edward Haley's *Revolution and Intervention: The Diplomacy of Taft and Wilson with Mexico* (1970) discusses 1910–1917. Lloyd C. Gardner's *Safe for Democracy: The Anglo-American Response to Revolution, 1913–1923* (1984) contains useful material on Mexico. Volumes two through five of Arthur Link's massive *Wilson* (1947–) contain many chapters on United States–Mexican relations. Peter Calvert's *The Mexican Revolution, 1910–1914* (1968) explains the international environment of the revolution. Kenneth Grieb's *The United States and Huerta* (1969) covers 1913–1914. Robert E. Quirk's *An Affair of Honor: Woodrow Wilson and the Occupation of Vera Cruz* (1962) explains the April 1914 embroglio. Robert Freeman Smith's *The United States and Revolutionary Nationalism in Mexico* (1972) is comprehensive. Friedrich Katz's *The Secret War in Mexico* (1981) has a good international perspective. John Womack's *Zapata* (1972) presents excellent social history of the roots of revolution.

THE FIRST WORLD WAR AND THE VERSAILLES PEACE, 1914–1920

The question of American entry into the First World War inspires bibliographies. See Richard Leopold, "The Problem of American Intervention, 1917: An Historical Retrospect," *World Politics* (1950); and Ernest May, *American Intervention: 1917 and 1941* (1960). Warren Cohen's *The American Revisionists* (1966) is a historiographical record of what dissenters said about American entry into the First World War from 1917 to the late 1940s.

Arno Mayer's "World War I," in C. Vann Woodward, ed., *The Comparative Approach to American History* (1968), is indispensable for understanding the meaning of the First World War. William A. Williams, *Tragedy of American Diplomacy*, rev. ed. (1962), presents a revisionist account.

Several works trace the development of Wilson's ideas of diplomacy. The most recent is Thomas J. Knock, *To End All Wars: Woodrow Wilson and the Search for a New World Order* (1992). Two excellent studies by Lloyd E. Ambrosius are *Woodrow Wilson and the American Diplomatic Tradition* (1987) and *Wilsonian Statecraft* (1991). See also Edward Buehrig, *Woodrow Wilson and the Balance of Power* (1955); N. Gordon Levin, *Woodrow Wilson and World Politics* (1968); Laurence Martin, *Peace Without Victory: Woodrow Wilson and the British Liberals* (1958); and Martin Schwarz, *E. D. Morel and the Union for Democratic Control of Foreign Policy* (1971).

Other figures appear in Daniel Smith's *Robert Lansing and American Neutrality* (1958). There is yet no good biography of Edward M. House, but see Charles Seymour, *The Intimate Papers of Colonel House* (1926–1928). John Garry Clifford's *The Citizen Soldiers: The Plattsburgh Training Camp Movement 1913–1920* (1972) discusses preparedness. William Widenor's *Henry Cabot Lodge* (1980) and John Garraty's *Henry Cabot Lodge* (1953) treat a major opposition figure. Merlo J. Pusey's biography *Charles Evans Hughes,* 2 vols. (1951), discusses the election of 1916.

The standard accounts of the diplomacy of neutrality are Ernest May, *The World War and American Isolation* (1959); Lord Patrick Devlin, *Too Proud to Fight: Woodrow Wilson's Neutrality* (1975); and Arthur S. Link, *Wilson,* III, *The Struggle for Neutrality, 1914–1915;* IV, *Confusions and Crises, 1915–1916;* and V, *Campaigns for Progressivism and Peace, 1916–1917.* John Milton Cooper's *The Vanity of Power: American Isolation and the First World War* (1969) is a quicker survey.

The American mood on the eve of the Great War is discussed in Henry May, *The End of American Innocence* (1959); Charles Forcey, *The Crossroads of Liberalism* (1961); Ronald Steel, *Walter Lippmann and the American Century* (1980); David Noble, *The Progressive Mind* (1980); and Richard Hofstadter, *The American Political Tradition and the Men Who Made It* (1948). Radical dissent appears in Theodore Roszak, ed., *War and the Intellectuals: Writings of Randolph Bourne* (1961).

The American approach during the war consciously differed from that of other belligerents. The best assessment of Wilson's outlook is in Arno J. Mayer, *Political Origins of the New Diplomacy* (1959). N. Gordon Levin's *Woodrow Wilson and World Politics* (1968) expands Mayer's analysis.

The origins of Wilson's Fourteen Points receive attention as well in books dealing with wider subjects. Ronald Steel's *Walter Lippmann and the American Century* (1980) and Lawrence Gelfand's *The Inquiry: American Preparations for Peace, 1917–1919* (1963) examine the role of outside experts in advising the government.

Developments at home are explained best in David Kennedy's *Over Here: The Home Front in the First World War* (1980). What happened to dissenters is discussed in Nick Salvatore, *Eugene V. Debs: Citizen and Socialist* (1982); Melvin Dubofsky, *We Shall Be All: A History of the Industrial Workers of the World* (1968); and Carl Bode, *Mencken* (1969). Propaganda efforts are treated in George Blakey, *Historians on the Homefront: American Propagandists and the Great War* (1970); James R. Mock and Cedric Larson, *Words That Won the War: The Story of the Committee on Public Information* (1938); and Carol S. Gruber, *Mars and Minerva: World War I and the Uses of Higher Learning in America* (1976). Mobilization practices appear in Daniel R. Beaver, *Newton D. Baker and the American War Effort, 1917–1919* (1966). Economic mobilization for total war is well covered in Jordan A. Schwarz, *The Speculator: Bernard M. Baruch in Washington, 1917–1965* (1981). Washington politics are covered in Seward W. Livermore, *Politics Is Adjourned: Woodrow Wilson and the War Congress, 1916–1918* (1966).

American diplomats still had to deal traditionally with partners in the war effort. Accounts of these activities include Wilton B. Fowler, *British-American Relations, 1917–1918: The Role of Sir William Wiseman* (1969); David Trask,

The United States in the Supreme War Council (1961); and Michael Fry, *Illusion of Security: North Atlantic Diplomacy, 1918–1922* (1972).

The story of intervention in the Russian civil war appears in George F. Kennan, *Soviet-American Relations, 1917–1920,* 2 vols. (1956–1958), and *Russia and the West Under Lenin and Stalin* (1961); Richard H. Ullman, *Anglo-Soviet Relations, 1917–1921,* 3 vols. (1961–1971); Betty M. Unterberger, *America's Siberian Expedition, 1918–1920* (1956); William A. Williams, *American-Russian Relations, 1781–1947* (1952), *The Tragedy of American Diplomacy* (1962), and *America Confronts a Revolutionary World* (1978). Lloyd Gardner's *Safe for Democracy,* mentioned above, is a sophisticated account of intervention in Russia.

Negotiations leading toward the armistice appear in Harry Rudin, *Armistice 1918* (1938); and a newer work, Arthur Walworth, *America's Moment: 1918* (1978).

The best work on the social, economic, and political context of the peace conference is Arno J. Mayer's *Politics and Diplomacy of Peacemaking* (1967). The most recent scholarship appears in Arthur J. Walworth, *Wilson and His Peacemakers* (1986). Charles J. Mee's *The End of Order: Versailles 1919* (1980) is breezy, and Harold Nicolson's memoir of the conference, *Peacemaking, 1919* (1931), is enjoyable. John Maynard Keynes's *Economic Consequences of the Peace* (1920) is bitter, while James T. Shotwell's *At the Paris Peace Conference* (1937) expresses the undimmed faith of an old Wilsonian. Thomas A. Bailey's *Woodrow Wilson and the Lost Peace* (1944) is sympathetic to the president without ignoring his faults. A physician, Edwin A. Weinstein, has written *Woodrow Wilson: A Medical and Psychological Biography* (1981) to explain some of the president's behavioral quirks.

The Bullitt mission and relations with Russia are treated in Beatrice Farnsworth, *William C. Bullitt and the Soviet Union* (1967). Peter Filene, *Americans and the Soviet Experiment, 1917–1933* (1967), covers a range of subjects.

The following describe the reception of the treaty in the United States: Lloyd Ambrosius's *Woodrow Wilson and the American Diplomatic Tradition,* previously noted; William C. Widenor, *Henry Cabot Lodge and the Search for American Foreign Policy* (1980); and Robert James Maddox, *William Borah and American Foreign Policy* (1969).

Wilson's economic diplomacy in the period after the armistice is described by Carl Parrini in *Heir to Empire: United States Economic Diplomacy, 1916–1923* (1969).

THE INTERWAR PERIOD, 1921–1939

Two works place the interwar period into proper context: E. H. Carr, *The Twenty Years' Crisis, 1919–1938: An Introduction to the Study of International Relations* (1939); and Gordon Craig and Felix Gilbert, eds., *The Diplomats,*

1919–1939 (1993). L. Ethan Ellis, *Republican Foreign Policy, 1921–1933* (1953), offers a good introduction to the twenties.

Economic issues and relations with Europe are discussed in Carl Parrini, *Heir to Empire* (1969); Herbert Feis, *The Diplomacy of the Dollar: The First Era, 1919–1933* (1950); Marc Trachtenberg, *Reparations in World Politics* (1980); Melvyn Leffler, *The Elusive Quest: America's Pursuit of French Security and European Stability, 1919–1933* (1979); Joseph Brandes, *Herbert Hoover and Economic Diplomacy: Department of Commerce Policy, 1921–1928* (1966); Joan Hoff Wilson, *American Business and Foreign Policy, 1920–1933* (1971); and Henry Blumenthal, *Illusion and Reality in FrancoAmerican Diplomacy* (1986).

The secretaries of state in the twenties are treated in Merlo J. Pusey, *Charles Evans Hughes* (1951); and L. Ethan Ellis, *Frank B. Kellogg and American Foreign Relations* (1961).

The development of the Foreign Service and the Rogers Act are covered by Warren Frederick Ilchman, *Professional Diplomacy in the United States, 1789–1939* (1961); Robert D. Schulzinger, *The Making of the Diplomatic Mind: The Training, Outlook and Style of United States Foreign Service Officers, 1908–1931* (1975); Richard Hume Werking, *The Master Architects Building the United States Foreign Service, 1890–1931* (1977), and Martin Weil, *A Pretty Good Club: The Founding Fathers of the Foreign Service* (1978).

The Middle East in the twenties is covered well by John A. De Novo's *American Interests and Politics in the Middle East, 1900–1939* (1963).

Cultural and political relations with Asia appear in Akira Iriye's *After Imperialism: The Search for a New Order in the Far East 1921–1931* (1965). Rodman Paul's *The Abrogation of the Gentlemen's Agreement* (1936) explains the connection between immigration and foreign policy in the early twenties.

Many of the works listed for the earlier period deal with United States policy in Latin America in the twenties. Others are Dana G. Munro, *The United States and the Caribbean Republics in the 1920s* (1972); Joseph S. Tulchin, *Aftermath of War: World War I and U.S. Policy Toward Latin America* (1971); Arthur C. Millspaugh, *Haiti Under American Control* (1930); William Kamman, *A Search for Stability: United States Diplomacy Toward Nicaragua, 1925–1933* (1968); and Neill McCauley, *The Sandino Affair* (1967). Harold Nicolson's *Dwight Morrow* (1935) contains a good portrait of Coolidge's emissary to Mexico. Jules Benjamin's *Hegmony and Development: The United States and Cuba, 1890–1934* (1977) offers a radical analysis.

The Washington Conference and naval rivalries are discussed by Thomas H. Buckley, *The Washington Conference, 1921–1922* (1970); Roger Dingman, *Power in the Pacific: The Evolution of Japanese and American Naval Policies* (1975); Stephen Roskill, *Naval Policies Between the Wars, I, The Period of Anglo-American Antagonism, 1919–1929* (1968); and John Chalmers Vinson, *The Parchment Peace: The Unites States Senate and the Washington Conference, 1921–1922* (1955).

Plans for peace and the maintenance of the old Wilsonian flame are discussed with sympathy by Denna Fleming in *The United States and World Organization, 1920–1933* (1938), disdain by Robert Ferrell in *Peace in Their Time: The Origins of the Kellogg-Briand Pact* (1952), and optimism by James T. Shotwell in *War as an Instrument of National Policy and Its Renunciation* (1929). Hamilton Fish Armstrong's memoirs, *Peace and Counterpeace: From Wilson to Hitler* (1971), provide the observations of a chastened Wilsonian.

The international effects of the economic collapse receive a whimsical discussion in John Kenneth Galbraith's *The Great Crash* (1955, 1966). Charles Kindleberger's *The World in Depression* (1974) is the standard account.

The diplomatic distress of the Hoover administration is well told in Robert Ferrell's *American Diplomacy in the Great Depression: Hoover-Stimson Foreign Policy, 1921–1933* (1957). Richard Current's *Secretary Stimson: A Study in Statecraft* (1954) is a biting assessment of Hoover's principal adviser.

The best general account of FDR's foreign policy is Robert Dallek, *Franklin D. Roosevelt and American Foreign Policy, 1932–1945* (1979). Robert Divine's *The Reluctant Belligerent* (1979) and *The Illusion of Neutrality* (1962), both good, provide a less detailed overview. William Leuchtenburg, *Franklin D. Roosevelt and the New Deal* (1962); James MacGregor Burns, *Roosevelt: The Lion and the Fox* (1960); Frank Friedel, *Roosevelt*, 2 vols. (1952–1956); and Arthur M. Schlesinger, Jr., *The Age of Roosevelt,* 3 vols. (1957–1960), all have good foreign policy material.

Far Eastern affairs received attention under both Hoover and Roosevelt. The best accounts of the Manchurian crisis are Armin Rappaport, *Henry L. Stimson and Japan, 1931–1933* (1963); and, especially, Christopher Thorne's *the Limits of Foreign Policy: The West, The League and the Far Eastern Crisis of 1931–1933* (1973). Dorothy Borg's *The United States and the Far Eastern Crisis of 1933–1938* (1964) and Dorothy Borg and Shumpei Okamoto, eds., *Pearl Harbor as History, Japanese-American Relations, 1931–1941* (1973), extend the story to 1941. Stephen Pelz, *Race to Pearl Harbor* (1974), covers naval competition in the Pacific; and James R. Leutze, *Bargaining for Supremacy* (1977), adds British naval policy to the Far Eastern arms race.

The New Deal's flawed attempts to reach international monetary accord are covered by Herbert Feis, *1933: Characters in Crisis* (1966); and Alfred E. Eckes, *A Search for Solvency* (1977). Lloyd C. Gardner's fine *Economic Aspects of New Deal Diplomacy* (1964) is comprehensive, while Frederick C. Adam's *Economic Diplomacy: The Export Import Bank and American Foreign Policy, 1933–1941* (1976) is a good special study.

Recognition of the Soviet Union and subsequent U.S.-Soviet relations are covered by Edward Bennett, *Recognition of Russia* (1970); Beatrice Farnsworth, *William C. Bullitt and the Soviet Union* (1967); William A. Williams, *American-Russian Relations, 1781–1947* (1952); and Joan Hoff Wilson, *Ideology and Eco-*

nomics: U.S. Relations with the Soviet Union, 1918–1933 (1974). For what happened to the Foreign Service officers who went to the Soviet Union, see George F. Kennan, *Memoirs, 1925–1950* (1967); and Hugh De Santis, *The Diplomacy of Silence: The American Foreign Service, the Soviet Union and the Origins of the Cold War 1933–1947* (1980).

The movement for neutrality legislation and nonintervention is treated by Selig Adler, *The isolationist Impulse* (1957); Warren Cohen, *The American Revisionists* (1966); Jordan A. Schwarz, *The Speculator: Bernard M. Baruch in Washington, 1917–1965* (1981); and John E. Wiltz, *In Search of Peace: The Senate Munitions Inquiry, 1934* (1963). Betty Glad's *Key Pittman: The Tragedy of a Senate Insider* (1986) uses insights from social psychology to trace a colorful career.

The growth of FDR's Good Neighbor policy is covered by Irwin F. Gellman, *Good Neighbor Diplomacy and the Rise of Batista* (1974); David Green, *The Containment of Latin America* (1971); and Bryce Wood, *The Making of the Good Neighbor Policy* (1961).

The domestic and diplomatic reaction to the Spanish Civil War is covered by three books: Allen Guttmann, *The Wound in the Heart: America and the Spanish Civil War* (1962); F. Jay Taylor, *The United States and the Spanish Civil War, 1936–1939* (1956); and Richard P. Traina, *American Diplomacy and the Spanish Civil War* (1968).

The minimal response to the plight of refugees from Hitler first received attention in Arthur Morse's inflammatory *While Six Million Died* (1968). More scholarly but equally damning treatments are Henry Feingold, *The Politics of Rescue: The Roosevelt Administration and the Holocaust, 1938–1945* (1970); and David S. Wyman, *Paper Walls: America and the Refugee Crisis, 1938–1941* (1968).

Arnold A. Offner's *American Appeasement: United States Foreign Policy and Germany, 1933–1938* (1968) charges the Roosevelt administration with blindness to the dangers of Germany. Patrick J. Hearden presents a New Left interpretation of American dreams of a commercial empire in *Roosevelt Confronts Hitler: America's Entry into World War II* (1987). Martin Gilbert's *The Roots of Appeasement* (1966) discusses the social bases of appeasement in Britain with some application to the United States.

THE SECOND WORLD WAR, 1940–1945

Many of the general works on FDR listed above apply to the Second World War. Of them, Robert Dallek's *Franklin D. Roosevelt and United States Foreign Policy, 1933–1945* (1979) is superb. Warren Kimball's *The Juggler: Franklin Roosevelt as World Statesman* (1991) is highly sophisticated. Gerhard L. Weinberg, *A World at Arms: A Global History of World War II* (1994), is massive. Gaddis

Smith's *American Diplomacy in the Second World War* (1985) is a quick survey, and James MacGregor Burns's *Roosevelt: The Soldier of Freedom* (1971) covers the war years.

Special studies of domestic politics during the neutrality period are Wayne S. Cole, *America First: The Battle Against Intervention, 1940–1941* (1953), Geoffrey Smith, *To Save a Nation: American Counter-Subversives, the New Deal and the Coming of World War II* (1973), and Manfred Jonas, *Isolationism in America, 1935–1941* (1967).

The general diplomatic history of the years immediately before Pearl Harbor is covered in two controversial volumes by William Langer and S. Everett Gleason, *The Challenge to Isolation, 1937–1940* (1952) and *The Undeclared War, 1940–1941* (1953). The writers, both former State Department officials, received access to papers denied to other researchers.

Revisionists like Charles Beard, *Franklin D. Roosevelt and the Coming of the War* (1948); Charles Tansill, *Backdoor to War* (1952); and Harry Elmer Barnes, *Perpetual War for Perpetual Peace: A Critical Examination of the Foreign Policy of Franklin D. Roosevelt and Its Aftermath* (1952), criticize such "court history" while arguing that Roosevelt maneuvered the United States into war. A recent account based on declassified intelligence documents is Waldo Heinrichs, *Threshold of War: Franklin Delano Roosevelt and American Entry into World War II* (1988).

For relations with Germany, see James V. Compton, *The Swastika and the Eagle: Hitler, the United States and the Origins of World War II* (1967), and Saul Friedlander, *Prelude to Downfall: Hitler and the United States, 1939–1941* (1967). The Atlantic Conference between Churchill and Roosevelt is explained best by Theodore Wilson's *The First Summit: Roosevelt and Churchill at Placentia Bay, (1941)* (1971).

Relations with Japan before Pearl Harbor are discussed in Dorothy Borg and Shumpei Okamoto, eds., *Pearl Harbor as History: Japanese-American Relations, 1931–1941* (1973), a series of essays by specialists on the military, economic, and diplomatic background of war between the United States and Japan. Gordon Prange, *At Dawn We Slept: The Untold Story of Pearl Harbor* (1981), over twenty years in the writing, supersedes all previous accounts. Roberta Wohlstetter's *Pearl Harbor: Warning and Decision* (1962) explains what Americans knew and when they knew it about the impending attack. Herbert Feis's *The Road to Pearl Harbor* (1950) represents a conventional interpretation by a former State Department official. The works by Harry Elmer Barnes, Charles Beard, and Charles Tansill listed above raise grave charges against Roosevelt.

Roosevelt's leadership of the anti-Axis coalition is covered in Eric Larrabee's *Commander in Chief: Franklin Delano Roosevelt, His Lieutenants and Their War* (1986). The president's complicated relationship with Winston

Churchill emerges best in Warren Kimball, ed., *Churchill and Roosevelt: The Complete Correspondence*, 3 vols. (1984). Herbert Feis, *Churchill, Roosevelt, Stalin* (1957), is still useful on the Big Three. See also Robert Beitzell, *The Uneasy Alliance: America, Britain and Russia, 1941–1943* (1973); Randall B. Woods, *A Changing of the Guard: Anglo-American Relations, 1941–1946* (1990); and Mark Stoler, *The Politics of the Second Front: American Military Planning in Coalition Warfare, 1941–1943* (1977). Planning for the postwar period is covered by Diana Shaver Clemens, *Yalta* (1970); Russell Buhite's *Decision at Yalta* (1986); and John Lewis Gaddis, *The United States and the Origins of the Cold War, 1941–1947* (1972); Lloyd Gardner's subtle *Architects of Illusion: Men and Ideas in American Foreign Policy, 1941–1949* (1970); Richard Gardner, *Sterling-Dollar Diplomacy* (1956); Robert Hathaway, *Ambiguous Partnership: Britain and America, 1944–1947* (1981); George C. Herring, *Aid to Russia, 1941–1946* (1976); Godfrey Hodgson, *The Colonel: The Life and Wars of Henry Stimson, 1867–1950* (1990); Gabriel Kolko, *The Politics of War, 1943–1945* (1968); and Michael Sherry, *Preparing for the Next War* (1977), a major departure.

The war in the Far East and American attitudes toward colonialism and Asia are covered by John Dower, *War without Mercy: Race and Power in the Pacific War* (1986); Akira Iriye, *Power and Culture (1980); William Roger Louis, Imperialism at Bay: The United States and the Decolonization of the British Empire* (1978); Michael Schaller, *The U.S. Crusade in China, 1938–1945* (1979); Kenneth Shewmaker, *Americans and the Chinese Communists, 1927–1945: A Persuading Encounter* (1971); Christopher Thorne, *Allies of a Kind: The United States, Great Britain and the War against Japan, 1939–1945* (1979), a brilliant book, and Barbara Tuchman, *Stilwell and the American Experience in China, 1911–1945* (1971).

Petroleum politics and the Middle East are discussed in Irvine H. Anderson, *Aramco, The United States and Saudi Arabia* (1981); Aaron David Miller, *Saudi Arabian Oil and American Security, 1939–1948* (1980); and Michael Stoff, *Oil, War and American Security: The Search for a National Policy on Foreign Oil, 1941–1947* (1980).

Special studies on the war in Europe include David S. Wyman, *The Abandonment of the Jews: America and the Holocaust, 1941–1945* (1984); Herbert Feis, *The Spanish Story* (1948); William Langer, *Our Vichy Gamble* (1947); Robert Murphy, *Diplomat Among Warriors* (1964) (Murphy was Eisenhower's representative in North Africa); Milton Viorst, *Hostile Allies: FDR and Charles de Gaulle* (1965); Dorothy Shipley White, *Seeds of Discord: de Gaulle, Free France and the Allies* (1964); and Julian Hurstfield, *America and the French Nation, 1939–1945* (1986). James E. Miller's *The United States and Italy, 1940–1950* (1987) bridges the Second World War and the Cold War.

Intelligence gathering and covert operations attract enormous attention from authors. The literature is of generally low quality, but some of the better are Allen Dulles, *The Secret Surrender* (1966); Bradley F. Smith, *The Shadow*

Warriors: The OSS and the Origins of the CIA (1983); R. Harris Smith, *OSS: The Secret History of America's First Central Intelligence Agency* (1972); and Anthony Cave-Brown, *The Last Hero: Wild Bill Donovan* (1983).

The development of strategic bombing, the surrender of Japan, and the use of atomic diplomacy are covered in several works. Start with Michael J. Hogan, ed., *Hiroshima in History and Memory* (1996). Michael Sherry's *The Rise of American Airpower* (1987) is superb. Gar Alperovitz, *Atomic Diplomacy: Hiroshima and Potsdam* (1965), is a revisionist work which argues that an inept Truman used the bomb to frighten the Russians and mask his own inadequate grasp of international relations. Herbert Feis, *The Atomic Bomb and the End of World War II* (1966), challenges Alperovitz. Martin J. Sherwin's prize-winning *A World Destroyed: The Atomic Bomb in the Grand Alliance, 1941–1945* (1975) elegantly weaves diplomatic and scientific history and supersedes earlier accounts. Robert Butow, *Japan's Decision to Surrender* (1954), discusses internal Japanese politics.

POST–WORLD WAR II AMERICA: GENERAL STUDIES

Several works are useful for treating the post–Second World War period as a coherent whole. Start with Michael Schaller, Virginia Scharff, and Robert D. Schulzinger, *Present Tense: The United States Since 1945* (1992), which blends culture, politics, and foreign policy. For foreign affairs, see Stephen E. Ambrose, *Rise to Globalism* (1992); Seyom Brown, *The Faces of Power: Constancy and Change in United States Foreign Policy from Truman to Reagan* (1983); John Lewis Gaddis, *Strategies of Containment* (1982) and his *The Long Peace* (1987). Walter Isaacson and Evan Thomas trace the Cold War through the actions of six members of the foreign policy establishment in their book *The Wise Men* (1986). William A. Williams, *The Tragedy of American Diplomacy* (1962), the major revisionist statement, is still valuable.

Useful recollections and recommendations by participants are George W. Ball, *The Past Has a Different Pattern* (1982), which covers forty years; George F. Kennan, *Memoirs,* 2 vols. (1967, 1972); and J. William Fulbright, *Old Myths and New Realities* (1964) and *The Arrogance of Power* (1966).

The revolutionary effects of nuclear weapons are discussed by Marc Trachtenberg, *History and Strategy* (1991); Alexander George and Richard Smoke, *Deterrence in American Foreign Policy* (1974), a definitive study; Henry A. Kissinger, *Nuclear Weapons and Foreign Policy* (1957), a dated account by an important man; and two splendid surveys by Michael Mandelbaum, *The Nuclear Revolution* (1980) and *The Nuclear Question* (1979).

For the changing international economic environment, see Richard Barnet and Ronald Mueller, *Global Reach* (1974); C. Fred Bergsten, *The Dilemmas of the Dollar* (1975); Diane B. Kunz, *Butter and Guns: America's Cold War*

Economic Diplomacy (1997); and Robert Solomon, *The International Monetary System, 1945–1976* (1976).

THE EARLY COLD WAR, 1945–1952

The origins of the Cold War ignited as sulphurous a debate among historians as did the earlier controversy over American entry into World War I. Thomas Paterson's *On Every Front* (1979) is the best introduction. Lloyd Gardner, Hans Morgenthau, and Arthur Schlesinger, Jr., *Origins of the Cold War* (1970), present the revisionist, realist, and orthodox sides. An account of the historiographical debate is in Charles S. Maier, "Revisionism and the Interpretation of Cold War Origins," *Perspectives in American History* (1970).

More detailed works offering contrasting accounts of the origins of the Cold War are, among others, Lloyd C. Gardner, *Architects of Illusion: Men and Ideas in American Foreign Policy 1941–1949* (1970); John Lewis Gaddis, *The United States and the Origins of the Cold War, 1941–1947* (1972); Fraser Harburtt's *The Iron Curtain: Churchill, America and the Origins of the Cold War* (1986), which is good on the transatlantic context; Deborah Larsen's *Origins of Containment: A Psychological Explanation* (1985), which breaks new ground; Melvyn P. Leffler, *A Preponderance of Power: National Security, the Truman Administration and the Cold War* (1992) and his *The Specter of Communism: The United States and the Origins of the Cold War, 1917–1953* (1994); Thomas J. McCormick, *America's Half-Century* (1989); Thomas G. Paterson, *Soviet-American Confrontation* (1974); Hugh Thomas, *Armed Truce: The Beginnings of the Cold War, 1945–1947* (1987); and Daniel Yergin, *Shattered Peace: The Cold War and the Origins of the National Security State, 1943–1949* (1978). See also works on World War II.

For the policies and personalities of the Truman administration, see Dean Acheson, *Present at the Creation: My Years at the State Department* (1969), Robert C. Donovan's two fine volumes, *The Presidency of Harry Truman* (1977–1982); Joseph C. Goulden, *The Best Years: A Social History of 1945–1950* (1975); Walter Hixson, *George Kennan: Cold War Iconoclast* (1989); David Mayers, *George Kennan and the Dilemmas of U.S. Foreign Policy* (1988); David McClellan, *Dean Acheson* (1976); David McCullough, *Truman* (1992); Robert L. Messer, *The End of an Alliance: James F. Byrnes, Roosevelt, Truman and the Origins of the Cold War* (1982); Wilson D. Miscamble, *George F. Kennan and the Making of American Foreign Policy, 1947–1950* (1991); Forrest Pogue, *George C. Marshall, Statesman, 1945–1947* (1987); Gaddis Smith, *Dean Acheson* (1972); Anders Stephenson, *Kennan and the Art of Foreign Policy* (1989); J. Samuel Walker, *Henry A. Wallace and American Foreign Policy* (1976); and Richard J. Walton, *Henry Wallace, Harry Truman and the Cold War* (1976).

Accounts of domestic politics, the search for subversives, and the origins of the Cold War are Richard Freeland, *The Truman Doctrine and the Origins of McCarthyism* (1972); Richard M. Nixon, *Six Crises* (1963); David Oshinsky, *A Conspiracy So Immense: The World of Joe McCarthy* (1983); Michael Parenti, *The Anti-Communist Impulse* (1971); Ellen Schrecker, *No Ivory Tower: McCarthyism and the Universities* (1986); Athan Theoharis, *The Yalta Myths* (1971) and *The Specter* (1974); and Allen Weinstein, *Perjury: The Chambers-Hiss Case* (1976), a well-researched but controversial study concluding that Hiss supplied documents to Chambers.

The ideas of conservative dissenters from the prevailing assumptions of the Cold War are covered by Justus Doenecke, *Not to the Swift: The Old Isolationists and the Cold War* (1979); Ronald Radosh, *Prophets on the Right* (1975), and Robert Taft, *A Foreign Policy for Americans* (1952).

Special studies on the reorganization of the foreign affairs bureaucracy are William R. Corson, *The Armies of Ignorance* (1977); I. M. Destler, *Presidents, Bureaucrats and Foreign Policy* (1972); John Ensor Harr, *The Professional Diplomat* (1969); Harry Howe Ransome, *The Intelligence Establishment* (1970); Rhodri Jeffriys-Jones, *The CIA and American Democracy* (1989); and Harold Stein, *American Civil-Military Decisions* (1963).

Atomic issues are treated by Paul Boyer, *By the Bomb's Early Light: American Thought and Culture at the Dawn of the Atomic Age* (1985); Gregg Herkin, *The Winning Weapon: The Atomic Bomb in the Cold War, 1945–1950* (1980), the best account; Joseph I. Lieberman, *Scorpion and Tarantula: The Struggle to Control Atomic Weapons, 1945–1949* (1970); Michael Mandelbaum, *The Nuclear Revolution* (1980); and George H. Quester, *Nuclear Diplomacy: The First Twenty-Five Years* (1971).

Studies on United States relations with Europe in the Truman administration include Leonard Dinnerstein, *America and the Survivors of the Holocaust* (1982); John Lewis Gaddis, *Strategies of Containment* (1982), a sympathetic exposition of Kennan's thought; Michael J. Hogan, *The Marshall Plan: America, Britain and the Reconstruction of Western Europe, 1947–1952* (1987), which is richly detailed; Robert A. Pollard, *Economic Security and the Origins of the Cold War* (1985), which also treats the Marshall Plan; Lawrence Kaplan, *The United States and NATO: The Formative Years* (1984); George F. Kennan, *Memoirs*, 2 vols. (1967, 1972); Bruce Kuklick, *American Policy and the Divison of Germany* (1972); Walter Lippmann, *The Cold War* (1947, rev. 1973); Thomas A. Schwartz, *America's Germany; John J. McCloy and the Federal Republic of Germany* (1991); Ronald Steel, *Walter Lippmann and the American Century* (1982); Lawrence Wittner, *American Intervention in Greece, 1943–1949* (1982).

On the Middle East, see Michael Cohen, *Truman and Israel* (1990); Bruce Kuniholm, The Origins of the Cold War in the Near East (1980); Mark Lytle, *The Origins of the Iranian-American Alliance, 1941–1953* (1987); John

Snetsinger, Truman, *The Jewish Vote and the Recognition of Israel* (1974); Steven L. Spiegel, *The Other Arab-Israeli Conflict: Making America's Middle East Policy from Truman to Reagan* (1985); and Robert Stookey, *The United States and the Arab States* (1975).

Asian relations from 1945 to 1953 are treated by Nick Cullather, *Illusions of Influence: The Political Economy of United States–Philippines Relations, 1942–1960* (1994); William Border, *The Pacific Alliance: United States Foreign Economic Policy and Japanese Trade Recovery, 1947–1955* (1984); Bruce Cumings, *The Origins of the Korean War,* 2 vols. (1981–1991), which places the conflict in its international setting; Rosemary Foot, *The Wrong War: American Policy and the Dimensions of the Korean Conflict, 1950–1953* (1985), and her *A Substitute for Victory* (1991), based on recently opened archives; Marc S. Gallicchio, *The Cold War Begins in Asia* (1988); Lloyd C. Gardner, *Approaching Vietnam: From World War II Through Dienbienphu, 1941–1954* (1988), a good place to start studying the Vietnam war; Gary R. Hess, *The United States' Emergence as a Southeast Asian Power, 1940–1950* (1987); Burton Kaufman, *The Korean War* (1986), a good general account; Robert Newman, *Owen Lattimore and the "Loss" of China* (1991); Andrew Rotter, *The Path to Vietnam: Origins of American Commitment to Southeast Asia* (1988); Michael Schaller, *The American Occupation of Japan* (1985), which places the occupation in context of the Cold War in Asia; the same author's *Douglas MacArthur* (1989); William Stueck, *The Korean War: An International History* (1995); Nancy Bernkopf Tucker, *Patterns in the Dust: Chinese-American Relations and the Recognition Controversy, 1949–1951* (1983), splendidly researched.

FROM EISENHOWER'S NEW LOOK TO ESCALATION IN VIETNAM, 1953–1968

The cultural milieu of the Cold War is captured in Elaine Tyler May's *Homeward Bound: American Families in the Cold War Era* (1988).

Policies and personalities of the Eisenhower era are covered by Charles Alexander, *Holding the Line: The Eisenhower Administration* (1975); Stephen E. Ambrose, *Eisenhower,* 2 vols. (1983, 1984); H. W. Brands, *Cold Warriors: Eisenhower's Generation and American Foreign Policy* (1988), and his *The Specter of Neutralism: The United States and the Emergence of the Third World, 1947–1960* (1989); Robert Divine, *Eisenhower and the Cold War* (1981), a rehabilitation of the president; Townsend Hoopes, *The Devil and John Foster Dulles* (1973), highly critical; and Blanche Weissen Cook, *The Declassified Eisenhower* (1981), good on covert operations. Richard H. Immerman, ed., *John Foster Dulles and the Diplomacy of the Cold War* (1990), presents excellent essays. Stephen E. Ambrose's *Nixon,* 3 vols. (1987–1991) contains much material on foreign affairs.

John Lewis Gaddis, *The Long Peace* (1987), contains penetrating essays on Eisenhower's foreign policies.

Defense, nuclear weapons, and scientific policies of the Eisenhower administration appear in Robert Divine, *Blowing on the Wind: The Nuclear Test Ban Debate, 1954–1960* (1979); Samuel Huntington, *The Soldier and the State* (1957) and *The Common Defense* (1961); Edward Kolodziej, *The Uncommon Defense and Congress, 1945–1963* (1966), a response to Huntington; James R. Killian, *Sputnik, Scientists and Eisenhower* (1977), and Warner Schilling, Paul Hammond, and Glenn Snyder, *Strategy, Politics and Defense Budgets* (1962). Michael Beschloss, *Mayday: Eisenhower, Khrushchev and the U-2 Affair* (1986), is a fast-paced account, weaving espionage, science, and diplomacy.

Covert operations in Guatemala and Iran are discussed by Richard H. Immerman, *The CIA in Guatemala: The Foreign Policy of Intervention* (1982); Stephen G. Rabe, *Eisenhower and Latin America: The Foreign Policy of Anticommunism* (1987), discussing the entire hemisphere; James Bill, *The Eagle and the Lion: The Tragedy of American Iranian Relations* (1988), the best account of the 1953 coup; Kermit Roosevelt, *Countercoup* (1980), which records the operation in Iran; Barry Rubin, *Paved with Good Intention: The United States and Iran* (1980); and David Wise, *The Invisible Government* (1964).

Relations with the Middle East during Ike's term are explained in Chester Cooper, *The Lion's Last Roar: Suez, 1956* (1978); Miles Copeland, *The Game of Nations* (1970), memoirs of a CIA agent; Robert Engler, *The Politics of Oil* (1961); Peter L. Hahn, *The United States, Great Britain and Egypt, 1945–1956* (1991); Diane B. Kunz, *The Economic Diplomacy of the Suez Crisis* (1991); Selwyn Lloyd, *Suez* (1978), a memoir by Britain's foreign secretary at the time of the invasion; Kennett Love, *Suez: The Twice-Fought War* (1969); Harold Macmillan, *Riding the Storm 1956–1959* (1971); Richard E. Neustadt, *Alliance Politics* (1970), a comparison of the Suez affair and the 1962 Skybolt missile controversy, Anthony Sampson, *The Seven Sisters: The Great Oil Companies and the World They Shaped* (1975); Robert Stookey, *America and the Arab States* (1975); and Hugh Thomas, *The Suez Affair* (1966).

Relations with Asia are discussed in Gordon H. Chang, *Friends and Enemies: The United States, China and the Soviet Union, 1948–1972* (1990); Dennis Merrill, *The United States and India's Economic Development, 1947–1963* (1990); and William O. Walker III, *Opium and Foreign Policy* (1991). On Indochina, see George C. Herring, *America's Longest War: The United States and Vietnam, 1950–1975* (1996); Stanley Karnow, *Vietnam: A History* (1991), and Robert D. Schulzinger, *A Time for War: The United States and Vietnam, 1941–1975* (1997).

Detailed works on the first Indochina war include Melanie Billings-Yun, *Decision Against War: Eisenhower and Dienbienphu, 1954* (1988); Ellen Hammer, *The Struggle for Indochina, 1940–1955* (1966); Bernard Fall, *Street Without Joy* (1972), a vivid description of the fighting, and *Hell in a Very Small Place* (1966), the classic account of Dienbienphu; Melvin Gurtov, *The First Vietnam Crisis, 1953–1954* (1967); and Edward Lansdale, *In the Midst of Wars* (1972), the bizarre account of an American adviser. Robert F. Randle, *Geneva, 1954* (1969), is the best discussion of the peace conference. The most comprehensive account of U.S. policy after Geneva appears in David L. Anderson, *Trapped by Success: The Eisenhower Administration and Vietnam, 1953–1961* (1991). See also the works listed below on American escalation in Vietnam.

Major figures in the Kennedy and Johnson administrations receive attention from Michael Beschloss, *Kennedy and Khrushchev: The Crisis Years* (1991); James N. Giglio, *The Presidency of John F. Kennedy* (1992); Diane B. Kunz, ed., *The Diplomacy of the Crucial Decade: American Foreign Relations during the 1960s* (1994); Herbert Parmet, *JFK: The Presidency of John F. Kennedy* (1984), based on the documentary record; Thomas Paterson, ed., *Kennedy's Quest for Victory, American Foreign Policy, 1961–1963* (1989); Thomas Schoenbaum, *Waging Peace and War: Dean Rusk in the Truman, Kennedy and Johnson Years* (1988); and Warren Cohen, *Dean Rusk* (1979), which places Rusk's diplomacy in the context of liberal ideology. See also David Halberstam, *The Best and the Brightest* (1972), filled with remarkable anecdotes; Roger Hilsman, *To Move a Nation: The Politics of Foreign Policy in the Kennedy Administration* (1964); Theodore Sorensen, *Kennedy* (1965), by the president's principal speechwriter; Arthur M. Schlesinger, Jr., *A Thousand Days* (1966) and *Robert F. Kennedy and His Times* (1978); Richard Walton, *Cold War and Counter-Revolution: The Foreign Policy of John F. Kennedy* (1972), highly critical; Richard Barnet, *Intervention and Revolution* (1972), equally damning; Henry Trewhitt, *McNamara* (1971), a sympathetic portrait of the defense secretary; Philip Geyelin, *Lyndon B. Johnson and the World* (1968), by a journalist; Randall Bennett Woods, *Fulbright: A Biography* (1995), a laudatory study; and Merle Miller, *Lyndon: An Oral Biography* (1980), containing interesting anecdotal material. Walt W. Rostow's *The Diffusion of Power* (1972) is a spirited defense. Richard D. Mahoney, *JFK: Ordeal in Africa* (1983), has important details. Thomas W. Zeiler, *American Trade and Power in the 1960s* (1992), subtly discusses economic diplomacy.

For relations with Latin America, see Gaddis Smith, *The Last Years of the Monroe Doctrine, 1945–1993* (1994). For Cuba, see Thomas G. Paterson, *Contesting Castro: The United States and the Triumph of the Cuban Revolution* (1994); Trumbull Higgins, *The Perfect Failure: Kennedy, Eisenhower and the Bay of Pigs* (1987); Wayne S. Smith, *The Closest of Enemies: A Personal and Diplomatic History of the Castro Years* (1987); Richard E. Welch, *Response to Revolution: The United States and the Cuban Revolution, 1959–1961* (1985); and Peter Wyden, *Bay of Pigs* (1979). For the Alliance for Progress, see Jerome Levinson and Juan de Onis, *The Alliance That Lost Its Way* (1970). On the intervention in the Dominican Republic, see Piero Gleijeses's brilliant *The Dominican Crisis* (1978); Abraham Lowenthal, *The Dominican Intervention* (1972); and Jerome Slater, *Intervention and Negotiation: The United States and the Dominican Revolution* (1970).

On the Cuban missile crisis and its effects on relations with the Soviet Union and the NATO allies, see Elie Abel, *The Missile Crisis* (1966). Graham Allison, *Essence of Decision: Explaining the Cuban Missile Crisis* (1971), applies theories of bureaucratic politics. David Detzer, *The Brink* (1979), is lively. Abram Chayes, *The Cuban Missile Crisis* (1974), is by an international lawyer. Herbert S. Dinerstein, *The Making of a Missile Crisis* (1969), looks at anticommunism. Irving Janis, *Victims of Groupthink* (1972), awards Kennedy high marks; and John Newhouse, *De Gaulle and the Anglo Saxons* (1971), explains the French leader's distress at his exclusion from great events. Edward Kolodziej, *The Politics of Grandeur* (1975), is the best account of French foreign policy under de Gaulle and Pompidou.

The Americanization of the War in Vietnam from 1961 to 1968 has generated a large and growing literature. Start with the books by George Herring, Stanley Karnow, and Robert D. Schulzinger already mentioned. See George McT. Kahin, *Intervention: How America Became Involved in Vietnam* (1986), and contrast it with Larry Berman, *Planning a Tragedy: The Americanization of the War in Vietnam* (1983), and his *Lyndon Johnson's War* (1989). R. B. Smith, *An International History of the Vietnam War*, 3 vols. (1983–1991), treats the subject from an international perspective. Gabriel Kolko, *Anatomy of a War: Vietnam, the United States and the Modern Historical Experience* (1986), places the war in a revolutionary context. Other good general accounts are by James P. Harrison, *The Endless War: Vietnam's Struggle for Independence* (1989); and Marilyn B. Young, *The Vietnam Wars* (1990).

Significant episodes and personalities in the war are covered by Ellen J. Hammer, *A Death in November: America in Vietnam, 1963* (1987), which discusses the overthrow of Diem. An American soldier's story appears in Neil Sheehan, *A Bright Shining Lie: John Paul Vann and America in Vietnam* (1988). William C. Berman describes how a senator came to oppose the war in *William Fulbright and the Vietnam War* (1988). David L. DiLeo's *George Ball, Vietnam and the Rethinking of Containment* (1991) analyzes the activities of a dissenter. Seymour Hersh, *My Lai 4* (1970), describes the massacre. Don Oberdorfer, *Tet* (1971), is an eyewitness report.

For domestic consequences of the war, look at Lawrence Baskir and Peter Strauss, *Chance and Circumstance: The War, the Draft and the Vietnam Generation* (1978). Charles DeBendedetti with Charles Chatfield, *An American Ordeal: The Antiwar Movement of the Vietnam Era* (1990), is encyclopedic. Tom Wells, *The War Within: America's Battle over Vietnam* (1994).

FROM DETENTE TO A NEW COLD WAR:
FOREIGN POLICY SINCE 1969

The best overviews of the years since 1969 appear in John Lewis Gaddis, *The United States and the End of the Cold War* (1992) and Raymond L. Garthoff, *Detente and Confrontation: American-Soviet Relations from Nixon to Reagan* (1992). William Hyland offers a participant's perspective in *Mortal Rivals: Superpower Relations from Nixon to Reagan* (1987). Tad Szulc, *The Illusion of Peace* (1978), is a detailed and highly critical account of Nixon's foreign policy. Two good biographies of Nixon are by Stephen E. Ambrose, *Nixon*, 3 vols. (1987–1991); and Herbert Parmet, *Richard Nixon and His America* (1990). For memoirs of the Nixon and Ford administrations, consult Richard Nixon, *RN: The Memoirs of Richard Nixon* (1977); and Gerald R. Ford, *A Time to Heal: The Autobiography of Gerald R. Ford* (1978). On Henry Kissinger, consult his own story in his memoirs, *White House Years* (1979) and *Years of Upheaval* (1982). Studies of Kissinger include those by Seymour Hersh, *The Price of Power: Kissinger in the Nixon White House* (1983); Walter Isaacson, *Kissinger* (1992); and Robert D. Schulzinger *Henry Kissinger* (1989).

Relations between the executive branch and Congress from the sixties to the late seventies are covered in a superb book, Thomas Franck and Edward Weisband, *Foreign Policy by Congress* (1979).

For changes in the international economic environment, see works listed at the beginning of the section on the post–World War II period. See also Paul Kennedy, *The Rise and Fall of the Great Powers* (1987); and Clyde V. Prestowitz, Jr., *Trading Places: How We Allowed Japan To Take the Lead* (1988).

On strategic arms negotiations and conventional arms sales, see Raymond Garthoff, *Detente and Confrontation* (1992); Gerard Smith, *Doubletalk: The Story of the First Strategic Arms Limitation Talks* (1980); and Andrew Pierre, *The Global Politics of Arms Sales* (1982).

On covert activities in the Nixon and Ford administrations, see Thomas Powers, *The Man Who Kept the Secrets: Richard Helms and the CIA* (1979); and J. Anthony Lukas, *Nightmare: The Underside of the Nixon Administration* (1976). John Stockwell, *In Search of Enemies* (1979), explains CIA actions in Angola. John Dinges and Saul Landau, *Assassination on Embassy Row* (1980), reveals covert activities by Chileans in the United States.

The end of the war in Vietnam is discussed by the general works on the Nixon and Ford administrations. Consult the bibliography in George Herring's *America's Longest War* and Robert D. Schulzinger's *A Time for War*. See also William Shawcross, *Sideshow: Kissinger, Nixon and the Destruction of Cambodia* (1979); Arnold R. Isaacs, *Without Honor: Defeat in Vietnam and Cambodia* (1983); Nguyen Tien Hung and Jerrold Schechter, *The Palace File* (1986), which argues that the United States betrayed Saigon after 1973; and Robert

Shaplen, *Bitter Victory* (1986), an incisive journalist's account of the postwar world. The Nixon administration's treatment of the antiwar movement receives good coverage in Melvin Small, *Johnson, Nixon and the Doves* (1988).

For the Middle East before 1977, see William Quandt's *Decade of Decision* (1978) and Steven L. Spiegel, *The Other Arab-Israeli Conflict: The Making of America's Middle East Policy from Truman to Reagan* (1985), both of which discuss the Arab-Israeli conflict. James Bill, *The Eagle and the Lion* (1988), has useful information on the growth of Washington's commitment to the shah of Iran.

For foreign policy in the Carter administration, start with Gaddis Smith, *Morality, Reason and Power: American Diplomacy in the Carter Years* (1986); and Jerel Rosati, *The Carter Administration's Quest for Global Community* (1987). Consult the memoirs by the principals: Jimmy Carter, *Keeping Faith* (1982); Zbigniew Brzezinski, *Power and Principle* (1983); Cyrus Vance, *Hard Choices* (1983). Human rights are covered by Sandra Vogelgesang, *American Dream, Global Nightmare* (1980); Immigration and refugee issues in Gil Loescher and John Scanlan, *Calculated Kindness* (1986), and David Reimers, *Still the Golden Door: The Third World Comes to America* (1992).

For relations with Central America, consult, on the Panama Canal treaties, Walter LaFeber, *The Panama Canal* (1979); and J. Michael Hogan, *The Panama Canal in American Politics* (1986). On Nicaragua, Robert Pastor, *Condemned to Repetition: The United States and Nicaragua* (1987); and Anthony Lake, *Samoza Falling* (1989).

Arms control and defense policies are covered in Raymond Garthoff, *Detente and Confrontation*, previously mentioned; and Michael Krepon, *Strategic Stalemate: Nuclear Weapons and Arms Control in American Politics* (1984).

For the Camp David accords, look at William B. Quandt, *Camp David: Peacemaking and Politics* (1986); and memoirs by participants: Ezer Weizman, *The Road to Peace* (1980); Moshe Dayan, *Breakthrough* (1981); and Anwar Sadat, *In Search of Identity* (1980).

For Iran, see James Bill, *The Eagle and the Lion*, previously noted; Barry Rubin, *Paved with Good Intentions: The United States and Iran* (1980); and Gary Sick, *All Fall Down: America's Tragic Encounter with Iran* (1986), the story as seen by the Carter administration's expert on Iran at the National Security Council.

On the conservative counterattack in the 1980 election, consult Theodore H. White, *America in Search of Itself, 1956–1980* (1982); and Norman Podhoretz, *The Present Danger* (1980).

The literature on the Reagan administration already is large. Start with Raymond L. Garthoff, *The Great Transition: American-Russian Relations and the End of the Cold War* (1994); Haynes Johnson, *Sleepwalking Through History: America in the Reagan Years* (1991); and Michael Schaller, *Reckoning with Reagan* (1992).

The memoirs of the Reagan years contain useful information on foreign affairs. See Alexander Haig, *Caveat: Reagan, Realism and Foreign Policy* (1984); Constantine Menges, *Inside the National Security Council* (1988); Donald Regan, *For the Record* (1988); George P. Shultz, *Turmoil and Triumph* (1993); Larry Speakes, *Speaking Out* (1988); and Caspar Weinberger *Fighting for Peace: Seven Critical Years at the Pentagon* (1991).

Expert observations of the Reagan foreign policy appear in Strobe Talbott, *Deadly Gambits* (1984); Michael Mandelbaum and Strobe Talbott, *Reagan and Gorbachev* (1987); Kenneth Oye et al., *Eagle Defiant: U.S. Foreign Policy in the 1980s* (1983); and I. M. Destler et al., *Our Own Worst Enemy: The Unmaking of American Foreign Policy* (1984).

Covert operations and the Iran-contra affair receive treatment in Theodore Draper, *A Very Thin Line: The Iran-Contra Affairs* (1991); John Tower et al., *The Tower Commission Report* (1987); and Bob Woodward, *Veil* (1987).

On the Reagan administration's Central American policy, see Kenneth Coleman and George Herring, eds., *The Central American Crisis* (1985); Walter LaFeber, *Inevitable Revolutions: The United States in Central America* (1983); and Robert Pastor, *Condemned to Repetition*, previously mentioned.

On the Middle East, refer to Spiegel's *The Other Arab-Israeli Conflict*, noted above; Wolf Blitzer, *Between Washington and Jerusalem* (1985); Itamar Rabinovich, *The War for Lebanon, 1970–1983* (1984); and Avner Yaniv, *Dilemmas of Security: Politics, Strategy and the Israeli Experience in Lebanon* (1987).

The profound changes in world politics since 1989 are covered in Michael Beschloss and Strobe Talbott, *At the Highest Levels* (1993); and Michael Hogan, ed., *The End of the Cold War* (1992). Discussion of post–Cold War issues appear in Richard Benedick, *Ozone Diplomacy: New Directions for Saving the Planet* (1991); Paul Kennedy, *Preparing for the Next Century* (1993); and Misha Glenny, *The Fall of Yugoslavia* (1992). For information on the Bush administration, see Raymond Garthoff's *The Great Transition*, cited above. James A. Baker III, *The Politics of War* (1995), is the secretary of state's memoirs. Philip Zelikow and Condoleezza Rice, *Germany Unified and Europe Transformed* (1995), is an insiders' account of the Bush administration's policy toward the collapse of communism in Central Europe. Bruce Jentleson, *With Friends Like These: Reagan, Bush and Saddam, 1982–1990* (1994); Lawrence Freedman and Efraim Karsh, *The Gulf Conflict, 1990–1991* (1992); and Bob Woodward's *The Commanders* (1991) discuss the wars in the Persian Gulf and Panama. Little work on the Clinton administration's foreign policy has appeared in book form. See Jonathan Clarke and James Clad, *After the Crusade: American Foreign Policy for the Post-Superpower Age* (1995). Until scholarship based on documentary evidence appears, consult articles in *Current History, Foreign Affairs*, and *Foreign Policy*. These journals, as well as the high-quality British newsweekly *The Economist*, also carry intelligent reviews of books on contemporary international affairs.

Index